95

D0561501

$\checkmark$

Milk Is Not for Every Body: Living with Lactose Intolerance

Facts On File, Inc.
11 Penn Plaza
New York NY 10001

Library of Congress Cataloging-in-Publication Data

Carper, Steve.
  Milk is not for every body : living with lactose intolerance /
Steve Carper : foreword by Robert Kornfield.
      p. cm.
  Includes bibliographical references and index.
  ISBN 0-8160-3127-4
    1. Lactose intolerance—Popular works. 2. Lactose intolerance—
Diet therapy—Recipes. I. Title.
  RC632.L33C37 1995
  616.3'998—dc20   95-9950

Facts On File books are available at special discounts when purchased in bulk quantities for businesses, associations, institutions or sales promotions. Please call our Special Sales Department in New York at 212/967-8800 or 800/322-8755.

Jacket design by Catherine Hyman

VB TT 10 9 8 7 6 5 4 3 2 1

This book is printed on acid-free paper.

Printed in the United States of America

MILK IS NOT FOR EVERY BODY

Living with Lactose Intolerance

Steve Carper

Foreword by Robert Kornfield, M.D.

Facts On File, Inc.

AN INFOBASE HOLDINGS COMPANY

CONTENTS

ACKNOWLEDGMENTS

Compiling the information necessary for a book such as this is an exercise in relying on the kindness of others. The few names listed here represent only a fraction of all I contacted, but they stand out from the crowd because they gave me more of their time and expertise than I had a right to expect. This in no way diminishes my thanks to the dozens of others who answered my phone calls or responded to my letters. They were patient with my badgering them for odd and ungainly nuggets of information they may not even have known they possessed, and I am sorry they cannot be individually named. A salute goes to the staff of the Science Division of the Rochester Public Library for their unfailing courtesy and assistance. And as always, eternal gratitude to Linda Saalman, who saw this book through every stage from proposal to publishing and whose help made it better than I could possibly have managed on my own.

Special thanks to: Chris Angie, Rochester Genesee Hospital; Dr. George Baker, Mead Johnson; Cy Caine, Physicians' Desk Reference; Dr. Michael Kaplan, McNeil Consumer Products; Chris Kilbane, Sterling Winthrop; Dr. Robert Kornfield; Dr. Richard Lawrence; Thomas A. Mekus, Diehl Specialties International; Jeff Reiter, Dairy Foods Magazine; Jan A. Remak, Vitasoy (U.S.A.), Inc.; Dr. Dennis Savaiano; Dr. Pol Vandenbroucke, Bayer Consumer Care Division.

FOREWORD

If you picked up this book expecting to read about a serious medical problem, you may be surprised to discover that only two chapters are given over to doctors, and they are the last two in the book. Nothing is wrong with the priorities here. Lactose intolerence (LI) is in many ways not a medical condition at all.

I am a practicing gastroenterologist, a physician specializing in diseases of the digestive tract and liver, the "gastrointestinal system," but I rarely am called in by a primary physician just because a patient may have LI.

This is partly because awareness of LI, which was little known even among the medical community 20 or 30 years ago, has become as common as the condition itself. Your primary physician can often make a preliminary diagnosis of LI just by knowing your medical and family histories and by listening to your description of your symptoms. The gradual loss of the ability to digest milk products is a natural genetic problem that is prevalent in many ethnic groups and near universal in some. If your parents were LI, then the odds are that you will become so as well. What many adults do not realize is that they can start seeing symptoms at any age. As the average lifespan increases, more and more adults will find themselves becoming LI. No medical problems are involved in any case, merely a need to reduce or restrict the dairy products in one's diet.

Doctors, however, have an additional set of concerns. The fragility of the body's ability to produce the lactase enzyme makes LI a possible complicating factor whenever intestinal problems occur. A host of diseases that are becoming more prevalent in our society, from Crohn's disease to AIDS enteropathy, can also damage the intestines sufficiently badly that a so-called Secondary LI can result. It is because of such triggers of Secondary LI that I see an increasing overall incidence of LI in my practice. The possiblity of Secondary LI is a major reason why self-diagnosis of LI is not a wise idea.

While some Secondary LI will vanish when the originating cause is cleared up, for most people LI is a permanent condition. I can review with my patients what changes need to be made to their diets, but even the partial removal of dairy products from one's daily life can be more complicated than most people think. Steve Carper goes far beyond the standard lactose-free diet sheet that doctors typically hand out. He covers all the questions and problems that can arise, including social, consumer and behavioral ones that few doctors have time to focus on. *Milk Is Not for Every Body* contains what my patients need to know for the months and years after they leave the doctor's office.

Robert Kornfield, M.D.

v

IF 3,000,000,000 PEOPLE IN THE WORLD ARE LACTOSE INTOLERANT, THEN WHY AREN'T WE RICH?

In 1978, when I was first diagnosed as being lactose intolerant, I had never heard the term before. Today it's so common that I stumble across it every time I turn on my television. Ads for lactose intolerance run during the national news. Characters on *Seinfeld, Murphy Brown, Grace Under Fire* and *The Simpsons* suffer from it. Jay Leno, Conan O'Brien and David Letterman play the term for laughs during their skits, confident that everyone will get the joke. Small wonder that *Rolling Stone* magazine proclaimed lactose intolerance to be 1992's "hot disorder." By no co-incidence whatsoever, 1992 was also the year in which sales of products aimed at the lactose intolerant burst through the $100 million barrier, spurred by a multi-million dollar advertising battle between two multina-tional pharmaceutical giants.

None of this was true back in 1978 when I was busily devouring milk in all its myriad forms. I had no notion that dairy products could be the root of the perpetual bloating, gas, cramps and diarrhea that had plagued my life for years. Milk! Milk had "something for every body." Milk was nature's perfect food. Milk was the all-American drink. Milk was so important that government subsidies kept the price of a half-pint in my high school cafeteria down to only three cents, so that everybody could afford to have it every day. Like other kids, I grew up snacking on milk and cookies. Milk was even *in* cookies, and in cakes and pizzas and breads and margarines and hot dogs and TV dinners and chocolates and gravies and a million other food products I never suspected. With perverse irony, well meaning friends advised me to drink milk to "soothe" my stomach. Each day, possibly each meal, I had milk, milk and more milk, some visible, much hidden, making it impossible for me to isolate any particular food as the source of my distress.

Finally, a young doctor at a clinic heard my story. He explained that many people could not digest lactose—the sugar that is found in milk and only in milk—because their bodies no longer produced a sufficient quantity of lactase, the enzyme that breaks down the lactose. To determine if I was one of these people, he ordered an immediate test. That test required me to drink a solution of about two ounces of lactose in water (an amount equal to that in a quart of milk). When I staggered back two hours later, the actual testing was a mere formality. I was so utterly sick and miserable that it was obvious lactose and I were a very bad match.

Products aimed specifically at the lactose intolerant may have existed in 1978, but I never found any. Instead, I began a fanatically milk-free diet, checking labels on every package in the supermarket, severely restricting what I could eat in restaurants and making myself a trying guest at friends' and relatives' homes.

Going from a milk-laden to a milk-free diet overnight meant that I needed to learn a lot in a hurry. Unfortunately, I couldn't find any books to help me, and articles on lactose intolerance in the popular press were about as frequent as those on Etruscan irregular verbs. For a long time I felt uncomfortable and isolated, a curiosity with a rare disease that was mostly too embarrassing to talk about. Poking around in odd corners of libraries comes naturally to me, though. After much searching through medical journals, histories of food, nutrition textbooks and piles of handouts from the National Dairy Council, I began to put together an understanding of lactose intolerance broad enough to use in my everyday life. Much of what I learned surprised me.

▉ LACTOSE INTOLERANCE: THE FACTS

Lactose intolerance is not a disease, not a syndrome, not even a disorder. It is not a sign that something is wrong with you or your body. It is certainly not rare or unusual. In fact, the vast majority of adults in the world, 70% or 3 billion by some estimates, are lactose intolerant. It is the normal state of humanity and always has been throughout history. Far from naturally being milk drinkers for life, our genetic programming assumes that we will encounter milk only for the first few years of childhood. Adult lactose intolerance very likely was still universal as recently as 10,000 years ago. It is a mere fluke of history that anyone is capable of drinking milk past the age of five or so, and an equal fluke that a concentration of adult milk-drinkers can be found in the United States.

For that matter, "lactose intolerants" is not even a very good name for who we are, because it implies a negative. Medical journals are full of other equally negative names—lactase deficiency, lactose maldigester—invented by doctors who thought they had identified a disease. I keep using lactose intolerance because it's by far the most familiar term, ubiquitously used outside the medical literature. No such popular equivalent name exists for the ability to digest lactose, just as there is no term for the state of not having a broken leg. Lactase persistence is probably the most neutral of the available terms, since it doesn't give the impression of normality or superiority.

For the rest of the book I will use LI to refer to lactose intolerance (or lactose intolerant), and LP to refer to lactase persistence (or lactase persistent). Please remember that this is only convenient shorthand. Lactose intolerance is not quite the same thing as lactose maldigestion, which is subtly different from lactase deficiency. *(See Glossary, page 312)* Technically speaking, lactose intolerance is the appearance of symptoms after the consumption of lactose, without regard to the quantity of lactase that is present. It is possible for people to get LI symptoms even when they have sufficient lactase, while others who presumably have insufficient lactase live their lives symptom-free. Almost any set of symptoms—or the lack of them—may result when you drink milk, no matter what category you think you are in [*see box*]. Self-diagnosis can be unwise, and possibly dangerous.

HIGH LACTASE = FEW SYMPTOMS; LOW LACTASE = MANY SYMPTOMS?

If you're sure you get LI symptoms after drinking milk, you might assume that a test to prove you're a low lactase producer is simply unnecessary. Fortunately, scientists are trained not to assume anything, which is why they sometimes do what appear to be obvious and totally unnecessary experiments. Their reward, as in this case, is to discover that the seemingly obvious is sometimes not at all true.

In a recent study ("Correlation of lactose maldigestion, lactose intolerance, and milk intolerance," A. O. Johnson *et al.*, *American Journal of Clinical Nutrition*, 1993; 57:399–401), researchers tested 164 volunteers, all of whom claimed to get LI symptoms after drinking a cup or less of milk.

Each test subject drank a solution containing lactose equivalent to the amount found in two cups of milk and then took a standard lactose tolerance test (*see Chapter 14*). Doctors also noted whether they actually exhibited any typical LI symptoms during the test.

Surprise! While the 164 volunteers may have thought of themselves as one large cohesive group, the testing split them into *four* separate categories:

	Had Symptoms	Had No Symptoms
Low Lactase Producer	50%	8%
High Lactase Producer	15%	27%

Only half, exactly 50%, fit into the group most of us would have placed everyone in. Only half, that is, did indeed have low lactase production and did get symptoms after drinking a lactose load (technically, any liquid or solid containing lactose). Look at what happened with the rest. A full 42% of a group who said they always had problems with milk produced high levels of lactase. And over a third of the lactase producers still suffered from diarrhea, gas, bloating or other symptoms normally thought of as resulting only from a lack of lactase. The number in the upper right corner of the grid is also interesting. Eight percent—one of every twelve people in the test— produced little or no lactase, drank a heavy lactose load and came out of it with no symptoms whatsoever.

Why such variation in a situation so seemingly straightforward? The best answer is that the role food plays in our lives is far more complicated than the stripped down abstraction tested in laboratories. Yes, a low level of lactase is the most likely explanation for any symptoms that follow milk drinking. But it is not the only one. Milk can create digestive problems for reasons other than LI; conversely, digestive problems may be due to other foods and have nothing whatsoever to do with milk.

We're also conditioned by earlier experiences. If we once had a bad reaction that we attribute to milk, we're likely to approach drinking it at a later time with trepidation, whether it is the culprit or not. Indeed, it has been suggested that a person's reactions to milk may be as much psychological as physiological. Some of the high-lactase people who associated digestive problems with milk drinking may fall into this category.

I read this study as proof that proper testing is critical, and self-diagnosis potentially dangerous. Low levels of lactase are a normal part of aging for most people, but other digestive problems can be serious. You may be LI because of damage to your intestines, or the diarrhea and other symptoms caused by LI may be worsening an existing medical condition. Or you may not be LI at all. Please see your doctor to be sure.

■ LACTOSE INTOLERANCE: FREQUENTLY ASKED QUESTIONS

Today, in the mid-1990s, LI has few secrets left. Except for some of the most arcane technical details, the role lactose and lactase play in the body is well understood. Over the course of this book I'll try to supply you with the most accurate and complete information on every facet of LI ever assembled in one place. In addition, I'll be presenting a wealth of information about milk that is difficult to find anywhere else. Since many people must avoid or look out for dairy products for reasons other than LI (see box), I've been careful to keep those needs in mind as well.

Let's start with the basics. What follows are the brief answers to the most frequently asked questions about lactose intolerance; the answers I wish I had in 1978. Much more detail on every area is provided in later chapters.

What Are Lactose and Lactase?

All food on the earth, whatever its source, is composed of the same basic nutrients: proteins, fats and carbohydrates; water; and a sprinkling of vitamins and minerals. Water, vitamins and minerals are directly absorbed by our digestive tracts, but the other molecules are too large and complex to be used that way. To absorb them our bodies must manufacture specialized proteins called enzymes to split the protein, fat and carbohydrate molecules into their basic building blocks: amino acids, fatty acids and simple sugars, respectively. This is the process we call digestion.

As a sugar, lactose is part of the carbohydrate family. It's fairly small and simple compared to some of the other carbohydrates, but not quite simple enough. Each molecule of lactose is made by joining two simpler sugars, glucose and galactose. Digestion makes the lactose usable by splitting it back into these component parts. Digestive enzymes are named for the molecule that they specifically target—that's why lactose's enzyme is called lactase. No other enzyme will digest lactose.

Most digestive enzymes are present in more than sufficient quantity to take care of any amount of their target nutrient molecules. Lactase is the major exception. Even those who normally have no trouble digesting milk have only half as much lactase as they do enzymes for other sugars. Those of us with LI have on average only one-tenth of that half-portion.

THE OTHER MILLIONS WHO NEED THIS BOOK

Living in a metaphorically milk-drenched society places special demands on those who cannot or will not drink milk. Some people face all the problems of those who are LI and then some, either due to personal beliefs or because the consequences of their intake of dairy products can be much more serious than an upset stomach. For people with such needs, special care has been taken throughout this book to indicate the presence of dairy-derived products in addition to lactose in the foods discussed.

Milk Allergies: True allergies to cow's milk protein are rare, but a small number of people risk severe medical problems even from the tiny amounts of milk protein that are commonly used in packaged and processed foods.

Enzyme Deficiency Diseases: Certain rare childhood diseases can require the elimination of all milk from the diet. Those with galactosemia may have to avoid all milk products even as adults.

Vegans: While many vegetarians feel comfortable with the use of dairy products, some, known as vegans, refuse all products that originate in connection with an animal.

Religious Dietary Laws: Those who try to keep kosher cannot mix dairy products and meat in the same food or in the same meal. There are other religious traditions which ban the consumption of animal products as well.

What Happens without Sufficient Lactase?

To prevent dehydration, we need many quarts of water in our diets even if it is hidden in soups or fruit or as the liquid measure of milk. Virtually all of that water is absorbed by the intestines, with just enough moisture reaching the colon (the large intestine) to keep our stools from being so hard that they hurt. Undigested lactose disrupts this process. It reverses the flow, actually pulling additional water out of the surrounding tissue into the digestive tract and sluicing the lactose down to our bowels. Digestion is normally very slow, with food creeping through the intestines at the pace of a very sluggish snail in order to give the enzymes the maximum opportunity to work. When excess water speeds the process it is even less likely that the lactose and lactase will have time to find one another. Adding insult to injury, the additional water also creates an uncomfortable bloated feeling.

Consequently, what reaches the colon is a large volume of lactose-laden water rather than a small volume of semi-dry solid. Trillions of normally beneficial colonic bacteria leap upon the lactose as if it were a gourmet meal. They too have to break down the lactose to make it usable but they do it in a two-step reaction that essentially ferments the sugar. This produces bubbles of gas for hours on end in a process that cannot be stopped until all the lactose is removed.

Gas and bloating are bad enough, but excess water and gas in the colon causes diarrhea. Their resulting pressure can lead to an almost immediate need to explosively expel loose, watery stools. Even without diarrhea, the continual production of trapped gas can also produce an accompanying and long-lasting medley of bloating, pain, cramps and borborygmi, those embarrassing rumbling noises from moving gas that make you wonder what in the world is going on inside your body. Of course, the range and severity of symptoms will vary enormously depending on any number of factors, including how much lactose you've eaten, how much lactase your body still produces, whether you've eaten the lactose with a meal, the amount and variety of bacteria in the colon and your individual health. In practice, this can mean that some people will have minimal symptoms or none at all (constipation is even possible) while others will suffer through pain and cramps that even a doctor has described as "unbearable."

Is Everybody Born with Sufficient Lactase?

Our bodies and lactase have a pretty shaky relationship right from the beginning. Lactase activity in the fetus as late as the eighth month may be only 30% of what it will be in a one-year-old. This level does shoot up right before birth, though, and may be higher in the newborn than anytime thereafter.

Premature babies are therefore born with intestines still struggling to manufacture lactase. Fortunately, this lack of lactase does not normally become a medical problem. The first feedings trigger a rise in lactase output so that it soon reaches optimum levels. Mother's milk reflects this lag by containing less lactose, among other differences, immediately after birth than a few days later. And newborns in any case lack intestinal bacteria, so undigested lactose can't be fermented to cause typical LI symptoms.

It is possible, however, for a baby to be born with a complete absence of lactase. Until artificial lactose-free formulas were developed at the beginning of this century, infants with this condition, known as Congenital Lactose Intolerance, were doomed to a quick if horrifying death by starvation. Congenital LI must always have been extremely rare, as it would have been impossible for such babies to grow to adulthood and pass their genes on to children of their own. The first known case does not appear in the medical literature until 1959 and only about 40 more cases are known worldwide. Today, Congenital LI can be identified immediately after birth and lactose-free formulas allow these babies to thrive.

When Do Most People Stop Producing Lactase?

With lactase the last and weakest among intestinal enzymes, it's hardly surprising to learn that it is also the first to go. Generally speaking, those populations with the greatest frequency of LI in adults will also have lost their lactase at the youngest age. The lactase-making ability of a few may diminish in their first year of life. Many more will keep their lactase high through age five and only then see a drop. In others, lactase production may fall very, very gradually throughout life so that symptoms from milk will not be noticed until adulthood. A few people have first reported lactose intolerance in their seventies. And many people simply keep producing sufficient lactase and never have LI at any time in their lives.

Who Is Likely to Develop LI?

Whether you maintain a high level of lactase production or switch it off early in life is genetically controlled. Anyone whose ancestors were born in Great Britain, France, Germany or Scandinavia is very, very unlikely to be or become LI. Those whose families originated in eastern Europe, northern India or anywhere along the Mediterranean shore are about as likely to be LI as LP. Except for a few isolated populations, LI is omnipresent in all the world's other ethnic groups.

Scientists hypothesize that it can be no coincidence that the areas with the lowest LI levels are also those where dairying has been a tradition for thousands of years, any more than it could be chance that LI is nearly universal wherever no milkable animals are to be found. That moderate levels of LI are found in populations who historically processed their milk into low-lactose forms only strengthens the hypothesis.

The U.S. is a milk-drinking nation with generally low levels of LI precisely because the vast majority of Americans are descended from northwestern Europeans who brought their cows and their LP genes with them when they settled the country. Even so, LI is probably at its highest levels today since the time when the universally LI Native Americans were the sole inhabitants of the continent. Immigration has greatly increased the number of Americans with ancestry from historically moderate and high LI areas of the world, such as Africa, Asia, Arabia and southern and eastern Europe. Intermarriages of these people with those of northwestern European descent has somewhat reduced the percentages of LI among these groups in the U.S. because the LP gene is dominant, meaning that children will likely be LP if either one of their parents is.

The inevitable conclusion is that eventually the LP gene will triumph everywhere except in a few isolated pockets of humanity. Until that day arrives, knowing your ancestors is still your best clue to your odds of being LI.

Will All Dairy Products Create LI Symptoms?
If being LI meant having no lactase at all, the answer would probably be yes. Few, if any, people truly have no lactase. The rest of us can produce at least a small amount of lactase and so can digest at least a small amount of lactose. We each have a lactose threshold, and up to a certain point lactose will create no symptoms at all. Exceed your threshold, however, and the symptoms will rapidly worsen with every new bit of lactose in your system.

For example, whole milk straight from the cow is about 5% lactose. The amount of lactose in half a standard 8-ounce glass of milk can be safely ignored by almost everyone. About one-fifth to one-third of people with LI develop symptoms from a whole glass. But two glasses of milk will cause symptoms in about 90% of those who are LI. Overindulging in any dairy product will almost assure unpleasant consequences.

Not all dairy products will do this equally, though, for their lactose contents vary tremendously. Butter is almost entirely milk fat; cheese is made from milk protein and it loses what little lactose remains through processing and aging. After eating the five or more pounds of cheese or butter needed to equal the lactose in two glasses of milk, LI symptoms would be the least of your worries. Traditional "soured" milks, including yogurt, kumiss, kefir and acidophilus milk, contain bacterial cultures that make a form of lactase of their own. The bacterial lactase breaks down 30%–40% of the lactose, mostly into the lactic acid that gives sour milks their tart taste, and in doing so it lowers the milks' lactose content below the threshold of many people. Dried milk products, on the other hand, are up to 80% lactose. Even the small amounts of these (or of lactose itself) that are used in packaged foods may be enough to produce a reaction.

Can Anything Be Done to Cure LI?
No. It is a natural consequence of aging, not a disease. No one has ever found a way to restart or increase lactase production once it has declined.

Can Anything Be Done to Alleviate LI Symptoms?

Yes, but to do so you have to focus on the true problem. Antacids aren't the answer, because they work on stomach gas rather than gas formed in the colon. Antidiarrhea medicine is not really helpful, because you want the offending lactose out of your system as soon as possible. Antiflatulents may be of some help in controlling the worst gas pains but they don't combat any of the other symptoms. In short, by the time you start feeling the symptoms, it's almost too late to do anything useful about them.

Prevention is the key. You can reduce symptoms either by reducing the amount of lactose entering your intestines (by eating lower-lactose foods or smaller portions of dairy products) or by increasing the amount of lactase available to break it down before it can do any damage.

Since you can't get your body to produce more lactase, a reliable outside source of it is needed. Scientists realized that certain microorganisms could be put to work in the laboratory to produce lactase under controlled conditions. Bacterial lactase works best as drops that can be added to milk to pre-digest the lactose there. A host of commercial low-lactose dairy products that have been pretreated with lactase are also widely available. Yeasts make a slightly different form of lactase that enables you to take it as a pill with food. While the pills should be taken with the lactose-containing food for greatest effect, some relief of symptoms may be possible if taken after consumption or even when symptoms are first felt.

How Serious a Problem Is LI?

If you believe everything you read, LI may be the most widespread medical condition in the U.S. Sales of lactase enzyme pills, reduced-lactose milk products and nondairy milk alternatives now exceed a fat $200,000,000 a year. The gigantic advertising campaigns that launched the lactase wars of the early 1990s proclaimed (in large type) that 1 in 4 adult Americans—some 50,000,000 people—suffered from LI. Other players in this business dropped the modifying "adults" and simply stated that 25% of all Americans have LI, which would place the number over 60,000,000. Estimates in print run as high as 80,000,000 people (*see box*), or as many as voted for Clinton and Bush *combined* in the 1992 presidential election.

If you believe the doctors, these numbers are wildly inflated. Dr. Michael Levitt, a veteran in gastrointestinal research, says that the marketers are "overdoing the severity of the problem." Another well-known LI scholar, Dr. Douglas McGill, says, "From my perspective, lactose intolerance has been a fad for 30 years now. There is nothing new except that business is after it."

Both sides, I should add, can back up their beliefs with a vast array of top-notch scientific research, years of professional experience and facts that are absolutely incontrovertible.

So who should you believe?

Neither side. They're both wrong.

LI people make up a very small percentage of the patients seen even by specialist gastroenterologists for a number of reasons: too few people know about the effects of LI; they have complaints they consider to be annoying or disruptive rather than a serious medical problem; they're embarrassed to talk about anything as personal as gas and diarrhea; they've stopped consuming milk because of the problems it caused; they already use lactase to be able to have milk again; LI is often likely to be diagnosed as a side issue after other, more dangerous, illnesses are involved.

Adults do not die from LI, nor do they need extensive testing, prescription drugs, or hospitalization. Nor does LI itself lead to more serious problems, although someone falsely ascribing debilitating symptoms to LI may wind up not getting attention for the true underlying cause until it worsens. From a doctor's point of view, LI is hardly a sexy issue (nor a very profitable one, if you want to be cynical). Doctors can't fairly be blamed for considering LI to be a relatively minor concern.

That the marketers take the exact opposite approach and ballyhoo the largest possible number of LI sufferers is also easy to understand. They want retail stores to make shelf room for their products, which will happen only if store owners think that those products will draw sufficiently large numbers of customers into the stores.

The truth lies somewhere in the middle. For millions of Americans LI is a real problem. Needing to think about every morsel of food you put into your mouth, needing to deal with the consequences if enough milk slips by, needing to look for special products and needing to adapt recipes and forego some favorite foods makes LI a constant trial, even with the wealth of milk alternatives and lactase products on the market. For many it is easier to not have milk than to hope you've gauged a dose of lactase correctly or to remember to carry lactase with you at all times. Children are especially sensitive to being thought of as different due to their LI. For the LI, a world in which milk is easier to avoid would be preferable to one in which measures must constantly be taken to avoid feeling ill.

LI may be a problem, but it is not one of an epidemic scale. Those 50 or 60 or 80 million people never did descend onto their local supermarkets demanding alternatives to high-lactose milk. That big a market just doesn't exist. But if only a conservative 20% of those who are LI get symptoms from a glass of milk, then we number 10 million strong. That's a vast pool of dollars that could be swung toward restaurants that feature milk-free meals, bakeries that market milk-free breads and desserts, food giants that list amounts of lactose on their products' nutrition labels or smaller firms who target the LI in their advertising. Our numbers are large enough to command attention and respect if only we could make our voices heard.

The national ad campaigns of the early 1990s managed to quadruple the sales of milk alternatives in only two years. We have a long way to go,

LI: RUNNING THE NUMBERS

How do you count the number of people who have LI when most of them have never even heard of it? You don't. Any number given is, at best, an estimate.

The truth is that the number of people who have LI—in the U.S. or in the world—is, just like the number of homeless, battered women, kidnapped children, philatelists and Madonna fans, essentially unknowable. For one thing, there is no one accepted definition of "a person with LI." Is it someone whom a doctor has tested and shown to be lacking lactase? Is it someone who has already experienced symptoms from milk? Is it anyone who would develop symptoms if given a sufficiently large dose of lactose? Even if we could somehow freeze time and magically check every individual in the U.S., these three definitions would result in three different counts.

Here's how I believe the widely accepted figure of 50,000,000 was produced. Scientists have roamed the world testing every conceivable group of people to determine whether or not they can digest lactose and in what amounts. Despite the lack of uniformity in test procedures, the results paint a remarkably consistent picture of the amounts of LI in groups with different ethnic heritages (*see Appendix I*).

More than perhaps any other country, the U.S. is home to vast numbers of immigrants or descendents of immigrants from all parts of the world. Luckily, ancestry is one of the questions asked by the U.S. Census Bureau. By applying the range of percentages found in ethnic studies, and factoring in the knowledge that children in those groups with the highest percentage of LI become LI earlier than those from mostly LP populations, it is a straightforward if tedious mathematic calculation to determine how many people are theoretically LI.

The result, however, is the proverbial educated guess rather than a true count, due to several serious shortcomings in the available data.

I found the appropriate numbers from *The Statistical Abstract of the United States* and attempted to apply them to the studies summarized in Appendix I. But those studies cover only a small fraction of the world's population. I dug out other results from other studies but still had holes left for which I could only estimate percentages. The census data was just as problematic. Many millions of Americans either refused to answer the question, gave vague replies (like "European" or "white") that cannot be neatly assigned to any specific study, or provided two or more countries of ancestry. One estimate led to another, extrapolation followed extrapolation. In the end I grouped similar-sounding answers as best I could, knocked off a percentage for children too young to likely be LI and multiplied the remaining number times a "high" and "low" percentage of LI for each group to cover the range of results given by different studies. The final numbers were then scaled back to account for multiple answers.

I ended up with an estimate of 40 to 70 million people in the U.S. who are, or are likely to become, LI, just as advertised. Even though the exact number may never be known, there are certainly tens of millions of individuals in the U.S. who are at risk for LI symptoms and who therefore can benefit from the products aimed at the LI and the kind of information gathered in this book.

however. Those reached were still just a small fraction of the potential market. Unfortunately, ad expenditures of that magnitude cannot be continued indefinitely; the smaller campaigns that followed lost the power to reach others with LI who have not yet gotten the message.

Informed consumers are powerful. They know whom to approach to satisfy their needs, they recognize what to demand and what to reject and they can articulate why it is important to them. The rest of this book is devoted to turning you into an informed consumer. All of us can then work together to take it from there.

2

THE SCANDALOUS HISTORY OF LACTOSE INTOLERANCE

That I had never even heard of LI when I was first diagnosed in 1978 says much about the newness of the term, which hadn't even appeared in the medical literature until the 1960s. I would guess that the term was therefore equally unfamiliar to a great many doctors in the 1970s. Dr. Norman Kretchmer, a pioneer in the study of LI, once wrote that "this general adult deficiency in lactase has come as a surprise to physiologists and nutritionists." He attributed this ignorance "to a kind of ethnic chauvinism."

The ethnicity in question is that of those white northern Europeans males and their counterparts in the U.S. who have long dominated the world of medicine. LI was ignored purely and simply because the leaders in medical research did not suffer from it. For centuries they had focused their research on themselves and their own problems, ignoring even white northern European women, let alone the inhabitants of the Europeans' far-flung colonies. This tunnel vision probably owed as much to pure arrogance as to conscious racism; a belief in their status as representatives of the pinnacle of humanity precluded any thought that those less fortunate could inspire findings of broad-based medical significance. They would have dismissed a time traveler's report informing them that in the future they would be known to be in the global minority.

▮ 2,000 YEARS OF PROBLEMS WITH MILK

Today such an attitude is referred to as Eurocentrism, the belief that the body of ideas that are considered to be the accumulated wisdom of western civilization ever since the time of the ancient Greeks and Romans does not need to be opened to new influences, even in the multicultural, multiethnic, multiracial late twentieth century United States. The worldwide prevalence of LI proves how small-minded that attitude is. If those happily milk-drinking doctors and researchers had been willing to look beyond their own bodies 100 years ago, perhaps a great deal of suffering due to LI could have been avoided.

It is frustrating to look back and realize that all the information a conscientious researcher would have needed to recognize the relationship between lactose and LI was available by the first years of the twentieth century. Some of the clues had been there for centuries and should have been well known, for their source ironically lay in the writings of those same Greek and Roman natural philosophers revered as the founders of western science.

Hippocrates, the Greek "father of medicine," said in his aphorisms (around 400 B.C.) that "Milk is bad for patients with fever, those whose bellies are distended and full of rumbling." Six centuries later, Galen, the Greek-born Roman whose work dominated medical thought for 1,500 years, gave a perfect description of LI in his warning that milk:

> should not be given to all, but only those who digest it well . . . [I]f sometimes it [milk] should ever be taken alone without bread, it both goes through more quickly and is flatulent. But somebody was sick all the time, no matter in what way he prepared it. And somebody else, similarly trying to use the milk, had no trouble, for he digested it well, and had no hyperacidity, or eructation [belching], or gas . . .

There, in a single concise paragraph, is all a doctor would need to make a preliminary diagnosis even today. Why Galen's clear description of the problem was forgotten is not clear. Perhaps this sound advice was discarded with the many truly incorrect ideas he had about the human body. Perhaps it was merely that the study of the digestion of milk lost all urgency when the cutting edge of science moved to northern Europe, where LI was not an issue.

More probably, the specific problems caused by LI were lost in a jumble of warnings against all dairy products in general and fluid milk in particular. The 17th century English author Robert Burton said, "Milk, and all that comes of milk, as butter and cheese, curds, etc., increase melancholy." Around the same time a French physician wrote that "men of the highest dignity from too constant indulgence in cheese have brought about their own death," one of many such stories quoted in Martin Schook's 1664 treatise, *The Dislike of Cheese*. Even one of milk's strongest advocates, the eminent 18th century physician Frederick Hoffmann, was forced to temper his enthusiasm:

> Although there is no better nourishment for man or beast than milk, so that it well deserves to be called the prince of foods, nevertheless there is hardly any in the whole list of foods that is so unsafe, so deadly, and which presents an opening for so great and so serious diseases, as does milk.

Fluid milk's rapid spoilage in the days before refrigeration was so well known that even in temperate northern Europe most milk was immediately converted into forms in which it could be stored and shipped with comparative safety—cheese and butter. Perhaps it is no coincidence that these are also forms that are low in lactose and tolerated even by the LI.

By the mid-19th century, however, the industrial revolution helped fluid milk make a comeback. Although refrigeration remained an inventor's dream, the early morning milk train that speedily connected dairy farms with large cities put fluid milk into the hands of everyone, rich and poor. But the rich got the first choice while the poor had to be satisfied with a product we would barely recognize, one that was transported on open trailers and arrived looking like dirty cheese. Adulterated and often disease-ridden, milk was responsible for a continuing series of epidemics of typhoid fever, diphtheria and septic sore throat well into the 1930s. For these same decades, Louis Pasteur's pasteurization process remained more of a laboratory curiosity than a standard part of milk production.

Even so, Pasteur made biochemistry and experimental medicine two of the hottest topics for bright young science students to dabble in, and milk received more than its fair share of the attention. If only they or their physiologist and nutritionist colleagues had pushed a little harder they could have made the breakthrough then and there.

As early as 1860, German scientists discovered that milk sugar gave dogs diarrhea. (Milk sugar received the formal name of lactose when its chemical composition was worked out in 1927.) By the 1890s, scientists knew about lactase in the intestines and that only young animals, no old ones, showed lactase activity. In 1903, they nailed down the mechanism by which undigested lactose created diarrhea.

Though these findings came from experiments on animals, milk sugar's effect on people had not gone unnoticed. Abraham Jacobi, professor of the Diseases of Children at Columbia University, was the first to sound a warning, in his speech to the Children's Section of the Thirteenth International Medical Congress in 1900. He advised his fellow pediatricians to add cane sugar to cow's milk to make it as sweet as mother's milk and therefore more acceptible to babies, rather than follow the usual practice of adding milk sugar. Milk sugar was known to cause diarrhea; doctors used it as a laxative for constipated babies. Analysis showed that much of the milk sugar was passing through the intestines undigested. Jacobi even understood that the quantity of milk sugar present was linked to the severity of the problems it caused.

Oddly, this admonition about milk sugar's role was given over and over again to no effect. In 1921, John Howland, then president of the American Pediatric Society, in the very same medical journal that had in 1901 printed Jacobi's speech, wrote that it was "a perfectly fair criticism to make in this very field of discussion that, while it is now generally appreciated that sugars initiate and perpetuate diarrhea and are capable of doing a great amount of damage, it took many years to arrive at this realization and almost all the other ingredients of milk were held responsible before the sugar.''

Although doctors developed soy milks and other nondairy substitutes to serve as infant formulas for babies who could not digest milk, it evidently entered no one's mind that adults might have similar problems and similar needs. Even the spark that finally ignited the medical community's awareness of LI came from a 1959 report of two babies who had had LI from birth—a condition that had never before been reported in the medical literature.

After that bombshell a major new discovery hit the journals every year. First came reports that various intestinal surgeries could temporarily or permanently shut down the body's ability to produce lactase. Then lactase deficiency was found in adults with healthy intestines. Surprise turned to shock in 1966 when a study found that 70% of ''Negro'' subjects but only 5% of whites proved to be LI. Two years later, another study found that 95% of ''Oriental'' adults living in the U.S. were LI. By the end of the 1960s scientists were swarming all over the globe testing every conceivable ethnic group for LI. To their amazement, they found it everywhere they looked.

■ A WORLD THAT IS LACTOSE INTOLERANT

Far from the rarity it was once thought to be, LI is closer to being a universal condition. Every group, nationality, ethnic heritage and race that has ever been tested has contained individuals with LI.[1]

Some patterns are immediately apparent from the results of over 100 studies in Appendix I. First, there can be no question that being able to digest lactose from birth is the norm. Except for maybe one baby in every 100,000,000, all humans are born with enough lactase to digest mother's milk. We start losing lactase remarkably quickly, however, with some infants becoming LI in their first year of life. (LI is occasionally referred to as ''adult-onset lactose intolerance'' in medical journals, but this is another case of Eurocentrism, true only for a minority of those with LI.) Each year thereafter a few more children become LI so that a majority of teens are LI along with an overwhelming number of adults in almost every corner of the globe. Clearly, the ability to produce lactase is genetically designed to last only as long as a child might expect to be breast fed by a

---

[1]The range of those studied is so great that it is highly unlikely any untested group will break this pattern. I'm hoping that the gaps (the largest is the former USSR, where very little testing has ever been reported) will soon be filled in, if only because knowing the distribution of LI in these areas may answer other puzzling questions.

mother. Check the entries listed under Bangladesh in Appendix I for a perfect illustration of rising LI with age.[2] By the age of five, LI is universal in that country.

Second, different groups start showing high percentages of LI at different ages. The groups who show the highest levels of LI as adults also become LI at a younger age. Conversely, while you can become LI at any age, odds are that if you can still drink milk as an adult, you will always be able to do so.

Third, which group you belong to appears to depend almost entirely on geography. People in certain parts of the world, along with travelers or immigrants from those countries, are much less likely to have high rates of LI than people from Bangladesh or other Asian countries. A sizable third group appears to have moderate percentages of LI. The geographic boundaries of these groups have a great deal to tell us about the origin of LP. How one thinks of these boundaries, however, changes the story they have to tell.

Your Ancestors and LI

The simplest, glibbest way of sorting out LI from LP is to split the world up by race. If you are white, especially of northern or western European heritage, you are unlikely to be LI. If you are nonwhite, it is highly probable that you are LI. And if you are either of mixed racial heritage or descended from brown- or olive-skinned peoples from the area around the Mediterranean Sea, you come from groups whose percentages of LI are between the first two. Dividing the world this way tells us little about LP, although it helps to explain why LI was so long ignored.

It's interesting to note how closely the populations with moderate to high levels of LI mirror the groups targeted by restrictive U.S. immigration laws, themselves influenced by notions of racial inferiority. Until after the Civil War, most settlers were overwhelmingly from northern Europe, while nonwhites were excluded or brought in only as laborers or slaves. A late nineteenth century shift in immigration patterns toward eastern and southern Europe engendered such resentment that a way to end the influx was contrived. The excuse was found in the low marks routinely scored by recently arrived immigrants on English-language intelligence tests. A 1924 law drastically reduced immigration from exactly those areas of the world where we now know LI levels to be moderate or high. Without that law,

---

[2]Note for the technical-minded: The perfect numerical correlation in Bangladesh is probably due to those studies being conducted by a single set of researchers. In other countries, different studies of different subgroups by a variety of scientists using different techniques are lumped together, creating a messier picture. Still, no exception to the general trend has ever been found, which, given the difficulties of doing field studies on human subjects, produces an overwhelmingly strong case.

the increasing numbers of such peoples might have triggered awareness of LI as a majority issue decades before it was finally recognized as such.

The exceptions and anomalies that complicate the racial approach soon drove most researchers to a more sophisticated way of viewing the issue that involved dividing the world into zones that are historically dairying or non-dairying. Milking animals (except possibly for ritual reasons) was once an unknown practice in the Americas, Australia and Oceanea, all of eastern Asia and in a wide belt across central Africa. Virtually the entire populations of each of these areas have proved to be highly LI. (Scholars once dismissed the cramps and diarrhea these nonmilkers developed after drinking milk by calling them "psychosomatic.") The rest of the world has been milking animals for many thousands of years, and these areas correspond almost perfectly to the regions of low and moderate LI.

This correlation is tantalizing, but doesn't provide an answer for any of the critical questions. Why did anyone start drinking animal milk in the first place? Why are humans the only mammals to exhibit LP? Did we always have this ability or did drinking milk as adults cause it to develop? Was it instead simply a chance mutation among a few? And if it was, could it really have spread from a presumed handful of people to a billion adults throughout the world so quickly?

Over the past two decades scientists in both the medical and anthropological communities have built on each other's efforts to formulate a strong and convincing explanation for the appearance of milk-drinking populations. In some ways it reads like the last chapter of a classic whodunit, in which the detective weaves together a series of clues that no one else would have noticed to build an airtight case against the least likely suspect. The explanation will take us across time and around the world, drawing connections between the relationship of English to Sanskrit, the explanation of the prevalence of pork in Chinese cuisine, the change in climate that allowed the Sahara desert to expand and the reason why sea lion cubs don't develop rickets. (James Burke, eat your heart out.)

If you're a closet anthropology buff you need no more excuse to read the following section. Those who aren't as enamored by anthropology can skip ahead to the next chapter. But you'll be missing a great yarn.

▌ THE ORIGINS OF MILK-DRINKING

We All Started with Mother's Milk
Mammals' ability to produce milk for their babies separates them from every other creature on earth.

All mother's milk is custom-designed as a nearly perfect food, necessarily so as it is the sole nourishment that the infant will receive during its period of greatest growth and greatest risk. Despite the tremendous value of mother's milk, it is a temporary resource. After a few days, or weeks, or years, the mother ceases producing milk, forcing her babies to stop suckling and move on to whatever solid food their species normally eats.

It may seem odd (and often tragic in the wild) that a mother withdraws such a nutritionally perfect, not to mention handy and mobile, food supply so early in a child's life. Mothers know best in this case. Lactating mothers require extra food and expend more energy, a drain on their resources that they must balance against ensuring their offsprings' survival until the children are old enough to fend for themselves. Presumably, mothers who never stopped lactating were too weak to successfully bear and raise more children; those who stopped too soon condemned their first batch. The ones with the best timing won out and lived to pass along more of their genes.[3]

Mammals, including certain upright primates who in the past several million years spread out of Africa and across the globe, have continued the cycle of nursing and weaning for the entire 200 million or so years that they've existed. In a harsh world where there was often literally feast or famine, the primates who would evolve into *homo sapiens* had a tremendous advantage: They were omnivores. Everything that they encountered became food, from the flesh and marrow of animals that they could hunt or scavenge, to the insects and grubs that also nourished their simian relatives, to an entire biosphere's worth of plant diversity—the hundreds of varieties of greens, roots, tubers, fruits and vegetables. (They undoubtedly would have drunk milk as adults as well, but lacked any access to it.) Only this utter lack of finickiness could have kept them alive through hard times and hard climates. By 10,000 B.C. they could be found in every inhabitable site on earth.

A New Source of Milk Appears

Somewhere around that time—the archaeological evidence is scant, but compelling—humans started domesticating other animals. Cattle, sheep, water buffalo, goats, camels, llamas, yaks and less familiar animals, whatever animals happened to be locally available were put to use. Keeping the animals penned nearby instead of hunting them down one by one saved time and energy. Animals provided meat, fur, leather, transportation and—in times of dire emergency—milk that might keep a baby alive if the women in the tribe had none to spare.

The human willingness to try any source of nourishment when the old standbys fail must have provoked the next logical step, which was for an adult with no other source of food to try drinking milk. (Killing all the

---

[3]Note for the technical-minded: It was once assumed that lactase production continued as long as lactose remained present in the diet. The loss of that trigger at the time of weaning was believed to be what prevented LP in animals. The predominance of experiments fail to bear this out; lactase production stops regardless of lactose intake.

animals for their meat was unthinkable, an absolute last resort. Dead animals could not produce offspring to keep the cycle going in future years. Animal-less tribes were soon doomed.) Most people who tried this must have regretted it, for if LI individuals drank enough to truly nourish themselves, they undoubtedly grew very, very sick in the process. But desperate people will resort to desperate measures, and it is better to be sick than dead. To their surprise, a few people must have found themselves neither sick nor dead. They could have their milk and drink it too, and that enabled them to survive when others did not.

Why Milk Drinking Spread around the World

The milk drinkers, though they could not have known this, had a quirk in their genetic makeup. In place of a gene that stopped the production of lactase when they were just a few years old, they had a gene that never sent that signal. As far as we know, there was no reason for this difference, nothing otherwise special about these people. The change simply came from a random mutation (*see box*). The mutation made the gene dominant as well, so that children who inherited it also could drink milk as adults.

GENETIC MUTATION AND NATURAL SELECTION

Our genetic material defines us absolutely uniquely. Passing along that identity to our children is surprisingly difficult. To conceive a child, a sperm must fertilize an egg. We assume that each of the hundreds of eggs or millions of sperm that we pump out over the course of a lifetime are tiny but exact copies of us. But with every egg and sperm having 23 chromosomes comprised of thousands of genes each with their own strands of DNA millions of amino acids long, the opportunities for slip-ups are abundant. Every difference between the copy and the original is called a mutation.

That makes mutations not just common but inevitable, a process that is known as genetic drift. The fact that children are so similar to their parents is proof that very few mutations are the harmful or deadly bogeymen of legend. Most, in fact, are neutral and invisible.

The LP gene was an example. The original LI gene sends out a signal shutting down the production of the lactase enzyme sometime after early childhood. The LP gene does not. For almost all of human history, this was a distinction without a difference. In a time in which no adult drank milk, the continuing presence of lactase had no noticeable effect at all. At some critical point, the availability of milk in a time of need revealed that a few adults had the ability to drink milk without getting ill. This gave them a totally unexpected evolutionary advantage.

Evolution is the unveiling of the effects of chance mutations by environmental changes. Much confusion stems from misunderstanding this

---

concept. Arguments against evolution almost invariably get cause and effect reversed: One food historian, for example, could not believe that "the lactase continues to be produced for generation after generation in the Micawberish hope that, some day, some lactose will turn up." Nevertheless, once you subtract out the anthropomorphic word "hope" this is exactly what happens.

Evolutionary changes occur automatically by means of natural selection. The process of natural selection can be stated very simply for all its incredible complication in actual practice: Those who survive to produce healthy offspring pass on their genes. If there is something special about those genes that offers an advantage—being more likely to live to become a parent, living longer to have more children, being better able to bear children without dying—those genes will over time appear in a greater and greater percentage of the population.

In other words, a random mutation to the LI gene produced the LP gene. At first the change went unnoticed, but eventually a few people with the LP gene were aided by milk's nutritional advantages to live to produce more children who in turn were LP. In just a few thousand years, the world had split into two groups: those with LP genes and those with LI genes.

Genes that exist in the population in a variety of types are called polymorphic, with each type known as an allele. Perhaps the best known example of polymorphic genes are the A, B, AB and O blood groups, the reasons for whose origins are lost in history. But it may be meaningful that the current frequencies of these four alleles show a regular gradation across Europe and correlate with the spread of farming from its source in the Middle East—exactly as the LI and LP gene alleles do.

The combination of the convenient presence of milk from domesticated animals, the nutritional advantage that milk can offer and the genetic dominance of the LP gene form the basis for the current scientific consensus that natural selection pressures account for the astoundingly high percentages of LP in certain corners of the world today. Once set into motion, the spread of milk-drinking appears to be inevitable, having happened at least twice in different ways in different parts of the world.

All that is necessary is that the following three conditions (set out by John D. Johnson, Norman Kretchmer and Frederick J. Simoons in "Lactose Malabsorption: Its Biology and History," *Advances in Pediatrics*, 1974; 21:197–237) be in place. LP is almost certain to appear whenever a cohesive group of people:

1. Have a plentiful milk supply;
2. Do not process their milk into products that are low in lactose; and
3. Cannot readily obtain from other available foods essential nutrients that milk does provide.

Milk, All Day, Every Day

The situation that would clearly create the greatest selection pressure is the one in which a group has literally nothing else to eat other than milk.

Impossible as it might seem, there are many such groups, all of them tribal nomads on the fringes of the Sahara desert. Take the Beja, who live in the Sudan between the Nile and the Red Sea. As recently as 5,000 years ago, northern Africa had a much wetter climate. When the rains dried up, so did the land, leading to a spread of the desert into traditional nomadic pastoral lands. Agriculture became impossible in this desert setting. Only animals could eat the few plants that naturally grew and no other food sources were available (condition 3). Yet the Beja survive as long as their animals do. During the dry season that may last as long as nine months, they live almost entirely on the milk of their camels and goats, up to three quarts per adult per day (condition 1). Milk processing and storage in forms that are low in lactose is impossible given the desert temperatures and the nomadic Beja lifestyle; all the milk must be drunk fresh (condition 2). As the Beja clearly satisfy all three conditions, they must have faced enormous selection pressures over the centuries in favor of those tribal members who could drink milk without getting sick. Today, over 80% of the Beja test as LP.[4]

Nor are they alone. Other nomadic desert peoples who have high frequencies of LP include the Bedouins in Arabia and the Libyan desert, Kabbabish in the western Sudan, Tuareg in the central Sahara and the Fulbe (Peulh) in the northern Sahel. (Whether each is an independent example of LP evolution or whether intertribal mixing of genes occurred is not clear.) Because their particular tribal cultures and unique histories have determined their powerful dependence on milk, this explanation for their LP is known as the "culture historical hypothesis."

Milk's Place in the Sun

Although it is possible that African nomadic tribes with similar histories and customs may have intermarried to be similarly LP, no one believes that they could also be responsible for the Scandinavians being 95% LP. It is equally unbelievable that milk was the only food available to those living in northern and western Europe 5,000 years ago. Does the underlying sequence of events in Europe also meet the conditions set out by Johnson and his colleagues for a natural selection advantage?

Both agriculture and the domestication of animals first appear in the archaeological record in the Near East about 10,000 years ago, a date that

---

[4]Note for the technical-minded: Given the inadequacies of LI testing in the field, it is likely that the remaining 20% of Beja are also LP, although some may simply have a high tolerance for milk due to the composition of their intestinal bacteria (*see* Chapter 7).

keeps getting pushed back farther and farther with each new discovery. Nomads-turned-farmers typically have a population boom serious enough so that some newly married couples or disgruntled factions want—or need—to strike off on their own for less crowded lands or less played-out soil (a smaller scale version of the same process that first took humans out of Africa).

According to anthropologist Colin Renfrew, the result was a slow diffusion of peoples deeper and deeper into the rich farmlands of Europe rather than a heroic journey of Neolithic explorers deliberately setting off to search for the fabled ice-covered lands of the Arctic. The edge of the developed areas may have been pushed out only a few miles on average during each generation but that was sufficient to blanket the continent over the course of 100 generations. The same early crops which reached Greece between 6,000 and 5,000 B.C. were distributed across today's Germany and Poland a scant 1,000 years later and reached Scandinavia and Britain between 4,000 and 3,000 B.C. The progression appears to have followed two broadly defined routes: an early one that moved north from Greece into the Balkans before turning west; and a somewhat later movement that we can trace westerly along the Mediterranean before it finally pushed north (*see box*).

Knowing that northern European agriculture and animal domestication had its origins in the sunny Near East gives useful clues to the type of foods and farming methods familiar to the northerners. It also alerts us to watch for adaptations these early farmers must have been forced to make as they wandered up from the Mediterranean into a climate that was dangerously different.

Americans often forget just how far north Europe truly is. Rome is at about the same latitude as New York City, while London, Paris and Berlin are north of any point in the continental U.S., and the Scandinavian capitals are as close to the North Pole as Anchorage, Alaska. While much of Europe is kept temperate by the warming effects of the Gulf Stream, its extreme northern latitudes not only make it the winter sports capital of the world but also result in winter nights far longer than any in the continental U.S. The lack of sun, worsened by northern Europe's extreme cloud cover, created a severe problem in a way that is not at all obvious.

The body produces natural vitamin D through the action of ultraviolet (UV) rays on chemicals just under the top layer of skin. Africans and the Semitic populations in the Near East were and are very dark-skinned, a protective adaptation against constant sun and the skin cancers it can cause. Although dark skin lessens vitamin D production by reducing the amount of sunlight's UV rays it lets through, this is hardly a concern in lands where a few minutes a day in the noontime sun could keep levels high.

THE PECULIAR PAIRING OF LANGUAGE AND LP

English is a member of the Indo-European family of languages, as are the majority of languages in Europe. The dispersion of Indo-European languages, as they swept west from their ancestral home in Turkestan in central Asia and across the upper Near East, follows, according to anthropologist Colin Renfrew's reconstruction, strikingly similar routes to those taken by the movement of agriculture across Europe. One branch started near Greece and can be traced north into the Balto-Slavic languages and then west through the Germanic languages; the other went through Greece and then followed the course of Latin and its Romance language descendants as they moved west to Spain and north into France. Eventually, of course, the two prongs would rejoin and become modern English after the Norman Conquest in 1066.

It would not seem to be mere coincidence that, except for descendants of those nomadic African tribes, every major group in the world with low levels of LI speaks an Indo-European language and every major group with moderate LI levels speaks either an Indo-European tongue or one of the Semitic languages that got their start in the lower Near East. In fact, given the spread of European genes after their frenzied three centuries of colonizing other continents, dividing populations into Indo-European speaking or non-Indo-European speaking may be the most sensible way of understanding who in today's world is likely to be LP or LI.

As the farmers moved north and encountered cooler summers and devastating winters, however, they were forced to cover more skin for longer periods of the year, cutting them off from what little direct sunlight was available and leaving them with a dangerously diminished vitamin D capacity. Among other effects, a lack of vitamin D lowers the body's efficiency in absorbing the calcium present in its diet. The result is the bone deformity and bowing of the long bones of the legs that is associated with the disease known as rickets in children and osteomalacia in adults. By far the earliest evidence of rickets in humans comes from Neolithic burial sites in Denmark. Woman were especially at risk, for even those who survived adolescence could easily die from the stress that childbirth put on weakened bones.

We've clearly discovered another situation in which natural selection pressures would be strong. The people with the reproductive advantage would be those with mutations that reduced their resistance to sunlight or improved calcium absorption. The problem must have been nearly overwhelming, for the survivors were the ones with both genetic advantages (*see box*).

The ever-present danger of skin cancers tended to kill people with fair-skinned mutations in Africa, but any such disadvantage in northern

Europe was more than overshadowed, so to speak, by the life-giving properties of increased vitamin D production. Fair skins developed as a particular, local adaptation to lack of sun and nothing more.

Calcium is a different issue. Two different issues, actually, for the Europeans not only needed to better absorb calcium, they needed a steady supply of the hard-to-come-by mineral in the first place. Other cultures derived calcium from mineral-rich water or from high-calcium plants that the agriculture of early Europe was not well-suited to. The Europeans found their own solution: milk.

Milk does not contain any significant amount of vitamin D (that's why the milk you buy in stores must be artificially fortified with it) but it is absolutely one of the best sources of calcium. Finding foods that contain calcium and being able to digest those foods are separate problems, however, and the extremely large percentages of LP found in northern Europeans would not have developed in a mere few thousand years were there not one further benefit to be gained from milk.

Lactose, it seems, actually improves calcium absorption—but only if lactase is present.[5] The evidence for this is somewhat mixed, although the majority of reports support this position. One study concluded that injesting calcium with lactose increased calcium absorption by 59% over plain calcium in those who were LP but *decreased* it by 18% in those who were LI.

Milk's crucial role in providing strong bones is a clear and powerful stimulus for the selection of individuals who are LP. This explanation for the European affinity for milk drinking is known as the "calcium absorption hypothesis."

Europe's Unique Dairy Culture

The early northern Europeans were surrounded by milkable livestock—sheep, goats, reindeer and, somewhat later in history, cows—whose milk helped build strong bones. This satisfies two of the three conditions needed for the spread of the LP gene in a population.

One question remains unanswered. Why did the early Europeans start drinking milk in the form of milk in the first place? They knew nothing of vitamins and minerals or their role in the body and they were not totally dependent upon fluid milk as a food source. Nor is the mere presence of livestock the answer. Many cultures around the world have milkable animals and never use milk. Why drink milk if it makes you sick?

The only answer can be that dairy products didn't make the early Europeans sick, even though they were not, at first, highly LP.

When the Bible talks about the "land of milk and honey," the milk it

---

[5]This characteristic of lactose may help explain why natural selection favored the production of lactose over other simpler or easier to digest sugars in the first place.

EAT YOUR LIVER IF YOU DON'T DRINK YOUR MILK

Europeans could be dark-skinned today, and thereby suffer far fewer incidents of skin cancer than they do, if only they had had a way of increasing the vitamin D in their diet. None lay close to hand, however. The best dietary sources of vitamin D are marine fish oils and sea mammal liver, but a high-seafood diet was not an option for farmers pushing their way across the interior of a continent. Eskimos, who did primarily live on such a diet, undoubtedly satisfied their vitamin D requirements in this manner just as their fulfilled their calcium needs by learning to gnaw on animal bones and eating their fish bones and all. (This is an extreme and marginal solution not to be taken by anyone with an easier calcium source close to hand.) With no selection pressures toward milk drinkers, you would therefore expect Eskimos to be predominately LI, and this proves to be the case.

We can even take this a step further and clear up the mystery of why the Pinnipedia—California sea lions, seals and walruses—are the only higher mammals whose milk contains no lactose. Their livers are loaded with vitamin D because their entire diet consists of marine fish. And, unlike that of all other mammals, their milk too is rich in vitamin D. With an assured supply of the vitamin to encourage calcium absorption, there was no selection pressure to develop lactose and lactase for the purpose.

The need to be able to absorb the calcium in the diet has been one of the most powerful forces shaping mammalian existence throughout history.

---

refers to is in the form of yogurt, laban, kefir or other fermented or "sour" milks, a term which itself is used in the Bible. The origins of yogurt and its variations are not completely certain (*see Chapter 7 for more information*), but these products have been known in the Arabian desert for thousands of years.

Sour milks were originally developed solely because they took longer to spoil in the desert heat. They soon became a staple because, in addition to their distinctive taste, they were both nutritious and easy to digest: highly fermented yogurts are low in lactose. Thus the selection pressures for LP were small, though not entirely zero. Indeed, the percentage of today's Semitic peoples who are LP is intermediate between that of northern Europeans and of peoples who never incorporated any dairy products into their diets, exactly as theory would predict.

Probably, then, the farmers who moved out of the Near East into Europe in the first place already had a tradition of using dairy products. Milk keeps better in the cold of winter than in the heat of summer, so the northerners would have had less need to sour their milk to keep it from spoiling, allowing them to drink it as is.

Or perhaps milk drinking developed as a part of butter-making. A prized liquid (called buttermilk, although it is a different product from the commercial buttermilk of today [*see Chapter 6*]) remained after the rest of the milk was churned into butter. Heated and strained it made cheese; pigs fed on it produced prime quality pork. Butter itself became a daily necessity to provide fat in lands where the olives that supplied the oil ubiquitous along the Mediterranean could not grow. Even so, a herd of dairy cows can produce more butter than a farm family or village can possibly use. Containers of salted butter, buried to preserve them for lean years that never came, have been dug up from peat bogs all over Europe. It's not hard to imagine how milk itself could be added to the repertoire in cultures that cherished everything that came from the cow.

Both explanations may be true at different times and different places. Either way, the Europeans do satisfy condition two: They did not process all their milk into products that were low in lactose. And they spread their genes and their love of dairy all over the world.

A QUICK LOOK AT MILKLESS CULTURES

No test of the natural selection theory can be complete without examining cultures who have lived with domesticated milkable animals for millennia without turning to them for fluid milk. They must fail to fulfill at least one of the three conditions laid out earlier for the theory to be true. Anthropologists have gone into these questions in enormous detail, but I'll keep it down to two examples.

India
Cattle may have been domesticated in India almost as early as they were in the Near East. By the time of the Vedas, a cattle and farming people who dominated northern India starting 4,000 years ago, cows were part of daily life. Today's India may contain 200 million cattle, more than any other country in the world, plus an additional 50 million milkable water buffalo.

India's reputation as the home of the "sacred cow" is misleading. The laws prohibiting the slaughter of cattle are real and perhaps half the population are vegetarians, but only a very few religiously abstain from the use of all animal foods. Dairy products are not just a major part of Indian cuisine, but one of the chief protein sources in the country. Yet the incidence of LP is only low to moderate in the tropical south and no more than moderate to high in the temperate north. It is assuredly no coincidence that northern India contains both the point of the easternmost spread of moderate LI groups and the eastern boundary of the Indo-European language family, as represented by Sanskrit. It is even conceivable that just as English is a descendant of Sanskrit, today's milk drinkers are the progeny of the original speakers of that language.

The word tropical is an important clue to the differences between India and Europe. All of India is far closer to the equator than any point in Europe. Long winters and lack of sunshine never limited the natural vitamin D supply, as evidenced by the populations' still-dark skins. The warmer climate also allowed the mostly vegetarian south to make calcium-rich vegetables and legumes a principal part of their diet, along with many varieties of seafood, which would also contribute vitamin D.

Milk is more commonly used in northern India, but there it is typically processed into various low-lactose forms: a water-buffalo yogurt called *dahi*; cheeses known as *chenna* or *paneer*; and *ghee*, a type of highly clarified butter. Nowhere in India is there evidence of any inexorable pressure to become LP to survive.

China

China would perhaps seem to be an even more difficult case to explain than India. Tropical does not apply here: Northern China can be as bitterly cold and snowy as Europe. Latitude is the key. Beijing, China's most northerly great city, is farther south than is Rome; Canton, in southern China, is closer to the equator than any point in the continental U.S. The combination of longer winter days and a generally sunny climate allowed the Chinese to receive sufficient sun for vitamin D production.

Chinese agriculture also leans heavily toward green, leafy vegetables and soybeans, both good providers of calcium. With both their calcium and vitamin D needs met, the Chinese, like the Indians, were under no pressures to change or add to their diets. The crucial difference is that the Indians choose to incorporate milk while Chinese cuisine is virtually devoid of dairy products.

Cattle and water buffalo have other uses that win them a place in Indian society—as plow animals, for instance. The Chinese certainly knew of these animals but did not have the space and resources in their densely populated land to allow their presence in large numbers. They instead turned to an animal that could easily be kept in a small village while being fed on otherwise useless household garbage: the pig. Pigs are not milkable animals, for they have no udders and so no place for storing milk. China exhibits none of the conditions necessary for developing high LP populations.

Competing Theories

It's only fair to end by saying that what I've given here is not the last word on the origin of milk drinking, still an area replete with speculation. Unlike capital T Theories, like the Theory of Gravity or the Theory of Evolution, which are presumed to be the facts upon which all the rest of science is based, small t theories are still in their own process of evolution. I wove together a consensus view that, even ignoring my necessary simplifications, contains elements that some disagree with.

A minority view, for example, places the origin of milk-drinking on the Arabian peninsula. In this theory the selective advantage doesn't involve milk as a food or calcium source but stems from the fact that milk would provide an additional source of water and electrolytes that would help those who were LP better survive the recurrent epidemics of diarrheal diseases, such as cholera.

Population geneticists use powerful mathematical analysis to aid a much more sophisticated critique. These scientists see a coevolution between the genetic trait of LP and the cultural option of milk-drinking, and note that coevolution can be mathematically shown to require a substantially longer period than a strictly genetic one. Plugging the numbers from the archaeological evidence into their equations gives results that argue that the relatively recent development of dairying in Scandinavia does not allow sufficient time to spread the LP gene so thoroughly through that population. Recent discoveries that dairying in Europe may be much older than the 5,000 years previously thought may remove this objection. In addition, other simplifying assumptions they use to make the equations manageable may not adequately reflect complex reality.

One older theory that has been superseded but seemingly never actually refuted may be the most radical theory of all, for it does not depend on natural selection. According to this "reversed-cause" argument, dairying is adopted by precisely those populations who can tolerate it, where the LP gene is already common because of genetic drift. This would allow a much longer period for the spread of the gene. On the other hand, if LP truly came first you would expect to find some high LP populations that were not traditionally milk drinkers, but none of these have ever been identified.

Part of the reason for these differences in opinion stems from the lack of cooperation among the medical researchers, anthropologists and population geneticists, each of whom cannot help but approach the problem from their discipline's narrow perspective. Better information and evidence would also help. Many of the studies of LI and LP percentages are based on unrepresentative populations, use tests less reliable than those available today, or are otherwise not strictly comparable. Many populations still have not been tested at all. Moreover, the whole field of Neolithic anthropology is in ferment, with new dating techniques and more precise methodology revamping older notions of the spread of agriculture and dairying. As equations are only as good as the numbers plugged into them, new assumptions and new findings could radically change their output.

One way or the other, however, it is clear that lactose holds a unique position in the human diet. It appears both to be supremely important and a general nuisance, depending on time and place. Over the new few chapters I'll take a closer look at lactose and at milk and the roles they play in nutrition and digestion.

3

STARTING WITH A SWEET TOOTH: LACTOSE AND MILK

Lactose is the sugar found in milk and in milk alone. The beauty and usefulness of this fact is somewhat obscured in English, where the term "milk sugar" is all but obsolete, but it allows you to bypass the appalling lack of translations of the word lactose in foreign language phrasebooks by piecing together the readily available words for milk and sugar. Thus in Germany, one can try to avoid *Milchzucker*, in France, *sucre de lait* and in Lithuania, *piencukris*. On the other hand, the word to look out for in Portuguese is *lactose*.

If we can digest it, milk—and when I say milk without further explanation I'll always be referring to cow's milk—is among our most valuable foods. High in a wide range of nutrients, able to be formed into a cornucopia of dairy products, an almost inevitable component of French and Italian and Mexican cuisines, milk is virtually unavoidable. The catch is that milk is designed to be a children's food. Lactose is, for adults, probably the least useful part of milk, making the problems it causes doubly ironic.

Know your enemy, as the saying goes. In this chapter I'll look at milk sugar from the perspective of both milk and sugar. Sugar first.

■ LACTOSE AND OTHER SUGARS

Who first knew of sugar's ability to make foods sweet is lost deep in the very beginnings of food history. We trace our modern word "sugar" back through Middle English to Old French to Medieval Latin to Old Italian to Arabic to Persian and finally to Sanskrit. Sanskrit is the base from which all Indo-European languages evolved; speakers of Indo-European languages also brought with them into Northern Europe the ability to drink milk. Words that can get traced back to Sanskrit are among the root words of western culture.

Sugars are equally fundamental in importance to the human body. Lactose's presence in mother's milk makes it the first sugar we encounter and the only one our bodies may deal with for many months after birth. It is in this period that lactose is most essential to life.

Lactose itself is formed out of the two simpler sugars glucose and galactose and is split back into them during digestion. As lactose is found only in milk, it's not surprising that the word itself comes from the Latin word for milk. (Galactose is derived from the Greek word for milk.) It was discovered in milk by Bartoletti in 1619 but not identified as a sugar until Scheele did so in 1780.

Galactose has little purpose on its own but glucose is nothing less than the basic energy source of the human body. A fair amount of everything involved in the digestive process can be said to exist solely to rip foods apart and turn the pieces into glucose. Lactose is in mother's milk partly to make it a tad sweeter and more appealing to the baby who depends on it but mostly to afford the newborn a constant supply of glucose (*see box*).

GLUCOSE IN THE BLOODSTREAM

Right this minute, as you're sitting here reading this, approximately one-fifth of an ounce of glucose is floating through your bloodstream, available for cells to grab whenever they need energy. That doesn't sound like very much and in everyday terms it isn't, but the body is almost fantastically efficient, able to make tiny amounts go a long way. The energy in our total blood glucose is equal to a mere 22.7 Calories, equivalent to that in almost exactly half a tablespoon of ordinary table sugar. Calories are very energy-intensive, however. The chemical energy contained in 22.7 Calories is sufficient to raise the temperature of 50 pounds of water by 1.8°F.

The demands of keeping the body at a constant temperature while simultaneously running the respiratory, circulatory, digestive and other systems and repairing and maintaining cells depletes energy at a fearful rate. Those 22.7 Calories can't last forever, and after about 15 minutes the energy supply must be replenished with more glucose. Since we don't eat 22.7 Calories every 15 minutes, the body needs a way to store glucose, which it does as a starch called glycogen. In between meals glycogen is broken back down into glucose (in a process called glycolysis) and dribbled out into the bloodstream. The pancreas, of all things, then gets involved, since it produces the insulin hormone which regulates the level of sugar in the blood to insure that it never rises to dangerous levels.

If we had to deal solely with glucose, life would be very much simpler. But even though glucose can be found in nature—in many sweet fruits and honey—it's available in fairly limited quantities compared with the many other sugars that exist. The upshot is that our digestive systems have to be able to recognize all the various sugars and other carbohydrates and know how to deal with them. That's where the problems arise.

TABLE 1 SIMPLE AND COMPOUND SUGARS				
SIMPLE SUGARS				
Chemical Name	Common and Alternate Names		Direct Food Sources	Sweetness
				(sucrose = 1)
Fructose	Fruit sugar; Levulose		Fruits; vegetables; honey	1.73
Galactose			Plants	0.32
Glucose	Blood sugar; Dextrose		Fruits; honey	0.74
Mannose			Manna ash tree	*
(* Mannose is always converted into a compound called mannitol before use.)				
COMPOUND SUGARS				
Chemical Name	Component Sugars	Common Names	Direct Food Sources	Sweetness
Lactose	Glucose + Galactose	Milk sugar	Milk	0.16
Lactulose	Galactose + Fructose		(not found in nature)	
Maltose	Glucose + Glucose	Malt sugar	Malt; grain; fruits	0.32
Sucrose	Glucose + Fructose	Cane sugar; Beet sugar	Sugar cane; sugar beets; maple sap	1.00

Notes to Table 1:

If a packaged food label says simply "sugar," the sugar it's referring to is sucrose. Any other sugar must be mentioned by name.

Other sugars you may find in foods:

Invert sugar: Mixing two simple sugars together is not the same thing as chemically combining them. Mixing glucose and fructose yields not sucrose but "invert sugar," with a sweetness of 1.3. Honey is a form of invert sugar, about 50% glucose and 50% fructose, although some varieties have more fructose and some may also contain a small percentage of sucrose.

Corn syrup: The starch in corn is made from long strings of glucose. These can be broken down to produce a syrup which is a mixture of various percentages of glucose and maltose.

High fructose corn syrup: Manufacturers who want a sweeter syrup can use an enzyme to convert some of the glucose in corn syrup into fructose. High fructose corn syrup contains about 52%–55% fructose, 42%–43% glucose and 3%–5% other sugars.

Molasses: This somewhat bitter and sticky liquid is concentrated sugar cane juice with roughly equal parts of sucrose and invert sugar.

Brown sugar: Not to be confused with raw sugar, which is similar in color but merely unrefined sucrose, brown sugar is made by coating crystals of sucrose with molasses. A small percentage of invert sugar may be present.

Sugars come in two varieties: simple sugars, or monosaccharides, and compound sugars, or disaccharides (*see Table 1*). Glucose is, not unexpectedly, a simple sugar, saving the body from having to take yet another step to break it down. The chemical formula for glucose is $C_6H_{12}O_6$. Oddly enough, this is also the chemical formula for galactose and every other familiar simple sugar. (Some foods contain five-carbon sugars, but their rarity puts them outside our scope.) Tiny differences in the placement of the oxygen and hydrogen atoms in the three-dimensional molecule account for all of the variations in the sweetness and other properties of these sugars.

As I said, lactose results from the chemical combination of the simple sugars glucose and galactose. Lactose has a chemical formula of $C_{12}H_{22}O_{11}$. (Its full formal name is O-β-D-galactopyranosyl-[1 → 4]-D-glucopyranose.) Logically, you might think that you could just double all the numbers in the formula for a simple sugar to get the formula for a compound sugar. Not quite. Combining simple sugars into compound ones, or condensation, forces out a molecule of water, H_2O, accounting for the missing atoms. The addition of a molecule of water is therefore required to split lactose back into its component parts. This process is known as hydrolysis. The hydrolysis of large molecules into smaller ones is in fact the exact definition of digestion. If your body cannot hydrolyze lactose you get the symptoms of LI (*see Chapter 5 for more details*).

Lactose is not terribly sweet for a sugar. Sugar sweetnesses don't play by ordinary rules. Since lactose is formed from glucose and galactose you might think that it would be as sweet as both of them put together or, alternately, that it would be as sweet as the average of the two would be. Instead, for reasons which are still not clear, lactose is less sweet than either. Powdered lactose is almost tasteless, one of the reasons it is so valuable as an additive in commercial baking.

When nutritionists scream about there being too much sugar in our diets, they're usually referring to sucrose, the sugar that is added to pop and cereals and baked goods and most everything else, including places you'd probably never suspect. If you check the ingredient labels on some salt packages, for instance, you'll find sugar listed.

Sucrose is an excellent anticaking agent, meaning that it can keep the salt grains from sticking together on humid days. Not all sugars work this way (fructose tends to pack into solid lumps) but lactose is just as good an anticaking agent. For some applications lactose may be even better since it is tasteless—artificial sweeteners, for example. They are so strong that a quantity equal in sweetness to a tablespoon of sucrose would barely be visible to the naked eye. Lactose is the perfect carrier for an artificial sweetener to give it the appearance of a free-flowing powder. All the brands I've checked, however, use either glucose or the corn-derived maltodextrins for the purpose, with one exception: Equal tablets (not packets or pouches) list lactose as the first ingredient. It is good to get into the habit of checking labels yourself.

For similar reasons lactose is used in the manufacturing of pills and tablets to bulk out the tiny active ingredients. (More on the use of lactose in medicines in *Chapter 13*. A listing of over 300 prescription medications that contain lactose will be found in *Appendix III*.)

Food scientists love lactose. Creating food in mass quantities that can sit in cans, bottles or bags for weeks or months on grocery shelves and still come out tasting more or less like what you can make in your own kitchen is quite a chore, but lactose helps in a dozen ways. Lactose is generally regarded as being a better carrier of flavor than fructose, glucose or sucrose. Since it has no characteristic flavor of its own it's compatible with many other food flavorings and additives and is especially good with fruity flavors. Added to baked goods lactose can contribute to flavor, texture, appearance and shelf-life. Lactose-enriched nonfat dry milk increases the tenderness and volume of cookies and doughnuts. Since lactose is not fermented by baker's yeast, it can be sprinkled on baked goods to produce a perfect brown crust without adding excess sweetness. French-fried potatoes need to caramelize a bit of sugar to produce the golden brownness we love with our burgers—in the United States sucrose or dextrose (the commercial name for glucose) is almost always used but lactose would also work perfectly well.

Finally, lactose adds that mysterious something known as mouth feel. Fats do this, too, as anyone who has tried the various low-fat or fat-free substitute products on the market knows. Even if the taste doesn't change too much, the substitutes never quite feel as rich or smooth in the mouth. Lactose can be a cheap and less fattening way of getting some of the texture back.

▌ MAMMALS AND MILKS

Human beings, like dogs, cats, bats, rats and sperm whales, are mammals. Mammals have a number of things in common that no other kind of animal on earth has. Fur, for example. All mammals have some hair; no other animal does. But Linnaeus, the scientist who invented the classification system we still use today, was even more impressed by their ability to give milk and so gave the group a name that comes from the Latin word meaning breast. (This strikes no one today as odd, but the mammals are the only major group named after a female characteristic, a bold move indeed for an 18th century male chauvinist who was a mammal himself.)

After childbirth, the mother's breasts produce milk. This internally generated, portable food supply gives mammals a tremendous advantage over other animals. The young of fish and reptiles and amphibians have to be able to fend for themselves from birth. Birds are limited in the area they can search for food because they have to return to the nest to feed their helpless chicks. Mammals are not. When times get rough, a mother mammal can prowl for food with her babies clinging to her or carried by her. As soon as she eats, they do. This is the kind of competitive advantage that helped mammals to survive even when they were no more than pests to the ruling dinosaurs and enabled them to dominate when the dinosaurs disappeared.

Most Americans, I'm sure, think of milk as milk, a constant, uniform product that comes from a cow. Probably not until they are confronted with their first child are they forced to realize that human milk and cow's milk are very different products and that baby formulas little resemble what's available in the local supermarket's dairy case. Each animal's milk is customized to best suit the needs of its own young, needs which vary tremendously. Table 2 compares the major constituents of mother's milk with that of a number of common animals that have been used for milking in various cultures. (Milk differs in other ways as well, some that affected history. Mare's milk has twice the vitamin C of human milk and four times that of cow's milk. The nomadic Mongols, whose diet was virtually devoid of fruits and vegetables, might have died out from vitamin deficiency diseases if they had depended on cattle. Instead, they made the horse the center of their culture and had both the health and mobility to conquer most of Asia.)

Scientists love numbers because their patterns, far from being cold and impersonal, actually tell stories about the ways of the world. Those in

TABLE 2
MILK FROM MANY MAMMALS

MAMMAL	LACTOSE (%)	FAT (%)	PROTEIN (%)	CALORIES/100 g*
Humans	6.94	4.62	1.23	73
Asses	6.20	1.50	2.10	46
Horses	6.00	1.60	2.20	47
Llamas	5.30	3.20	5.20	65
Indian Buffalos	4.90	7.45	3.78	100
Cows				
Guernsey	4.70	4.65	3.65	75
Frisian	4.60	3.50	3.25	62
Yaks	4.60	7.00	5.20	100
Goats	4.40	4.50	3.30	71
Sheep	4.40	7.50	5.60	105
Camels	4.10	4.20	3.70	70
Reindeer	2.40	22.50	10.30	250

*Scientists always use the metric system, whose unit of weight is called the gram (g). There are 454 grams in a pound; 28.375 grams to the ounce. In addition, 1 milligram (mg) = 1/1000 of a gram; 1 microgram (mcg) = 1/1,000,000 of a gram = 1/1,000 of a milligram.

(Adapted from *Milk and Milk Products in Human Nutrition,* 2nd rev. ed. Food and Agricultural Organization of the United Nations, FAO Nutritional Studies No. 27. Rome: S.K. Kon, 1972.)

Table 2 allow for deep insights into evolutionary history. Human babies are small and helpless for months after birth, but other mammals expect that their young will be up and moving in a much shorter time. Human babies require some 180 days to double their birth weight, while calves need only 50 and lambs do it in a mere 15. In growing that fast lambs need a constant and tremendous supply of protein and so the protein content of sheep's milk is very high. We slow-growing humans can get along with a much smaller percentage of protein. There's a tradeoff here. Generally speaking, the higher the protein content, the lower the lactose, and vice versa.

A similar relationship holds for fat and lactose. Fat contains more Calories than sugar does, so it's a more concentrated source of fuel. Cold-climate animals like the reindeer have an overriding need for the warmth those Calories can provide and so natural selection favored those individuals whose milk had the highest fat content. Aquatic mammals, especially arctic ones, need even higher levels of fat in their milks. Sea lion milk is 35% fat.

If you were to deduce that sea lion milk is extremely low in lactose, you'd be right. Except for the very primitive mammals known as the monotremes, which include the duck-billed platypus and other oddities, whose ancestors evidently appeared before lactose evolved, the Pinnapedia (including the sea lion and its close relations) are the only mammals whose milk is entirely lactose-free. (We first learned this fact in 1933, when a baby walrus was being shipped from Alaska to California. Not having any spare walrus milk lying around, the handlers fed it cow's milk. The young walrus grew extremely debilitated from what must have been one of the worst cases of diarrhea in history, but recovered when it rejoined other walruses at the zoo, inspiring scientists to do a fast analysis of walrus milk.)

No milk is terribly sweet, at least not by the standards of colas or even fruit juices, but of all the milks, human milk is the sweetest that exists, with a reported lactose content as high as 7.5%. We're all born with a sweet tooth. Why we need all that sugar isn't quite clear. Monkey milk is almost as high in lactose, so the answer lies somewhere back in our evolutionary heritage rather than being a part of the uniqueness of humanity.

With milk being so customized, it's obvious that no other milk will be as right for an animal as that from its own mother. Fortunately, unlike that poor baby walrus, humans can still get some value out of animal milk. Measures exist to compare the nutritional usefulness of various foods, including biological value (BV) and net protein utilization (NPU). With mother's milk set equal to 100, cow's milk has a BV of 84.5 and an NPU of 81.6. Not bad.

But not perfect. Far be it for me to cast aspersions on the advertising profession, but in reference to cow's milk the slogan, "Milk is the perfect food," just ain't so. Human milk beats it in a number of ways. It has less of a protein called casein, giving it a curd that is lighter and easier to digest.

Breast feeding may help prevent or delay the onset of allergies and is a rich source of bacterial and viral antibodies. The vitamin contents are also slightly different. "Mother's milk is the perfect food" would be a lot closer, but even that isn't quite true. For one thing, all milks are low in iron and most are deficient in vitamin D.

Supposedly, when billionaire John D. Rockefeller grew very old he hired wet nurses and lived his last years of life on mother's milk, proving something no doubt very profound about the value of huge piles of money. Even if this were desirable, it's hardly feasible for the rest of us. In the U.S. we make do by supporting a wide-ranging dairy industry and drinking oceans of cow's milk. Cow's milk's strengths are that it provides a broad spectrum of the nutrients most people need, is easily obtainable and, thanks to a vast array of subsidies, costs relatively little for the food value it possesses.

In part, milk has become such a huge part of our daily diet because of its versatility. We use liquid milk, dried milk, cultured milk, soured milk, frozen milk, sweetened milk and condensed milk in literally hundreds of different forms. (All the major varieties will be included in *Chapter 6*.)

And while cow's milk may not be the perfect food, it is at least an extremely good one. Dairy products are not irreplaceable, but cutting

TABLE 3 PERCENTAGE OF TOTAL U.S. INTAKE OF NUTRIENTS THAT IS SUPPLIED BY DAIRY FOODS (EXCLUDING BUTTER), 1988	
NUTRIENT	PERCENTAGE
Carbohydrate	5
Fat	12
Protein	20
Minerals	
Calcium	75
Iron	2
Magnesium	19
Phosphorus	34
Zinc	19
Vitamins	
Vitamin A	16
Thiamin (Vitamin B_1)	8
Riboflavin (Vitamin B_2)	33
Niacin	2
Vitamin B_6	10
Vitamin B_{12}	18
Vitamin C (Ascorbic acid)	3
Folate (Folic acid)	8
Vitamin E	3
Energy (Calories)	10

them out leaves a very large hole in the diet that needs to be filled. On a national level, we get a third of our phosphorus and riboflavin from dairy foods and a whopping three-quarters of our calcium (*see Table 3*). This means that if you have already stopped using dairy products, your diet may not be as healthy as it should be. If you seriously plan to do without milk, you need to be careful to make healthful changes to your diet at the same time. To do this you need to know something about good nutrition and the intricacies of the digestive system. Nutrition first, though. That's the subject of the next chapter.

4

....

NUTRIENTS: GOOD HEALTH
WITH OR WITHOUT LACTOSE

If you are what you eat—and, jokes aside, there's plenty of evidence that you are—how do you decide what needs to be replaced and what you can do without if you are going to eliminate or greatly reduce milk in your diet?

On the very simplest level, milk is water, lactose, proteins, fats and vitamins, with the remaining tiny percentage of minerals and miscellaneous lumped together as "ash." Water is water and lactose is lactose: After that, the complications begin. Milk contains three distinct families of proteins totalling 18 different amino acids; a variety of fats plus related compounds called lipids; over a dozen vitamins and some 30 macrominerals and trace elements in the ash. Milk naturally contains both silver and aluminum, not to mention pseudoglobulin and ketonogenic glycerides. Are they necessary? What happens to you if you don't include them in your diet? Where do you go to order a side dish of ketonogenic glycerides if you don't drink milk? To be honest, nobody really has the answers to these questions.

And the process of investigation is not a job for the squeamish. The basic techniques by which it is possible to discover whether something in our food is vital to health include studying people who have eaten staggeringly deficient diets for long periods of time; examining patients who through genetic defects, illnesses or surgery have lost the ability to process a nutrient; or depriving volunteers of that component of their diets. The one study of experimentally induced magnesium deficiency (on cancer patients who had to eat a special formula) brought forth symptoms involving nausea, muscle weakness, irritability and mental derangement. And that is a fairly mild list as such things go. As it may take a very long time to deplete the body of its store of a nutrient, such studies have to be conducted over periods of months, even years. Volunteers do not flock to nutrient deficiency studies.

When you consider that milk alone may have 100 components worthy of someday being named essential nutrients, it's not surprising that our knowledge of those well down the list is lacking. Even so, determining essentiality is a breeze compared to determining exactly how much of any of those nutrients should be included in a diet to bring about the highest conceivable state of health in a person. Nutrients interact with one another to such a degree that a thorough study would involve pairing every nutrient on the list with every other, running through all possible variations in dosages and then starting over again looking at them three at a time. And even then all the work would have to be customized to our individual circumstances which change, sometimes radically, over time.

The foregoing may give you a shadow of a clue as to why the battles over what should and shouldn't be in your food and in your diet are acrimonious, noisy and never-ending. To examine issues of especial concern to the LI, I'll be using as my base the summarized wisdom of the last hundred years of research into nutrition—the Recommended Dietary Allowances (RDAs).

■ HOW MUCH GOOD HEALTH CAN ANY ONE BODY TAKE?

The RDAs are put out by the Food and Nutrition Board of the National Academy of Sciences-National Research Council (NRC). They're good, sound advice, conservative in the non-political sense, and the best available today. The last revision was completed in 1989 and is shown in Table 1. To put this mass of figures into perspective, Table 2 shows the percentages of RDA found in a glass of milk.

Any discussion of nutrition has to start with the RDAs, not least because you see them listed on all nutrition labels on packaged foods and the ingredients labels of vitamin and mineral supplements. A surprising number of Americans do not get sufficient amounts of certain nutrients in their diets and the latest data show that the vast majority of us need to improve our eating habits. Making the RDAs universally available provides a constant series of gentle nudges toward a better diet.

For all their value, the RDAs have numerous critics from every position. Some of the flaws can't be denied. Our knowledge and understanding of nutrition changes and expands rapidly and constantly, leaving the RDAs lagging until the controversies settle. Even so, too little is still known about the dozens of components of food beyond the 19 currently in the RDAs to establish firm recommendations for them. The RDAs are divided into 18 age- and sex-related categories, undoubtedly too few rather than too many, lumping far larger groups of people together than would be ideal. The fine print states that, "The allowances, expressed as average daily intakes over time, are intended to provide for individual variations among most normal persons as they live in the United States under usual environmental stresses," a statement that contains as many hedges as a English garden maze.

Does LI or a physical ailment mean that you are not normal? What is a usual environmental stress? I'm 44 years old, but does the group labeled "males 25–50" apply to me? On the other hand, it is so nearly impossible to determine the exact amount of any nutrient in your daily diet that fine tuning the RDAs is (except in special, individual, cases) hardly worth your time. If you want to make the effort or if you think you have a special situation or needs, the NRC puts out a whole book, *Recommended Dietary Allowances, 10th edition*, (write to National Academy Press, 2101 Constitution Ave., NW, Washington, DC 20418 or order through your local bookstore), that explains the reasoning behind every recommendation and allows you to customize the RDAs more closely to your individual requirements.

It used to be so much simpler. Many of you will remember the time when these numbers were no more than Minimum Daily Requirements. As humorist Dave Barry has said, they were "based on the requirements of the Minimum Daily Adult, a truly pathetic individual that the government keeps in this special facility in Washington, D.C., where he is fed things with names like 'riboflavin.'"

Today, however, the objective is not to establish minimum requirements, but optimal values to ensure your health. A worthy goal, and one that I'll keep in mind as I discuss the individual nutrients as they apply to someone I like to call the Mythical Average Person (MAP).

▎ CARBOHYDRATES

The sugars, mono- and disaccharides, described in Chapter 3 are one form of carbohydrates. Polysaccharides, also known as complex carbohydrates or starches, are long strings of sugars hooked onto one another. Potatoes and other root vegetables, whole grain breads and flours, pasta, rice, peas and beans, and fruits and vegetables in general are all good starch sources. Dairy products are the only major animal source of carbohydrates in the diet.

Each gram of carbohydrate—sugar or starch—provides only 4 Calories, less than half that of fats. The complex carbohydrates are now recognized as "good things." In the 1950s, a diet plate might consist of a hamburger (with up to 75% of its Calories from fat) and cottage cheese (with 30%–40% of its Calories from fat) but no bread. Starches, it was then thought, made you overweight. Today, the advice is just the opposite. You should plan your diet around complex carbohydrates. Foods containing complex carbs come loaded with other nutrients, generally have little fat and are low in Calories for their bulk, so they fill you up without putting on pounds, and are digested more slowly than simple sugars, thereby giving you an energy boost for longer periods of time.

In general, carbohydrates should provide 55%–60% of the daily Calories in the MAP's diet, up from about 45% today. The bulk should be from starches, with no more than 10% from sugar. (No sugar, whether

TABLE 1
FOOD AND NUTRITION BOARD, NATIONAL ACADEMY OF SCIENCES – NATIONAL RESEARCH COUNCIL
RECOMMENDED DIETARY ALLOWANCES,[a] Revised 1989
Designed for the maintenance of good nutrition of practically all healthy people in the United States

Category	Age (years) or Condition	Weight[b] (kg)	(lb)	Height[b] (cm)	(in)	Protein (g)	FAT-SOLUBLE VITAMINS Vitamin A (μg RE)[c]	Vitamin D (μg)[d]	Vitamin E (mg α-TE)[e]	Vitamin K (μg)
Infants	0.0–0.5	6	13	60	24	13	375	7.5	3	5
	0.5–1.0	9	20	71	28	14	375	10	4	10
Children	1–3	13	29	90	35	16	400	10	6	15
	4–6	20	44	112	44	24	500	10	7	20
	7–10	28	62	132	52	28	700	10	7	30
Males	11–14	45	99	157	62	45	1,000	10	10	45
	15–18	66	145	176	69	59	1,000	10	10	65
	19–24	72	160	177	70	58	1,000	10	10	70
	25–50	79	174	176	70	63	1,000	5	10	80
	51+	77	170	173	68	63	1,000	5	10	80
Females	11–14	46	101	157	62	46	800	10	8	45
	15–18	55	120	163	64	44	800	10	8	55
	19–24	58	128	164	65	46	800	10	8	60
	25–50	63	138	163	64	50	800	5	8	65
	51+	65	143	160	63	50	800	5	8	65
Pregnant						60	800	10	10	65
Lactating	1st 6 months					65	1,300	10	12	65
	2nd 6 months					62	1,200	10	11	65

	WATER-SOLUBLE VITAMINS							MINERALS						
	Vitamin C (mg)	Thiamin (mg)	Riboflavin (mg)	Niacin (mg NE)[f]	Vitamin B6 (mg)	Folate (µg)	Vitamin B12 (µg)	Calcium (mg)	Phosphorus (mg)	Magnesium (mg)	Iron (mg)	Zinc (mg)	Iodine (µg)	Selenium (µg)
Infants	30	0.3	0.4	5	0.3	25	0.3	400	300	40	6	5	40	10
	35	0.4	0.5	6	0.6	35	0.5	600	500	60	10	5	50	15
Children	40	0.7	0.8	9	1.0	50	0.7	800	800	80	10	10	70	20
	45	0.9	1.1	12	1.1	75	1.0	800	800	120	10	10	90	20
	45	1.0	1.2	13	1.4	100	1.4	800	800	170	10	10	120	30
Males	50	1.3	1.5	17	1.7	150	2.0	1,200	1,200	270	12	15	150	40
	60	1.5	1.8	20	2.0	200	2.0	1,200	1,200	400	12	15	150	50
	60	1.5	1.7	19	2.0	200	2.0	1,200	1,200	350	10	15	150	70
	60	1.5	1.7	19	2.0	200	2.0	800	800	350	10	15	150	70
	60	1.2	1.4	15	2.0	200	2.0	800	800	350	10	15	150	70
Females	50	1.1	1.3	15	1.4	150	2.0	1,200	1,200	280	15	12	150	45
	60	1.1	1.3	15	1.5	180	2.0	1,200	1,200	300	15	12	150	50
	60	1.1	1.3	15	1.6	180	2.0	1,200	1,200	280	15	12	150	55
	60	1.1	1.3	15	1.6	180	2.0	800	800	280	15	12	150	55
	60	1.0	1.2	13	1.6	180	2.0	800	800	280	10	12	150	55
Pregnant	70	1.5	1.6	17	2.2	400	2.2	1,200	1,200	300	30	15	175	65
Lactating	95	1.6	1.8	20	2.1	280	2.6	1,200	1,200	355	15	19	200	75
	90	1.6	1.7	20	2.1	260	2.6	1,200	1,200	340	15	16	200	75

[a] The allowances, expressed as average daily intakes over time, are intended to provide for individual variations among most normal persons as they live in the United States under usual environmental stresses. Diets should be based on a variety of common foods in order to provide other nutrients for which human requirements have been less well defined.

[b] Weights and heights of Reference Adults are actual medians for the U.S. population of the designated age, as reported by NHANES II. The median weights and heights of those under 19 years of age were taken from Hamill et al. (1979). The use of these figures does not imply that the height-to-weight ratios are ideal.

[c] Retinol equivalents. 1 retinol equivalent = 1 µg retinol or 6 µg β-carotene. [d] As cholecalciferol. 10 µg cholecalciferol = 400 IU of vitamin D.

[e] α-Tocopherol equivalents. 1 mg d-α tocopherol = 1 α-TE. [f] 1 NE (niacin equivalent) is equal to 1 mg of niacin or 60 mg of dietary tryptophan.

TABLE 2			
FOOD VALUE IN A GLASS OF MILK			
	PER 8 OZ. WHOLE MILK		
NUTRIENT	**AMOUNT**	**UNITS**	**PERCENTAGE RDA***
Protein	8.03	g	16%
Fat-Soluble Vitamins			
Vitamin A	307.	IU	38
Vitamin D**	100.	IU	25
Vitamin E	Trace		0
Vitamin K	Trace		0
Water-Soluble Vitamins			
Vitamin C	2.29	mg	4
Thiamin	0.093	mg	8
Riboflavin (B_2)	0.395	mg	30
Niacin	0.205	mg	1
Vitamin B_6	0.102	mg	6
Folate	12.	mcg	7
Vitamin B_{12}	0.871	mcg	44
Minerals			
Calcium	291.	mg	36
Phosphorus	228.	mg	29
Magnesium	33.	mg	12
Iron	0.12	mg	1
Zinc	0.93	mg	8
Iodine	10.49	mcg	7
Selenium	9.76	mcg	18

g = grams; mg = milligrams; mcg = micrograms; IU = International Units
*RDA is that for female, age 25–50.
**Added during processing.

honey or brown sugar or raw sugar, has worthwhile amounts of other nutrients.)

One other form of complex carbohydrate has been in the news steadily for the past several years: fiber. Fiber crazes are nothing new: Kellogg's cereals were first formulated as cure-alls by the good Dr. Kellogg at his sanatorium in Battle Creek in the early part of the century. The doctor was preoccupied by the need for cleaning out the intestines on a regular basis and found that high-fiber diets did the trick.

There are two kinds of fiber, however. Fruits, with their high water content, along with beans and oats, are higher in pectins and gums, fiber that dissolves in water. There is some evidence that this type of fiber may actually be able to lower the level of cholesterol in the blood (*see the section on fats and lipids*). Grains are especially high in insoluble fibers like cellulose, hemicellulose and lignin, as are vegetables in general. Bran, the husk of the grain that is eliminated in the production of white flour and white rice, has become practically synonymous with fiber. The insoluble fibers trap several times their weight in water as they move through the intestines, producing a laxative effect as well as stools that are larger but softer and therefore easier to eliminate. Others have claimed that fiber can aid diabetics by controlling blood sugar and that it may help prevent colon cancer.

No RDA exists for fiber, but we should eat probably two to three times as much as the MAP does now. Although those with LI may not feel they need anything more in the way of a laxative effect, fiber's water-trapping ability is probably helpful. To avoid diarrhea, increase the amount of fiber in your diet very slowly. On the other hand, fiber also shortens the time that it takes food to pass through the intestines, making lactose digestion more difficult (*see Chapter 4*). In general, you should probably avoid eating high-fiber foods with dairy products (as in the classic combination of bran cereal and milk) and get your fiber only from foods with complex carbohydrates, never from bulk fiber supplements.

▌ PROTEINS

Half the non-water weight in the body of the MAP consists of proteins. Hair, nails, skin and cartilage are formed from proteins. Muscle is mostly protein, which makes muscle meats (steak, for example) major protein sources. Digestive enzymes (including lactase) are proteins. Blood and milk are part protein. In fact, protein is found in every cell of the body. Even plants contain some protein.

Just as starches are made up of smaller sugars strung together, proteins are formed from smaller pieces called amino acids. Whereas starches and fibers just string one glucose after another, the vastly more complicated proteins are built up from 22 known amino acids, like letters of an alphabet. While there are only a few polysaccharides, the amino acid alphabet can form as many proteins as letters do words, giving proteins a versatility that no other nutrient shares.

Protein is not stored in the body, so we need regular supplies of it in the diet. That's easy. A 12-ounce sirloin steak alone contains all the protein an adult male requires in a day. Our meat-heavy diet therefore provides far more protein than is necessary for health. On average, the MAP needs only 8%–9% of daily Calories from proteins but actually gets 12%–14% that way.

Is that too much for good health? The controversy rages. Some say that, except for certain people with kidney problems and high-protein diets, there is no evidence that even 20% of daily Calories from protein would be harmful. On the other hand, protein has 4 Calories per gram just as carbohydrates do and excess protein can be similarly converted to fat, something that most of us do not need. Few people realize that the foods in which most animal proteins are found lug around far more Calories from fat than from protein. A T-bone steak gets 20% of its Calories from protein, the other 80% from fat.

Best current thought suggests that you aim for 12% of Calories from proteins. Note that growing infants and children need more protein per pound of weight than do adults. Pregnant and lactating women also should increase their protein intake. Otherwise, healthy adults—even athletes—probably get more than enough. Potatoes, sweet potatoes, spinach, broccoli, and corn are good plant sources of protein so a diet focusing on these will be high in complex carbohydrates and maintain protein needs even if you cut back on meat.

One warning to those contemplating going to a purely vegetarian diet: The human body can manufacture only 13 of the 22 amino acids. The other nine must be part of the diet. These nine—histidine, isoleucine, leucine, lysinc, methionine, phenylalanine, threonine, tryptophan and valine—are called "essential" amino acids. That's unfortunately confusing: All 22 are essential for health.

Animal proteins are "complete"; that is, they have sufficient amounts of all the essential amino acids. Plant proteins are "incomplete." Most plants are missing or are very low in one or more of the essential nine. Luckily, your body is capable of assembling a complete set of amino acids as long as the essential amino acids are present in the various foods eaten together at a meal (or at least within a few hours of one another). A plant that is high in lysine but low in methionine can "complement" one that is high in methionine but low in lysine. Most cultures around the world already have a staple dish that does this: corn-flour tortillas and beans in Mexico; soybean tofu and rice in China and Japan; lentils and rice in India; and Middle East hummus, made from chickpeas and sesame seeds. Peanut butter on whole wheat (not white) bread does the same trick.

As a rule of thumb, grains—rice, wheat, corn, rye, bulgur, oats, barley, buckwheat—should be combined with legumes—black-eyed peas, chickpeas, split peas, peanuts, lentils, sprouts and black, broad, kidney, lima, navy, pea and soy beans—to create a meal containing all the essential amino acids. Vegans need to be careful even then. The body digests proteins solely from plant sources less efficiently than it does from the typical mixed diet of plant and animal proteins. Those on a meat-heavy diet can think about reducing protein consumption, but if you get no animal protein at all, you need to be especially careful to get your full RDA of protein.

■ FATS AND LIPIDS

"Diets low in fat are associated with the reduced risk of cancer," proclaims the FDA. Worried about heart attacks? Saturated fats may be worse for you than cholesterol. High-fat foods contribute to obesity, itself a risk factor for heart disease. "Fat-free" foods proliferate in every aisle of the supermarket, including fat-free potato chips and fat-free brownies. Is there anything at all good to say about fats?

Yes, but don't blink or you'll miss it. Fats insulate the body and provide a cushiony layer for our internal organs. Fats keep your skin and hair from drying out. Fats contribute components for a number of regulatory compounds and are needed to absorb several vitamins. And most of all, fats supply energy for our muscles and the muscles of the animals we eat. Well-marbled meats contain more fat than protein. That fine porterhouse steak is tender enough to cut with a fork for the same reason that a warm block of butter is.

You don't need much fat to meet the body's needs: the equivalent of a tablespoon a day is sufficient. The MAP gets six to eight times that much. And not only do Americans in general get too much fat, they get too much of the wrong kind of fat. A quick fat lesson is in order.

Just as proteins are made of amino acids, fats are made of fatty acids, usually three of them, connected to a framework called glycerol, earning them the technical name of triglycerides. And just as sugars vary depending on the number and arrangement of their carbon, hydrogen and oxygen atoms, so do fats, the major difference being that fats contain much less oxygen relative to the carbon. This makes fats a more concentrated source of energy. Fats have 9 Calories per gram, more than protein and carbohydrate put together. Your body likes this, because it can store the greatest amount of fuel in the least amount of space, but it also means that it's way too easy to eat many more Calories of fat than we need or are even aware of.

The hydrogen in fatty acids raises another issue. A fatty acid with two or more pairs of missing hydrogen is polyunsaturated; a single missing pair of hydrogens creates a monounsaturated fatty acid. Saturated fats have their full complements of hydrogen. The additional hydrogen works to solidify the fat. Every fat in our food supply is a mixture of different percentages of poly, mono and saturated fatty acids. Animal fats, including those in dairy products, are usually highly saturated and therefore solid. (Butter turns solid when released from the milk it is part of.) Fats which are liquid at room temperatures are called oils and most vegetable oils are indeed liquid and low in saturated fats. (Coconut "oil" and palm kernel "oil" are misnamed fats, solids much higher in saturated fat than butterfat.) Hydrogenation, adding hydrogen, will turn an oil into a fat by saturating it, the secret behind the partially hydrogenated oils found in most solid margarines.

The three essential fatty acids are similar to the nine essential amino acids in being dietary necessities. The body can't manufacture arachidonic acid or linolenic acid, but the most essential is linoleic acid, found in corn, safflower and soybean oils, since the body can use it as a base to make the other two. All three fatty acids are polyunsaturated, by the way. The body requires no saturated fat in the diet at all.

Both polyunsaturated and monounsaturated fats appear to have relative health benefits, prompting a boom in highly monounsaturated oils like canola and olive, polyunsaturated omega-3 fish oils and the high polyunsaturated oils. Liquid margarines are preferable in this sense to solid margarines or butter. Margarines and oils are still as much nutrient-free carriers of empty Calories as sugars are, however; going out of your way to add them to the diet makes no sense.

Fats do not dissolve in water, making them part of a larger class called lipids. Another example of a lipid is sterols, including the dread cholesterol. Dread or not, cholesterol is found in—and needed in—every single cell in our bodies; it is in the bodies of animals generally but not in any plants. It's not an essential nutrient, though, because the liver can manufacture all the cholesterol we need, fortunately for the vegans who survive without the intake of any foods derived from animals.

Animal-food eaters can easily get so much excess cholesterol in their diets that it causes problems. Specifically, cholesterol can cling to the insides of our arteries, clogging them like the pipes in your kitchen sink. If they become totally closed off, the result can be a heart attack or stroke, the leading killers in the United States.

In recent years, the direct relationship between blood cholesterol and heart disease has been questioned, or at least understood to be oversimplified. As a lipid, cholesterol can't travel through the water-based bloodstream by itself. The liver manufactures carriers called lipoproteins that transport the cholesterol where it's needed. High-density lipoproteins (HDL) seem to be more efficient at this than low-density lipoproteins (LDL). You can think of the LDLs as dropping cholesterol along the arteries in their path, while the HDLs not only hold on better, but even sweep out the deposits left behind. Therefore it is not merely your total cholesterol count that is at issue, but your ratio of HDL to LDL as well. Scientists are now finding that high levels of blood triglycerides may be an even better predictor of heart disease than high cholesterol. Saturated fats both stimulate LDL production and raise cholesterol and triglyceride counts, while polyunsaturates favor HDL transport and may lower cholesterol counts.

Little wonder that low-fat diets are the latest craze. Some authorities contend that no more than 10% of the Calories in your diet should come from fat. More conservative advice, as usual, comes from the NRC. There's no RDA for fats, although they're studying setting RDAs for individual fatty acids, but they do recommend that no more than 30% of daily Calories come from fat, split more or less evenly among poly, mono and saturated fats, and that dietary cholesterol should be no more than 300 mg/day. This does not mean that every single food you eat must have less than 30% or 10% or whatever your Calories from fat target is. Even with the occasional treat, an overall healthy diet you can stick with is better than a rigid one you keep falling off.

▌ VITAMINS

Vitamins' healthful effects were known long before they were named, or even thought of, from the days when British sailors were nicknamed "Limeys" because they drank lime juice on long sea voyages to prevent scurvy. This "antiscorbutic vitamin" is still called ascorbic acid, or, more familiarly, vitamin C. Scurvy is just one of a long line of so-called deficiency diseases, from beriberi to pellagra to rickets, now mostly unknown in the United States, which are prevented by regular doses of vitamins.

The 13 known vitamins are absolutely essential to good health despite being needed only in extremely tiny doses. How tiny? Well, an ounce of vitamin D is a 15,000-year supply for the average adult. A daily supply of all 13 vitamins is barely visible to the naked eye. (Vitamin pills are largely filler, huge mostly so the manufacturer can stamp its logo on them.) So little of any vitamin is present in any food that isolating vitamins foiled chemists until the early years of the twentieth century. Vitamin A was named in 1913 and alphabets of vitamins seemed to follow. Decades went by until testing proved that many of the "new" vitamins were really identical to older ones and that some of the others thought to be related weren't. By that time it was far too late to start over with a sensible naming system. In consequence, we have vitamins E and K, but not F or G, and vitamin B_{12} but not B_{11}. The trend lately is to go back to calling the vitamins by their chemical names and avoiding the letters and numbers as much as possible. I'll give both versions to avoid confusion, with the more commonly used one first.

Vitamins are classed into two large groups depending upon whether they are water-soluble or fat-soluble. Water-soluble vitamins are not stored well in the body, so you constantly need to replenish your supply of these vitamins through the foods you eat or through supplements. Both vitamin C and the B-complex vitamins are water-soluble. The B complex includes Thiamin (B_1), Riboflavin (B_2), Niacin, B_6 (Pyridoxine), Folate (folic acid, folacin), B_{12} (Cyanocobalamin), Pantothenic Acid (B_3), and Biotin (B_7), the last two of which do not yet have RDAs. All the B vitamins are involved in processing carbohydrates, proteins and fats and helping to use that energy in the growth and maintenance of all cells. They're also generally found in the same types of foods, especially liver, dried peas and beans, green leafy vegetables and whole-grain cereals and breads. Despite sufficient similarities to fool the namers, we now know that many of the Bs are not chemically related, another reason why the B numbers are being de-emphasized.

Milk contains all the B vitamins, but is a major dietary source only of riboflavin, B_6 and B_{12}. If you don't use dairy products, see Table 3 for the best alternative sources. Warning to vegans: The only non-animal sources of B_{12} are from foods fermented by bacteria, such as the fermented soybean paste, miso, or from foods which have had the vitamin specifically added, including some cereals and fortified soy milks.

Water-soluble vitamins are easily washed out during cooking or processing, which makes raw, pressure cooked, microwaved or steamed vegetables better sources than boiled ones.

Because we can't store B and C vitamins, we are also in little danger of overdosing on them: even if you try to take more than the body needs, say in the hope of warding off colds or more serious diseases, the excess is rapidly excreted in the urine. There are limits. Enormous megadoses (100 or 1000 times the RDA) of C and some of the B vitamins have been shown to produce a variety of ill effects.

Vitamins A, D, E, and K work a little differently. They require an internal fat supply to enable them to be absorbed into the body, but once there they get stored indefinitely. The fat-soluble vitamins can be found in most animal fats and get concentrated in the liver. Yes, cod liver oil *is* good for you, if you happen to need vitamin A, but polar bears are the champs. Early arctic explorers are rumored to have died from overdoses of vitamin

TABLE 3
NONDAIRY SOURCES OF VITAMINS THAT ARE PRESENT IN LARGE QUANTITIES IN DAIRY PRODUCTS

VITAMIN	ANIMAL SOURCES	VEGETABLE SOURCES
Vitamin A (Retinol; Beta Carotene)	Liver, egg yolk, fish oils, kidney	Spinach, broccoli, carrots, sweet potatoes, kale, cantaloupe, peaches
Riboflavin (B_2)	Liver, oysters, eggs, salmon	Green, leafy vegetables, dried peas and beans, asparagus, whole-grain cereals and breads
Vitamin B_6 (Pyridoxine)	Muscle meats, poultry, fish, liver	Wheat germ, soybeans, nuts, bran cereals, avocados, green vegetables, potatoes
Vitamin B_{12} (Cyanocobalamin)	Lean meats, liver, kidney, fish, shellfish, eggs	Miso, fortified soy milk and cereals
Vitamin D (Calciferol)	Cod-liver oil, salmon, liver, egg yolk, tuna, mackerel, herring, sardines	Fortified foods

A after eating polar bear liver. No plants contain vitamin A, but many have beta carotene, which can be converted in the body to vitamin A. Claims have been made imbuing beta carotene with a host of benefits, although recent studies have cast shadows over some of its more miraculous properties.

Dairy foods are naturally poor sources of all the fat-soluble vitamins except A, but milk and vitamin D do have a connection. Vitamin D is of concern to us because it is the vitamin which controls the way calcium enters growing bones (*also see the following section on calcium supplements*). Young children who don't get enough vitamin D can develop rickets, a disease in which bones stay soft enough to cause deformities. Osteomalacia (literally, "soft bone" and not to be confused with osteoporosis) is the adult form of rickets.

Raw milk contains only tiny amounts of vitamin D, but virtually all fluid milk sold in the United States is fortified with the equivalent of a child's RDA in every quart because of the importance of the vitamin to younger children, the biggest milk drinkers. (The RDA now gives the vitamin D requirement in micrograms, but most milks and vitamin supplements still list it in the older International Units, or IU. Ten micrograms equals 400 IU.) Other dairy products, including most cheeses and yogurts, are not fortified. There are no good plant sources for vitamin D; vegans have to rely on foods to which the vitamin has been added.

Fortunately, the body also has a mechanism for forming vitamin D in the skin from the ultraviolet rays of the sun. Cholesterol, of all things, is involved in this. Allowing 15 minutes a day of summer sun to hit most of your body should produce a year's worth of vitamin D—as long as you don't apply a sunblock. Sunblocks, of course, screen out ultraviolet rays. Despite the very real connection between tanning and skin cancer, consistently denying yourself all sun is counterproductive to good health. The institutionalized elderly, and others who do not get sufficient sun exposure, are prone to osteomalacia. Moderation is the key.

See Table 3 for non-milk sources of vitamins A and D.

▌ MINERALS

Nearly half of the 90 plus natural elements are found in milk, most in incredibly tiny amounts. Only seven of these have had RDAs established for them, even though it is quite likely that others will be shown to be essential to good health. That's one of the major reasons nutritionists emphasize so strongly that even the LI should continue to drink some milk if they possibly can: Do you really want to go out and take arsenic pills to replace the arsenic you're missing by doing without dairy products?

Of the seven, by far the most significant is calcium because it has so few other good dietary sources. Calcium rates an entire section of its own, following this one.

The other RDA minerals are phosphorus, magnesium, zinc, iron, iodine and selenium, with dairy products being a significant source only of the first three and possibly selenium. Phosphorus, necessary for the growth and repair of body cells, is almost as important to the body as calcium, a major component of bones and present in all soft tissues. Bones have a significant supply of magnesium as well and the mineral has an enormous number of roles to play in metabolism. Phosphorus, magnesium and calcium have so many closely related functions that maintaining a proper balance of the three is important, since deficiencies or excesses in one can affect the others. So little zinc is required (the RDA for phosphorus is up to 24,000 times larger) that it is referred to as a "trace element," but its presence in numerous enzymes makes it vitally important nonetheless.

See Table 4 for non-milk sources of phosphorus, magnesium and zinc.

 ## CALCIUM

What is a full supply of calcium? The RDA for adults is 800 mg/day. That may be too low. Virtually the entire nutrition community was shocked when the 1989 revision of the RDA failed to raise the recommendation for calcium. The 1984 Consensus Conference on Calcium, sponsored by the National Institutes of Health, recommended 1,000 mg/day for women nearing menopause and 1,500 mg/day for postmenopausal women. Those numbers appear sound for men, too. And the elderly of both sexes absorb calcium more poorly than those younger do.

If you do not drink milk or eat dairy products, you almost certainly have a calcium problem. Even if you have some dairy products in your diet, you probably have a calcium problem. The vast majority of Americans—65% of adult men, 75% of women over 40 and an astounding 90%

TABLE 4
NONDAIRY SOURCES OF MINERALS THAT ARE PRESENT IN LARGE QUANTITIES IN DAIRY PRODUCTS

MINERAL	ANIMAL SOURCES	VEGETABLE SOURCES
Phosphorus	Meat, poultry, fish, eggs, organ meats	Dried peas and beans, peanut butter, soybeans, broccoli, whole grains
Magnesium	Seafood	Raw leafy green vegetables, nuts, bananas, avocados, wheatgerm
Zinc	Oysters, lean meat, poultry, organ meats	Lima beans, whole grain breads and cereals

of teenage girls, whether LI or not—fail to get their RDA of calcium. Even 50% of children, whom you'd expect to be milk drinkers, fall short on calcium intake. Most people fall way short. Adult women get, on the average, no more than half the RDA of calcium.

Virtually all of the calcium in your body, some 99% plus, is in your bones and teeth, with the other less than 1% scattered through your cells and in the bloodstream for ready use. Without calcium your body can't regulate your heartbeat, stimulate blood clotting, help your muscles flex or facilitate vitamin B_{12} absorption, nerve impulse coordination and hormone response. Calcium is so crucial that the body is more concerned about keeping the bloodstream supply high than keeping bones strong. If the blood level of calcium declines by as little as 3%, the calcium bank in your bones is raided to make up the difference. Just as you need a steady income to avoid dipping into your savings account, your body requires its RDA of calcium to prevent bone loss. Too much bone loss results in the condition known as osteoporosis.

Bones are living and changing tissue, not dead sticks; as much an active part of your body as your heart or liver. Like all living tissue (except nerve cells) it is constantly broken down and reformed. Osteoporosis isn't normally a problem for someone growing up, except in extreme cases of anorexia or malnutrition. Just the opposite. Throughout adolescence and early adulthood more bone is formed, through a process called bone remodeling, than lost. Bone mass is added through your mid-thirties, well after you reach adult height.

Two types of bone are made. Although every bone in the body has both kinds, the long arm and leg bones are mostly cortical bone, while the bone ends and the vertebrae in the spine are mostly the lighter trabecular bone. Each has its own function. Trabecular bone resembles the inside of a sponge or a honeycomb, providing stiffness and strength without weight, while cortical bone is more like smooth solid steel.

By the time you hit your forties, however, bone remodeling losses outweigh gains. For men, the rate of bone loss gradually increases with age. Women experience a huge acceleration of bone loss for the five or six years following menopause, related to decreased estrogen levels. Type I osteoporosis, which only occurs in women, hits trabecular bone hardest and is characterized by easily crushed vertebrae. Small-framed women, typically thin Caucasian or Asian women, or those who have had a hysterectomy or early menopause, are at greatest risk. Type II osteoporosis, sometimes referred to as ''senile'' osteoporosis, is a natural result of aging. Both cortical and trabecular bone is affected, so fractures of the hip and the long bones become common in addition to vertebral damage. Everybody who lives long enough will develop osteoporosis, though to very different degrees. Men can only get Type II, but its effects are still seen far more often in women, since the average woman is smaller than the average man and has a quarter to a third less bone mass to begin with. An estimated 90% of women have osteoporosis by age 75. With far greater numbers of both men and women living to advanced ages than ever before, osteoporosis has suddenly emerged as a major health care issue.

Consider these facts:

- Some 15 million to 24 million Americans over the age of 45 have osteoporosis.
- Osteoporosis is responsible for approximately 1.3 million fractures of the vertebra, hip or arm each year. One of every three women will fracture a vertebra by age 65.
- 150,000 women and 75,000 men fracture a hip annually. Twelve to 20% of those with hip fractures die as a result of complications.

Although some bone loss due to aging is inevitable, much of it appears to be the result of lifelong deficiencies in calcium intake. Past age 35, there is little evidence that high calcium diets alone can increase bone mass or make up for earlier deficits.

The time to start increasing calcium intake is during childhood, while bone formation predominates. So critical is this period that the RDA for children as young as one year is as large as it is for an adult. Those 11 to 24 have RDAs fully half again as large (*see Table 5*). The pressure for thinness that already afflicts teenage girls with anorexia and bulimia also manifests itself in a calcium-poor diet that sets the stage for future osteoporosis. One study of adolescent girls showed that increasing daily calcium intake from 80% to 110% of the RDA also increased bone mass by several percent a year. As all the evidence indicates that a stronger skeletal base provides significant protection against osteoporosis, an early healthy diet could make a major difference later in life.

Though by middle age increasing your bone mass is no longer possible, minimizing natural calcium loss is. Calcium is swept out of the body every day, mostly in the urine but also in sweat, saliva, mucus and other bodily fluids. Up to one-fourth of the RDA for men and women over 25 vanishes in this fashion. Maintaining a calcium supply in the diet relieves the body of the need to remove it from the bone bank. In addition, the body's ability to absorb the calcium it gets decreases with age, a double whammy since the elderly typically consume less calcium than those younger.

As with all the other vitamins and minerals, calcium is affected by every aspect of your diet. Bad health habits seem to have a particularly negative effect on calcium. Doubling protein intake leads to a 50% increase in urinary calcium loss. Excessive caffeine consumption, say 10 to 20 cups of coffee a day, also increases the amount of calcium in the urine. So does a high-sodium diet. Smoking and alcohol abuse are bad for you in so many

TABLE 5 NONDAIRY DIETARY SOURCES OF CALCIUM		
TYPE	RATING	SOURCE
Breads and Flours	Good	Calcium-fortified flours.
	Fair	Lime-processed corn flour, yeast-leavened breads and baked goods.
	Poor	High in phytic acid: Whole grains, nuts (except chestnuts).
Seafood	Excellent	Canned fish with bones (herring, mackeral, salmon, sardines, smelt).
	Good	Clams, dried salted cod, oysters, salmon, shrimp.
Tofu	Excellent	Calcium sulfate-processed tofu.
Vegetables	Excellent	Bok choy, broccoli, collard greens, dandelion greens, kale, mustard greens, okra, turnip greens.
	Good	Artichokes, asparagus, brussels sprouts, cabbages, endive, kohlrabi, leeks, parsley, rutabagas, salsify, tomatoes.
	Fair	Carrots, cauliflower, celery, green peas, lettuce, radishes.
	Poor	High in oxalic acid: Beets and beet greens, eggplant, green beans, onions, rhubarb, sorrel, spinach, swiss chard.
	Poor	High in phytic acid: Black or green gram beans, corn, great northern beans, haricot beans, kidney beans, lima beans, pinto beans, red mexican beans, brown rice, soybeans, white beans, wild rice.
Water	Good	"Hard" tap waters, mineral waters.

Note: Foods labeled "poor" contain naturally occurring chemicals that reduce the digestibility of the calcium. You need not shun them entirely, as most are good sources of other nutrients. Merely avoid reliance on them as your *primary* calcium source. They may still provide some usable calcium. I have not been able to determine the oxalic or phytic acid content of any of the raw seaweeds (hijiki, kombu, wakame and others) listed in food composition tables as being high in calcium.

ways that osteoporosis is almost a minor factor, but both also severely reduce bone mass and increase the risk of fractures.

Calcium in the Diet

From where should you get your calcium? Experts agree that because of the additional nutrients available, dairy products are far and away the best source of dietary calcium. Not only does milk have among the highest levels of calcium, milk products are more popular and better tasting than the alternatives. At least 75% of all the calcium intake in this country comes from dairy products. This puts those who are trying to cut back significantly on milk or trying to eliminate it altogether at serious risk for an inadequate calcium supply.

There are three roads the LI can take to avoid this. One would be to continue to eat dairy products in ways which cause less distress. Most people go this route, not just for the calcium and other nutrients, but to keep from having to eliminate their favorite foods from their diet. This is such a big topic that Chapters 6 and 7 will cover various tips and tricks for a lactose-reduced diet.

Your other choices are to find nondairy sources of calcium or to take calcium supplements. (They're not mutually exclusive, of course. I do all three: eat some dairy, try for other high-calcium foods and take a daily supplement.) See Table 5 for a summary of important nondairy sources of calcium. The comprehensive nutrient listing in Appendix I not only gives the calcium content for several hundred foods but also allows you to pick out ones which give you the best value of calcium in the least number of Calories.

With 99% of calcium in bone, your first thought might be to go out and find some bones to crunch on. Cultures all over the world find ways to incorporate bone into the diet, whether by gnawing on large bones, munching on the ends of chicken wings or the haute gourmet style of eating tiny but whole roast birds. Eating hard bones can be dangerous; softened bone, usually processed, is safer. Canned sardines and canned salmon are probably the most common sources of high-calcium, edible bone. Shellfish, as their name implies, wear their bones on the outside, as shells. Oyster shells are a major commercial source of calcium, but nothing you'd want to eat directly. Some people crunch on the shells of fried shrimp, but the flesh of shrimp, oysters and clams are themselves moderately high in calcium and probably a lot better tasting.

Our high-vitamin friends, dark-green leafy vegetables and dried peas and beans, often turn up on lists of good sources of calcium. I need to make a distinction here that is often ignored: Not all foods that contain calcium are also good sources of calcium. Only those foods whose calcium comes in a form that is easily digestible by the body qualify as good sources. I hate to give kids yet another reason to avoid spinach, but it contains six times as much oxalic acid as it does calcium. The oxalic acid binds with the calcium to produce the non-digestible calcium oxalate. Technically speaking, the calcium in spinach has a low bioavailability. Most peas, nuts and beans, as well as whole-grain breads and cereals, contain phytic acid, which binds the calcium into calcium phylate. Yeast destroys the phylates that result, making yeast-leavened breads a better calcium choice than other grains. Fortunately, there's no evidence that these acids affect any calcium not in the original food. The calcium in a glass of milk drunk with a meal containing spinach should still have high bioavailability. Table 5 summarizes which foods are useful calcium sources and which to avoid.

Calcium also shows up in places you might not expect, ones which don't get always get covered in lists of high-calcium foods. Hard (mineral-rich) tap water can be an excellent calcium source, depending on where you live. Bottled mineral waters are also often high in calcium. Some tofu manufacturers use calcium sulfate to coagulate the soybean "milk" during processing, resulting in calcium more bioavailable than that in dairy foods. Similarly, the lime used to soften corn used to make the flour for corn tortillas also enhances the calcium bioavailability of the tortilla. And alligator meat contains a full day's allowance of calcium in every serving.

With the increasing awareness of the need for calcium to combat osteoporosis, many foods are appearing in calcium fortified varieties. Cereals, flours, orange and grapefruit juices and even milk can be found with added calcium.

Calcium Supplements

Calcium supplements are highly controversial, not least because many people appear to ignore the word "supplement" and take them as a substitute for a good balanced diet. This circumstance is not unique to calcium, of course; whole stores exist that appear to contain little but bottles of increasingly exotic "nutrients." Strictly as a supplement, however, calcium pills can be useful for the LI.

All calcium, even that in food, comes naturally combined as part of a calcium salt. There are four basic types: calcium carbonates (natural-source or refined); calcium phosphates or bonemeals; dolomite; and "chelated" calciums, which essentially covers everything else. Because the calcium is only part of a whole, the percentage of "elemental calcium" must be known to compare among types. (RDAs are also given as elemental calcium equivalents.) Table 6 compares various common calcium sources.

The label on the supplement bottle will say something like "450 mg elemental calcium" or "1,250 mg Calcium Carbonate provides 500 mg elemental calcium." (If only a single number is given without specifying that it is the amount of elemental calcium, think twice about buying that brand.) Since the RDA for adults is 800 mg, one such pill would probably make up any difference between the calcium in your diet and the RDA. The higher concentration of calcium in calcium carbonate allows you to take fewer pills, so it's not surprising that most of the big name national brands use this as their source.

Adjusting the number of pills you take will even out differences so that the total amount of elemental calcium is equivalent. Perhaps more significant is the bioavailability of the calcium. More controversy erupts here. Some reports claim that calcium citrate is somewhat better absorbed

TABLE 6
PERCENTAGE OF ELEMENTAL CALCIUM IN VARIOUS SOURCES
USED IN SUPPLEMENTS

SOURCE	PERCENTAGE OF CALCIUM
Calcium carbonate	40
Calcium phosphate, tribasic	38
Bonemeal	32
Calcium phosphate, dibasic	23
Dolomite	22
Calcium citrate	21
Calcium lactate	13
Calcium levinulate	13
Calcium gluconate	9
Calcium gluceptate	8
Calcium glubionate	6.5

than calcium carbonate and carbonate better than phosphate. Other reports put calcium lactate on top. (You may read that those who are LI should avoid calcium lactate supplements. This is a simple misunderstanding of the difference between lactate and lactose or perhaps the misreading of the use of lactose as a filler.) There is an almost total absence of hard evidence to back up any of these claims, except in the most unusual of cases. In fact, one study found that variations in calcium absorption ability among individuals was at least as significant as variations among the supplements themselves.

The only factor which may truly influence bioavailability is whether the supplement is taken with meals. Some experts say that calcium carbonate and the calcium phosphates should be taken after meals, because stomach acidity is highest then. People with low stomach acid production and the elderly, whose production of acid may cease with age, are therefore sometimes advised to avoid calcium carbonate. As long as the pill is not taken on an empty stomach, however, the absorption level should be satisfactory. The chelated calciums will work equally well regardless of acidity levels. They may be taken either at meals or at bedtime.

A related issue is dissolvability. Creating a calcium pill that dissolves properly in the stomach is a challenge. Starches help tablets break up in the stomach, but also make the already bulky calcium pills gigantic. Most companies have now taken other fillers, like sugars, out so that they can label their pills as containing "no sugar," partly to reassure the LI that no lactose has been used. Some manufacturers have been known to shellac pills to make the chalky calcium easier to swallow. Because of this, a study done a few years ago found that several major name brands flunked USP standards. The U.S. Pharmacopeia (USP), a nonprofit organization that sets standards for drugs, requires that at least 75% of a calcium tablet dissolve in the stomach within 30 minutes. Most companies have reformulated their coatings and this should not now be a problem even for house brands. Calcium tablets that are marketed as food supplements with no therapeutic claims are not regulated as drugs and are not required by law to meet the USP standard. Check the package label for confirmation if you have a concern. Table 7 lists a number of major brand names by type that meet USP standards.

Some calcium supplements come with added vitamin D, usually in the amount of 400 IU. This, not coincidentally, is the quantity of the vitamin thought to be necessary for our bodies to process calcium most efficiently. (Because of the need to simplify label information, virtually all vitamin supplements equate 400 IU with 100% of the RDA for vitamin D. The RDA for those under 25 is 400 IU; for those 25 and over it is only 200 IU.) Whether you should opt for a calcium supplement with vitamin D depends on your other sources of the vitamin. Paradoxically, very high levels of vitamin D, 2000 IU per day or more, can actually cause bone loss. Taking calcium with vitamin D, plus a multivitamin with vitamin D plus vitamin D in the diet plus vitamin D from sunshine may be overkill. Calcium with vitamin D is usually only recommended for those elderly who, because they are on a reduced diet or are not active outside, do not get an adequate supply of the vitamin.

One other issue regarding calcium supplements must be addressed. For over a decade, the FDA has been warning the public to limit intake of calcium supplements, especially those produced from dolomite and bonemeal, because of potentially high levels of lead. All types of calcium supplements are likely to contain some lead, mostly from natural sources. Animal bones—and bonemeal is literally ground animal bone while much calcium carbonate comes from oyster shells—absorb lead from the air the animal breathes and the food the animal eats. As leaded gasoline has been largely phased out in the past few years, lead pollution has dropped significantly. Two major studies that made headlines in 1993 tested whether this drop was reflected in lower lead levels in calcium supplements. At a glance one seemed to say yes and the other no; a closer reading shows that it's not that simple.

Testing bonemeal products alone, *Consumers Reports* found that all were within FDA guidelines of 5 parts per million (ppm) for lead and only three exceeded the more stringent USP guideline of 3 ppm. Their conclusion: "Lead concentrations in bone-meal products have dropped enough to make the health threat negligible for most adults." But a study in the *American Journal of Public Health* (AJPH) warned that "the use of dolomite, bonemeal, and, to some extent, natural source calcium-rich products for the production of mineral supplements would have to be reevaluated."

Which to believe? Both. As so commonly happens, the studies used

TABLE 7
COMMONLY FOUND BRAND NAMES OF CALCIUM SUPPLEMENTS
(In all cases, generics, house brands or natural foods brands that meet USP standards may also be available)

UNITED STATES	CANADA
Calcium Carbonate	
BioCal	Apo-Cal
Calcarb 600	Calcite 500
Calci-Chew	Calcium 500
Calciday 667	Calsan
Calcilac	Caltrate 300
Calcium 600	Caltrate 600
Calglycine	Caltrate Chewable
Caltrate 600	Mega-Cal
Chooz	Nu-Cal
Dicarbosil	Os-Cal
Gencalc	Os-Cal Chewable
Mallamint	
Nephro-Calci	
Os-Cal 500	
Oysco	
Oysco 500 Chewable	
Oyst-Cal 500	
Oyst-Cal 500 Chewable	
Oystercal 500	
Rolaids Calcium Rich	
Super Calcium 1200	
Titralac	
Tums	
Tums E-X	
Calcium Chloride	
(none listed)	Calciject
Calcium Citrate	
Citracal	(not commercially available
Citracal Liquitabs	in Canada)
Calcium Glubionate	(as Calcium Glucono-Galacto
Neo-Calglucon	Gluconate)
	Calcium-Sandoz
Calcium Gluceptate and Calcium Gluconate	
(not commercially available in the U.S.)	Calcium Stanley
Calcium Gluconate	
Kalcinate	(none listed)
Calcium Glycerophosphate and Calcium Lactate	
Calphosan	(not commercially available
	in Canada)

TABLE 7 (Continued)	
UNITED STATES	**CANADA**
Calcium Lactate	
(none listed)	(none listed)
Calcium Lactate-Gluconate and Calcium	Calcium Sandoz-Forte
Carbonate	Gramcal
(not commercially available in the U.S.)	
Dibasic Calcium Phosphate	(not commercially available
(none listed)	in Canada)
Tribasic Calcium Phosphate	
Posture	(not commercially available
	in Canada)

(Source: USP DI-Volume II—Advice for the Patient: Drug Information in Lay Language, Edition 14, 1994. Brand name products continually leave and enter the market. The purpose of this listing is to indicate the range of products available. No endorsement of any brand name is implied.)

different measures to look for different things and so can't be directly compared. The AJPH study concentrated on whether young children who got their total RDA from calcium supplements would be subjected to too much total lead, rather than whether any individual pill exceeded the guidelines. Children are more sensitive to low-level effects of lead and assimilate lead more efficiently than do adults.

For children under six years of age then, the recommendation would be to use chelated calcium supplements, which had the lowest levels of lead. (Refined calcium carbonates were about as low, but all the products used in the study were Canadian.) Bonemeals had highly varying lead levels, but are probably not a significant danger to adults. One major caveat here: Bonemeal powders advertised in health food stores as "food supplements" can easily get overused. An FDA study found that 90% of the individuals consuming large quantities of bonemeal were women aged 50 or over, presumably to ward off the effects of osteoporosis, and that daily intakes five to ten times the RDA were not uncommon. Lead poisoning can be the result.

Some general advice concerning calcium supplements:

- All supplements currently appear to be safe for adult use. For children, or those worried about lead intake, the chelated calcium supplements may be preferable.
- Take supplements with or, even better, after meals to improve absorption. If you are sure you can absorb calcium well on an empty stomach, the chelated supplements can also be taken at bedtime to provide calcium at a time when none is being absorbed from food.

- Do not take supplements within 1 to 2 hours of taking other medications by mouth. Doing so may prevent the medicine from working properly.
- Do not take supplements within 1 to 2 hours of eating large amounts of fiber-containing foods, especially if you are being treated for hypocalcemia (insufficient blood calcium).
- There is no good evidence that your total calcium intake, including that from foods, needs to exceed 1,500–2,000 mg/day.
- Because there is a slight possibility of large amounts of calcium causing diarrhea, do not take more than 500–600 mg of calcium at any one time.
- Only the elderly and housebound have a real need to aid absorption by taking calcium supplements containing vitamin D. Extremely large doses of vitamin D are potentially dangerous, however.
- Antacids with calcium carbonate are perfectly good and potentially inexpensive calcium supplements. Do not use antacids containing sodium bicarbonate, aluminum hydroxide or magnesium hydroxide for the purpose, however.
- Calcium carbonate may decrease iron absorption so it should not be taken together with iron supplements.
- There is no evidence that calcium supplements interfere with magnesium absorption.
- Consult a doctor before taking supplements if you have a history of kidney stones or infections or a family history of kidney stones.

Osteoporosis

A few years ago, it would have been impossible to escape the deluge of articles and books touting the wonders of calcium in controlling or curing osteoporosis. Like the Mississippi River after the 1993 floods, this deluge left behind a lot of obscuring mud, a bad odor and some ruined lives.

Osteoporosis does not have a single cause, so it can have no single cure. Inadequate calcium intake certainly plays a major part, but other factors come into play: the amount of bone mass you start with, for example; the rate at which you lose calcium through the urine; the amount of exercise you get; for women, the estrogen loss during and after menopause.

Today's advice for combating osteoporosis concentrates more on preventing bone loss than any other factor. In large part the advice is the same no matter your age or the condition of your bones: good diet and exercise.

The best way to prevent osteoporosis is to start with healthy bones in a healthy body. Especially during the crucial years of bone formation, you will build stronger bones by ensuring that you get a full supply of calcium. Even the RDA of calcium will not be enough if the rest of the body is neglected, though. Calcium works in concert with magnesium, zinc, fluoride and phosphorus in the formation and maintenance of good bones and teeth. Too much protein, sodium, fiber, caffeine and alcohol, on the other hand, can rob the body of calcium. That's one of the reasons I've touched on all the various nutrients in this chapter. A balanced diet means exactly that: an adequate or optimal supply of all the numerous nutrients in food.

Calcium supplements may be necessary to achieve recommended levels if you're avoiding dairy products, but they alone will not ward off osteoporosis. A. Li Wan Po, head of the Pharmacy Practice Research Group, Queen's University of Belfast, has said that "recommending calcium supplements for this purpose is largely an act of faith although, on balance, a small positive effect is consistent with the available data." In other words, the consequences of osteoporosis are so severe that anything that might help, however minimally, is worth doing.

A better long-term preventive for osteoporosis—right up there with an overall healthy, high-calcium diet—is exercise. Strong muscles and strong bones go together. Dr. Robert Heaney, a scientific advisor to the National Osteoporosis Foundation, has said that, "One of the best kept secrets in this field is the fact that there is a nearly constant ratio of bone to muscle in a woman's body. Women who have a subnormal amount of bone . . . have an equally subnormal amount of muscle. This association points to the importance of a life-long program of vigorous physical activity."

Exercise works in two ways, with the lack of it actively harmful and a regular program of it actively beneficial. The muscle tissue loss from the lack of exercise can increase bone loss. A sedentary lifestyle and excess weight go together, putting an additional strain on the weakened bones. Those who are bedridden or otherwise immobilized may lose 30%–40% of their bone within a few years. In contrast, regular exercise increases the flow of blood and therefore of nutrients to bones and creates a heavier musculature which leads to denser bones.

Any kind of exercise at any age will be beneficial. Some authorities suggest concentrating on weight-bearing exercises—lifting weights, running, aerobics—to concentrate on strengthening the muscles most directly involved with the bones most at risk. Most, however, make no distinctions. Exercise is good for you, period. To be sure, if you have neglected exercising for a very long time, have medical problems, or are sufficiently osteoporotic that your bones are at risk, consult your doctor or ease into exercise very gradually. There is no one whom exercise cannot help, however.

Women have one other line of defense to consider: estrogen. Why estrogen replacement therapy (ERT) may reduce osteoporosis-related fractures by up to 60% is not completely clear. The evidence that it does is overwhelming. Moreover, the combination of ERT and calcium supplementation may be even more effective, especially for those women who do not receive the RDA of calcium in their regular diet.

While prevention of osteoporosis is one of the approved uses of ERT, controversy continues to surround the appropriateness of such treatment. Estrogen is a powerful drug with the potential to affect the body in many ways, both positively and negatively. Studies have associated ERT with a decreased risk of osteoporosis and coronary heart disease while simultaneously increasing the risk of a form of uterine cancer and possibly breast cancer as well. That it appears that ERT will save many more lives than cause deaths and that the use of progestin, another female hormone, may reduce the cancer risk, is hardly sufficient to issue a blanket recommendation for this treatment. Any woman considering ERT—and it should be considered for any woman who is hypoestrogenic, i.e. with diminished estrogen capability—should see her physician and thoroughly investigate how these risks and benefits may apply to her individual case.

5

LACTOSE DIGESTION: THE INSIDE STORY

Rumblings, gases, noises, explosions, rushing water and general commotion—a bout of LI makes my insides feel like Tokyo in the midst of an attack by Godzilla. Amazingly, all that sound and fury comes not from a 100-foot-tall monster, but from a mere fraction of an ounce of sugar hidden in a delicious and nutritious meal. I've made it a priority over the years to find out everything I could about what lactose does in my insides. I was surprised to discover just how much turned out to be involved.

You can define LI simply as letting your lactose intake exceed your production of an enzyme called lactase, but that's like dismissing the national deficit as nothing more than letting spending exceed taxes. It's true as far as it goes, but if you want to do anything about the deficit it helps to know some basics about economics, party politics and what a trillion is. Digestion, fortunately, is somewhat simpler to explain and about a trillion times easier to do something about. By studying digestion, a number of ways of alleviating the symptoms and problems of LI pop into view.

If you want, you can skip this chapter and go right on to the next two where I'll lay out a smorgasbord of tips for living with LI. If you're like me, however, you want to know as much as possible about the workings of the digestive system and why you need the lactase enzyme. For that matter, your first question might be: Just what is an enzyme anyway? The answer is in an intoxicating story.

ENZYMES

The discovery of enzymes and how they worked was one of the great triumphs of nineteenth century medicine. All the big questions—how did the body grow and develop, how was food changed into nutrients, how did life itself come into being—proved to require an understanding of enzymes for their answer. Like so many of the giant leaps made by science, the starting point was a seemingly simple question. In this case, Why did grapes turn into wine?

Wine-making may be almost as old as the domestication of animals for milking. Someone, somewhere, some 10,000 years ago, noticed that the juice of crushed grapes, if left untended for days or weeks, transformed itself into a drink that tingled the belly and muddled the head. By paying closer attention, our budding proto-scientist must have seen that a slow procession of bubbles started to roil the surface of the juice within a few hours of the grapes being crushed. After a few days everyone could see the skins and seeds floating on the surface churning so vigorously that they seemed to froth and foam. A boldly experimental finger would discover that the foam had become warm to the touch. Magically, however, a calm, clear liquid eventually resulted, although there was also a layer of sediment left behind at the bottom of the vessel.

They called this sediment "yeast," a word that, like sugar, goes back to the Sanskrit language, from their word meaning "it boils." Nobody knew back then that the sediment contained living organisms far too tiny to see (which we now also call by the name of yeast). Over centuries, various cultures used similar processes to turn grain into beer, potatoes to vodka, or milk into yogurt. The process became known as fermentation. Moreover, the yeast could be recovered and added to a fresh batch of the juice, grain, potatoes or milk to restart the fermentation process all over again. Oddly, the yeast itself never seemed to be used up; it was as present at the end of the reaction as at the beginning.

That was the mystery. By the nineteenth century, enough about chemistry was known to make it clear how unusual this process was. Chemists had two classic and opposing models of chemical reactions. Putting two or more chemicals together might produce completely different chemicals as an end product. Or, one chemical might be broken down with heat or acids into its component parts. Proceeding along these lines, scientists eventually understood that during fermentation the sugar in wine was breaking down into ethanol and carbon dioxide. Ethanol gave the wine its alcohol content, carbon dioxide gas produced the bubbly fizz. Even so, the reaction fit neither model. No other chemical was reacting with the sugar nor was anyone adding acid or heat to get the reaction started. In fact, it would give off its own heat, seemingly from out of nowhere.

Among those to work on the problem was Louis Pasteur, already renowned for his work in microbiology. In 1858, Pasteur captured in a sentence the relationship between fermentation and the processes of life:

The globules of yeast are true living cells, and may be considered to have as the physiological function correlative with their life the transformation of sugar, somewhat like the cells of the mammary glands transform the elements of the blood into the various constituents of milk in connection with their life functions.

Though Pasteur failed to predict that we would soon be able to synthesize the enzymes and so not need living microorganisms, he otherwise had it exactly right. Life is a constant cycle, in which food is broken down to its component parts and then reassembled where and when needed in exactly the proper form. Enzymes are the engines that do this work.

The German chemist Emil Fischer determined just how enzymes accomplished this. He revealed that enzymes (which take their very name from the Greek words meaning "in yeast") make chemical reactions happen by being catalysts.

To illustrate, let's look at lactose. Lactose, if you remember from Chapter 3, is a double sugar, made up of the simple sugars glucose and galactose, which join their ends together after squeezing out a molecule of water. Adding back that molecule of water splits the lactose into simple sugars again. This is important, because it means that the reaction works in both directions.

Some chemical reactions are easy to start, others very hard. Putting pure sodium into room temperature water creates an enormous, instant and very dangerous reaction. Placing lactose into room temperature water normally gives you nothing but wet lactose. Wait a while, though—not hours or days, but years—and you'll eventually find both glucose and galactose in that water, implying that the bond that had held the simple sugars in place had spontaneously split. Some heat energy exists in the water even at room temperature. If that energy strikes the bond at just the right place, it breaks, a molecule of water gets grabbed and two simple sugars form from the one molecule of lactose.

If we had to wait years for lactose to break down spontaneously, we'd all be LI. Nor would we be very happy if our bodies used high heat or acidity to force the molecule to split. Fortunately for our innards, the lactase enzyme speeds up lactose breakdown by about a million times. And the enzyme itself remains unchanged by the process, so a single lactase molecule can be used repeatedly, just as the yeast sediment in wine can start new fermentations over and over again. Chemicals that work this way are called catalysts.

Fischer was studying sugars and their structure. I said in Chapter 3 that all the simple sugars have exactly the same chemical formula but behave very differently nonetheless. Fischer realized that this could be explained by assuming that the atoms in the sugars were arranged in distinct patterns, just as a six-room ranch house has the same number of rooms as a six-room colonial but a totally different ambiance. Compound sugars were unique as well, in a way that depended on the bond their components formed. Fischer's other insight was that this must mean that each enzyme also had to be unique, that it and the molecule it worked on had to fit together like a lock and key.[1]

There was the answer. It was as if you had a high school corridor several miles long, lined with lockers that had both keyholes and combination locks. Needing to guess the combination for each locker would require years as well as an enormous expenditure of energy to open them all. Armed with the master key, however, you could unlock them as fast as you could go from one to the next. And your key would still be just as good when you got the last one open.

The body makes such extensive use of enzymes precisely because they're so energy-efficient. Only a relative few molecules of each enzyme must be made, just as a school janitor can get by with just a small set of keys. The drawback to this cozy scenario is that when you lose your key, you're really stuck. LI is also called lactase deficiency because the body stops producing as much lactase as it did when you were a child. Since both lactose and lactase are unique, there's no alternative. Without the lactase key, you can't unlock the lactose that you're putting into your digestive system. On a larger scale, the body's need for tens or hundreds of thousands of different enzymes offers many ways things can go wrong, and indeed, numerous other enzyme deficiency disorders exist.

Just as keys lock as well as unlock, chemical reactions also work in both directions. Digestive enzymes help break larger molecules into smaller ones, other enzymes ease the way for smaller molecules to join together and form larger ones. As Pasteur predicted, it is an enzyme in the mammary gland that joins together glucose and galactose to create the lactose that's present in mother's milk. You are the center of a vast set of cycles that tear down food brought into the digestive system to nourish all the cells in the body and build up the proteins that make up the organs that make enzymes that digest food that . . .

And so on. But strictly speaking, the body doesn't use "food," it uses the nutrients hidden in food. The breakdown of food to nutrients is the process of digestion. The digestive system is our next target.

---

[1]Note for the technical-minded: The orientation of the lock and key is the reason that lactase is also called a beta-galactosidase. Sugars vary in the ways the hydrogen and oxygen atoms, or hydroxyl groups, are bound to the ring of carbon atoms. When two simple sugars link, the hydroxyl groups forming the bond can point either in the same or opposite directions, producing alpha and beta bonds, respectively. In lactose, the two hydroxyl groups have opposite orientations and so produce a beta bond, requiring a beta-galactosidase to unlock it. There is an alpha-galactosidase which, of course, has no effect on lactose but serves to split the sugars that are often found in beans. The lack of this enzyme is the cause of beans' famous propensity for forming gas. The process is similar to that of LI.

■ THE PIPELINE THROUGH YOUR BODY

Like a doughnut, the human body has an outside which receives all the attention and a hole through the middle that everybody takes for granted. The hole that runs through you from mouth to anus is called the alimentary canal. That's where digestion takes place.

The alimentary canal (or gut) includes the mouth and throat, the esophagus (or gullet), the stomach, the small intestine and the colon (or large intestine). The length of the complete system is a matter of definition. A pathologist may measure a relaxed gut at some 30 feet during an autopsy; muscle tone compresses it to about half that length during life.

Though each part plays its own specialized role in digestion, the physical makeup of the gut is similar throughout: a long tube that is revealed in cross-section to have three layers. On the outside is a protective coating called the serosa, which also serves to anchor the gut in place in the body with attachments called mesentery ligaments. Just inside are two muscle layers. The outer is made up of long bands of muscle that run along the length of the gut, while the inner muscles are circular. They cross at right angles just as the lines of latitude and longitude do on a globe. By contracting in coordination with one another the two bands cause ripplelike waves that serve to push food through the gut, somewhat in the way you would use your fingers to milk a cow. This is the process known as peristalsis. The innermost layer is the mucosa, which both provides the digestive juices and absorbs the nutrients.

More is involved in digestion and nutrition than just the gut. The liver and pancreas, for example, supply digestive enzymes of their own. Getting the nutrients to the rest of the body is just as crucial as producing them. Three large arteries lead in to the gut and a system of veins sweep the absorbed nutrients away to feed all the other cells. Lymphatic vessels do the same for fats. Excess water is carried through the bloodstream to the kidneys, where it is filtered and sent on to the bladder.

What's odd about this complex and interconnected arrangement is how little of it is necessary to keep us alive. People survive perfectly well with part or even all of their stomach missing or closed off. Yards of intestine can be surgically removed without putting a halt to digestion. Even so, the gut is fairly sensitive in certain ways and, just our luck, the production of lactase is one of the things most easily disrupted.

Digestion works similarly in the LI and LP alike. All our digestive systems are designed to handle lactose for the first few years of life and its basic structure does not change after that. To make what happens when one suffers from the symptoms of LI as clear as possible, I'll first go through the alimentary canal from top to bottom and show you what happens when everything works well. Then I'll explain what happens when someone who is LI takes in a load of lactose. Food, by the way, takes about 10 hours to make the trip. I'll try to complete it just a bit faster.

Converting Food into Something Useful

Digestion actually starts in the mouth, where an enzyme in saliva begins breaking down starches. The tongue pushes the semi-liquefied food through a sphincter into the esophagus. Sphincters are one-way valves, made up of the thick, circular muscle tissue of the gut and scattered at critical junctures all the way through the gut, serving two major functions. By staying tightly closed until the right signal is given, sphincters maintain an orderly flow through the various sections of the alimentary canal. Teaching babies how to control the sphincter that we call the anus makes civilization possible. In addition, sphincters keep food flowing in the right direction. Vomiting and heartburn are examples of what can happen if the valves fail to work correctly.

The sphincters at each end of the gut, in the throat and anus, are under our command, but all voluntary control vanishes once food enters the esophagus. You can't make your stomach digest at will nor can you force your intestines to produce lactase. For the most part you can't even tell when digestion is taking place or where.

The esophagus is the smallest piece of the gut, only 8 or 10 inches long and maybe an inch in diameter. Peristalsis pushes food down the esophagus in an average of about seven seconds. Though that may sound slow compared to the fraction of a second food would need to hit a plate if dropped from that height, one of the nice things about peristalsis is that it *doesn't* depend on gravity. Astronauts eat perfectly well in the weightlessness of orbit and we can sip soda lying on our stomachs at the beach or standing on our heads if we choose. Birds can't do this, by the way, which is why they tilt their heads back when they swallow. This nifty feature wasn't developed just so you can pig out on the sofa, of course. Certain animals like sloths and opossums live upside down, hanging from trees. If it weren't for peristalsis they wouldn't be here today and the world would have been deprived of Walt Kelly's Pogo.

The Stomach

Whether your belly hangs down over your belt or is washboard flat has nothing to do with your stomach: That's just body fat (or the lack of it). To find your real stomach, spread your hand out as wide as it will go, put your thumb on your throat and your little finger a bit left of center. That's your stomach, just about where most people think their heart is. If you feel your ribcage, fine; the lower five ribs protect the stomach. Nor does the stomach lie horizontally. It sits upright instead, approximately the shape of a boxing glove whose fingers are pointing down.

Empty, the stomach's volume is surprisingly tiny, only large enough to hold an ounce or two of liquid. The reason you feel overstuffed after

Thanksgiving dinner is that you really are; a meal that big may swell your stomach to 50 times its resting size, to a half gallon or more. The stomach can easily handle smaller amounts of food without a change in pressure.

Digestion is a process that is part physical and part chemical. Although the roles aren't completely separated, for the most part the mouth and stomach do all the physical work and the small intestine is responsible for virtually all the chemical action. The stomach is more like a food processor, pulverizing food so that its nutrients are more accessible. Unfortunately, most of us have had the opportunity to see what food looks like after it's been in the stomach for a time. Vomiting is normally a protective mechanism that quickly removes potentially harmful substances from the body. What emerges depends of course on both the stomach's contents and how long it's been there, but it generally consists of a thick watery slurry with perhaps a few recognizable chunks of food. This soupy paste is called chyme (pronounced with a k sound).

All food must be completely converted into chyme before it can be passed on to the small intestine. Liquids move quickly; nine-tenths of what you drink may disappear in an hour. Solids can take four to six hours. Volunteers willing to give their all for science have shown that solid indigestible objects can sit for 48 hours before the stomach finally gives up and sends them on. Parents of curious babies have probably found this out for themselves.

Just as the tantalizing aroma of that Thanksgiving turkey can cause your mouth to water before you taste a single bite, your stomach starts working as soon as it gets the signal that food is coming down the hatch. Some 35 million tiny glands in the mucosa that lines the stomach begin secreting gastric (stomach) juices, which start working on the incoming food the moment it arrives. Scientists were amazed to discover that the major component of gastric juice is one of the most potent acids known—hydrochloric acid (HCl). Even the relatively weak 0.5% solution produced by the stomach is 3 million times more acidic than the blood: strong enough to burn holes in your carpet. The muriatic acid that bricklayers use to clean mortar from bricks is just HCl under a different name.

Tuning in television at suppertime is an invitation to be bombarded by antacid commercials promulgating the absolute dire need to neutralize stomach acid. I can hardly blame anyone who believes that any acidity in the stomach is an evil thing, but the notion is quite incorrect. The proper amount of acidity is needed to activate an enzyme called pepsin, which is an absolutely vital part of the digestive process, especially of protein digestion.

Scientists therefore long puzzled over the fact that the stomach, which is made of proteins, stays whole and healthy, even though food made from the stomachs of other animals, such as haggis or tripe, gets digested as quickly as any other food. Finally, microscopic examination showed that the gastric glands produce a sticky substance called mucin, which collects as a thick impervious layer of mucus lining the stomach walls. Cracks in this lining are called ulcers and may become sore and inflamed when bathed by HCl. As people grow older they produce less mucin, which is why gastric ulcers are more likely to be found in the elderly.

The acid in gastric juice can cause one other common problem. If the sphincter between the esophagus and stomach is weakened, the acid juice can splatter backwards and injure the esophagus, which does not have the protective lining. The resulting burning pain is located where most people believe their hearts to be and so has become known as heartburn. During the late months of pregnancy, the uterus can become enlarged sufficiently to press a bit of stomach up through the hiatus or gap in the diaphragm through which the esophagus also passes. This is the condition known as hiatus hernia and it can also lead to acid spilling back into the esophagus. Antacids will treat the symptoms and the end of pregnancy also means the end of this pressure. If the condition becomes chronic, however, a doctor's care is needed.

(I haven't said anything about sugar so far, because the stomach has no role in carbohydrate digestion: Sugars remain intact well into the small intestine.)

After a meal, peristaltic contractions slowly sweep through the stomach at a rate of about three a minute, squeezing liquids out and into the small intestine. Liquids move through the alimentary canal much faster than solids do and, in a feedback loop, trigger waves of peristalsis of their own. This helps explain why, despite digestion supposedly being such a slow process, eating a meal often seems to trigger the need to find a bathroom in a hurry. Solids larger than about one-tenth of an inch stay behind, though, churning gently in the stomach until small enough to be safely let through. The stomach has one other function somewhat less glamorous than protein digestion and the breaking down of food into chyme. It acts simply as a storehouse, a place for the remains of a large meal to sit for hours while tiny sprays of chyme are sent on for further processing.

The Small Intestine

True digestion begins in the small intestine, where the chyme mixes with a long series of digestive enzymes. The body takes advantage of the extraordinary length of the intestine to extract every possible bit of nutrient and ensure that the end products—amino acids, fatty acids and simple sugars—are absorbed.

Though that lump that flops over most of our belts is thought of as the stomach, under the fat are actually some 15 feet of folded and coiled intestine. (Because of the enormous variations among people, all lengths listed in this chapter are averages only.) Why "small" then? Because it is only 1½ to 2 inches in diameter, much narrower than the large intestine is.

It may seem odd to picture the equivalent of a 15-foot fire hose coiled up inside your gut, but the reality is far stranger. Like a magic satchel in a fairy tale, our insides are many times bigger than our outsides. The inner wall of the small intestine is covered with millions of microscopic fingerlike projections called villi (VIL-eye), almost like a thick shag carpet. Secreting enzymes and absorbing nutrients, the villi mark the spots where digestion truly occurs. Individually tiny, collectively the villi vastly increase the surface area of the small intestine. Various estimates place its total area from 3,000 to 5,000 to 9,000 square feet. It's as if every square inch of every floor in every room of your house were devoted to the job, spectacular confirmation of how vital digestion is.

The small intestine is somewhat arbitrarily divvied up into three sections. The first 10 to 11 inches are called the duodenum; the remaining length is split into the jejunum and the ileum. The duodenum ends and the jejunum begins at a sharp angle called the ligament of Trietz, which I mention only because lactase activity is higher here than anywhere else in the small intestine. A doctor taking a biopsy sample for a lactase test will snip off a piece here. (More on this in Chapter 13.) Nothing quite as noticeable as the ligament of Trietz marks the division between the jejunum and the ileum. Most references put the ileum at about half again as long as the jejunum, making it, say, 12 to 15 feet to the jejunum's 8 to 9 feet, although you may also read that the jejunum is actually longer.

The Duodenum

The duodenum is only 3% of the length of the entire alimentary canal, but it is by far the most important piece. If digestion is technically the hydrolyzing of proteins, fats and starches into their most basic components, then virtually all digestion takes place in the duodenum (except that of sugars, which wait for the jejunum). Everything above the duodenum is there simply to break food down so the duodenum can work on it; everything after is there simply to absorb the basic nutrients and get rid of the wastes. If the duodenum fails, we're in trouble.

The surprise, as Samuel Johnson once said in another context, is not so much that it's done well, but that it is done at all. Getting the duodenum to work is a production equivalent to putting on a live broadcast of a three-ring circus in the middle of an active volcano. In both, a number of complex events that need to be perfectly coordinated occur simultaneously, while at the same time requiring shelter from violent natural forces.

Every 20 seconds, for hours after every meal, a spray of highly acid chyme shoots in from the stomach through the pyloric sphincter. The duodenum lacks the stomach's protective lining, so the acid has to be immediately neutralized or else ulcers can form. (In fact, 90% of all ulcers occur in the first inch and a half of the duodenum.) Help comes from the liver and pancreas, the digestive system organs that are outside the alimentary canal.

Although the stomach's motor activity has actual control over gastric emptying, it looks to conditions in the duodenum as a trigger. When the acidity rises with the introduction of the chyme, the pyloric sphincter sees that as a signal to shut tightly, preventing any more acid from entering the duodenum. Simultaneously, the liver and gall bladder discharge bile salts and the pancreas pours in pancreatic juice. Both are alkaline, the chemical opposite of an acidic solution just as a base is the chemical opposite of an acid. Mixing one with the other produces a neutral solution.

With the chyme neutralized, the pancreatic juice enzymes for digesting starches, fats and proteins can do their jobs, which amounts to the bulk of actual digestion. The pancreas just doesn't get its due for its importance. The liver is equally unappreciated; it has about 500 different jobs and ties in to almost every system in the body. The bile salts, by the way, are not digestive enzymes but detergents. They break large globules of fats down to tinier ones to enable the enzymes to properly latch on in the lock and key fashion I talked about earlier. (Bile is also known as gall: The gall bladder concentrates and stores bile in between meals.)

When a sufficient amount of the acid has been neutralized and the chyme digested and moved on, the lowered acidity triggers the pyloric sphincter to open once again and restart the cycle. The duodenum may spend five hours in continuous action after a meal.

The Jejunum, Villi and Absorption

In the jejunum, the small intestine gets to contribute a few enzymes of its own to digestion. The ones we're concerned with are called disaccharidases because they split disaccharides—compound sugars—into the simple sugars that the body can absorb. Lactase is a disaccharidase. Lactose is a disaccharide. Here, finally, is where lactose is digested.

Digestion and the absorption of the nutrients that are formed are the responsibility of the villi that line the jejunum walls. The villi are in constant motion, waving back and forth to churn the chyme so that the enzymes are evenly distributed and absorption of nutrients speeded. Though a cross section of the small intestine really does look remarkably like a rolled up carpet sample, in action the villi more resemble those ghostly wormlike tube plants found undulating on the ocean floor.

Villi may require a microscope to be seen but are extremely complex inside and out. Each individual villus contains a network of blood capillaries to whisk amino acids and simple sugars off to the liver for processing and a lacteal which conveys fatty acids to the lymphatic system. The cells that cover the villus, only a single layer deep, have openings or pores between them through which the nutrients enter. Vitamins and minerals, by the way, are also swept up through the pores of the villus. I haven't mentioned them earlier because they are small enough that they don't need hydrolysis.

The villi themselves are covered with finger-like protuberances called microvilli, so tiny that they can be seen only through an electron microscope. Think of putting on a glove. Your fingers correspond to the blood and lymph vessels at the core of a villus connecting it to the rest of the body while the fabric of the glove equates with the surface of the villus where the nutrients are absorbed. The microvilli would be like a nap on the fabric's surface which brush against the stream of oncoming nutrients. Indeed, the microvilli are often referred to as the brush border. Microvilli increase the surface area of the small intestine even further.

Finally, we've hit the point at which lactase is found, lactose is split into glucose and galactose and those simple sugars are absorbed into the villi and swept off to be put to good use. All the enzymes which split compound sugars are also here in the brush border.

Why the jejunum rather than the duodenum? It seems that the microvilli are packed together so tightly that large molecules would have a difficult time reaching them. The intestine overcomes this by using the duodenum as a kind of mortar and pestle to break down large molecules and send only the smaller end products out into the jejunum. Something as small to begin with as lactose simply drifts through the chaos of the duodenum and lets itself be carried onward in the intestinal juices, but other compound sugars such as maltose are part of starches and require hydrolysis in the duodenum first. In this way, the digestive system can bunch all its disaccharidases together in the jejunum for efficiency. The compound sugars fall out of the juices flowing freely through the jejunum and latch onto the enzymes that are sitting in wait on the brush border.

That doesn't mean that all sugars get equal attention or handling. Lactase is known to be the enzyme whose production is most easily disrupted by intestinal diseases or surgery. In addition, lactase production even in healthy LP adults is at best never more than one-half that of sucrase, the enzyme that works on sucrose, and only one-quarter that of maltase, the enzyme which works on maltose. This may be because lactase is truly needed only for the digestion of limited amounts of mother's milk.

All the remains of our food along with all the internal juices we add for processing flow across the tremendous surface area the villi afford us until virtually all the available nutrients in our diet are picked out and packed away. Over the course of a day, our small intestines handle an amazing volume of liquids. The solid food and water in the daily diet of our mythical average person total about 2 quarts. Our salivary glands contribute an additional quart and a half to the liquids in the digestive system, 2 more quarts come in from the stomach as gastric juice, a combined 2 quarts enter from the liver and pancreas and the duodenum throws in 1½ quarts of its own intestinal juices. Fortunately, our recycling is excellent.

Most of this liquid, along with most of the minerals and nutrients, is reabsorbed by the villi in the jejunum. The ileum is responsible for the absorption of vitamin B_{12} and the bile salts. By the end of the ileum there is only a pint or so of leftovers to be taken care of. And that is the job of the colon.

The Colon

The small intestine ends rather low in your body not all that far from your rectum, a matter of only a few inches in fact. A few inches aren't enough for the colon, a name more commonly used today than large intestine, to do even the few simple tasks that are given it. So the five foot length of the colon actually rises (the ascending colon) from the point where the small intestine ends, runs right to left along the top of the small intestine and directly under the stomach (the transverse colon) and then angles down again (the descending colon) almost back to its start, where with another angle it turns into the rectum which leads out to the anus. The small intestine runs into the side of the colon, about 2½ inches above where it begins. The little pouch that is formed below that juncture is called the cecum and the appendix hangs off of it. The cecum and appendix are extremely important in animals such as the rabbit since that is where the cellulose in plants is digested. Scientists are still puzzling over whether these vestigial pieces have any function in humans.

Overall, the colon's one main function is to absorb most of the water that made it through the small intestine. By taking in the water, the body also gets the benefits of any dissolved vitamins and minerals although the colon is not technically involved in digestion. As is true of most of the rest of the alimentary canal, you can get along pretty well without your colon.

Once most of the water is absorbed, all that's left is feces. Feces contains the rest of the water (necessary since soft stools do less damage to the anus on the way out) along with substances our bodies consider indigestible: cellulose, other so-called nondietary fibers, unprocessed nutrients, mucus, bile pigments (which give it that familiar color) and whatever baby has managed to swallow when you weren't looking.

That accounts for about half the mass of feces. The other half (although the percentage may vary greatly depending upon what you've been eating and whether you've been taking antibiotics) consists of trillions of dead bacteria. The publicity given recent outbreaks of bacterial gastrointestinal diseases have given these bacteria a bad name but, like cholesterol, the presence of some bacteria is not just helpful but absolutely essential to health. Our intestinal bacteria produce the blood-coagulating vitamin K, for example.

Bacteria, both good and bad, come in with our food. Newborn babies have absolutely sterile intestines. From the first few days of life, however, some bacteria escape the killing action of stomach acid and make their way through the intestines. Our colonic bacteria have adapted so that they feed on what is otherwise indigestible by the small intestine: fiber for the most part, but also any lactose that may have made it through. Most of the problems we associate with LI are produced by the action of particular colonic bacteria on lactose. (Ironically, some different varieties of colonic bacteria may play a major role in helping the LI tolerate milk even if they can't digest it [see Chapter 7]).

All the wastes sitting in the colon are pushed into the rectum, where they are stored until their weight and volume start sending increasingly urgent signals. How often a healthy adult defecates can easily range from three times a day to three times a week; there is no normal frequency. This puts the colon almost constantly at work. By the time it gets rid of the remains of one meal, it probably has already been long at work on the next couple.

Most of us learn very early in life how to control the anal sphincter that seals off the rectum. And most of the time we produce a semi-solid stool that is easy to control. You don't have to be LI to know that the presence of gas and excess water in the colon can put excruciating pressure on your sphincter.

THE INSIDE SCOOP ON LACTOSE

At this point, I hope you're thoroughly impressed by the incredible abilities of your digestive system. The fact that you're here and able to read this is testimony that it has been working remarkably well for years on end. But let's face it, none of us ever sits around and talks about how invisible and unnoticed our digestive systems have been. Things that hum along functioning perfectly tend to get ignored while the slightest variation away from that perfection draws our immediate notice. Gas and diarrhea certainly do have a way of focusing attention on our intestines to the exclusion of almost everything else. The discomfort and pain that the symptoms of LI can bring about are sure indicators that something is spoiling the beautiful picture of the digestive system working in perfect harmony. It's time to swallow some lactose, technically known as a lactose load, and see what happens to turn the stuff of life into the carrier of pain.

To make things as simple as possible, imagine drinking a glassful of a solution of lactose in water. This in fact is what you might drink if you were being tested for LI. As a liquid, it will move fairly quickly through your stomach and into your duodenum. No digestion takes place, however, because no proteins, fats or starches are involved. The lactose therefore moves unchanged into the jejunum.

So far, what I've described is the same for everyone. What happens next depends entirely on how much lactase you produce. If you produce enough, then the lactose is split into glucose and galactose, gets absorbed and everything is fine.

"Enough" is a relative term, however. Virtually everyone produces some lactase, but even LP adults produce no more than half as much as they do of some of the other enzymes which split compound sugars. It is therefore easier for the lactase to be overwhelmed by the contents of the intestine than other enzymes. Sucrase, for example, is the enzyme that splits sucrose (table sugar) into glucose and fructose. Most of us can eat dozens or even hundreds of times as much sucrose as lactose because so much sucrase is produced by the villi. By contrast, lactase at best can just keep up with the task at hand. If the jejunum contains more lactose than there exists lactase to digest it, the unsplit lactose will simply stay in the intestinal juices as they flow toward the colon.

The intestinal juice has four major components when it hits the jejunum: water; absorbable nutrients (including amino acids, fatty acids, vitamins and minerals); indigestible fibers and whatnot; and compound sugars. Each gets handled slightly differently. Indigestible fibers just keep moving through to the colon. Nutrients get absorbed through the pores of the villi, while water is able to diffuse right through the villi's walls. Water always moves from the region with fewer numbers of particles per unit of water to the region with greater numbers of particles per unit of water. Those quarts and quarts of intestinal juices make for a very dilute concentration indeed so that water normally flows from the gut into the body.

That changes when a lactose load hits. In the absence of lactase to split it into absorbable glucose and galactose, the lactose particles just sit there in the gut. Now that the liquid in the intestine is more concentrated than that of the surrounding tissues, water is drawn from the body into the intestine.[2] The volume of the small intestine can increase fivefold. Worse, this excess water stimulates peristalsis, moving the lactose through the intestine faster and allowing even less time for it to come into contact with whatever lactase might be present.

---

[2]Note for the technical-minded: You may want to raise an objection at this point. Digested lactose, split into glucose and galactose, has double the number of particles of undigested lactose. So if water flows toward the direction of higher particle count, then why should the worst effects be produced by the lower number of undigested lactose particles? The answer is found in an extremely thin but vital layer of stagnant water adjacent to the brush border of the villi where the lactase is produced, allowing the lactase to sit in place rather than being carried off in the churning stream of juices. The glucose and galactose that are produced stay in this stagnant layer as well. An additional effect is also at work. Unabsorbed lactose appears to keep sodium and other electrolytes from being absorbed. The end result is that the volume of fluid passing through the ileum is about three times greater than would otherwise be the case.

The large volume of lactose-laden water has nowhere to go but the colon. There the colonic bacteria go to work fermenting the lactose. The bacteria can produce their own lactase to hydrolyze the lactose into glucose and galactose. The problem is that the colon, unlike the jejunum, can't absorb simple sugars. They remain instead as food for the bacteria, which metabolize them into what are known as short-chain fatty acids. The higher acidity stimulates more peristalsis and causes still more water to flow into the colon. Peristalsis and water in the colon is a combination which results in diarrhea.

Meanwhile, the bacteria are busy splitting one of the acids produced, formic acid, into carbon dioxide and hydrogen gases and, in some people, methane as well. Most of the resulting gas escapes through the nearest opening, either by itself, which doctors politely call flatulence, or propelling the loose, watery stools that are part of the diarrhea. (Some of the hydrogen is absorbed into the bloodstream where it quickly makes its way to the lungs. This means that our breath, normally hydrogen-free, suddenly contains hydrogen as a result of LI. This is a wonderful diagnostic tool, covered in Chapter 13.) The result is bloating, pain, cramps and borborygmi, those embarrassing rumbling noises from moving gas that make you wonder what in the world is going on.

An 8-ounce glass of milk contains about 12 g of lactose. A test lactose load can be huge by comparison, with as much as 50 g of lactose. Not surprisingly, its effects are often felt quickly and severely. Within 30 minutes of a huge lactose load, you might start to feel bloated. Children, who are usually the only ones to show vomiting as a symptom of LI, may vomit at that time. Abdominal pain and flatulence will hit within one to two hours. Not everyone experiences diarrhea, but those who do will also start to feel it in the first couple of hours. Symptoms may persist for hours, even days.

By the time you start feeling the effects of undigested lactose it's too late to do much of anything about it. Antacids, which are designed to neutralize stomach acid, aren't going to be effective against colonic gas. Taking diarrhea remedies might seen like the most logical course, but may actually work against you. Uncomfortable as it might be, you want the water, lactose and offending bacteria to be swept out of the colon as soon as possible. Slowing down the process may temporarily relieve symptoms only to prolong the discomfort. If the diarrhea persists to a second day, after the lactose is pretty well gone, taking a remedy to ease any continual spasming may bring the episode to a close. Antiflatulents containing simethicone may help relieve some symptoms, since simethicone works to combine small gas bubbles into larger ones that are easier to expel, but again this does not attack the cause. It may be possible to gain a small measure of relief by taking lactase pills (discussed in Chapter 8) when the symptoms start, but don't get your expectations too high.

The symptoms of LI are likely to make you exquisitely miserable. If every dairy product affected the LI this way every time, you'd have to be fanatic about avoiding milk.

But it just doesn't work that way. Many people, even in countries where virtually the entire population can be presumed to be technically LI, have dairy products on a regular basis, without harm. LI is much more complicated than a simple equation of lactose comsumption = symptoms. What symptoms you get, if any, and when, turns out to depends not only on who you are but what you eat, when and how often. We've looked at lactose as lactose. In the next chapter, we'll take a look at lactose as food, as a piece of the many forms of milk. Chapter 7 talks about which forms of milk are easiest to tolerate.

6

THE WONDERFUL WORLD OF DAIRY PRODUCTS—

I've said it before, but it bears repeating: If you are LI you should become an expert on milk. Whether you want to continue having dairy products, but in as safe a manner as possible, or whether you are looking to eliminate them from your diet altogether, milk and its byproducts have to be at the center of our attention.

What follows is an exhaustive list of all the various types of dairy products you are likely to encounter either on their own or as ingredients in packaged foods. Whey, for example, is something you'll seldom see on the shelf but is absolutely critical for you to know about. I've provided a description and the lactose percentage for the types of dairy product, wherever possible. Remember, everything else being equal, it's the total amount of lactose that you respond to, not the total amount of food. An 8 ounce glass of milk contains far more lactose than an 8 ounce chunk of ripened cheese, but may have less lactose than another product that's had half an ounce of dried whey added.

For the most part it should be clear which products are high in lactose and which low. With certain types of products, however, there can be some surprising variations in lactose content from brand to brand as the result of different recipes and manufacturing processes. Some yogurts, ice creams and processed cheeses may have two or more times the lactose of other brands. Without knowing the exact manufacturing process used, it is usually impossible to say which are which.

Milk is astonishingly versatile and food scientists constantly invent new variations and find new uses for older products. And milk is in an enormous number of commercial products under aliases that may disguise its identity entirely. Here is milk's entire family tree.

▌ FLUID MILKS

Whole Milk
When the electric guitar came along, the ordinary guitar known for centuries magically acquired the modifier "acoustic" to distinguish it from

DON'T DRINK YOUR MILK?

In 1992, the Physicians Committee for Responsible Medicine (PCRM), joined by baby guru Dr. Benjamin Spock and Dr. Frank A. Oski, director of pediatrics at Johns Hopkins University, rocked the medical and nutritional communities by declaring war on milk. "Parents should be alerted to the potential risks to their children from cow's milk products," the PCRM statement said. "Milk should not be required or recommended in government guidelines." Dr. Oski, author of *Don't Drink Your Milk*, added, "There is no redeeming feature to cow's milk that should make people drink it."

Around that time, studies in *The New England Journal of Medicine*, inspired by an outbreak of vitamin D poisoning that left one person dead, found that some milks and infant formulas tested had several times too much vitamin D added. Only a minority had a vitamin content within the accepted range.

Milk was soon under attack again after the use of the growth hormone BST was approved for dairy cattle. Consumers' groups, lawmakers and parents rose in fury and demanded that hormone-free milk be made available and clearly labeled as such.

Latching on to the popular mood, magazines feature pun-filled articles ("holy cow?" being a favorite) linking milk to everything from juvenile diabetes to non-Hodgkin's lymphoma to increased mucus production.

Is milk the next worst thing to drinking rocket fuel? The case is far from proven. What we do know is that headlines are as bad a source of medical information as schoolyard gossip. Health is a field of nuances and individual variances. The simplistic generalizations crammed into attention-getting headlines are often belied by the very stories they highlight. Digging beneath the headlines is a requirement.

First, you should take note of who is making the accusations. It is not at all a coincidence that the PRCM also advocates a strict vegetarian diet or that the strongest supporters and popularizers of its position share those views. The debate over the value—nutritional and moral—of vegetarian diets has been increasing in volume for several years. Attacks on milk would seem to be part of a larger strategy. Bonnie Liebman, director of nutrition for the Center for Science in the Public Interest, itself no friend to the medical establishment, noted her fear that "the committee's dietary advice is influenced by its animal-rights agenda."

A second major issue is the penchant for taking a single study's findings as proof when in fact they may be too inconclusive or based on too small a sample to be meaningful. The juvenile diabetes study that raised so much fuss is a prime example. Dr. George Eisenbarth, executive director of the Barbara Davis Center for Childhood Diabetes in Denver, said that it was "too preliminary to warrant withholding milk from children, even children with a family history of diabetes." Sara King, the research director for the Juvenile Diabetes Foundation, said she was "very uncomfortable taking a stand against dairy products for young children."

Newspapers, to be fair, do usually include dissenting views in their articles to provide balance. Too often, however, these quotes are buried so deeply in the article that few casual readers ever get to them. Too bad, for they can change the tone of the entire debate. You might expect establishment groups like the American Medical Association, the American Academy of Pediatrics and the American Dietetic Association to attack the PRCM report. But you may not have read Dr. Oski quoted as saying, "It is relatively safe to drink milk after about a year or a year and a half," or that Dr. Spock's stance against milk only amounted to a recommendation that breastfeeding was preferred and whole milk should not be given to infants under a year old—the exact position of the American Academy of Pediatrics.

It's often said that if aspirin were invented today, the FDA would never approve it as a drug because of the number of problems it causes. Nevertheless, aspirin appears to do an enormous amount of good in many people. Milk falls into the same category. It is hardly "nature's perfect food." Dairies and dairy farmers may require closer supervision. Lower-fat versions are undoubtedly healthier for adults. Future research may confirm its dangers for selected individuals. But it remains a major source of nutrients that can only be obtained elsewhere by diligent effort and in less palatable forms.

Controversy over milk is sure to continue. Just remember that headlines are meant to grab your attention, not to inform. Dig deeper, listen to both sides and make your decisions through reason and understanding rather than fear.

---

its amplified descendent. In the same way, milk straight from the cow is called "whole" milk by the dairy people to distinguish it from the dozens of variations that exist. After processing to meet certain minimum legal standards, whole milk contains 3.7%–5.1% lactose. Whole milk and most other fluid milks have vitamin D added.

The FDA allows concentrated milk, reconstituted milk, and dry whole milk to be listed as "milk" in ingredients lists. (To reconstitute a product, you add water to its dry form. Water plus dry whole milk equals reconstituted milk. Reconstituted products will contain about the same amount of lactose as their originals, so reconstituted milk should be equal in lactose to whole milk.)

Lowfat Milk

Whole milk must contain, under federal standards, not less than 3.25% milkfat. If the percentage of milkfat is reduced to 2.0%, 1.5%, 1.0%, or 0.5%, the resulting product is lowfat milk. "Protein fortified" lowfat milk has had nonfat milk solids added. Lowfat milk contains 3.7%–5.5% lactose.

Removing the milkfat also removes vitamin A. Replacement vitamin A must be added before shipping so that lowfat milk has the minimum of 2,000 IU that is found naturally in whole milk.

Skim or Nonfat Milk
When you take as much milkfat away from milk as technologically possible, the result is skim or nonfat milk (the terms are interchangeable). Skim milk contains 4.3%–5.7% lactose. On an ingredients list, concentrated skim milk, reconstituted skim milk and nonfat dry milk may be referred to as "skim milk" or "nonfat milk."

Reduced Lactose Milks
There are numerous varieties of reduced lactose milks on the market today. In general, they have been treated with the lactase enzyme to remove typically 70% of the lactose in the original variety of milk. Since reduced lactose milk now comes in whole, 2% and 1% lowfat and nonfat varieties, the lactose content will vary to a degree. Expect a range of approximately 1.1%–1.6% lactose. Reduced-lactose milk may also come fortified with calcium. A 100% lactose-free milk is now available commercially. See Chapter 8 for more information on reduced-lactose milk products.

Flavored Milk
In years past, this category consisted only of chocolate milk but today the dairy industry has gone beyond ordinary chocolate or strawberry to set a course for the outer limits of our taste buds. To wit, Bart Simpson now can covet a Butterfinger Chocolate-Peanut Butter Low Fat Milk that others better not lay a finger on. Flavored milks are otherwise similar to the type of milk—whole, lowfat or skimmed—that they are made from. Lowfat varieties are the ones most commonly found in stores. Chocolate milk has a lactose content similar to that of its constituent unflavored milks, about 4.1%–4.9%.

Eggnog
Eggnog is officially a mixture of milk products, egg yolk, egg white ingredients and nutritive carbohydrate sweetener, no matter what your Christmas recipe might say. Salt, flavoring, color additives and stabilizers may be added. Eggnog must be at least 6% milkfat and the egg yolk solid content may be not less than 1% by weight of the finished food. The lactose content of eggnog will vary considerably by recipe, but is likely to be in the same range as other fluid milk products. I have seen lactose-free eggnog in supermarkets, however.

Low Sodium Milk
Ninety-five percent or more of the sodium in milk can be removed for those people on low-sodium diets. Whole milk is normally used as the starting point. The lactose content should not be not affected.

CREAMS

Technically, there is no longer any one product known as "cream." Cream represents a whole spectrum of high fat milk products containing not less than 18% milkfat. In general, the higher the fat content for fluid milk or cream, the lower the lactose content, and vice versa. The FDA says that reconstituted cream, dried cream, and plastic cream (sometimes known as concentrated milk fat) may be called "cream" on an ingredients listing.

Light Cream

Light cream, also known as coffee cream or table cream, is the lightest of the creams, containing at least 18% but less than 30% milkfat. It has somewhat less lactose than milk, or 3.7%–4.0%.

Light Whipping Cream

Whipping cream or light whipping cream must contain at least 30% but less than 36% milkfat. Light whipping cream normally contains 2.8%–3.0% lactose, but citations range as high as 3.6% for cream that is only 30% fat. Whipped cream topping, ready-to-use whipped cream sold in aerosol cans or tubs in stores, is a blend of various milk products. The lactose percentage will vary according to the product, but one figure I've seen is 13.3%.

Heavy Cream

Heavy cream or heavy whipping cream is heavy indeed, containing at least 36% milkfat. The higher fat content reduces its lactose content to below that of light whipping cream. The same source that gave a 3.6% figure for light cream gave 3.1% for cream that is 40% fat.

Half-and-Half

Half-and-half, as its name implies, is not milk or cream but a mixture of both. It contains at least 10.5% but less than 18% milkfat. Half-and-half is the preferred whitener for coffee. Many restaurants today have moved away from using tiny containers of nondairy creamer and are substituting half-and-half instead. Half-and-half contains 4.0%–4.3% lactose.

CULTURED AND ACIDIFIED MILK PRODUCTS

Milk is cultured by the addition of appropriate bacterial cultures. Milk is acidified when it has been soured with an acid (lactic or citric acid, for example) with or without the addition of cultures. The terms therefore overlap to a certain extent but acidified and cultured milk products differ both in flavor, depending upon final acid content, and in consistency. Virtually any milk product can also be found in a cultured or acidified form.

Cultured or soured milks are found in many regions where LI is prevalent. They stay drinkable longer than fresh milk and are better tolerated by the LI because their lactose content, due to the lactase action produced by the bacteria, will drop 50%–80% or more from that of the starter milk in the first few days or even hours of culturing. The acidification process can also be designed to produce alcohol. Kefir and kumiss are cultured acidified milks with an alcohol content of 1.5%–2.5%. (Traditionally, these names referred to products from specific animals— *kefir* from fermented mare's milk and *kumiss* from camels, along with such variations as *airan* from yaks—but those distinctions are unlikely to hold for today's commercial beverages.)

Sour Cream
If cream is cultured with bacteria and fermented until the acidity is at least 0.5%, the result is sour cream, also called cultured sour cream, containing 3.0%–4.3% lactose. Variations include acidified sour cream, sour half-and-half, and acidified sour half-and-half.

Yogurt
Yogurt is a cultured milk product, usually made commercially by starting with skim or whole milk and adding about 30% milk solids in the form of non-fat dry milk. *Lactobacillus bulgaricus* and *Streptococcus thermophilus* bacteria cultures are added to ferment the milk mixture. The final product is plain yogurt, which can then be sweetened or mixed with fruit. Federal standards specify that "yogurt" contains not less than 3.25% milkfat, "lowfat yogurt" may contain from 0.5%–2.0% milkfat and "nonfat yogurt" must contain no more than 0.5% milkfat, before any bulky flavors are added.

There are so many varieties and styles of yogurt that their lactose contents also vary significantly. Whole-milk yogurt has 4.1%–4.7% lactose. Lowfat yogurts are considerably more common and so vary considerably more; 1.9%–6.0% lactose have been found in various brands. Traditional yogurts have about half the lactose content of commercial yogurts.

Even many severely LI people can eat yogurt with few or no ill effects, despite its lactose content. You'll find an extensive section on yogurt in the next chapter.

Cultured Buttermilk
Once buttermilk was the liquid left over when cream was churned into butter. Today's buttermilk is very different, a cultured product usually made from lowfat or skim milk with nonfat dry milk solids added. It can also be made from fresh whole milk, concentrated milk or reconstituted nonfat dry milk. Buttermilk contains 3.6%–5.0% lactose. Sweetcream

buttermilk, concentrated sweetcream buttermilk, reconstituted sweet-cream buttermilk and dried sweetcream buttermilk may be declared as "buttermilk" on ingredients lists.

Acidophilus Milk
Acidophilus milk has a history similar to that of buttermilk. An older variety, known as acidophilus cultured milk or fermented acidophilus milk, was yet another variation on the widespread idea of souring milk to keep it unspoiled for a longer time. It is little seen today because of its tart and, to most people, unpalatable taste. *Lactobacillus acidophilus* bacteria are added to skim or lowfat milk and incubated until a soft curd forms, producing the pronounced cooked and acidic flavor. A newer process eliminates the flavor changes that fermentation brings by growing the bacteria culture first and then adding it directly to cold milk. This product, called sweet acidophilus milk (SAM), preserves both the natural flavor and consistency of the original milk.

The existence of two similarly named products has led to endless confusion over acidophilus milk's value to the LI. Some sources strongly recommend it; others dismiss it as being as bad as regular milk. Here's the full story.

Traditional sour milks of all kinds tend to have much less lactose than their unfermented equivalents. How much the lactose content has been reduced relates directly to the length of the fermentation period. Usually, the longer the fermentation, the lower the lactose content—and also the sourer the milk.

One study done with fermented acidophilus milk found that it had only half the lactose content (2.4%–2.6%) of lowfat milk. Not surprisingly, it was better tolerated than the lowfat milk as well.

Toleration by the small intestine is a different issue than toleration by the taste buds. It is extremely unlikely that you will find fermented acidophilus milk anywhere outside of specialty health food stores. The standard commercial acidophilus milk is SAM. Because it is not fermented, SAM cultures do nothing to the lactose content. The evidence is overwhelming that SAM is tolerated no better than the (usually) lowfat milk it is made from.

For years, *Lactobacillus acidophilus* cultures have been ascribed virtually magical powers for treating gastrointestinal disorders. There does not appear to be a sound consensus of medical studies supporting these claims, however. Even if there were, it is not at all clear that SAM would be any more effective in this respect than it is in relieving the symptoms of LI. For now, soured milks are in the realm of home remedies—literally, since you almost have to make them at home to even hope to get their supposed benefits.

CONCENTRATED MILKS

Evaporated Milk

Evaporated milk is a misnomer. Milk isn't evaporated, but about 60% of the milk's water content is. What's left is subjected to a complex scheme of homogenizing, standardizing, vitaminizing, stabilizing, and canning. The sealed can is heat-treated to sterilize it completely, so that it can sit unopened on a shelf almost indefinitely. Evaporated whole milk must contain at least 7.5% milkfat and 25% total milk solids. Evaporated skimmed milk must contain at least 20% milk solids but no more than 0.5% milkfat. Both contain 9.7%–11.0% lactose, or about twice that of fluid milks.

Concentrated Milk

Concentrated milk, also known as condensed milk, is a kind of evaporated milk in which the process has been stopped before the sterilizing stage. This means that concentrated milk will spoil if not refrigerated. It is intended for bulk use by industry and very little of it is sold through retail outlets. The removal of water drives up the lactose content of the remainder, to 14.7%.

Sweetened Condensed Milk

Cans of sweetened condensed milk are not sterilized and yet they can sit on grocery shelves as long as cans of evaporated milk can. How do they do it? With sugar (sucrose). Lots of sugar, about 40%–45% of the condensed milk, so much that no bacteria can grow in it. Be careful not to confuse evaporated with condensed milk in cooking, as the sugar content in the condensed milk will muck up your recipe unless called for specifically. The lactose concentration is high, too, about 11.4%–16.3%.

DRY MILKS

Nonfat Dry Milk

If at least 95% of the water in skim milk is removed, a powder is formed which is far less bulky, almost as nutritious, and less expensive than the fluid milk. Both the standard powdered milks on supermarket shelves and thousands of commercial food products contain nonfat dry milk.

Because so much water is removed, the solids which remain in the dry product are extremely high in lactose: 49.0%–52.3%. Instant nonfat dry milk is a variation designed to disperse immediately in cold water. It typically contains 49.5%–54.0% lactose. The final concentration of lactose in a commercial food product depends on the amount of water or other filler added, but it is safe to say that nonfat dry milk appearing high on an ingredients list is a warning sign for anyone with severe LI.

Dry Whole Milk

The same process which makes nonfat milk dry can also make powdered whole milk. The lactose content is appreciably lower, about 36.5%–38.4%, although that is still high by ordinary standards.

Dry Cream

Removing water and water only from pasteurized milk and/or cream creates dry cream. It contains 40%–75% milkfat and no more than 5% moisture. I do not have a lactose percentage for it but all other dried milk products are extremely high in lactose.

Dry Buttermilk

Dry buttermilk is obtained by drying liquid buttermilk only and cannot contain or be made from nonfat dry milk or dried whey or anything else. It has a protein content of not less than 30% and a lactose content of 46.5%–49.0%. Dry buttermilk product is identical except that its protein content must be lower than 30% and so its lactose content is slightly higher: 48.0%–55.0%.

 ## BUTTER AND MARGARINE

Butter

Butter is a combination of milkfat, buttermilk and water, but mostly fat. Most butter is made from cream, since cream has 10 times the butterfat content of milk. Grade AA butter, the best, is made from high-quality fresh sweet cream. This is the grade usually found in supermarkets. Grade A butter is made from fresh cream and Grade B butter from sour cream. In any case, butter has a fat content of over 80%.

Since butter is so high in fat, it should be no surprise that it is low in lactose. Estimates vary, but none places the percentage of lactose over 1.0%.

Margarine

All margarines are made of oil and fat, a liquid, emulsifiers and usually preservatives, artificial butter flavoring, coloring and added vitamins. If the liquid is plain water, then the margarine probably contains no lactose. Most margarines, however, use a milk product as the liquid. Even so, since margarines, like butter, are over 80% fat, their lactose percentages will also be similar to butter's, almost certainly 1.0% or under.

FROZEN MILKS

Ice Cream, Soft Ice Cream and Frozen Custard

Sure, ice cream was once actually made from fresh sweet cream, but today's run-of-the-mill supermarket product may very well use whole milk, skim milk or any one of 25 other milk product variations, as well as five forms of the milk protein casein. Ice cream also contains air, sometimes lots of it, in percentages varying from near zero to over 50%. Nutritionally, soft ice creams aren't much different from their harder counterparts, although they do contain less air and slightly less sugar. In addition, ice cream must contain less than 1.4% egg yolk solids. More egg yolk turns the product into frozen custard, alternatively known as french ice cream and french custard ice cream.

As with so many other milk products, all these variations make it difficult to put a firm figure on lactose content. One study estimated 6%–7% lactose for plain vanilla ice cream. Other studies, working with a greater variety of flavors, brands and styles, found a lactose range of 3.4%–8.4%.

Ice Milk
Since ice cream may be made from milk as well as cream, the only real difference between it and ice milk is that the latter is lower in fat, having a maximum fat content of 7% (and a minimum of 2%), compared to ice cream's minimum of 10%. Because of changes to FDA product labeling regulations, the name ice milk will probably be phased out and replaced by light, reduced-fat, lowfat or nonfat ice cream as a descriptor. One test of ice milk found a lactose content of 7.6%; individual brands may be much higher or lower.

Sherbet
In America sherbets almost always contain some milk solids along with their fruit flavoring. Indeed, federal regulations state that its milkfat content must be between 1%–2% with total milk-derived solids between 2%–5%. Low in protein and calcium, sherbet is high only in Calories, from the huge amount of sugar (over one pound per gallon) added to give it sweetness. U.S. sherbets contain 0.6%–2.1% lactose.

Mellorine
According to the Code of Federal Regulations, "Mellorine is a food produced by freezing, while stirring, a pasteurized mix consisting of safe and suitable ingredients including, but not limited to, milk-derived nonfat solids and animal or vegetable fat, or both, only part of which may be milkfat." In other words, whatever this stuff may be, it probably contains some variation on skim milk and therefore contains lactose.

■ CHEESES

Hundreds if not thousands of different cheeses are produced around the world, a large percentage of which can be found in America's specialty cheese shops. All cheeses start with milk, of course, and the basic process changes little whatever the animal the milk is obtained from. I only have lactose percentages for cow's milk cheeses, but I doubt that the goat's milk or sheep's milk cheese that you occasionally see will be radically different.

Cheese is made by using an enzyme called rennet to coagulate the milk protein casein, thereby separating the milk into a semi-soft solid, the curds, and a liquid, the whey. Most of the fat, casein and vitamin A in milk, plus about two-thirds of the calcium, wind up in the curds. Most of the lactose, water-soluble proteins, vitamin C, thiamine and riboflavin, along with the remaining third of the calcium, stay in the liquid, which is mostly water.

Heating the whey coagulates the soluble proteins and allows a soft cheese to be made. Known as recuit and serac in France and Quarg (or Quark) in Germany, in the United States it usually goes by its Italian name of ricotta. As a whey cheese it has the highest lactose content of any natural cheese, up to about 5.1%. Real Italian ricotta may be acceptable for someone with a non-severe casein allergy, as 96% of the casein in milk goes into the curd. Be warned, though, that in the U.S. some curd is often added to make the cheese smoother and moister.

Boiling ten parts of whey with one part of sheep's milk produces a cheese known in various parts of the eastern Mediterranean as skuta, puina, mizithra, noor and anari. The mysost found in Scandinavian countries is virtually a caramelized lactose made from concentrated whey. A few other whey cheeses may be found.

All other cheeses, and the vast majority of common ones, are made from the curd. A bewildering variety of schemes for classifying cheeses have been proposed but for our purposes we need only sort cheese into one of two categories, unripened or ripened.

Unripened Cheeses
Stopping the cheesemaking process just after the curd separates creates most of the familiar soft cheeses. All are fairly high in lactose because some of the remaining whey gets trapped inside the curds. Cream cheese and Neufchatel are just under 3% lactose, nearly as high as whipping cream. Cottage cheese normally runs 2.5%–3.5% lactose, with the 2% lowfat variety even higher, at 3.6%. Pot cheese and farmer cheese are similar.

Ripened Cheeses
The more whey removed from the curds, the firmer the cheese. Once most of the whey is gone, and the lactose with it, cheeses are pressed into forms and aged, or ripened using molds or bacteria that give the cheese its distinctive flavor. For example, by law cheddar cheese must be aged at least 60 days (unless made from pasteurized milk). Even after two months of aging, a cheddar is still considered mild. Four to six months of aging produces a medium cheddar, while sharp or extra sharp cheddars may be aged 6 to 12 months or even longer.

For all cheeses, the longer the aging, the lower the lactose content. Many eminent authorities say flatly that aging removes all the lactose from cheese, even from cheeses that have only been ripened for a few days. At the same time, I have seen figures for the lactose content of aged Cheddar cheese, as well as Emmentaler and other Swiss cheeses such as Gruyere, of 1.4%–2.1%. Try cheese cautiously and find your personal tolerance levels.

The maximum lactose percentages I have found for various cheeses are: American Blue, a sharp and usually crumbly cheese, 2.5%; Camembert, a semi-soft cheese with a crust formed by the mold used to ripen it, 1.8%; Gouda, semi-soft when young, firmer when aged, 2.2%; Edam, something like a skimmed milk version of Gouda, 1.4%; Colby, a variation on Cheddar, 2.5%; Parmesan, a good grating cheese, often aged for years in Italy, but usually sold when younger in America, 3.7%; Stilton, an English cheese, blue-veined from mold, 0.8%; and Romadur, a German cheese similar to Limburger, usually served very young, 2.5%.

Most of these cheeses, and most of the others, for that matter, are sold in a number of varieties which have been aged for differing amounts of time. In any case, a small cube, wedge or slice of an aged cheese is likely to have a minuscule lactose content. To reduce symptoms as much as possible, always go for the most aged ones available if you have a choice.

Processed Cheese
Several types of processed cheese can be found on the market, each farther away from natural cheese than the last. The first three types below (and their variations) have federal standards to which manufacturers must conform.

Pasteurized process cheese is the closest to real cheese, made by "comminuting and mixing, with the aid of heat, one or more" hard cheeses and adding emulsifiers. The fat and moisture contents must be about the same as the natural cheese from which it is made.

Pasteurized process cheese food is similar but may contain less fat. (Grated American cheese food can be made only from cheddar, colby, washed curd or granular cheeses but is also a lower-fat product.)

Pasteurized process cheese spread must be spreadable at 70° F. It has less milkfat and more moisture than a cheese food.

Pasteurized process cheese products have no standard of identity. Although they must be based on dairy products, almost anything else goes, and any additive allowed in foods can be used. Cheese products usually are lowfat and low Calorie and are aimed at the diet market.

If vegetable oil is substituted for the milkfat, the word "imitation" must be on the label if the product is called cheese. To avoid using the dread word imitation, some manufacturers simply don't bother to call what they make cheese. Artificially Flavored Pasteurized Process Slices are available under a variety of brand names. They contain some cheese, but are mostly whey, vegetable oil, and casein.

It's next to impossible to give any meaningful lactose contents for this bizarre array of cheese near-foods. The estimates I've seen range from a tolerable 0.8% to a high 14.2%. All the "cheese foods" I examined in a recent trip to the supermarket had whey added to them, so they are likely toward the high end of this range.

▌ WHEY PRODUCTS

If you do not already know that whey is a milk product, then this section may be one of the most important for you in this entire book. If you just read the section on cheese, you saw that whey is the liquid left over when the solid curds form in cheesemaking. Fresh liquid whey is approximately 93% water, so it has a lactose content of 4.5%–5.0%, not much different from that of whole milk, with the other 2% or so made up of milk proteins as well as most of milk's minerals and water-soluble vitamins. This makes whey a valuable, versatile and relatively inexpensive ingredient in thousands of commercial food products.

But transporting heavy and bulky water across country is not very efficient and most whey is dried before shipping. Taking the water out leaves little in the final product other than lactose. Whey products generally have the highest percentage of lactose of any product used in foods other than lactose itself. In fact, commercial lactose is normally obtained from whey.

The FDA allows concentrated whey, reconstituted whey and dried whey to be represented as "whey" on food labels. Although there may be some foods which would use the relatively low-lactose liquid product, my assumption is that in the commercial food industry, "whey" is almost always a form of dried whey. The presence of whey on a food label is therefore a warning that almost pure lactose has been used in its preparation.

How much whey is in any individual product is impossible for the consumer to ascertain. Unlike sugar, whey is seldom listed first on an ingredients list and it is the very last ingredient listed on a large number of products. Whey is found in nearly every conceivable variety of food product, both those you would expect to find dairy products in—cookies, margarines, baked goods, candies—and those which might surprise you—canned soups and vegetables, meat products and sausage, even carbonated and citrus beverages. The American Dairy Products Institute, to whom I am indebted as a source for this section, calls the use of hydrolyzed whey permeate in the brewing of beer the new frontier for whey utilization.

Dry Whey

Dried whey comes in two distinct forms. Dry (sweet-type) whey has an insignificant portion of the lactose converted into lactic acid. Typically, its lactose content is 63%–75%. Dry (acid-type) whey has more of its lactose converted into lactic acid and so has a slightly acid flavor and a slightly lower lactose content, typically 61%–70%. Both are obtained by drying fresh pasteurized whey.

Concentrated Whey
Removing some of the liquid in whey without changing the relative proportions of anything else results in concentrated whey. I do not have a typical lactose range for it, but, depending on the amount of water removed, its lactose percentage should run intermediate to dried whey and fresh liquid whey.

Reduced Lactose Whey
Well, reduced is a relative term. The lactose content of reduced lactose whey cannot exceed 60%, if that's any comfort to you, but is typically 52%–58%. This variation can also come in fluid, concentrated, or dry form.

Reduced Minerals Whey
Ash is the non-organic component of foods, which mostly means minerals. Whey normally has 7%–14% ash, but reduced minerals whey is limited to 7% ash. The difference seems to be made up with lactose: reduced minerals whey is typically 70%–80% lactose. A variant is partially demineralized whey solids.

Whey Protein Concentrate
By boosting the protein level to a minimum of 25%, whey becomes whey protein concentrate. It may come in liquid, concentrated or dry forms. Because of the many ways it can be formulated, whey protein concentrate shows the greatest typical lactose range of any milk product, from a low of 10% all the way up to 55%.

Whey Protein Isolate
Nearly pure protein, whey protein isolate must be at least 90% protein and it has a tiny 0.5% lactose content.

Dairy Product Solids
Dairy product solids are modified dairy products (permeates and products derived therefrom) obtained by the removal of protein and/or lactose, and/or minerals from milk or whey. They have a typical lactose range of 65%–85%.

Dried Dairy Blend
A combination of dried whey and the milk protein calcium caseinate, the lactose content of dried dairy blend will vary with the blender, but expect it to be high.

MILK SOLIDS

Milk solids include the protein, carbohydrate (lactose), fat, vitamins and minerals, in short, everything in milk but the water. Solids of one sort or another are commonly added to food. I've seen milk solids, skim milk solids, buttermilk solids, sour cream solids, butter solids and whey solids, and other variations undoubtedly exist. All are likely to be similar in lactose content to the dry version of the same form.

MILK PROTEINS

Milk doesn't contain an enormous amount of protein, only about 3.3% on the average, but it is very high quality protein, furnishing all the amino acids essential for nutrition and many others besides.

Most of the milk protein, some 76%–78%, comes from casein, a family of related proteins. Casein concentrates in the curds from which cheese is formed, making cheese a higher protein food than milk itself. In fact, many food processors throw a little casein into their products so that the numbers on the nutrition label look higher than they otherwise would. Casein also makes imitation products work more like the real thing and so is often included in so-called "nondairy" products.

If you're LI, the presence of casein shouldn't bother you. Casein comes from milk, and so it's possible, even likely, that some lactose has tagged along, but the chance of it affecting anyone with LI is quite small. Some of the sodium caseinate-containing nondairy products even say lactose-free on their labels. Of course, people with milk protein allergies, galactosemia or other rare disorders that require a rigorous abstention from all milk products should stay far away from anything with casein, despite the nondairy tag on the outside. Similarly, casein-containing products cannot be designated "pareve" or neutral for those who keep kosher (*see Chapter 10*).

The remaining 14%–24% of the milk protein comes out of the whey portion. Here, two families predominate, the lactalbumins and the lactoglobulins. Beta-lactoglobulin can cause even worse allergic reactions than casein. Oddly enough, while the lactose and casein in goat's milk are similar to that of cow's milk, the whey proteins are not. If you're sure you have only the whey protein allergy, then you might want to take a chance on goat's milk for a change of pace.

For those of us who are LI, goat's milk is out, but we're probably safe if the pure proteins lactalbumin or lactoglobulin appear by themselves on a product label. Remember, whey protein concentrate is not a pure protein, but merely a high protein version of whey, and very high in lactose. Whey protein isolate, on the other hand, is lower in lactose than butter.

Hydrolyzed casein is casein protein that has been treated, usually by breaking it down into individual amino acids, to make it less allergenic. It is found in many products, including some infant formulas. Under the new labeling rules, the terms hydrolyzed protein and hydrolyzed milk protein are no longer allowable because they were insufficiently descriptive.

MILK FATS

Most milk fat products are going to be low in lactose, if they contain any at all. Butter, which I've already mentioned, is 80%–85% fat and only a fraction of a percent lactose. Butter is sometimes disguised in foods as butter solids or natural butter flavor, and of course most margarines contain some milkfat.

Pure fats—milk fat, butterfat, and butter oil—are also sometimes added to foods. All are likely to be virtually lactose free. Both butter oil and anhydrous butterfat may be referred to as "butterfat" on ingredients listings, by the way.

Very occasionally you may see a milk fat identified by one of its chemical names. With over 500 different fatty acids identified in milk there is no way to list them all here. Fortunately, they fall into a few large families. Saturated fatty acids include myristic acid, palmitic acid, and stearic acid. Unsaturated fatty acids include oleic acid, linoleic acid, and linolenic acid. Any of these or their variations (sodium stearyl lactylate and glycerol lacto palmitate are two I've seen on food labels) probably are safe in terms of lactose reactions.

Milk fat intolerance, on the other hand, may be the underlying cause of symptoms for a select few. Some research has been done on intolerances to milk fat, none of it very conclusive. One study ("Do Lipids Play a Role in Milk Intolerance?" J. P. Costet, *et al.*, pp. 156–61 in *Milk Intolerances and Rejections*, ed. by J. Delmont, Basel: Karger, 1983) found that 9% of their test subjects could not tolerate milk fats, but that the "role of lipids in milk rejection thus appears moderate and of little importance." I've seen nothing since to contradict this finding. It remains an open question.

OTHER

Imitation and Filled Milk

Combining water, soybean protein, vegetable fat, corn syrup solids and some miscellaneous milk derivatives like casein, whey, or lactose can produce a fluid that looks a lot like milk. And, under new FDA regulations that took effect in May 1994, it must be nutritionally equal to milk, although fats and Calories may be reduced. But if it doesn't contain any actual dairy products, then it must be referred to as imitation milk.

Removing all or part of the milkfat from substitute milk products and replacing it with any fat or oil other than milkfat gives you filled milk.

Both imitation milk and filled milk are quite rare nowadays. I have never seen either included on any ingredients listing. The wide variation in the way they can be made makes it impossible to give a lactose percentage. You should be aware that the American Academy of Pediatrics considers imitation and filled milk products inappropriate for feeding infants and children under two years of age.

Lactic Acid

Lactic acid is what the bacteria in cultured milk products turn lactose into. For this reason, lactic acid is lactose-free. It appears in ingredients lists every once in a while, causing endless confusion, but by itself, it is perfectly safe.

TABLE 1 PERCENTAGES OF LACTOSE IN DAIRY PRODUCTS		
	LACTOSE PERCENTAGE	
	Range	Average
Fluid Milks		
Whole milk	3.7–5.1	4.7
2% milk	3.7–5.3	4.7
1% milk	4.8–5.5	5.0
Skim or Nonfat milk	4.3–5.7	5.0
Chocolate milk	4.1–4.9	4.5
Half-and-half	4.0–4.3	4.2
Light cream	3.7–4.0	3.9
Whipping cream	2.8–3.0	2.9
Reduced lactose milk	1.1–1.6	
Lactose-free milk	0.0–0.5	
Cultured Milk Products		
Sour cream	3.0–4.3	3.9
Buttermilk	3.6–5.0	4.3
Yogurt, commercial lowfat	1.9–6.0	
Yogurt, commercial whole milk	4.1–4.7	
Acidophilus, skimmed sweet	4.4	4.4
Kefir, commercial part-skim	4.0	
Dry Milks		
Nonfat dry milk	49.0–52.3	51.3
Instant nonfat dry milk	49.5–54.0	
Dry whole milk	36.0–38.5	37.5
Dry buttermilk	46.5–50.0	
Dry buttermilk product	48.0–55.0	

TABLE 1 (Continued)		
	LACTOSE PERCENTAGE	
	Range	Average
Concentrated Milks		
Sweetened condensed milk	11.4–16.3	12.9
Evaporated (whole and skim)	9.7–11.0	10.3
Frozen Milks		
Ice cream	3.1–8.4	
Ice milk	7.6	
Sherbet	0.6–2.1	
Butter	0.8–1.0	
Margarine	0.0–1.0	
Whey		
Dry whey (sweet-type)	63.0–75.0	
Dry whey (acid-type)	61.0–70.0	
Reduced lactose whey	52.0–58.0	
Reduced minerals whey	70.0–80.0	
Dairy product solids	65.0–85.0	
Whey protein concentrate	10.0–55.0	
Whey protein isolate	0.5	
Cheddar type whey	4.5–5.1	
Cottage cheese whey	4.5–4.9	
Lactose	>98.0	
Lactose product	93.0–97.0	
Cow's Milk Cheeses		
American	1.6–5.2	
pasteurized processed	0.0–14.2	
Blue	0.0–2.5	
Brick	0.0–2.8	
Brie	0.0–2.0	
Camembert	0.0–1.8	
Cheddar		
Mild	0.0–2.1	
Sharp	trace–2.1	
Colby	0.0–2.5	
Cottage		
Uncreamed	0.0–3.5	
Diet	3.4	
2%	3.6	
1%	2.7	
Creamed	0.6–3.3	
Cream Cheese	0.4–2.9	
Edam	0.0–1.4	
Feta	4.1	
Gouda	0.0–2.2	

TABLE 1 (Continued)		
	LACTOSE PERCENTAGE	
	Range	Average
Cow's Milk Cheeses *(continued)*		
Liederkranz	near 0	
Limburger	0.0–2.2	
Mozzarella part-skim, low-moisture	0.0–3.1	
Muenster	0.0–1.1	
Neufchatel	0.4–2.9	
Parmesan		
Grated	2.9–3.7	
Hard	0.0–3.2	
Provolone	0.0–2.1	
Quarg	3.0	
Ricotta	0.2–5.1	
Romadur	2.5	
Romano	0.0–3.6	
Roquefort	2.0	
Stilton	0.8	
Swiss	0.0–3.4	
pasteurized processed	0.0–2.1	
Velveeta	9.3	
Other Milk Solids[1]		
Proteins		
Casein, sodium caseinate, calcium caseinate, potassium caseinate	0.0	
Lactalbumins, lactoglobulins	0.0	
Fats		
Milk fat, butterfat, butter oil	0.0	
Other		
Lactic Acid	0.0	

1. While pure proteins and fats have no lactose content, those used in commercial food products have been separated from the rest of the milk through a variety of manufacturing processes. Depending on the process and the quality control, some lactose may—in fact, often does—remain in the finished product. I have seen figures of 0%–2% for the amount of lactose found in commercial caseins. Since caseins themselves are typically used only in small amounts, the actual amount of lactose present in a food containing caseins but no other dairy product is, in the language of federal regulations, "trivial."

7

— AND HOW TO EAT THEM

If the vast majority of the world's adults do not produce lactase as adults, if lactose affects them so severely and if milk is still so widely consumed, then why doesn't every bathroom in the world have a line of horribly anxious people standing outside of it?

The answer, of course, is that the symptoms I described at the end of Chapter 5 were a worst case scenario, just as our trip through the alimentary canal was a best case one. The reality, with humans, is never so simple and straightforward. Whether you are bothered with the symptoms of LI after a meal or snack depends upon several factors, some of which are even in your control. I've summarized them in the following chart.

GREATER SYMPTOMS	LESSER SYMPTOMS
large lactose load	small lactose load
rapid gastric emptying	slow gastric emptying
poorly tolerated food	easily tolerated food
poorly adapted colonic bacteria	better adapted colonic bacteria

As the bar indicates, each factor is really a continuum and you could find yourself at any point along it. The factors are also highly interactive. It's obvious that if you have no lactase activity, eat a large lactose load and have poorly adapted colonic bacteria you will certainly suffer for it. On the other hand, if you have a middling amount of lactase activity and swallow a small lactose load, but one of a poorly tolerated food, it's almost impossible for me to predict how that might affect you. You'll have to learn these things for yourself and the only way to do it is through trial and error.

What I can do is walk you through each of these factors so that you'll have the best possible idea of what may happen if you eat some lactose.

▌ LACTOSE LOAD

Many doctors dismiss LI as a problem. After all, they say with a shrug, most people can drink a glass of milk and not feel any effects. True enough. How many is most? The current consensus assumes that no more than 80% of the LI are this fortunate. Based on the guesstimate that 50 million Americans are LI, that still leaves 10 million who must worry over a glass of milk, or the equivalent of the entire population of Michigan.

How do you know if you're one of them? Or if you could drink two glasses without symptoms? Or only a half glass? You could keep taking lactose tolerance tests until you reach your threshold, but given the potential for symptoms that testing entails, few people would want to go through the test over and over with slightly different amounts of lactose, and few doctors would allow such a thing in the first place.

That's why college students were invented. Since most researchers are already on college campuses, student volunteers—generally young, healthy and in need of quick cash—are the guinea pigs in an amazingly high proportion of the studies reported in the medical literature. I found one such study[1] ("Cocoa feeding and human lactose intolerance," Chong M. Lee & Christine M. Hardy, *American Journal of Clinical Nutrition*, 1989; 49:840–4) that did what we would not. The researchers had volunteers (students from the University of Rhode Island and a nearby minority training center) keep drinking glasses of milk with more and more lactose added to determine exactly what amount of lactose they required to start exhibiting LI symptoms.

Of a mixed group of Caucasians, African-Americans, Asians, Latinos and Jews[2], 27% suffered symptoms after drinking a regular glass of milk (5% lactose); 43% stopped being tolerant at the 7.5% lactose level; 19% more showed symptoms at 10% lactose and the remaining 11% hit their limit at 12.5% lactose.

This is a prime example of the type of experiment sometimes cited to prove how small the LI "problem" really is. After all, three out of four of the volunteers in the experiment—everyone who required more than 5% lactose to produce symptoms—could drink a glass of milk. But as someone who himself is LI, I suppose I'm inclined to see the glass as half empty

---

[1]Note for the technical-minded: No one study by itself is ever truly meaningful, something that is often forgotten when individual studies make headlines in the newspapers. Those discussed in this chapter were picked because they are good, clear examples out of many which tend to reinforce similar conclusions. They are not meant to be definitive by themselves.

[2]Jews are not an ethnic group, but are often grouped as such because so many American Jews share a common eastern European heritage, which is the meaningful phenomenon when it comes to LI.

instead of half full. To me the really important number is the last one: only about one in eight could drink two glasses of milk without ill effects.

If seven out of eight of the LI will exhibit symptoms after the equivalent of two or fewer glasses of milk, and a full quarter after a single glass, then worrying about the amount of lactose you're getting at any one meal is not trivial and not dismissible. On the contrary, one's lactose threshold is a fine line that the vast majority of us may easily step over (*see box*).

There are two ways of reducing the lactose load to ensure that it stays under your threshold: have smaller amounts of dairy products at any one time or switch to dairy products that have less lactose to begin with. I went over the whole long list of dairy products in the last chapter, so I'll just summarize the information here:

- In general, the lower the fat content, the higher the lactose. Skim milk is about 5% lactose, half and half closer to 4%, whipping cream down around 3%. Butter, with the highest fat content of all, has a trivial amount of lactose.
- Aging lowers the lactose content in cheeses. Although some studies have found lactose in all cheeses, such familiar ones as Blue, Brie, Cheddar, Colby, Gouda, Mozzarella, Muenster, Provolone and Swiss have also tested out as containing no lactose. Eat cheeses aged as long as possible, as they are most likely to have little or no lactose. Avoid whey cheeses like ricotta or mysost, however.
- Dried whey, found in many packaged foods, is extremely high in lactose. In general, all dried milk products will be predominantly lactose.

STAYING UNDER YOUR LACTOSE THRESHOLD

No doctor's test will tell you what your exact lactose threshold is. A bit of trial and error is your best bet to come up with an approximate amount, close enough to give you the ability to judge how much is too much. Please note: This exercise is designed to help you judge your limitations after you know for sure that LI is your problem and your only problem. *It is not a substitute for a doctor's diagnosis or clinical testing.*

Start by drinking a glass of milk. Other milk products will do, but milk is easy to buy, doesn't vary much from one brand to the next, and can easily be taken in large quantities. (Whole milk, lowfat milk and skim milk will work equally well for this particular experiment, but don't use chocolate milk or a reduced-lactose milk.) Begin with an amount you're fairly sure you can handle, say, 4 ounces (½ cup) or 8 ounces (1 cup). (If you get symptoms from less than 4 ounces of milk, then just go straight to the chapters on lactase pills and milk substitutes.) Add a constant amount, say 2 ounces or 4 ounces, with each new trial. Keep careful records of exactly how much you drink throughout this experiment.

Drink the milk by itself, and preferably on an empty stomach, because taking it with meals will skew the results. Being consistent is important: Try to keep outside factors to a minimum. If you drink the milk in the morning the first time, then keep on doing so; don't alternate mornings and evenings. Wait an hour before eating other foods to allow your stomach time to move the milk into your intestines and for the first symptoms to be felt. The experiment will work best if you tailor it to your daily schedule. Your convenience is important, because you have to be willing to repeat the process in the same way until you get a result.

One other point before you start: Eating or drinking any additional lactose will throw off all your numbers. To make the experiment work, you must start without any lactose in your system (i.e. you cannot have eaten any dairy product for at least two days prior to testing) and you may not eat any other food containing lactose while the test is going on. This is bothersome, I know, but it should be for just a few days.

Now you're all set. Keep a record of how you feel during the entire test period. Note if you get any symptoms—gas, cramps, diarrhea or a general feeling of bloating or discomfort—from drinking the milk. Your individual symptoms may vary. For most people, symptoms will show up very quickly, within an hour or two. Others may have to wait overnight. If nothing happens, or the symptoms are so mild you're not sure they've been caused by the milk, try again, with a larger glassful. Continue until you start getting obvious or consistent symptoms. That amount is your Lactose Threshold (LT). Since milk is about 5% lactose, you can then figure out your Lactose Threshold Equivalent (LTE). (If you get symptoms right away, *decrease* the amount of milk until you *stop* getting symptoms. If any amount at all causes symptoms, then you belong on a lactose-free diet.)

The LTE is a device to help you estimate how much of any other milk product you can have without getting symptoms. As an example, say that you started getting symptoms after drinking 10 ounces of milk. Whole milk is close to 5% (or 0.05) lactose. To find out how much lactose there is in 10 ounces of milk, multiply 10 by 0.05 to get an answer of 0.5 or ½ ounce of lactose. Therefore, you would also be affected by any other food which contained ½ ounce of lactose: 25 ounces of a cheese which is only 2% lactose or 4 ounces of sweetened condensed milk at 12.5% lactose. Don't worry about the math: I've done it all for you.* The following table lets you just plug in the numbers.

---

*Here's how you can calculate an exact LTE. Let n equal your Lactose Threshold, the number of ounces of milk that causes symptoms. Let y equal the number of ounces of any other milk product you might want to try. Let L equal that product's lactose percentage. Therefore, $y = 0.05n/L$. Example: A person with a lactose threshold of 10 ounces of milk wants to eat a 2% lactose cheese. That makes $n = 10$, $L = 0.02$ and $y = 0.05 \times 10/0.02$. Therefore $y = 25$ and that person can gorge on up to 25 ounces of that type of cheese without feeling symptoms from the lactose, assuming, of course, that the cheese is the only lactose-containing food in the meal.

TABLE 1									
LACTOSE THRESHOLD EQUIVALENT CHART									
If I can have this many ounces of whole or skim milk:	**Then I can have this many ounces of a food whose lactose percentage is:**								
	1.0%	2.0%	3.0%	4.0%	5.0%	6.0%	8.0%	10.0%	12.0%	15.0%
2	10	5	3	3	2	2	1	1	1	1
3	15	8	5	4	3	3	2	2	1	1
4	20	10	6	5	4	3	3	2	2	1
5	25	13	8	6	5	4	3	3	2	2
6	30	15	10	8	6	5	4	3	3	2
7	35	18	12	9	7	6	4	4	3	2
8	40	20	13	10	8	7	5	4	3	3
10	50	25	17	13	10	8	6	5	4	3
12	60	30	20	15	12	10	8	6	5	4
14	70	35	23	18	14	12	9	7	6	5
16	80	40	27	20	16	13	10	8	7	5
18	90	45	30	23	18	15	11	9	8	6

How to use this chart: Find your Lactose Threshold (LT), the number of ounces of milk you can drink without symptoms, in the first column. Then move across that line to the column that matches the percentage of lactose in the food you want to eat. As an example, if your LT is 12, you could have as much as 20 ounces of cottage cheese, which is about 3.0% lactose, or 8 ounces of vanilla ice cream, which is closer to 8.0% lactose, but not both together. (All numbers have been rounded to the nearest ounce. Milk is assumed to be 5.0% lactose. Chapter 6 contains a complete chart of lactose percentages in various foods.)

▌ GASTRIC EMPTYING

The secret of life (which you probably never expected to find here) is that all food is interchangeable. This makes eminent sense. The sheer complexity of proteins, for example, make it unlikely that any two types of living beings would share exactly the same set. If our bodies could not tear down foreign proteins to provide the parts for the specific ones we need, humans—all living creatures—would be forced to become cannibals and life on Earth today would be very different. Fortunately, your body doesn't care whether the proteins it gets are from cows, nuts, fish or rye bread.

Your body is therefore free to regard whatever enters the alimentary canal as a potential source of nutrients. What form the food is in doesn't matter to the small intestine, since it's all been reduced to chyme before it gets there. (*Refer back to Chapter 5 for details on digestion*). How the stomach deals with the actual food differs from food to food, however, and that affords us a chance to take advantage of those differences.

The idea, once again, is to deliver lactose into the small intestine in manageable doses. The key lies in getting the stomach to empty the lactose it contains into the duodenum as slowly as possible so the lactase you do produce never gets overwhelmed. The simplest way to do this is wrap the lactose in a meal, even if that lactose is from a glass of milk.

Although this may sound obvious, it is anything but. Liquids are emptied from the stomach far more rapidly than solids. Liquids that are part of a meal don't go through quite as quickly as liquids by themselves, but they still move faster than the solids that are in the meal. Whatever delays are involved might not seem enough to make a difference. But they do.

An elegant experiment ("Reduced intolerance symptoms from lactose consumed during a meal," Margaret C. Martini & Dennis A. Savaiano, *American Journal of Clinical Nutrition*, 1988; 48:57–60) illustrated just how sensitive the stomach is to the presence of solids.

A group of a dozen people who tested as low lactase producers allowed themselves to be subjected to a series of five test meals: lactose in water (19 g lactose); skim milk (12 g lactose); a commercially manufactured food supplement (19 g lactose); a standard breakfast consisting of orange juice, whole wheat toast, peanut butter, jelly, and a banana (0 g lactose); and the same meal plus the food supplement (19 g lactose). Everybody, as you would expect, developed symptoms after drinking the lactose solution. At the other extreme, the lactose-free meal produced only mild symptoms in only one person.

What happened in between is the clincher. The skim milk, with its smaller lactose load, produced symptoms in 8 of the 12. The food supplement contained 50% more lactose—the same amount as the lactose solution—but had nonfat milk solids, corn sugar and sucrose added to its skim milk base. Despite the higher lactose content, the presence of the solids made it no more punishing than skim milk alone: only nine people developed symptoms after drinking it. Combining the supplement with the meal made it even easier to tolerate, and only three of the subjects reported any symptoms.

Anything that delays the rate of gastric emptying and gives you more time to let what lactase you have do its job will help relieve or prevent symptoms. Solids and semi-solids are emptied more slowly than liquids. The presence of amino acids and fatty acids in the duodenum send back powerful signals to slow the stomach, so fats and proteins move through more slowly. For this reason whole milk appears to produce fewer symptoms than lower-fat milks. (Perhaps someday we'll see an international chain of slow food restaurants catering specifically to the LI.)

Chocolate milk and other cocoa drinks are also known to produce fewer symptoms, even in low-fat varieties. Why this is isn't quite clear. Some studies have suggested that the cocoa solids slow the gastric emptying rate. Alternatively, cocoa might have an effect on our colonic bacteria, either by stimulating their natural lactase production or lowering the amount of gas they produce (*see the section at the end of this chapter*). Either way, it's nice to have an excuse to bring back a childhood favorite. Don't overdo it, though. Too many glasses of chocolate milk are just as likely to overwhelm your lactase as too many glasses of any other kind of milk.

Until then, if you drink milk, do so with a meal or at least a snack. If you are not watching fats, avoid skim milk and stick to the higher fat varieties. Or try chocolate milk or hot cocoa instead. Lactose that is part of the solid food in a meal (from the milk in a pancake or pie, for example) should also produce fewer symptoms because it will exit your stomach over a longer period of time.

One note: transit time—the time it takes food to move through your intestines—can also be a factor in the symptoms produced. A few people on extremely high-fiber diets may experience significantly decreased transit times. They may therefore see increased intolerance since their systems allow their lactase less time to come into contact with the passing lactose.

▌ TOLERATED FOOD

Both chocolate milk and whole milk are sometimes said to be better tolerated than other types of milk, because they tend to produce fewer symptoms in many people. Low lactose foods like ripened cheeses are also better tolerated than higher lactose Velveeta. But when it comes to tolerated foods, one is in a class by itself: yogurt.

More than 5,000 years ago, peoples in the Middle East had discovered that fermented or soured milk could be kept for weeks without spoiling. The Old Testament records Abraham serving sweet and sour milk to three visiting angels. Depending on such factors as the outside temperature and the specific bacteria involved, the curdled milk could produce either fine curds or coarse curds. Coarse curds ended up as cheese, but the fine curds became the *dahi* of India or the *taetta* of Scandinavia or the variety most familiar in the U.S.: yogurt (or yoghurt, a term which first surfaces in eighth century Turkish records). Yogurt itself is far older than the name. The ancient Assyrians called it *lebeny*, which was also their word for "life" itself.

Milk sours because bacteria ferment it, producing the sour-tasting lactic acid as a byproduct. Americans like even their sour foods sweet, so yogurt never really caught on in the U.S. until the Dannon Corporation introduced fruit-flavored yogurt in 1946. Even then it took the burgeoning health craze of the 1970s and the promotion of low-fat yogurt as a diet food to make it an everyday commodity. The American yogurt market expanded sixfold between 1970 and 1990. Commercial yogurts come in a staggering number of varieties, from plain and unmodified to those that come perilously close to being junk foods. Fortunately, all use a basically similar manufacturing process. Yogurt can also be easily made at home (*see box*) and purists insist that the commercial product bears little resemblance to the real thing. Whoever makes it, the differences in the way the end products are treated are crucial for the LI.

Yogurt begins with milk, usually cow's milk, although other varieties can be found. (The source of the milk makes little difference to the LI.) Whole milk tends to produce a somewhat creamier but higher Calorie yogurt than those made from low-fat or skimmed milk. Commercial yogurt manufacturers may then concentrate the milk with an additional 30% of milk solids—mainly proteins, calcium and lactose—to help thicken the yogurt. Yogurt therefore starts off higher in lactose than regular milk. The milk is then pasteurized, which heat-kills unwanted bacteria to insure that they do not spoil the final product. Two very specific strains of bacteria cultures are added to the milk after it's been cooled to about 113°F: *Lactobacillus bulgaricus* and *Streptococcus thermophilus*. (*Lactobacillus acidophilus* or other strains may also be added to some yogurts.) The mixture is incubated for several hours, the bacteria all the while fermenting the milk into a tart, creamy gel as they coagulate the casein protein into curds. The bacteria also manufacture lactase, which breaks down some of the excess lactose. The final yogurt product typically has about as much lactose as does milk.[3]

After the yogurt reaches the desired levels of tartness and creaminess, it is chilled to shut down the fermentation process, enabling you to let it sit in your refrigerator for about two weeks without changing flavor. The cold also stops the bacteria from producing any more lactase. (For this reason, you should allow the yogurt a half-hour to warm at room temperature before eating.)

Although most enzymes in foods are destroyed by stomach acid, somehow the yogurt buffers the lactase enzyme so that it slips through unimpaired. Once in the duodenum the lactase begins to go to work on the accompanying lactose. Yes, the duodenum and not the jejunum. This is a very different process from natural lactose digestion. For an hour after

---

[3]You may read elsewhere that the lactose content of yogurt, as well as other cultured products including kumiss, kefir and dahi (made from water buffalo's milk), is *lower* than that of the milk from which it's made, reduced by the natural lactase action of the bacteria, and that this accounts for its being better tolerated. It's true that traditional, non-commercial yogurts are lower in lactose than their starter milk and that this helps accounts for their widespread acceptance in populations who are mostly LI. (If you make yogurt at home, by the way, letting the mixture ferment longer further reduces its lactose content. This also produces a much tarter yogurt, however.) Even so, the lactase production of live cultures that I am about to describe is probably a major mechanism in the digestibility of all yogurts, and is the only factor than can explain the tolerance of the higher lactose commercial varieties.

you eat the yogurt, the lactase activity in your duodenum is high enough to digest 50%–100% of the lactose present in the yogurt. Studies show that on average only one-third the amount of lactose reaches the colon after yogurt is eaten compared to what gets there after drinking an equivalent amount of lactose in milk. Since most people can digest a small amount of lactose naturally, this reduction is sufficient to significantly reduce or even eliminate symptoms in all but the most sensitive LI. Yogurt works just as well when eaten alone or as part of a meal. Unfortunately, you can't count on the yogurt to digest more lactose than was in it in the first place. Drink a glass of milk with the yogurt and you'll probably have as many symptoms as you would from the glass of milk alone.

Yogurt depends on the presence of live bacterial cultures for any noticeable reduction in symptoms. The problem, from our point of view, is that manufacturers may further heat-treat their yogurt *after* fermentation to improve shelf life, thus killing off all the remaining bacteria. You have to read the label very carefully. The wording "made with active cultures" is meaningless: All yogurts are *made* with active cultures. Yogurts that still contain living bacteria will have labels that read "active yogurt cultures," "living yogurt cultures" or "contains active cultures." Heat-treated yogurts must, by FDA regulation, say on their labels "heat-treated after culturing."

On the other hand, none of the fruits, flavorings, stabilizers, thickeners, sweeteners and other manifestations of food technology that may be added to yogurt to target a manufacturers' desired audience should make any difference as long as the yogurt contains living bacteria. It is possible that liquid yogurt drinks may not work as well since it is speculated (although not proven) that a reduced rate of gastric emptying due to the yogurt solids also helps relieve symptoms.

Frozen yogurt presents other problems, though no longer in taste and flavor. The first commercial frozen yogurts were so horrendous that even after a decade without ice cream they couldn't lure me in. Today's frozen yogurts compare favorably with all but the best superpremium ice creams. Though they're now readily available in supermarkets, I was more delighted to find that in the seeming blink of an eye frozen yogurt outlets went from a novelty to never more than a mall's length away. Then several unpleasant experiences sent me scurrying for more research. The results I've found are mixed.

There is no guarantee you'll find active cultures in your frozen yogurt, unless it bears the National Yogurt Association seal (*see box*). Freezing in and of itself is not the problem; what happens just before the freezing is. Many commercial frozen yogurts go through a second pasteurization at that point to heat-treat the product, improving shelf-life. A common manufacturing technique adds starter culture to the pasteurized yogurt before freezing, allowing the product to be labeled "frozen yogurt with

---

THE NATIONAL YOGURT ASSOCIATION'S LIVE CULTURE SEAL

For the best possible assurance that the yogurt or frozen yogurt you eat has active cultures, look for packages that carry the National Yogurt Association's (NYA) Live and Active Cultures logo.

Companies wanting to display this logo, as well as the slogan, "Meets National Yogurt Association Criteria for Live and Active Culture Yogurt," must meet NYA standards as determined by an independent testing laboratory. Companies can retain the seal indefinitely, as long as they reapply annually and certify that no changes to the product have occurred. A material change in the product or its method of manufacture requires an immediate, new application.

Three of the criteria are of concern to LI:

1. At the time of manufacture, refrigerated yogurt must have a total viable count of 10^8 cultures per gram and frozen yogurt a total viable count of 10^7 cultures per gram;
2. The cultures must still be active at the end of the stated shelf-life;
3. At the time of consumption, total organisms in both refrigerated and frozen yogurt will still be at least 10^7 per gram.

The presence of active cultures is not a panacea. Even the 10^7 figure may not be high enough to ensure sufficient lactase production to make a significant difference for all who are LI. Nor does the absence of the logo necessarily mean a lack of active cultures. The application costs $2,500 per type of yogurt product, so smaller companies may not be able to afford it. But the logo does take away a lot of the guesswork. With luck, you should see the NYA seal on an increasing number of yogurts in the future.

---

active culture." This evidently does not give the cultures time to grow and produce lactase before the cold deactivates them.

One study, conducted by the trade journal *Dairy Foods*, found that refrigerated yogurts have the highest counts of viable yogurt cultures, with hard-pack frozen yogurt close behind, while soft-serve yogurt from fast-food franchises trailed in their dust. The veteran LI researcher Dr. Dennis Savaiano confirmed this for me and noted that fresh yogurt may have 100–1,000 times the number of cultures as do frozen yogurts. Trial and (necessarily) error are your best bets to find one that works for you. If you don't care to chance the error part, you should know that your homemade yogurt stirred with fruits and flavorings makes a fine frozen yogurt. Frozen yogurt can also be made in an ice-cream maker.

■ ADAPTATION OF COLONIC BACTERIA

Starting in the 1950s, global feeding programs by UNICEF, CARE and other agencies spread milk into every corner of the globe, inevitably into

HOMEMADE YOGURT

Yogurt can be made from any type of milk, either fresh or powdered reconstituted with water. The higher the fat content of the milk, the smoother, richer and thicker the final yogurt will be.

A small amount of either fresh yogurt with live bacteria or a dried culture is needed as a starter. Older live cultures will produce a more sour-tasting yogurt. Best results come from the freshest milk, sweetest culture and cleanest equipment.

Bring 1 quart of milk just to a boil in a saucepan, stirring to prevent a skin from forming. Remove from heat and allow to cool to approximately 113°F.

In a small bowl, blend a few tablespoons of the lukewarm milk and 2 tablespoons fresh live yogurt. Pour the mixture back into the saucepan and stir until well blended. If using dried culture, pour it directly into the pan and mix well into the lukewarm milk.

The milk must now be incubated for several hours at 113°F. If you do not have an electric yogurt maker, heat a wide-mouthed thermos by rinsing it with warm water, fill it with the milk and seal.

Check after 4 hours and then again once every hour to see if the mixture has developed a creamy, custardlike texture and slightly tart flavor. When it has, open the lid of the container and refrigerate it for 24 hours.

Any watery whey found floating on top of the yogurt after refrigeration should be poured off and discarded.

Flavorings such as ¼ to ⅓ cup honey, 3 tablespoons of chocolate syrup, 1 tablespoon of instant coffee mixed with sugar or vanilla extract may be added to the milk before heating, but this may delay or prevent coagulation. Otherwise, add flavorings or fruits if desired after chilling. If you do not flavor beforehand, put a small amount of unflavored yogurt aside in a jar in the refrigerator to act as starter for the next batch.

Yogurt will keep in a tightly covered container in the refrigerator for about a week.

(Adapted from *The Book of Yogurt*, by Sonia Uvezian.)

populations who, later research proved, became LI while still quite young. This wasn't the recipe for disaster that it may appear to be. As we've seen in this chapter, most people—and certainly most children—can handle small amounts of milk without symptoms of LI. Even so, complaints of gas and diarrhea were frequent at the beginning of almost every program. Then a strange thing happened. By the time milk had been part of their daily diets for anywhere from a few weeks to a year, virtually all the symptoms stopped—even among adults.

When scientists finally began to understand LI and went back to study these groups, they first thought that the milk might be stimulating a reawakening of lactase production. That notion was quickly shot down. All were as clinically lactase-deficient at the end of any study as they were in the beginning. If, through normal aging, you have naturally lost the ability to produce lactase, nothing (as study after study has shown) will bring that ability back to any significant degree. Yet millions of non-lactase producers consume milk as part of their daily diets with no ill effects.

So what's happening? Well, humans tend to adapt slowly, with changes in a population occurring over generations. This is true for all living creatures, from bacteria on up. One major distinction needs to be made, though: Generations for bacteria may be equivalent to overnight by human time. In other words, if the bacteria in our colon are what produce all the symptoms of LI, then you can avoid much grief by trading them in for a new set that doesn't produce these symptoms.

Let's see how this might work. Your intestines likely contain dozens of different species of bacteria. Many of these (at least 21 different species) can ferment lactose, an ability other bacteria lack. There will also be variation among the fermenters, with some having higher levels of lactase activities than others. If you've been avoiding dairy products regularly, but then drink a glass of milk, the sudden availability of lactose will stimulate the growth of the lactose-fermenting bacteria at the expense of the lactose non-fermenters. Fermentation will lead to the production of short-chain fatty acids and large amounts of carbon dioxide and hydrogen, helping to create the classic LI symptoms.

The colon, like the rest of the intestinal tract, is very sensitive to acidity. In a highly acid colon, the production of short-chain fatty acids stops completely and the production of hydrogen decreases by 75%. Even a smaller change in acidity will favor the growth of bacteria which prefer acid conditions. One group of acid-favoring bacteria in particular, the lactic acid bacteria (including species of *Lactobacillus* and *Streptococcus*, the very ones used in making yogurt), seem designed to be near and dear to the hearts of those who are LI: They have high lactase activity without producing the formic acid that creates so much of the offending gases.

Short-lived bacteria are highly sensitive to changes in their environments. If gas or diarrhea persuade you to stop drinking milk, colonic acidity will decrease and the gas-producing bacteria will quickly reappear, so that another dose somewhere down the line will probably trigger the symptoms all over again.

Regular doses of lactose, at least in theory, create a permanent shift in the type of bacteria packing the colon.[4] As long as the lactose keeps coming, tolerance remains high.

---

[4]Note for the technical-minded: Which types of bacteria are favored by a high-lactose colonic environment is a matter of controversy. Earlier research favored the lactic acid bacteria. More recent research points to a different group of bacteria, the *Bacteroides*, and their production of iso-butyric and iso-valeric acids as a major factor in creating tolerance to lactose. Since I know of no evidence indicating that anything you can do will cause one species to flourish over the other, for now the issue is relevant only to scientists.

Will this work for you? Once again, the evidence is mixed. In one very encouraging study ("Lactase in man: a nonadaptable enzyme," T. Gilat *et. al, Gastroenterology*, 1972; 62:1125–8), 10 LI volunteers drank milk several times a day, gradually increasing their total consumption. They suffered at first from "mild disturbances" but within a short period of time all could tolerate over a quart of milk a day without increased symptoms. Other published studies and ongoing research by Dr. Savaiano also indicate that daily doses of milk will reduce or even eliminate symptoms, albeit not immediately. According to Dr. Agu Tamm, "The patient must of course be prepared to accept the discomforts and complaints that develop during the first 7–14 days of treatment."

A separate review of the medical literature by Dr. Eivind Gudmand-Hoyer, however, noted that despite the positive studies reporting universal reduction of symptoms among their test subjects, "That this by no means applies to all lactose maldigesters is clearly demonstrated by investigations that show that many patients continue to experience abdominal complaints despite daily milk consumption."

For us, the real question is whether research study results can be translated into the real world, where other factors are likely to come into play, including all the other ways of increasing tolerance discussed in this chapter, individual variations among intestinal bacteria and the willingness to endure symptoms for the sake of hoped-for long-term improvement. Few of us, after all, are in the position of those recipients of CARE packages who adapted to the new-found milk in their diets. Dependent on these handouts for a reprieve from malnutrition, they were pretty much captive populations, with little choice but to keep drinking the milk for weeks or months until the LI symptoms eventually abated. Looking at the larger picture, it would be hard to argue that the overall improvement in their health did not outweigh the temporary symptoms suffered. Even the strongest advocates of these programs, however, are grudgingly forced to acknowledge that although the vast majority seemed to adapt very well sooner or later, a few people never stopped having symptoms.

Let's look closer to home at the results of a study conducted with American volunteers ("Adaptation of lactose maldigesters to continued milk intakes," A. O. Johnson, *et al.*, *American Journal of Clinical Nutrition*, 1993; 58:879–81). All were hard-core LI, who claimed a history of symptoms after drinking as little as a glass of milk and who were further screened by two preliminary studies to insure that they were truly and measurably intolerant. Each morning they drank a glass of milk that had been treated with lactase to control the amount of lactose in it. If they did not get any symptoms from the first glasses of low-lactose milk, the lactose content was gradually increased every few days until the volunteers either reached a lactose level at which the symptoms were too uncomfortable to continue or hit the end of the 12-week study.

Newspaper or television reports of studies like these tend to boil all the fine details down to a single sound bite: "Research proves more milk best for fickle tummies." Does it? It depends on which points you choose to emphasize.

For one thing, the study, as with almost all research studies, used only a small group, 25 people. How representative a group were they? All we know about them is that they were all adolescent or young adult African-Americans. Even though they all tested as clinically LI, it is possible that older adults, who may have lost even more of what little lactase they had left, would be somewhat less adaptable.

Even without knowing much else about them, we can infer that they were highly motivated. How many of us would volunteer for a third study that would involve drinking enough milk to make symptoms very likely? Could it be the rigors of the process that would make three people (12%) of a dedicated core group drop out of the study? Without more information, we can't say.

The reported results are equally subject to interpretation. Everybody was able to go from the starting point of 5 g of lactose, a little less than half that in a glass of milk, and get to tolerate 7 g of lactose. Five of the 22 hit their limit somewhere between 7 g and 12 g, the equivalent of a glass of milk. The other 17 adapted much better, and some managed a maximum daily dose of 20 g of lactose. A total of 77% of the group, therefore, wound up drinking large glasses of milk for weeks on end without complaint. That's a percentage big enough to justify favorable headlines and provide sufficient incentive to get you to try it.

Perhaps. But an even closer reading produces a few more details that have to be taken into account on one side or the other. Positive: The milk was evidently not drunk as part of a meal, which means you may be able to improve tolerance even more by doing so. Negative: The volunteers were on an otherwise lactose-free diet, which you may not be able to keep up in real life. Positive: They skipped weekends, implying that it's okay to miss occasional days without having to start all over and reaccustom oneself. Negative: There is no way of knowing how many days of no lactose would wipe out the gains or whether you would have to continue consuming lactose almost every day forever.

Although it's good to learn to read all studies with a skeptical eye, I've spent the time on this one only because of my concern that for many people the possibility of overcoming LI by actually *increasing* the milk you drink will be just too seductive to resist. Out-toughing one's problems is the fundamental American myth, celebrated in a hundred familiar slogans: Never give up; No pain, no gain; When the going gets tough, the tough get going. We hear the success stories—the airline pilot who conquered a fear of heights by taking flying lessons, the stand-up comedian who put aside terminal shyness to attend open joke night—repeated endlessly. The flaw in this rosy picture is that it is entirely one-sided. We know it works for the people it works for, and we never, ever hear about the failures or what it cost them.

I would love to be able to recommend to everyone that they go out and just drink milk and never mind all this LI foolishness. Nobody likes to live with restrictions and denial, Americans least of all. The potential consequences, even if they are in the realm of discomforts and not dangers, are just too great for me to do so. If you do want to try, start small, increase slowly, don't go on until your symptoms are at a minimum and be patient. You will also require a large amount of what I might be forced to call intestinal fortitude. Good luck if you're adventurous enough to give it a go.

If the thought of increased symptoms makes you blanch, however, turn to the next chapter for quick, quick, quick relief.

8

·····························

THE LACTASE PHASE

The Dutch have given the world cheese and tulips and chocolate. We now have one additional item to thank them for: The Dutch firm of Gist-Brocades gave us lactase.

Although LI isn't a disease, our inability to drink milk often makes it seem like one in a culture so in awe of dairy products that maintaining their protected status has been incorporated into its very body of law. Because most of the people around us can drink milk with impunity, our normal lack of the lactase enzyme is taken as evidence that there is something wrong with us, something that needs fixing. If there is a pill for every ill, then why not a lactase pill to cure LI?

Easier said than done. Since there appears to be a shortage of spare lactase-producing intestines on the black market, the alternatives are few. Pharmaceutical companies could make artificial lactase, but synthesizing enzymes is a logistical nightmare. Lactase, like all enzymes, is a protein, a huge, complicated and ungainly creature compared to the typical drug. One way of indicating its size is to look at a scientific measure called molecular weight. Lactose has a molecular weight of a slim 342. By comparison, lactase weighs in at about 280,000.

We're lucky that there is, relatively speaking, a simpler way. Humans are not the only creatures to make lactase naturally. A host of microorganisms in our intestines do a better job of it than we do. Why not put them to work manufacturing lactase as fast as their tiny bodies can pump it out and then harvest their crop? The Gist-Brocades researchers went on a search for the perfect lactase mini-machine.

They settled on the dairy yeast *Saccharomyces lactis* (now called *Kluyveromyces lactis*), used for centuries in Russia as a starter culture for fermented milk products, and put its lactase on the market under the brand name of Maxilact. That first product was the lactase enzyme in powder form,

---

NOTE: Listings of brands, varieties and flavors in this chapter and following chapters are accurate as of late 1994 but are subject to change. Their sole purpose is to illustrate the range of products available to fulfill LI needs. Companies listed are from author's survey or research. No endorsement of individual products is implied.

designed to be added to fresh milk to hydrolyze (break down) its lactose into glucose and galactose. In 1979 Gist-Brocades discovered how to produce the enzyme in a more convenient liquid form. By that time, the company was promoting its use in reduced-lactose milks and a wide variety of other dairy products. But the all-important lactase pill, the one that would work in the body rather than only in milk, continued to elude them.

The catch in having microorganisms produce lactase for human use is while all lactase hydrolyzes lactose, no two lactases have identical properties otherwise. (In the same way, humans can use animal milk in place of a mother's milk even though they are only similar, not perfectly identical.) Various lactases are at their most effective at different conditions of acidity (measured by pH) and temperature. Human lactase is meant to work in the small intestine, a location whose temperature is that of body heat, 98.6°F or 37°C. The intestines also have a pH value close to a neutral 7, because the stomach acids are neutralized by alkaline juices from the liver and pancreas when they enter the small intestine.

K. lactis lactase works at an optimum 35°–37°C and 6.8 pH. This preferred environment sounds perfect, and if we could put the enzyme directly into the intestine it might actually be. Pills must go through the stomach before they reach the intestines, though, and stomach acids would degrade the enzyme before it could do any good.

The search for a better lactase led to a fungus known as *Aspergillis niger*. *A. niger* lactase works at an optimum pH of 4.4, about that of the stomach. (The lower the pH, the more acidic.) But its optimum temperature was a distinctly unpleasant 55°–60°C or 140°F–150°F. It still works in the body but loses about 30% of its activity at body temperature. Nevertheless, *A. niger* lactase has a wide variety of commercial applications and has been occasionally used in lactase pills themselves.

Goldilocks must have been in on the search, for the third try was just right. The lactase produced by a related fungus known as *Aspergillis oryzae* proved to have an optimum pH of 4.5–5.5 and a stable range of 3.0–7.0, as well as an optimum temperature of 37°C. When taken with food, this form of lactase readily withstands the buffeting it takes in the stomach and survives to digest lactose in the small intestine. Today all major brands of lactase pills use *A. oryzae* lactase.

Lactase is classified as a food supplement rather than as a drug, although the FDA is currently considering whether enzyme tablets should be given drug status. Treating lactase as a drug would be helpful for those of us who want to know such basics as the strength of the pills we're taking. Measuring lactase activity is frustratingly difficult in the first place, compounded by the lack of a universally accepted method. If drug standards were imposed, the firms marketing lactase would be forced to use a uniform measure that would allow comparisons between pills.

Almost as important, standards for expiration dates would be established for the pills.

Most commercial brands of lactase pills use one of two units to state their strength. (The medical literature uses yet others.) One is FCC units, where FCC stands for the federal Food Chemicals Codex.[1] The other is the more familiar milligrams (mg). There is no way to directly compare the two units, however, or convert from one to the other. For that matter, it is not always possible to compare two brands giving lactase weight in milligrams. Lactase is sold by manufacturers in both a pharmaceutical grade and a less expensive food grade. The only difference is that the food grade is bulked out by fillers, which dilutes the activity per unit of weight. Proprietary studies by manufacturers claim that there is not necessarily any correlation between stated weight and actual lactase activity. While I wish everyone would use FCC units, some of the pills using milligrams have been shown in clinical studies to be equally effective with pills measured in FCC units.

To give you an idea of how varied strengths can be, a review ("Management of Lactose Intolerance," A. Tamm, *Scandinavian Journal of Gastroenterology*, 1994; 29(suppl 202):55–63) of various international reports on lactase enzymes found that:

> To hydrolyze about 90% of the lactose contained in one liter of milk, the following amounts of enzymes are needed: 0.25 g Maxilact LX 5000 produced by Gist-Brocades NV; or 2 ml of Lactozyme 3000 L, produced by Novo Industries of Denmark; or 2.6 g of LactAid (liquid form), produced by SugarLo Co Inc [now Lactaid]; or 0.64 g Lactase A (Takamine) by Miles Lab, Elkhart, IN; or 0.4 g of Lactase N produced by GB Fermentation Products Co, USA.[2]

There is no question that lactase works in the body to reduce the symptoms of LI, but not all lactase pills, drops or reduced-lactose dairy products are of equal value. You may have to test several for yourself to determine which is best for you.

▌ THE LACTASE INDUSTRY

Gist-Brocades put its lactase powder on the market in the early 1970s, still the dark ages of LI. Maxilact was a solution without a problem.

Enter Alan Klingerman, who grew up delivering milk for his family's

---

[1]Note for the technical-minded: An FCC unit is defined as "that quantity of enzyme that will liberate 1 micromol of o-nitrophenol per minute" when using the formal assay procedure prescribed by the Food Chemicals Codex. An FCC unit is sometimes referred to as a Neutral Lactase Unit (NLU).

[2]You cannot use these figures to compare products currently on the market, even if you could find them in the U.S., due to changes in manufacturing techniques and ownership of producing firms over the years.

Atlantic City dairy and majored in dairy science at Cornell University. His first major dairy innovation was Sugar-Lo, an ice cream for diabetics. While looking for new markets, he heard about a potentially huge one: people with LI. He soon learned about Maxilact, and acquired exclusive marketing rights for it in the U.S. in 1974 under the name of "Lact-Aid." The powder was sold at first only by mail order. Health food stores embraced the product and pharmacies soon joined them. After the liquid enzyme was developed, he introduced reduced-lactose "LactAid" milks in a few selected supermarkets in 1979.

After Klingerman finally got the lactase pills to market in 1985, the notion of products for the LI began to seep into the national consciousness at last. His troika of lactase drops to be added to fresh milk, lactase pills that could be taken with any dairy foods, and line of reduced-lactose milk and other dairy products overshadowed the rest of the industry. Other brands existed, notably Lactrase pills from Kremens-Urban (now a part of Schwarz Pharma), but Lactaid (the current spelling) and lactase were almost synonymous in people's minds.

The second biggest event in the U.S. history of lactase came in 1990, when Dairy Ease burst onto the scene to compete with Lactaid product by product. Competition was exactly what the musty LI industry needed, preferably a battle between companies with pockets deep enough to throw money at the problem. Dairy Ease qualified, since its pedigree was Winthrop Consumer Products, Glenbrook Laboratories, Division of Sterling Drug Inc., a pharmaceutical house picked up by Eastman Kodak in a spurt of diversification. (And since divested. See below.) Its enormous introductory promotional campaign included commercials on national television, ads in major magazines and literally hundreds of millions of coupons. Lactaid, whose marketing rights had been picked up by Johnson & Johnson's McNeil Consumer Products Co., was forced to retaliate with a multi-million dollar advertising blitz of its own. Awareness of LI skyrocketed, as did sales of most lactase products. A market estimated to be $35 million in 1989 grew to approximately $150 million in sales by 1993, mostly driven by double-digit percentage increases in sales of the lactose-reduced milks. (Pill sales were essentially stagnant, possibly because former pill users were now buying the milks instead.)

The problem with the lactase market is that it is driven by advertising, and the effectiveness of advertising on a national scale seems directly proportional to its expense. (Lactaid's hotline received 300,000 calls during its April to July 1993 ad blitz, a huge jump from 160,000 the entire previous year.) It's still not clear just how deeply the message has penetrated into the potential population of LI product users, but awareness has to be higher now than in the early 1990s when one study of different lactase pills found that 9 of the 10 test subjects had never seen or taken any of them.

The field is still essentially a two-firm race. In January 1994, Lactaid was estimated to hold a 62.8% share of the lactase pill market, followed by Dairy Ease at 29.9%. Other brands, include private label brands and brands no longer on the market, had 6.9%. (Lactrase is marketed primarily to physicians with little or no consumer advertising, so it has a tiny market share despite being one of the oldest national brands,)

Reduced-lactose milks have equal ills. Lactaid and Dairy Ease remain the only national brands, although a number of regional dairies have introduced their own reduced-lactose milks to only moderate success. The experience of Dean Foods, which markets Easy 2% reduced-lactose milk to a few midwestern states, is instructive. The trade journal *Brandweek* quoted a Dean executive as saying, "We have a small number of very loyal consumers who drink milk now because of us, but it's no more than 3% to 4% of our total milk sales. We thought it might get higher than that." Easy 2% had been available for four years at the time.

Loyal customers LI may be, but unless sales rise to match our potential numbers and clout we may see the few products addressed specifically to us fade away for lack of support.

One final note. The industry was shaken up yet again when, in a burst of divestiture, Eastman Kodak sold off all its drug subsidiaries in the summer and fall of 1994. Consumer pharmaceuticals, as represented by the now-named Sterling Winthrop and including Dairy Ease, were purchased by SmithKline Beecham, which immediately turned around and resold them to German giant Bayer AG, which was really much more interested in regaining the U.S. rights to Bayer aspirin than anything else. In the short term, customers shouldn't be affected. A spokesperson for the Bayer Consumer Care Division said in early 1995 that no changes to the Dairy Ease line were planned. As with any corporate pronouncement in these fast-moving times, that assurance is subject to the whims of the market, so the long-term picture is murkier. If you like and use a product—any product—make your preferences known to your local store manager and to the company that makes it.

▌ LACTASE PILLS

Sales of lactase pills were approximately $35 million in 1993, a surprisingly small number considering that the pills are probably the most versatile and therefore the most valuable of all the lactase products. After all, they work with everything made with dairy, not just fluid milk, they need no refrigeration and they can be carried with you to offer relief from symptoms whenever you are eating outside of your own house—and surveys tell us that that is as many as half of all meals. (They therefore allow you to be a polite guest, able to eat all foods your hosts serve.) While the bigger bottles are the least expensive per pill, smaller travel sizes are available to slip into a purse, backpack, briefcase or glove compartment, and there's always the option of just tucking a few into a pill case and slipping it into a pocket, as I do every day of my life. Perhaps their greatest psychological value is that they allow you to consume foods on impulse without worry. While there is an opposing psychological burden that comes from taking pills (and having to remember to take them) I don't see how anyone who is LI can afford to be without them.

Pills is an awkward word, but the lactase enzyme is available in so many forms these days that no other generic term fits. Lactaid comes as caplets, Lactrase has always been an openable capsule, Dairy Ease offers both chewable tablets and a harder-to-find caplet, and some companies offer softgel capsules as well.

Of course, each has its own advantages. Dairy Ease chose chewable tablets after their studies revealed that many people who were LI but didn't know it had been taking chewable antacids to try to relieve their symptoms. They could therefore switch directly to Dairy Ease without altering their habits. Even those without the habit may prefer a chewable tablet that does not require a liquid to wash it down. Alternatively, an openable capsule allows the contents to be sprinkled directly onto food. Softgels are easily swallowed. Caplets are small and can be stashed in a case for easy availability.

Whatever the outside shape or form, all lactase pills come with the same directions: Take with food.

"With food" has always seemed a bit ambiguous to me. Does that mean with the first bite of food? With the first bite of lactose-containing food? At anytime during the meal? At the end of the meal so that all the lactose would be present? Before the meal so the lactase would be waiting for it?

The clue to which is best lies in the knowledge that the presence of food in the stomach buffers the enzyme, allowing it to reach the intestine and get to work on the lactose. Taking lactase long after meals—when symptoms are being felt—is far less effective than swallowing it with the first bites of lactose-containing food. Pills can even be taken to good effect as much as five minutes before you start eating. (Too much earlier will run the risk of the enzyme being degraded before the food arrives to protect it from the ravages of an empty stomach.) The enzyme will likely be effective as long as the stomach continues to actively process food, given the variability of gastric emptying and how the lactose load is distributed in a meal.

Unfortunately, I'm sure we've all had the experience of having finished a meal without remembering the unopened bottle or pill case at our side. Is there really any point to grabbing for them then? I would have said that was too late, but, citing proprietary studies, Dr. Pol Vandenbroucke, director of Medical Affairs, Bayer Consumer Care Division, says that taking the pills at the first sign of symptoms may give some relief, although less than either taking them with food or just before the meal.

Taken correctly, however, lactase does work. Virtually every study I have ever seen confirms this. Lactase pills *will* reduce or eliminate the symptoms of gas, bloating, diarrhea and stomach pain that would otherwise result from undigested lactose in the intestines.

How many to take is your decision. For some reason, two pills per slice of pizza seems to be a common pattern with people who are seriously LI, but the later pills may not be necessary or have as much impact. Up to a point, there is a more or less linear relationship between the number of pills and their effectiveness. Twice as many pills will do twice as much good. Five times as many pills may not have five times the power, however, unless you were totally lacking in lactase to begin with, as few of us are.

Whether you must limit yourself to a maximum is more a matter of good sense than a medical decision. At one time, some package inserts warned against taking more than six pills at a sitting, but only because effectiveness studies of taking more than six pills had not been done. There are no known harmful effects from ingesting lactase in any amount, according to Dr. Vandenbroucke. He points out that lactase is a substance normally present in the human body without any safety problems associated with it. Furthermore, lactase, when taken in pill form, is not even absorbed into the body but stays in the gastrointestinal tract until broken down into harmless protein fragments. Even allergic reactions to ingested lactase seem to be unknown. One caveat: The fillers in the pills are standard ingredients not normally known to cause reactions, but it is possible for the rare individual to be allergic or sensitive to them.

Lactase will not work on every symptom in every person every time. Far too many variables are involved. As we've seen, when you take the lactase is critical; how much you take is just as important. Only you and your experience will enable you to gauge just how much lactose a lactase pill will digest, and which foods require more than your usual number of pills. The inserts that come with the various brands are deliberately vague on such details. Take one or two, they say. Or two or three. There's really not much more guidance they can give. Depending on other factors, such as the particular dairy product you're eating and whether it is part of a meal, an amount that is effective one time may not work at another. Less severely LI individuals, on the other hand, may not have these uncertainties at all. Over time, you should be able to judge how to adjust your lactase dosage to best suit your needs.

The lactase in pills also seems to be fussy, with some preparations reported to have poor stability over time. If you're getting your supply from a bottle past its expiration date, think about tossing it and dipping into a new one for your next meal.

LACTASE PRODUCTS

Supermarket and Pharmacy-oriented Products:

Bayer Consumer Care Division
Dairy Ease—3,000 FCC units
  caplets; chewable tablets

McNeil Consumer Products
Lactaid—3,000 FCC units
  caplets

Schwarz Pharma
Lactrase—250 mg
  capsules

Health Food Store–oriented products:

Country Life
Power Dairy-Zyme Caps—2,500 FCC units
  capsules
Green Life-Zyme Caps—750 FCC units
  capsules
KAL Lactase Enzyme—125 mg
  softgel capsules
Nature's Plus
Say Yes to Dairy—3,000 FCC units
  chewable tablets
Nature's Way Lactase Enzyme—3,450 FCC units
  capsules
Rainbow Light Nutritional Systems
All-Zyme + Lactase—750 FCC units
  capsules
Schiff Natural
Milk Digest-Aid—1,750 FCC units
  softgel capsules
Solgar Lactase—3,500 FCC units
  chewable tablets
Source Naturals
Essential Enzymes—5 mg
  capsules

The Best Lactase Money Can Buy

You know, you just know, that in some triple-locked vault at the end of a dimly lit corridor in the unused wing of an unheated warehouse sits a report that will never again be seen by human eyes. The report was commissioned by one of the pharmaceutical firms that makes lactase pills.

It was locked away because it spells out in no uncertain terms which lactase pill actually works the best. And it wasn't theirs.

That report is the Holy Grail of LI, but you and I are as likely to ever get to see it as we are to read the Sherlock Holmes stories that Dr. Watson tucked away in his dispatch box in the vaults of Cox and Co.

In the absence of secret in-house studies, published reports in the medical literature are the next best thing. Only two that I know of exist, and a poor, pale imitation they are. Small sample sizes, limited generalizability and contradictory outcomes make them almost worthless as a basis for broad pronouncements.

Those who blanch at the memory of their lactose tolerance test may shudder to hear that each of 20 adults, all known lactose maldigesters, went through five of them for this experiment, "Comparative Effects of Exogenous Lactase (β-Galactosidase) Preparations on *in Vivo* Lactose Digestion," M.-Y. Lin *et al.*, *Digestive Disease and Sciences* (1993; 38(11): 2022–27). For each trial they drank about a glass and a half of milk (20 g of lactose) and took with it, in random order: 1) two chewable Dairy Ease tablets; 2) two Lactaid caplets; 3) two Lactogest softgels; 4) four Lactogest softgels; or 5) two placebo capsules. (Four Lactogest softgels were equal in strength to two of either the Dairy Ease or Lactaid; they are no longer on the market.)

Equal strengths of all three lactase preparations produced remarkably similar results. All products cut symptoms by at least half. Flatulence was significantly reduced and diarrhea occurred less frequently. The only real difference among them was that all the larger doses significantly reduced stomach pain and breath hydrogen production, but the smaller dose of Lactogest did not.

Unfortunately, these findings cannot be easily generalized because no mention is made of the ethnic backgrounds of the volunteers, how long they had been LI or anything about their symptoms except the group averages. The results do correlate well with other studies concentrating on individual brands, however.

Somewhat more variation among brands was seen in the study reported in "All Lactase Preparations Are Not the Same: Results of a Prospective, Randomized, Placebo-Controlled Trial," F. C. Ramirez, *et al.*, *The American Journal of Gastroenterology* (1994; 89(4):566–570). The study design was very similar. Ten adult LI volunteers (five Blacks, three Caucasians, one Hispanic and one Asian) ate 1½ cups of vanilla ice cream (18 g of lactose) and took with it, in random order: 1) three chewable Dairy Ease tablets; 2) three Lactaid caplets; 3) two Lactrase capsules; 4) three placebo capsules. (They do not report why they thought that two Lactrase capsules, which lists its strength in milligrams rather than FCC units, would be equal in activity to three of the others.)

An odd split was seen in the test results. Only Lactaid significantly reduced breath hydrogen production. But Lactrase significantly reduced the maximum severity of both pain and bloating, while Dairy Ease significantly reduced the maximum severity of pain. (Lactaid did reduce severity of these symptoms but not to statistically significant levels.) All reduced diarrhea almost entirely, but none significantly influenced gas.

Odder still, every pill, *including the placebo*, made the subjects feel significantly better after eating lactose than they had in the past. And even though some of the results were not statistically significant, "Every lactase formulation was able to influence the symptomatic scores positively for each of the four individually assessed symptoms." Perhaps the high solids content of ice cream made it better tolerated, perhaps the study group was simply too small to be meaningful. Whatever the explanation, the results are too idiosyncratic to be used as a recommendation for or against any product, unless and until a number of other studies confirm the findings.

▌LACTASE DROPS

If you have a bit of patience, making your own lactose-reduced milk at home may be just the option for you.

If you've known about LI for more than a few years, lactase drops were probably the first lactase product that you ran into—unless you're a real old-timer and remember the powder that the drops replaced. You won't see the powder around at all anymore; the liquid form has greater stability and is easier to use.[3] Both are essentially similar in concept and function. They contain lactase enzyme made by the yeast *K. lactis* in an innocuous base. When added to fresh milk, the enzyme begins to hydrolyze the lactose into glucose and galactose. Doses are calculated so that five drops of the liquid will remove 70% of the lactose in a quart of refrigerated milk in 24 hours.

As with all do-it-yourself projects, there are advantages and disadvantages related to cost, convenience and customizability.

Advantages:

- The drops can be used with any variety of liquid fresh or reconstituted powdered milk: whole, 2%, 1%, nonfat and chocolate.
- Adding more drops hydrolyzes more lactose. The Dairy Ease insert says that 10 drops will remove 90% of the lactose in 24 hours and that 15 drops will remove 97+%. Lactaid says that 15 drops "should remove nearly all of the lactose."

---

[3]Lactrase-brand lactase capsules are designed so that they can be opened and the powder inside added to milk in the same way the drops are. Because their enzyme is derived from the *A. oryzae* fungus, it is not quite as effective when used in milk as the *K. lactis*-derived enzyme in the drops.

- The enzyme continues to hydrolyze lactose as long as it is in the milk so that its lactose content will decrease even further after 24 hours.
- Regular milk is sold in more outlets than reduced-lactose milk. A bottle of drops will guarantee you low-lactose milk wherever you travel.
- Regular milk is much cheaper than reduced-lactose milk. In my local supermarket, reduced-lactose milks cost 50¢–60¢ more a quart than the comparable regular milks. A five-drop dose of enzyme that will hydrolyze a quart of milk costs only 12¢–18¢.
- The milk becomes somewhat sweeter, since both glucose and galactose are sweeter than lactose. Most people find this acceptable; some, children especially, prefer the extra sweetness.
- Some studies suggest that you can reduce symptoms even if you do not add the drops until five minutes before drinking the milk. This method is less effective than taking the lactase pills; higher doses produce better results, however.

Disadvantages:

- The drops cannot be used in cultured milk products like buttermilk or yogurt because of their higher acidity.
- The milk carton must be opened to add the drops and then refrigerated for 24 hours, making it less convenient for transport.
- The drops must themselves be kept refrigerated after opening for maximum effectiveness.
- The drops are less effective if the milk is not fresh.
- Most varieties of milk now come in reduced-lactose forms, which are drinkable immediately upon purchase. Such milk is also widely available in Europe.
- The milk becomes somewhat sweeter. Some people find the taste unacceptable.
- The drops will not completely remove all lactose from the milk.
- Many store-bought reduced-lactose milks are UHT processed, giving them five times the shelf life of regular milk.

LACTASE DROPS

Bayer Consumer Core Division
    Dairy Ease Drops

McNeil Consumer Products
    Lactaid Drops

Commercially Processed Reduced-Lactose Milks

Reduced-lactose milks are the hottest category in the lactase world today. Sales reached approximately $90 million in 1993, a 15% increase over the year before. Perhaps three times as many people use the milks as use the lactase pills. They have the immense psychological advantage of appearing to be a normal food rather than a type of medicine, and of being drinkable immediately or on impulse.

The manufacturing process for a reduced-lactose milk is similar to what you would do with lactase drops in your kitchen, except on a much huger scale. The same *K. Lactis* enzyme is used, in amounts calculated to remove 70% of the lactose by the time the milk is placed on sale. There is one major difference. Most reduced-lactose milks are Ultra High Temperature (UHT) pasteurized. In UHT processing, milks are subjected to a normal pasteurization at 180°F for 30 seconds followed by steam infusion to 290°F for two seconds and vacuum treatment to render them bacteria-free. UHT processed milks have a 45–60 day shelf life compared to the 9–12 day shelf life of fresh pasteurized milk.

The extended shelf life is a real advantage. While families with kids may go through gallons of milk every week, adults are much less likely to devour quarts on a regular basis. Lactose-reduced UHT milks may stay drinkable longer than nondairy creamers do. It also allows for national distribution of a single brand from a single or small number of dairies, unlike the mostly local or regional cooperatives who produce regular milks. A smaller number of dairies allows for better control over the manufacturing process.

The disadvantage is that UHT processing changes milk's flavor to a slight degree, in addition to the extra sweetness imparted by splitting the lactose into sweeter glucose and galactose. Some of the smaller, regional dairies that have been moving into the field stick with fresh pasteurized milks. Dean Foods' Easy 2%, for example, is fresh, but it is only available in parts of the Midwest.

One other disadvantage of reduced-lactose milks will leap out at you: They are far more expensive than their regular milk counterparts. In my local supermarket they run 80%–90% higher, even in the half-gallon form that should give you a price break. Chocolate milk was the one exception, and even that was 40% more expensive. There would seem to be little hope of this changing. Economies of scale (reduced-lactose milks sell less than 1% as much product as regular milks) and lower transportation costs from local suppliers would keep regular milk far cheaper even if supermarkets did not often use it as a loss leader and price it at cost or below.

Reduced-lactose milks have caught up with the competition in one way: They now come in almost every format that regular milks do and must, of course, be vitamin-fortified in the same way. Currently on the market are

---

LACTOSE-REDUCED MILKS

National brands of lactose-reduced milks:

Dairy Ease—70% lactose-reduced
   Whole; 2% Lowfat; 1% Lowfat; Nonfat
Lactaid—70% lactose-reduced
   1% Lowfat; 1% Lowfat Chocolate Milk; Nonfat; Calcium Fortified
   Nonfat
Lactaid—100% lactose-reduced
   Nonfat

Regional brands of lactose-reduced milks:

Lehigh Valley Dairies
Mighty Lac—70% lactose-reduced
   1% Lowfat
Farmland
Easy Lac—80% lactose-reduced
   1% Lowfat; Nonfat

---

whole, 2% lowfat, 1% lowfat, Chocolate 1% lowfat, nonfat, Calcium-fortified nonfat, and a new 100% lactose-reduced nonfat.

That last is an exciting addition to the category, for several reasons. Many people who are LI cannot tolerate even the remaining 30% lactose (about 4 g per 8 ounce glass) that is in most reduced-lactose milks. A lactose-free milk offers possibilities only dreamed-of before. Those who were using nondairy creamers, even the fat-free varieties, now have a direct alternative with all the nutritional advantages of real milk. It is a nonfat milk, however, which means that the taste will come as a shock to anyone who has grown used to the higher fat nondairy creamers after years of use.

Please note: Despite the name, do not assume that every single molecule of lactose has been removed from 100% lactose-reduced milk. The milk has been treated with extra *K. lactis* enzyme to remove all but a tiny percentage of lactose, but complete hydrolyzation is difficult, if not impossible. The process is well over 99% efficient, however, which allows the milk to bear the 100% lactose-reduced label and still conform to state laws that permit up to 0.5% residual lactose. Allowances for such tiny leeways are common in labeling regulation: Federal package labeling laws define "fat free" to really mean "less than ½ gram fat per serving" and "sodium free" to mean "less than 5 milligrams per serving," for example. Actual lactose content of Lactaid 100% Lactose-Reduced Nonfat Milk is less than 60 mg of lactose per 8 ounce glass. You would have to drink 200 glasses to equal the amount of lactose in a glass of regular milk. Only the exceptionally rare individual with no lactase activity whatsoever is likely to feel any effect from such a

---

OTHER LACTOSE-REDUCED PRODUCTS

Dreyer's/Edy's Grand Ice Cream—70% lactose-reduced
Almond Praline; Cookies 'N Cream; Rocky Road; Strawberries 'N
Cream; Vanilla

---

minuscule amount. Even so, I would not recommend the product to galactosemics. (As a true dairy product, it is of course not pareve, acceptable to vegans or safe for those with milk allergies.)

Other Reduced-Lactose Products
Any product that uses milk can be made with reduced-lactose milk instead. So why aren't there reduced-lactose cheeses, cream cheeses, sour creams, yogurts, ice creams, frozen yogurts, evaporated milks, milk chocolate candy bars and all the rest of the million and one dairy products that bulge grocery shelves?

Because they don't sell, is my guess. Lactaid has marketed a reduced-lactose lowfat cottage cheese and American process cheese food but does not do so at the time of writing. All the other items I've seen over the years have also disappeared from my local supermarket. This circumstance may change. The trade press keeps announcing that both Dairy Ease and Lactaid plan to expand their lines past their current emphasis on fluid milk. When and where and what remain to be seen.

Their indecisiveness has allowed a competitor to beat them to the punch in a critical and glamorous area. In April 1994, Dreyer's/Edy's Grand Ice Cream introduced the first lactose-reduced ice cream. (The Dreyer's brand is marketed as Edy's in the eastern U.S. to avoid name confusion with the Breyer's brand ice cream sold there.) Interestingly, their research showed them that the LI were buying regular ice cream, although less often, rather than nondairy alternatives. Like the majority of milks, their ice cream is 70% lactose-reduced or less than 1 g of lactose per serving.

For further information on nationally-distributed lactase enzyme products and reduced-lactose dairy products, contact:

 ## SUPERMARKET AND PHARMACY-ORIENTED PRODUCTS:

Dairy Ease
Bayer Corporation Consumer Affairs Department
Morristown, NJ
800-331-4536

Dreyer's and Edy's Grand Ice Cream
5929 College Avenue
Oakland, CA 94618
Dreyer's—800–888-3442
Edy's—800–777-3397

McNeil Consumer Products
Camp Hill Road
Fort Washington, PA 19034
800-LACTAID

Schwarz Pharma
P.O. Box 2038
5600 W. County Line Road
Milwaukee, WI 53201
800–558-5114

 HEALTH FOOD STORE–ORIENTED PRODUCTS:

Country Life
28300-B Industrial Blvd.
Hayward, CA 94545
510–785-1196

KAL Inc.
Woodland Hill, CA 91365
800–755-4525

Nature's Plus
10 Daniel St.
Farmingdale, NY 11735
800–645-9500

Nature's Way Products Inc.
10 Mountain Springs Parkway
Springville, UT 84663
800–866-4404

Rainbow Light Nutritional Systems
207 McPherson St.
Santa Cruz, CA 95060

Schiff Products Inc.
Moonachie, NJ 07074
800–436-4333

Solgar Vitamin Co. Inc.
Lynbrook, NY 11563
516–599-2442

Source Naturals Inc.
Scotts Valley, CA 95066
800–777-5677

9

A CORNUCOPIA OF
NONDAIRY ALTERNATIVES

M ilk does have very real advantages for many people—not least of which is calcium and the lactose that aids in its absorption—but full and healthy lives are perfectly possible without it. Just about every dairy product has an analog that is lactose-free. Not only are there alternative milks, but butters, cheeses, ice creams, yogurts and more. About the only thing they have in common is the creativity through which they alert you to the particular product they are attempting to copy, since they must do so without actually being able to use the name. Milk turns into "nondairy creamer," butter into "margarine," cheese into "cheeze." The various alternatives have advantages and disadvantages of their own, of course. I'll try to cover them all and allow you to make your own decisions.

The differences among milk substitutes are more striking than the similarities. Just as your choice of a luxury car, small import, minivan or light truck probably says more about your philosophy of life than about your transportation needs, the type of milk alternative you favor will probably be guided more by your overall approach to buying food than by a taste-test. In acknowledgment of this likelihood, I'm splitting this chapter into two sections. The first will look at milk substitutes that are likely to be found in your basic suburban supermarket. The second will concentrate on products that were designed to appeal to shoppers at health food stores. You should be able to find a complete range of alternatives no matter where you shop, however.

All products mentioned in this chapter should be usable by the LI. Many do contain casein or whey proteins in some form, so they may not be 100% lactose free. Milk protein-containing products, remember, may not be acceptable to those with severe milk allergies or other ailments, those looking for pareve foods or those seeking to avoid animal-derived products. I will indicate the presence or absence of casein wherever I am aware of it.

▌ SUPERMARKET PRODUCTS

Alternative "Butters"
The first deliberately contrived artificial substitutes for dairy products were attempts to mimic butter.

The easy availability of vegetable oils blinds us today to the importance butter once had as the only source of fat in northern Europe. Fats are critical in cooking and impart rich flavor and texture to foods. Each community produced its own unique butter; farmers claimed to be able to tell from its taste which cow had produced the milk. Butter had symbolic value as well. It was the color of gold yet emerged from the pure whiteness of milk. When butter went bad it could only be because of magic, and witches took the blame. Food historian Margaret Visser sums up butter's allure as "irreproachable, unique and irreplaceable."

Only desperation could force the search for a replacement for the irreplaceable, and desperation prevailed after a cattle plague decimated herds in Europe in the 1860s. Just as it would in the 1960s, butter became the "high-priced spread." France's Emperor Napoleon III offered a prize for a cheap substitute. A food chemist with the magnificent name of Hippolyte Mège-Mouriès took up the challenge. He chopped sheeps' stomachs and cows' udders into beef fat, soaked the mixture in milk and suspended it in water and potash at body temperature. By pressing the goo between warmed plates, a runny liquid fat or oleine separated from a hard, white solid fat called margarine. The oleo could be churned and marketed.

The udders and stomachs were soon tossed from the process, but the beef fat became increasingly expensive itself, defeating the whole purpose. In the early twentieth century, though, chemists found the secret of hydrogenizing fats to harden liquid vegetable oils (see also Chapter 4). All vegetable oils were equal in this process and so the very cheapest available at any given time could be used. From then on the price of margarine plummeted. The dairy industry grew absolutely hysterical.

Despite milk's use in margarine manufacturing from the very beginning, milk lobbies around the world fought margarine with tactics that were as dirty as any of those of the steel or railroad barons. German food shops forced buyers to use a separate entrance for margarine purchases. Canada and New Zealand simply forbade the production of margarine. (Canada did not rescind that law until 1948 and still bans a variety of imitation dairy products. [see box pg. 146])

U.S. dairy interests had margarine labeled as a "harmful drug" so that stores had to be licensed to sell it. Several states hit upon the subtler tactic of protecting the "purity" of the naturally lard-white margarine by prohibiting manufacturers from coloring it yellow. Bullying became farce in the five states that forced margarine to be dyed pink.

Today seemingly anything goes. Margarine turns up in sticks and tubs and squeezable liquids, is whipped with air and blended with real butter, comes in low, lower and lowest-fat varieties. Fat-free margarine is even available, creating the existential and oxymoronic image of a fat-free fat.

For all this variety, one characteristic seldom changes: Most margarines continue to rely upon dairy ingredients to provide that all-important hint of butterness. Hint is the operative word. Margarines' high fat (or fat-replacement) content leaves room for little more than the maximum 1% lactose content that you'll find in butter itself.

True milk-free margarines are, at best, rare. Unsalted or "sweet" stick margarine has traditionally been milk-free, but is extremely difficult to find these days. Several companies make milk-free kosher margarines, the idea being that they can be eaten at meals containing meat. The rush to introduce lower-fat margarines has produced a number that are milk-free as well, with the market's current volatility guaranteeing that these and others will quickly come and go. Take the following listing just as a snapshot of a recent trip to the "dairy" case and confirm before you buy. None contains any casein.

ALTERNATIVE "BUTTERS"

Fleishmann's Lower Fat Margarine (tub but not sticks)
Fleishmann's Sweet Unsalted Margarine (sticks)
Mazola Sweet Unsalted Margarine (sticks)
Mother's Soft Margarine Sweet Unsalted (sticks and tub)
Nucoa Super Light Smart Beat Light Margarine (tub)
Promise Ultra 65% Less Fat (tub)
Shedd's Willow Run Soybean Margarine (sticks)
Weight Watchers Light Margarine (tub)

Alternative "Milks"

Only those with exceptionally refined palates would refuse margarine under any and all circumstances. The better margarines taste sufficiently like butter for everyday duties and may even have a few health advantages to boot.

The milk substitutes that sit next to regular milks in the dairy case have a long way to go before they reach that lofty status. Only a few even among the LI settle down with a tall cool glass of nondairy creamer and only the most ardent opponents of milk would ascribe health benefits to its imitators. No matter. As long as we remember that nondairy creamers are alternatives to milk and not milk itself, we can acknowledge that the new generation of substitutes is an enormous advance over its predecessors and so can play a useful role in the milk-free household.

So strong is the milk mystique, though, that the very existence of these products is enough to give otherwise rational consumer publications the heebie-jeebies. I greatly respect both *Consumer Reports* and the Center for Science in the Public Interest's *Nutrition Action Healthletter*, but they forfeit respect when they imply that the LI are so stupid that they can mistake a carton labeled "Non-Dairy Beverage" for one of lactose-reduced milk.

Long gone are the days when nondairy creamers were just that: thick, dense liquids stuffed full of coconut oil and other highly saturated fats to fats to evoke the richness of a splash of cream in a cup of coffee. The new formulations are closer to half-and-half than cream, while light and fat-free versions now compete in all-purpose versatility with 2% and skim milks. In some ways the manufacturers have outsmarted themselves. They've produced products close enough to milk so that people have begun to actually consider them as milk. Nondairy creamers are increasingly being used for entire families' everyday needs, even when not all are LI. Oddly enough, this sometimes creates a crisis for the manufacturers rather than the cries of triumph you might expect.

First, let me sound the requisite warnings. Supermarket milk substitutes are as artificial a creation of the food chemist's expertise as supermarket margarines. *Cooking Light's* look at Vitamite, a 2% Non-Dairy Beverage made by Diehl Specialties, was a masterpiece of faint praise, saying that "it does give the impression of drinking milk, and people might adapt to its taste." The *Nutrition Action Healthletter* was far less kind, as might be expected in a column headed "Food Porn." "What we've got here is a pseudo-food that's made by taking water and adding sugar, oil, potassium and calcium, and a couple of thickening gums and vitamins," it said. The horror of it all evidently overwhelmed the writer's command of English diction: "As a substitute for milk, it's pretty lousy. It's got no riboflavin, one-third the protein, half the potassium, and 20 percent less calcium." (Vitamite heroically managed to refrain from saying "Oh, yeah? Sez you," in its response: "As compared to a 2% milk, Vitamite is very similar in Calories, calcium and vitamins A and D, as well as fat. In addition, riboflavin and additional nutrients will be added to the product by the end of this year [1993] to make it even more healthful."

Consumer Reports gave Carnation Co.'s Coffee-mate and Rich Products Corp.'s Farm Rich the once over and concluded that "Neither creamer tasted much like milk or half and half, according to our trained tasters. Of the two, Farm Rich had more of the flavor of dairy products, with a slight vanillalike note. The Coffee-mate tasted bland, with a slight but distinct flavor of vegetable oil." They noted that both products had considerably more fat, although slightly less saturated fat, than whole milk.

No one can argue with those facts, but high fat warnings do not apply to low-fat or fat-free nondairy creamers. Although they cannot equal milk's overall nutritional superiority, the fat issue that so provokes the consumer magazines is rendered moot. I have not seen analyses of the nutritional value of any of the lower fat versions, perhaps for this very reason.

As nondairy creamers evolve into nondairy milks, they become more and more tempting to use by the glass as an overall milk substitute and not just by the tablespoonful in coffee. *Cooking Light*, for example, noted that Vitamite "worked wonderfully baked in a cream pie and cooked in cheese chowder." Nondairy creamers in general can substitute directly for milk or cream in almost any recipe.

Much as they might like to promote the total milkness of their products, the corporate entities behind them actually face a dilemma. The FDA's new nutritional information regulations specify that the serving size correspond to the way people actually use the product rather than an artificial number. The drawback is that with a larger serving size all the other numbers on the nutrition label increase as well. Staying with a 1 Tbsp serving size helps to keep potentially unseemly numbers, like those of fat, from growing large enough to call attention to themselves.

Current practice in nutrition reporting is mixed. Vitamite's nutritional information panel uses a serving size of 1 cup, just as milk does. Others, including Coffee-mate and Presto Foods' Mocha Mix, cling to the traditional 1 Tbsp serving size. Farm Rich, interestingly, uses two serving sizes and has two sets of nutrition information on its Light (but not Fat Free) cartons. (The presentation does not allow a direct comparison of nutritional information with that of milk, unfortunately.)

These corporate facts of life may account for the defensive tone that at the time puzzled me during my correspondence with the Carnation people. When Coffee-mate first appeared (long before a fat-free version was introduced), the buzz surrounding it involved its suitability on cereals. I dutifully poured some on and found that it worked quite well. My mistake lay in writing to let them know this. In response I received a smoothly written letter that never specifically said that Coffee-mate shouldn't be used on cereals but nevertheless powerfully downplayed the notion. Feeling as if I had entered the Twilight Zone, I wrote back to remind them that everything about Coffee-mate implied just the opposite. The text on the carton urged us to use it in cereals, reinforced by the picture of a bowl brimming with a white liquid. Its national advertising bade us to enjoy Coffee-mate "in more than just coffee. Try it on fruit, cereal, or in your favorite recipe." Another polite, noncommittal letter was the only response.

Cut to 1994. Coffee-mate cartons no longer bear any reference to cereals. Coincidence? Lawyers and potential FDA battles were probably 99.99% of the reason, but I report on my offstage role here just to reinforce my oft-repeated claim that companies do indeed pay close attention to informed consumers.

To be fair, let me quote the company position in those pre-Fat Free Coffee-mate days, as stated by one of its nutritionists:

> We always like to encourage as much milk consumption as can be tolerated. Beyond that limit, Coffee-mate Liquid can be used as long as the consumer is aware of the added Calories and fat to the total diet and the fact that Coffee-mate Liquid does not supply the nutrients of milk, nutrients which will have to be obtained from other sources.

Excellent summation, one that matches my general views on the use of nondairy creamers and beverages. They're convenient, they keep longer

---

ALTERNATIVE "MILKS"

Diehl Specialties—not available in all parts of U.S.
  Vitamite 2% Fat Non-Dairy Beverage—liquid; refrigerated; contains casein

Nestlé Beverage Company
  Carnation Coffee-mate Liquid Non-dairy Creamer—refrigerated; contains casein
    Fat Free; Regular

Carnation Coffee-mate Non-dairy Creamer—powder; contains casein
    Lite; Regular

Presto Food Products—west coast distribution only
  Mocha Mix Non-Dairy Creamer—liquid; refrigerated; no cascin
    Fat Free; Lite; Original

Rich Products Corp.
  Coffee Rich Non-Dairy Creamer—liquid; frozen; no casein
    Light; Original
  Farm Rich Non-Dairy Creamer—liquid; refrigerated; no casein
    Fat Free; Light; Original

---

than milk does and they have many uses. Used intelligently and sparingly they can relieve you of the possible worries of reduced-lactose milk. But the fact that they are not nutritionally equivalent to milk should always be kept in mind.

Flavored Nondairy Creamers
Following the success of coffeebeans and espressos and their multitude of flavors and flavorings, flavored creamers for the home could not be far behind. (I assume there is a technical reason why all those I've seen have been nondairy.) Conspicuously labeled with words redolent of the coffee bar experience—hazelnut and french vanilla, Irish Creme and Amaretto—they're obviously designed to evoke the wafting aromas even when it's just you, your coffee cup and an infomercial.

They are also notable for their intense sweetness, probably to mimic the sugar that gets added to mask the bitterness of strong espressos. If you unwittingly sugar your coffee and then add these creamers, you may find the cup undrinkable. Start with the creamer and then taste before going further.

All the flavored nondairy creamers use milk protein, and some use whey protein in addition to the more usual casein. Those with milk protein allergies may react differently or not at all to the whey protein.

FLAVORED NON-DAIRY CREAMERS

M. Star Inc.
  International Delight Gourmet Flavored Creamers—liquid; refrigerated;
  contains casein
    Amaretto; Cinnamon Hazelnut; Irish Creme; Suisse Chocolate Mocha
  No Fat International Delight Gourmet Flavored Creamers—liquid; refrigerated; contains casein
    No Fat Amaretto; No Fat French Vanilla Royale; No Fat Irish Creme;
    No Fat Hawaiian Macadamia

Nestlé Beverage Company
  Carnation Coffee-mate Flavored Creamer—powder; contains casein
    Amaretto; Cinnamon Creme; French Vanilla; Hazelnut; Irish Creme;
    Mocha Almond
  Carnation Coffee-mate Creamer—refrigerated; liquid; contains casein
    Amaretto; Hazelnut; Irish Creme
  Carnation Coffee-mate Fat-Free Creamer—refrigerated; liquid; contains
  casein
    Butter Rum; Irish Creme

Presto Food Products
  Signature Flavors Fat Free Creamers—refrigerated; liquid; contains whey
  protein concentrate and milk protein concentrate
    French Vanilla; Irish Cream; Kahlua; Mauna Loa Macadamia Nut

---

Alternative "Ice Creams"

A few short years ago, supermarket freezer cases were inundated by a wave
of nondairy frozen desserts. Most are long, long gone. Besides supplying
case histories for marketing classes at business schools, the rise and fall of
the nondairy dessert is an object lesson for those of us who want more
choices in the supermarket.

It all starts with tofu. Made from curdled soybean "milk," tofu has the
proper texture for creamy nondairy products, with little taste of its own to
get in the way. Many nondairy substitutes found in health food stores are
made from versatile tofu, but getting the flavor and texture right in a
frozen dessert proved extremely difficult.

The first tofu "ice cream" I know of was Ice Bean, introduced in 1976.
It took entrepreneur David Mintz, an orthodox Jew and Kosher caterer
always on the lookout for nondairy desserts, to break open the category on
a national scale. His Tofutti Brand Non-Dairy Frozen Dessert hit the
market in 1982 and created a sensation. Between 1983 and 1985 sales
zoomed from $300,000 to over $17 million. Wish you had bought stock?
Well, a couple of years later sales had dipped to only $5 million.

ALTERNATIVE "ICE CREAMS"

Presto Food Products
   Mocha Mix Non-Dairy Dessert—no casein
      Berry-Berry-Berry; Dutch Chocolate; Mocha Almond Fudge;
      Neapolitan; Strawberry Swirl; Vanilla

Tofutti Brands—all no casein
   Tofutti Frozen Dessert
      Better Pecan; Chocolate Cookies Supreme; Chocolate Supreme;
      Vanilla; Vanilla Almond Bark; Vanilla Fudge; Wildberry Supreme
   Tofutti Free—low fat
      Deep Chocolate Fudge; Special Strawberry; Swiss Mocha Coffee;
      Vanilla/Chocolate/Strawberry
   Tofutti Better Than Yogurt
      Chocolate Fudge; Coffee Marshmallow Swirl; Passion Island Fruite;
      Peach Mango; Strawberry/Banana; Vanilla Fudge
   Tofutti Frutti—fruit juice sweetened
      Apricot Mango; Three Berry; Vanilla Apple Orchard
   Tofutti Cuties—snack size sandwiches
      Chocolate; Vanilla

As is the fate of many pioneers, Mintz found a horde of competitors—over 30 at one point, many from giant corporations—jumping on his bandwagon. They created that wave of products I mentioned, and had enough money to buy shelf (or freezer) space in hopes of crowding out the competition. The frenzy, according to various industry publications, prevented customers from building brand loyalty. Sales never matched expectations and the rise of frozen yogurt as the preferred low-Calorie, low-fat alternative to ice cream finished off those firms that were in it for quick profit.

Today, frozen tofu is alive and flourishing in health food stores, as we'll see in the next section, but Tofutti is about the only brand left in conventional supermarkets. (I assume there are others with regional distribution that I am not familiar with.) Mintz himself is trying to rebuild by adding a new line containing bacteria cultures, Tofutti Better Than Yogurt, to his original and fat-free Tofuttis. All are pareve foods, which makes conventional cultures grown in a dairy product like yogurt unacceptable in them. Mintz found a way to make the acidophilus bacteria grow on a carrot base instead, allowing him to market a nondairy "frozen yogurt." I just wonder when the wave of competitors will hit the stores.

Not all nondairy frozen desserts use tofu as their base. The Presto people have adapted their Mocha Mix nondairy creamer recipe so that it will yield an equally milk-free "ice cream." It can be found from coast to coast in the U.S., but not in all states or all cities in the states it does reach.

The nondairy "ice creams" in your grocer's freezer case are known as hard packs in the industry. Soft serves, on the other hand, are those that swirl out of machines onto cones. Nondairy soft serves may occasionally be found alongside ice cream and frozen yogurt in shops that sell frozen desserts. None has had much national success, but if you do stumble across any be sure to give them a try and encourage the store manager not to give up on them.

The busy Mr. Mintz of Tofutti also markets nondairy "cream cheese" and "sour cream," both based on tofu.

It has been years since I've run across any other nondairy "sour creams," but they do turn up from time to time as regional products.

OTHER ALTERNATIVE NONDAIRY PRODUCTS

Tofutti Brands
    Tofutti Sour Supreme Better Than Sour Cream—no casein
      Plain
    Tofutti Better Than Cream Cheese—no casein
      Herbs and Chives; French Onion; Plain

For further information on nondairy supermarket products, contact:

Diehl Specialties International
24 N. Clinton St.
Defiance, OH 43512
419–782-5010

M. Star Inc.
5956 Sherry Lane
Dallas, TX 75225
800–441-3321

Nestlé Beverage Company
345 Spear St.
San Francisco, CA 94105
800-NESTLE-4

Presto Food Products
P.O. Box 584
18275 Arenth Ave.
City of Industry, CA 97148–1225
818–810-1775

Rich Products Corporation
Buffalo, NY 14240
800–356-7094

Tofutti Brands
P.O. Box 786
50 Jackson Dr.
Cranford, NJ 07016
908-272-2400

■ HEALTH OR NATURAL FOOD STORE PRODUCTS

Health food stores (a description seemingly preferred, from the evidence of industry brochures and promotional material, to that of natural food stores) were born as conscious alternatives to supermarkets, rejecting mainstream products as firmly as supermarkets disdained health food items. That was before the traditional retailers found that the buzzwords—organic, natural, preservative-free—that lured customers to health food stores were just as powerful a draw on their side of the street.

The two worlds now overlap to an extent difficult to imagine a decade ago. It's true that no one is likely to mistake a giant suburban supermarket for the less formal confines of typically urban (or college town) health food stores, but most supermarkets today carry at least a selection of soy beverages, tofu burgers and exotic grains and some do much more. Tellingly, a few health food superstores have emerged that are as big as supermarkets—or at least the size the supermarkets used to be before they hypertrophed. The Whole Foods Market, across the street from Stanford University in Palo Alto, contains everything from a gourmet deli to a selection of California wines along with a dozen different lines each of lactase pills and dairy alternatives. It's a complete shopping experience, one that would startle anyone whose ideas of such places were formed by a local co-op in their college days.

I should stress that the overlap is unidirectional; standard supermarket brands are hard to find even in the health food superstores. Although the stores may be fancier, they maintain their position as alternatives. It is the health foods firms that are reaching out to, one might even say proselytizing, conventional supermarkets. For today, as both a philosophical and practical distinction, it makes sense to speak of health foods as a separate category. For one thing, their spotty distribution in supermarkets makes locating any particular brand name frustrating. For another, firms in the industry work with the health food stores to espouse a collective culture. Ecological awareness, organic farming, the avoidance of animal products, community involvement, a commitment to recycling and the return of a portion of sales revenues to groups supporting similar goals are common themes. The "alternative" in these alternative foods takes on any number of meanings.

For more information about soy milk and other soyfoods, call the United Soybean Board Soy Hotline: 1-800-TALK-SOY.

Alternative "Milks"

For centuries, Japanese tofu shops have followed an ancient recipe. Grind presoaked soybeans with water to produce a puree, then mix with hot water and allow to cook for a few minutes. Strain and press to remove a creamy white liquid. Voila: soy "milk."

Commercial soy beverages resemble that traditional product in the same tenuous way that pasteurized, homogenized, vitamin-fortified, reduced-fat milk resembles the raw liquid that comes steaming from inside the cow. That is to say, both have been elaborately remade to suit the demanding American standards of taste, consistency and shelf life. Successfully so, too, since by 1994 soy milk sales were growing at a rate of 20% a year. Total sales approached the impressive $100 million mark, making them as large as the more mainstream lactose-reduced milks.

Though few know it, soybeans are the second-largest crop in the U.S. Although most get used as animal feed, the high protein, extremely versatile beans have commercial applications that go far beyond the traditional tofu, tempeh, miso and soy sauce. Soy has been used to make dairy-free infant formulas since Baltimore pediatrician John Ruhrah developed the first example in the early part of this century. (WARNING: Soy milk is NOT the nutritional equivalent of the specially fortified soy-based infant formulas. *Prolonged exclusive use of soy milk by very young infants will lead to malnutrition and even death*.) Henry Ford of auto fame tried to upgrade the soybean's then-lowly image into the Model T of food by serving the press a 14-course soybean banquet at the 1934 Chicago World's Fair. It didn't take.

At about the same time, the first modern soy milk plants were being built in China. After a long interruption for World War II, Asian entrepreneurs went to work, notably Taiwan's Dr. K. S. Lo. Dr. Lo's Vitasoy was a postwar phenomenon. For a time in the 1960s, it even displaced Coca-Cola from its position as the best-selling soft drink in Hong Kong.

Soy drinks' tendency to taste like soybeans delayed their success in the U.S. Food scientists were brought in to work their magic, and modern soy milks little resemble the product that you can make at home. Most natural foods stores sell that more traditionally made soy milk if you would like to try it before making your own, and many companies continue to provide that beanier variety for shops in the various North American Chinatowns.

The good news is that even commercial soy milks tend to be healthy products. They are mostly low-fat, or come in low-fat varieties, and none have more than a gram of saturated fat per 8 ounce glass. All are cholesterol-free because they have no animal fat. Soy milk's protein content can rival cow's milk's (and soy is very good plant protein) and many have more potassium and are fortified with calcium and vitamins A and C. They are undoubtedly more beneficial than the nondairy creamers.

ALTERNATIVE "MILKS"

Edensoy
    Edensoy Organic Soy Beverage
        Carob; Original; Vanilla
    Edensoy Extra Organic Soy Beverage
        Original; Vanilla
    EdenRice Rice Beverage
    EdenBlend Rice and Soy Beverage

Ener-G Foods
    Ener-G Foods Pure SoyQuik (soy flour beverage mix)
    Ener-G Foods NutQuik (almond meal beverage mix)
    Ener-G Foods Lacto-Free Beverage (corn syrup solids beverage mix)

Grainaissance
    Amazake Naturally Sweet Rice Drink
        Aseptic pack—Almond Shake; Organic Almond Light; Organic
        Original Light
        Containers—Almond Shake; Apricot; Cocoa-Almond; Mocha Java;
        Original Flavor; Sesame Shake; Vanilla Pecan; Rice Nog (seasonal)

Health Valley Foods
    Fat-Free Soy Moo Non-Dairy Soy Drink

Imagine Foods
    Rice Dream Non-Dairy Beverage Made From Organic Brown Rice
        Carob; Chocolate; Vanilla
    Rice Dream Lite
        Carob Lite; Chocolate; Organic Original Lite; Vanilla Lite.

Pacific Foods
    Pacific Lite
        Plain; Vanilla
    Pacific Select
        Plain; Vanilla
    Pacific Ultra-Plus
        Plain; Vanilla

Sovex Natural Foods, Naturally Tofu
    Better Than Milk?
        Chocolate; Light; Natural

Vitasoy
    Vitasoy Non-Dairy Soy Drink
        Creamy Original; Rich Cocoa; Vanilla Delight; Carob Supreme;
    Vitasoy Light
        Light Cocoa; Light Original; Light Vanilla

Westbrae Natural Foods
  Westsoy-Organic
    Original; Unsweetened
  Westsoy Lite
    Lite Cocoa; Lite Plain; Lite Vanilla
  Westsoy Plus
    Carob; Plain; Vanilla
  Westbrae Malteds
    Almond Malted; Carob Malted; Cocoa Mint Malted; Java Malted;
    Vanilla Malted
  Westbrae Lite Malteds
    Almond Lite; Carob Lite; Cocoa Mint Lite; Creamy Banana Lite;
    Vanilla Royale Lite
  Ah Soy Soy Drink
    Carob; Chocolate; Original; Vanilla

Wholesome and Hearty Foods
  AlmondMylk (almonds and brown rice syrup-based)
    Original; Vanilla

Despite the claims you sometimes see from enthusiasts, though, commercial soy drinks cannot equal milk's overall nutritional excellence. In the past, most comparisons were made to whole milk, which gave the zero cholesterol and relatively low-fat soy drinks an edge. The rocketing sales of skim milk have outdated these claims and most firms have rushed lite versions onto the market to give themselves still lower fat contents to promote. Most of these ''lite'' beverages are just watered-down versions of their originals, which serves to further depress their nutritional value. Table 1 compares soy and other vegetable milks with cow's milk using the components of the new nutrition labels on packaged foods to provide a head-to-head comparison.

Soy milks can substitute directly for milk in most recipes, although you will want to stick to the unflavored and unthickened varieties in order not to impart unwanted tastes to the final product.

Other vegetable ''milks'' have equally long histories but remain even less familiar to the general public than soy milks. Coconut milk was commonly used in India and Southeast Asia. Native Americans extracted a milky liquid from hickory nuts and pecans for use in gruels and maize cakes. In Europe, where access to dairy animals might be thought to have eliminated the need for milk substitutes, walnuts and almonds—blanched, pulverized and soaked in water—provided a milk used in many households at least until the end of the eighteenth century. Nut milks were so commonplace that when the thirteenth century traveler William of

TABLE 1
NUTRITIONAL COMPARISON OF NUT, RICE AND SOY-BASED "MILKS" WITH COW'S MILK

Based on 8 oz. serving Product	Calories	Calories from fat	Total fat (g)	Saturated Fat (g)	Chol-esterol (mg)	Sodium (mg)	Carbo-hydrates (g)	Fiber (g)	Sugars (g)	Protein (g)	Vitamin A (%)	Vitamin C (%)	Calcium (%)	Iron (%)
Nut/Rice Based														
AlmondMylk														
Original	80	40	4	0	0	190	8	2	6	2	2	2	<2	2
Rice Based														
Amazake Light Original	90	0	0	0	0	75	20	2	19	2	0	0	0	2
Amazake Light Almond	110	2	0	0	0	75	20	2	19	2	0	0	0	2
EdenRice	110	25	3	0.5	0	85	21	NG*	16	1	NG	NG	4	2
Rice Dream Enriched Chocolate	160	20	2.5	0	0	100	35	0	8	4	10	0	30	8
Rice Dream Chocolate	180	25	2.5	0	0	75	40	0	1	1	0	0	0	0
Amazake Almond	272	NG	7	NG	0	23	46	NG	NG	7	0	0	4	8
Soy Based														
Better Than Milk? Natural	100	55	6	1.5	0	140	10	0	3	2	0	0	25	0
Westsoy Lowfat Plain	100	18	2.5	NG	0	140	16	NG	NG	4	0	2	20	4
Westsoy Lite Plain	100	NG	2	<1	0	100	16	NG	NG	4	0	2	2	4
Health Valley Soy Moo	110	NG	0	NG	0	25	19	NG	NG	7	<2	<2	40	2

Soy Based														
Edensoy Original	133	34	4	1	0	104	13	3	NG	9	24	0	19	9
Edensoy Extra Original	133	34	4	1	0	114	13	NG	NG	9	0	0	9	9
Westsoy Lite Cocoa	140	NG	2	<1	0	95	27	NG	NG	3	0	2	2	6
Westsoy Original	150	NG	5	1	0	115	18	NG	NG	7	0	0	6	6
Westsoy Plus Plain	150	50	5	1	0	140	18	NG	NG	6	10	2	30	10
Vitasoy Rich Cocoa	208	NG	NG	NG	0	180	30	NG	NG	8	NG	NG	8	6
Westbrae Lite Malted Carob	213	NG	4	<1	0	187	36	NG	NG	7	0	5	13	5
Westbrae Malted Java	360	NG	15	NG	0	187	49	NG	NG	8	0	20	13	8
Soy/Rice Based														
Pacific Lite Plain	100	20	2.5	0	0	115	15	0	8	4	10	0	30	8
Pacific Select Plain	100	25	3	0	0	115	14	0	7	4	10	0	30	8
EdenBlend	120	30	3	0.5	0	85	16	NG	12	7	NG	NG	2	6
Pacific Ultra Plus Plain	160	45	5	0.5	0	120	22	0	11	6	10	0	30	15
Cow's Milk														
Skim	90	0	0	0	<5	125	13	0	12	8	10	4	30	0
1%	110	20	2.5	1.5	10	125	13	0	12	8	10	4	30	0
2%	130	45	5	3	20	125	13	0	12	8	10	4	30	0
Whole	150	70	8	5	35	125	12	0	12	8	6	4	30	0

*NG = not given

NONDAIRY ALTERNATIVES IN CANADA

We chauvinistic Americans often forget that Canada is a separate country with its own laws and customs. Conspicuous examples are the Canadian laws banning many imitation dairy products.

Provincial laws against dairy substitutes date from the days when even margarine was banned. Concerns about lack of nutritional equivalence with milk and overt protection of the dairy industry drove the laws. As margarine and other supermarket staples, including nondairy creamers, nondairy dessert toppings and infant formulas, may now be legally sold, health food products, especially nondairy cheeses, for some reason, disproportionately feel the weight of government action.

Individual customers may not be greatly affected by the ban on products such as soy or nut cheese because the laws are only enforced in response to complaints. Technically illegal products line the shelves of many stores, affording Canadians much the same range of choices as is available in the U.S.

In the long run, the dairy industry probably cannot prevail. U.S. firms are increasingly winning exemptions from Canadian provincial governments for their products and are getting support from the Canadian courts as well. Canadians who are LI may want to join in the effort by talking to their legislators and regulators about the need for and value of all nondairy products. In the meantime, Canadian consumers may have to search to find some of the products listed in this chapter.

Rubruck wrote of his experiences with the Mongols he described the taste of their *kumiss* (fermented mare's milk) as being like almond milk.

Today brown rice syrup provides the base for the majority of commercial non-soy milks. Only a few commercial almond milks exist, although almond is a common flavoring. Almond milk can be made at home, along with vegetable milks, out of almost any base including pumpkinseeds and pine nuts. Even proponents, however, say that the taste transition may be difficult to make in one leap if you are coming directly from milk or nondairy creamers. Experiment first with the various commercial varieties to see which are most pleasing to your taste buds.

These drinks have a slightly different spectrum of nutritional pluses and minuses than either soy milks or cow's milk (again, *see Table 1*) and offer the added benefit of being acceptable to those with allergies to soy. A few products blend rice and soy, which may be to further mask any beany taste residue from the soybeans.

Even non-fat dry milks have a counterpart in the form of powdered soy milks and nut milks. In addition, one powder, Lacto-Free Beverage, from Ener-G Foods, is made from corn syrup solids and canola oil. It should not be confused with the similarly named Lactofree, a lactose-free milk-based infant formula made by Mead Johnson.

Alternative "Cheeses"

Like alternative milks, most alternative "cheeses" are made from soy, usually in the form of tofu, although there is again a significant minority that is nut-based and one that is oil-based. Cheese is even harder than milk to copy; to get a product that "tastes, melts & stretches like cheese," as one manufacturer puts it, some form of the milk protein casein must be added to the recipe. Soy and nut cheeses even with casein are virtually lactose-free (99.98% lactose free, according to one claim; completely, according to another). Spreadable "cream cheeses," which in my experience all contain casein, are also available. Kosher casein-free products that are made in the same machinery as a firm's casein-containing products would have to be labeled "Kosher-Dairy," but are still milk-free.

If you want to avoid even casein, several truly vegan cheeses and cream cheeses are available. They do not pass the "stretch or melt" portion of the alternative cheese test, nor are they nutritionally equivalent to cheese. One further difference from the casein-containing cheese alternatives is that vegan cheeses cannot be frozen. Of course, none of this matters if all you want are slices or nibbles.

ALTERNATIVE "CHEESES"

American Natural Snacks
   Soya Kaas—soymilk & tofu-based; contains casein
      Hickory Smoked; Jalapeno Mexi-Kaas; Mild American Cheddar style; Mozzarella style
   Shredded Soya Kaas—soymilk & tofu-based; contains casein
      Mild American Cheddar style; Mozzarella style
   Fat-Free Soya Kaas—soymilk & tofu-based; contains casein
      Jalapeño Monterey Jack style; Mild American style; Mozzarella style
   Soya Kaas Spreadable Cream Cheese style—soymilk & tofu-based; contains casein
      Garden Vegetable; Garlic and Herb; Plain
   Vegie Kaas Spreads—no casein
      Regular; Smoked

Sharon's Finest
   TofuRella—tofu-based; contains casein
      Cheddar; Garlic-Herb; Jalapeño Jack; Monterey Jack; Mozzarella
   TofuRella Slices—tofu-based; contains casein
      Cheddar; Mozzarella

Sharon's Finest (*continued*)

AlmondRella—almond milk-based; contains casein
  Cheddar; Garlic-Herb; Mozzarella
Zero-FatRella—tofu-based; contains casein
  Cheddar; Jalapeño Jack; Mozzarella
VeganRella—brazil nut-based; no casein
  Italian; Mexican; (plain) Cream Cheese; Onion-Dill Cream Cheese

Galaxy Foods
  formägg—canola oil-based; contains casein
  Deli Varieties/5 lb. loaves
    Caesar's Italian Garden; Classic American; Old World Mozzarella; Old
    World Swiss; Vintage Provolone; Zesty Jalapeño
  Individually Wrapped Slices
    Swiss American; White American; Yellow American Flavored Slices
  Grated Parmesan Alternative
  Macaroni and Cheese Sauce
  Shredded Varieties
    Cheddar; Mozzarella

Galaxy/Soyco Foods division

  Lite 'n' Less—soymilk-based; contains casein
  Chubs
    Cheddar; Mozzarella
  Deli Varieties/5 lb loaves
    Cheddar; Monterey Jack; Mozzarella
  Grated Low-fat Parmesan
  Individually Wrapped Slices
    Mozzarella; Swiss American; Yellow American
  Macaroni 'n' Cheese
  Lite 'n' Free—fat-free; soymilk-based; contains casein
  Chubs
    Cheddar; Mozzarella
  Soymage—soymilk-based; no casein
  Chubs
    Cheddar; Mozzarella
  Sour Cream

White Wave

  Soy A Melt—tofu-based; contains casein
    Cheddar style; Jalapeño Jack style; Mozzarella style; Monterey Jack
    style; Garlic Herb style
  Soy A Melt Fat-Free—tofu-based; contains casein
    Mozzarella style, Cheddar style
  Soy A Melt Slices—tofu-based; contains casein
    American; Mozzarella-flavored

Alternative "Puddings"

Getting milk substitutes to set is often the bane of homemade recipes. Ready-to-eat, usually rice-based, "puddings" make for a convenient and fuss-free snack. Low-fat or fat-free, they are available in a host of flavors.

ALTERNATIVE "PUDDINGS"

Grainaissance
    Amazake Pudding—brown rice-based
        Almond, Almond Cinnamon, Cocoa, Lemon (nonfat)

Imagine Foods
    Dream Pudding—brown rice-based
        Almond; Banana; Butterscotch; Carob; Chocolate; Coconut; Lemon

---

Alternative "Yogurts"

Yogurt may be better tolerated than most other dairy foods, but soy and soy-rice "yogurts" are completely dairy-free, yet are made with the same bacterial cultures as traditional yogurts to retain whatever health benefits the cultures themselves may provide.

ALTERNATIVE "YOGURTS"

Springfield Creamery
    Nancy's Cultured Soy—soy- and brown rice-based
        Blackberry; Blueberry; Plain; Raspberry; Strawberry

White Wave
    Dairyless—soy-based
        Apricot Mango; Blueberry; Lemon Kiwi; Organic Plain; Peach;
        Raspberry; Strawberry; Vanilla

Alternative "Butters"

Even in the health food stores, alternative "butters" are called margarines. The difference is that these are all milk-free and made with a soybean oil or canola oil base that is non-hydrogenated. One restriction: You may not be able to fry with them.

ALTERNATIVE "BUTTERS"

Spectrum Naturals
    Spectrum Spread

ALTERNATIVE "ICE CREAMS"

Imagine Foods
  Rice Dream Non Dairy Dessert Pints—rice-based
    Cappuccino; Carob; Carob Almond; Carob Chip; Cocoa Marble
    Fudge; Lemon; Mint Carob Chip; Peanut Butter Fudge; Strawberry;
    Vanilla; Vanilla Fudge; Vanilla Swiss Almond; Wildberry
  Rice Dream Non Dairy Dessert Quarts—rice-based
    Cocoa Marble Fudge; Cookies N'Dream; Neapolitan; Vanilla
  Rice Dream Pies (cookie with Rice Dream filling)—rice-based
    Chocolate; Mint; Mocha; Vanilla
  Rice Dream Bars—rice-based
    Rice Dream Chocolate Bar; Rice Dream Strawberry Bar; Vanilla Bar
  Nutty Rice Dream Bars (nut-covered, chocolate-coated Rice Dream)—
  rice-based
    Chocolate Nutty Bar; Vanilla Nutty Bar

Sovex Natural Foods
  Naturally Tofu, Tofu Ice Cream—soy tofu-based
    Carob; Strawberry; Vanilla

Turtle Mountain
  Living Lightly Light Non-Dairy Frozen Dessert—soybean and brown rice
  syrup-based
    Almond Pecan; Carob Almond; Carob Peppermint; Chocolate; Choc-
    olate Almond; Espresso; Mint Carob Chip; Peanut Butter Cup;
    Raspberry; Vanilla; Vanilla Swiss Almond
  Sweet Nothings Nonfat Non-Dairy Frozen Dessert — brown rice syrup-
  based
    Black Leopard; Chocolate; Chocolate Mandarin; Espresso Fudge;
    Mango Raspberry; Raspberry Swirl; Tiger Stripes; Vanilla; Very Berry
    Raspberry

Alternative "Ice Creams"
Not too many years ago, a trip to any local supermarket would have turned
up as many as a half dozen different brands of alternative "ice creams."
Today they are few and far between. A far better selection in terms of sheer
number of brands is to be found at the average health food store. You will
again be able to find them in both soy- and rice-based varieties.

Other Alternatives
If you can make a nondairy cheese, then you can use it wherever cheese
itself is used. Pizzas and macaroni-and-cheese-like products are a growing
category.

Nondairy "sour creams" are much more difficult to find, but not
impossible.

OTHER ALTERNATIVES

Galaxy Foods
    formägg—canola oil-based; contains casein
    Macaroni and Cheese Sauce

Galaxy/Soyco Foods division

    Lite 'n' Less—contains casein
    Macaroni 'n' Cheese
    Soymage—soymilk-based; no casein
    Sour Cream

Jaclyn's Food Products

    Jaclyn's Fat-Free Pizza—contains casein

For further information on nondairy health food store products, contact:

American Natural Snacks
P.O. Box 1067
St. Augustine, FL 32085–1067

Earth's Best Inc.
P.O. Box 887
Middlebury, VT 05753
800–442-4221

Eden Foods Inc.
701 Tecumseh Rd., Box E
Clinton, MI 49236
800–248-0320

Ener-G Foods, Inc.
5960 First Ave. So.
P.O. Box 84487
Seattle, WA 98124–5787
800–331-5222/800–325-9788 (in Wash.)

Galaxy Foods
2441 Viscount Row
Orlando, FL 32809
800–441-9419

Grainaissance
1580 62nd St.
Emeryville, CA 94608
510–547-7256

Health Valley Foods Inc.
16100 Foothill Blvd.
Irwindale, CA 91706–7811
800–423-4846

Imagine Foods Inc.
350 Cambridge Ave., Suite 350
Palo Alto, CA 94306
800–333-6339

Jacyln's Food Products Inc.
P.O. Box 1314
Cherry Hill, NJ 08034
609–354-2267

Pacific Foods of Oregon Inc.
19480 SW 97th Ave.
Tualatin, OR 97062
503–692-9666

Sharon's Finest
P.O. Box 5020
Santa Rosa, CA 95402–5020
707–576-7050

Sovex Natural Foods Inc.
P.O. Box 2178
Collegedale, TN 37315–2178
800–227-2320

Spectrum Naturals Inc.
Petaluma, CA 94952

Springfield Creamery
29440 Airport Rd.
Eugene, OR 97402
503–689-2911

Turtle Mountain Inc.
P.O. Box 70
Junction City, OR 97448
503–998-6778

Vitasoy (USA) Inc.
99 Park Lane
Brisbane, CA 94005
800-VITASOY

Westbrae Natural Foods
1065 E. Walnut St.
Carson, CA 90746
310–886-8200

White Wave Inc.
1990 N. 57th Ct.
Boulder, CO 80301
800–488-9283

Wholesome and Hearty Foods Inc.
2422 SE Hawthorne Blvd.
Portland, OR 97214
800–636-0109

10

GOOD NEWS FROM WASHINGTON: NUTRITION AND INGREDIENTS LABELING

Living with LI means much more than simply cutting back on milk, more than merely trying to stop feeling sick. Those are negatives. Health and well-being (or wellness, for those who collect buzzwords) are positives. Whether your goal is reducing the lactose that you eat or the more challenging one of completely eliminating dairy products, you must ensure that your diet stays at least as nutritious as it was in the past. To do so, reading the labels of everything you buy is a must. Fortunately, these labels are more meaningful than ever before.

The Nutrition Labeling and Education Act of 1990 (NLEA) changed everything—and for the better. You can usually tell how good a law is for consumers by how loudly the affected industry screams in protest. By that standard NLEA rates a solid 10.

Consumers were also wary of talk of major changes being made to their favorite foods, even if only to the packaging. To some, the increase in information seemed like confusing overkill, full of percentages, metric equivalents and something called "% Daily Values" just when they were finally getting used to the ins and outs of the Recommended Dietary Allowances.

The new label requirements are worth all the fuss and bother, however. They cover three separate and important areas: product claims, nutrition information and ingredient lists.

Product claims are the most visible—those come-ons slapped in huge screaming typefaces across the fronts of packaged foods aimed at an increasingly health-conscious market. Everyone who was confused about what manufacturers meant by "light," "low fat" or "reduced sodium" can take comfort from the knowledge that these and dozens of other terms once splattered almost at random on packages now have specific meanings that will be consistent from product to product. The overly creative imaginations of marketers will soon find new words to hype (they're already substituting the unregulated word "right" for "light" on prod-

154

FOR MORE INFORMATION

The new food labeling rules and regulations cover a lot of ground. While all the changes are valuable, even critical, to many people, only a few of them have a direct bearing on LI. I'll cover those as completely as possible. If you are interested in the others, here are some easy-reading sources of additional information.

The FDA, working in conjunction with groups such as the American Heart Association and the American Association of Retired Persons, has available a number of free brochures covering various aspects of the new labels. If you only need one copy of any of the following, write to: FDA (HFE-88), 5600 Fishers Lane, Rockville, MD 20857. If you are ordering for a group, you can get 2 to 25 copies of each brochure by writing to FDA (HFI-40) at the same address, or you can fax your order to 301–443-9057. Please be sure to include the publication numbers (given in parentheses) when you order.

An Introduction to the New Food Label (FDA 94–2271). An overview of food labeling changes with a poster of the "Nutrition Facts" panel.

How the New Food Label Can Help You Plan a Healthy Diet (FDA 94–2273). An overview written at a fifth-grade reading level.

How to Read the New Food Label (FDA 93–2260). An introduction to food labeling changes, particularly those that apply to heart disease prevention. Also available in Spanish: *Cómo Leer la Nueva Etiqueta de los Alimentos* (FDA 93–2260S).

Using the New Food Label to Choose Healthier Foods (FDA 94–2276). A large-type brochure.

Brochures are also available from a variety of other groups. A free one I particularly recommend for its completeness is *Understanding Food Labels*, available from The American Dietetic Association, 216 West Jackson Blvd., Chicago, IL 60606–6995 (or phone 312–899-0040).

If a single brochure isn't enough, try *Focus on Food Labeling—An FDA Consumer Special Report* (FDA 93–2262), which contains a series of articles reprinted from *FDA Consumer* magazine (itself a good ongoing source of information on all matters relating to food.) Unfortunately, *Focus* is not free. Copies are $5 each. Write to Superintendent of Documents, P. O. Box 371954, Pittsburgh, PA 15250–7594.

ucts which don't meet the "light" standards) but their worst flights of fancy will be reined in for a while.

The nutrition labels found on the sides of packaged foods got the biggest overhaul, with virtually every aspect of them changed or brand new (*see box*). Those % Daily Values, for example, carry over from product to product. For the first time, you can quickly add up your total daily consumption of these nutrients from packaged foods. The resulting numbers may please or appall you, but it is now much easier to fine-tune them.

Changes to the ingredients lists have been more subtle, though some are of crucial importance to those trying to eliminate dairy products from their diet.

GOOD NEWS ON INGREDIENTS LABELS

Listings of ingredients on certain packaged foods have been required ever since the Federal Food, Drug, and Cosmetic Act of 1938. Today it would be difficult to find a food package that didn't contain one. Some of these listings go on for such extraordinary lengths and include so many different chemicals that you'd think you were looking at the side of a bottle of shampoo. I'm sure many food processors would rather that you didn't know what was in these conglomerations: That's probably why you see them printed in tiny type with green ink on purple labels, making them virtually impossible to read. My rule of thumb is that if it looks like the manufacturer doesn't want you to know what a product contains, you're better off without it.

In an odd way, the comprehensiveness of such lists is itself reassuring, seeming to imply that nothing could be left to reveal. The food industry counts upon such naivete. Those who complain about government regulations need to remember that some businesses will go to great lengths to conceal all information not specifically mandated to be given to consumers. A series of loopholes had allowed much potentially useful information to be left out of lists. As is the case with most obscure government regulations, the once-meaningful rationale has been lost in nearly forgotten history.

Standards of Identity and Other Crises
Back in 1938, far more foods were prepared in the home, from scratch, than is the case today. The stereotypical Mom did the bulk of both the cooking and the shopping in that era, and no one had any idea that a role fixed in tradition and necessity could someday become a demeaning stereotype. Quite the opposite. Insult Mom by implying she didn't know what went into familiar foods? That would be as bad as hinting that her Sunday dinners of high-cholesterol pot roast, boiled-into-submission vegetables and lard-based apple pie were somehow unhealthy.

The FDA, therefore, was less concerned about identifying the ingredients in familiar foods than in insuring that manufacturers were held to Mom's high standards when they made these foods for retail sale. Thus were standards of identity born. Take Mom's fruit jelly as an example. She sought that delicate balance of sweetness and bite by mixing roughly equal quantities of fruit and sugar. That made sense when the fruit came from a tree in the backyard, but fruit was the more expensive half of the equation for giant food processors. They always had the temptation to skimp on the good stuff and add more sugar to compensate.

What the 1938 act did was prescribe minimum standards for hundreds of foods. Any jar labeled "jelly" had to have at least 45% fruit. Peanut butter had to contain at least 90% peanuts. And so on and on and on, in painstaking detail. Manufacturers could make products as high over those minimums as they liked, but any products that didn't meet the standards had to wear conspicuous and off-putting "imitation" or "substitute" labels. A good deal for all: The public was protected and the food industry got a break.

Because the standards of identity were available for anyone to see— anyone who knew their way around the Code of Federal Regulations, that is—these standardized foods were also exempted from the labeling provisions of the Act when used as ingredients in other products. Until the new rules were passed, in other words, peanut butter jars had to list all the ingredients used within but a box of peanut butter cookie mix, say, could just list peanut butter with no further elaboration.

Times have changed. I do half the cooking and shopping in my household, but I've never made jelly or peanut butter from raw ingredients and I'm not likely to. Like most everyone else, I get my foods from supermarkets and specialty stores and I want to know exactly what is being put in them with no assumptions made about my level of knowledge.

The FDA (caving in to present-day realities or boldly casting off tradition, take your pick) now agrees. Under rules now in effect, all ingredients, even of standardized foods, have to be listed on all labels. (The U.S. Department of Agriculture also requires full ingredient labeling on all meat and poultry products under its jurisdiction.)

Why is this such an important change for those with LI? Because some standardized foods can contain dairy products.

Take margarine as a prime example. Margarine's status as a standardized food did not excuse manufacturers from placing full ingredients lists on the tubs, packages and squeeze bottles of margarine they made. However, when margarine was used as an ingredient in other foods no more than the bare word "margarine" needed to be listed. Was that margarine made with milk? There was usually no way to tell.

The new rules, which went into effect May 1994, eliminate any possible confusion. Margarine, even in other products' ingredients lists, must have its own ingredients spelled out. Any dairy products used in its manufacture will be there to see. Other potentially dairy-containing standardized foods—chocolate, for example—are treated the same way.

"Nondairy" – A Non-truth?

Another interesting and important rule change concerns casein (sometimes listed in the form of sodium, potassium or calcium caseinate). Casein is a milk protein, normally of no concern to those with LI. But it is of great concern to those with milk allergies, since it is specifically the proteins to which they are allergic. A great many others, from galactosemics to vegans to those trying to keep strictly kosher, also urgently need to know when any milk products might be present (*see box*).

Caseinates are in many foods, but nowhere is their presence more confusing than their use in so-called "nondairy" products. How can this be? Simple. The nondairy tag was needed to satisfy state law rather than a term regulated by the FDA. It's a holdover from the days when the dairy-producing states did things like refuse to allow manufacturers to add color to margarine, thereby ensuring that the naturally pale white oleo would look unappetizing compared with the more expensive butter. Forcing a "nondairy" label on milk substitutes was part of this strategy. The fact that certain ingredients might be derived from milk was not an issue.

No more. Under the new rules, any caseinate-containing product that carries a nondairy label must say in its list of ingredients "caseinate (a milk derivative)" or the appropriate equivalent. This is another example of the importance of always reading ingredients lists. Relying on the manufacturer's labeling, even if that label is "nondairy," just isn't enough.

Protein Hydrolysates

Hydrolyzed proteins have been broken down into their constituent amino acids before being added to foods. They have a million uses—leavening agents, stabilizers, thickeners, flavorings, flavor enhancers, even as nutrients in their own right. In the past, while you might have seen them specifically mentioned in an ingredients list, they were equally likely to be buried under "flavorings" or "natural flavors" or listed simply as "hydrolyzed protein." Generic hydrolyzed protein could be of either animal or vegetable origin. And if it came from an animal—you guessed it, we're talking hydrolyzed casein here.

The new rules state that the sources of all protein hydrolysates now must be identified. The largest audience for the new rules are those who need to avoid all foods derived from an animal source, rather than the LI: If processed casein has little in the way of lactose, casein that has been further processed by being broken down into its constituent parts will likely have even less. Since hydrolysates are used as a safe way to provide protein in infant formulas for allergic babies, the vast majority even of older children and adults who eat hydrolysate-containing foods should feel no ill effects.

LACTOSE AND CASEINATE

Caseins are a complex of milk proteins, a separate constituent of milk from the sugar, lactose. Both caseins and lactose are finely dispersed throughout liquid milk (technically, in a colloidal suspension) and will stay there indefinitely. Getting either out of the liquid they're floating in takes deliberate effort. Commercial processors use enzymes or acids to coagulate the casein and precipitate it out. Coagulated casein protein has a much more familiar—and friendlier—name: curds, which are the basis for most cheese. As I explained in Chapter 6, stopping the process there produces such familiar soft cheeses as neufchâtel and cream and cottage cheeses. They are relatively high in lactose, at least for cheese, because some of the remaining whey and the lactose it contains gets trapped in with the curds.

Commercial processors don't need to stop there, of course. If they choose, they can wash the casein curd to remove the remaining whey and then dry the residue to a granular powder. Although it can be used in that form as a protein supplement, casein has limited usability is most recipes because it will not dissolve in water. That's why it's usually converted to the sodium (or calcium or potassium) caseinate found on most package labels. How perfectly lactose-free the final product is will depend on the specifics of the manufacturer and the manufacturing process.

Belief in their processors is what allows some firms to state explicitly on their labels that sodium caseinate is not a source of lactose. Some caseinate does contain lactose, however; as much as the 0.4%–1.2% lactose researchers have detected in some studies. Is this a concern? As the caseinate will be only a small percentage of any given food, a small percentage of a small percentage is unlikely to cause a noticeable reaction even in someone severely LI.

Others, however, can be harmed even by these tiny quantities. People with milk protein allergies are usually sensitive specifically to the casein proteins. They should avoid products containing caseinate. While those with the rare metabolic disorder galactosemia will not be affected by proteins, they must avoid all traces of galactose in the diet. As galactose is found in lactose, texts on galactosemia warn that they must scrupulously avoid caseinates just in case. (*See Chapter 14* for more information on these ailments.)

The presence of caseinate is also sufficient to deprive a product of a pareve label and force a "Kosher-Dairy" label on it to maintain kosher certification. Vegans will also want to avoid caseinate-containing products.

Those with extreme allergic sensitivities should be very careful to check ingredients lists, for they may find casein mentioned where they would never have suspected it. The unspecified hydrolyzed protein in canned tuna, for example, was in the past often from casein and allergic reactions following its consumption have been documented in the medical literature.

"Not a Source of Lactose"

The caseinate rulings may not solve other potential confusion created by nondairy labeling. While the original purpose of the nondairy designation was to flag goods not made with butter, milk or cream, its more recent use appeared to allow so-called nondairy products to include as an ingredient any dairy product that did not contain milk fat. The most jaw-droppingly astounding example I have in my collection of bizarre product labels is one from something called "Evaporated Mellorine," whose label states that it is "not a dairy product but a blend of nonfat dairy solids and vegetable oil." First ingredient: skimmed milk. For those of us with LI, there were even worse examples. I have packets of several brands of powdered nondairy creamers which contain both sodium caseinate and reduced minerals whey. As reduced minerals whey is 70%–80% lactose its use in your coffee would be like starting the day with a laxative.

I can no longer find examples of such products on my local supermarket shelves today, implying that the FDA is gaining some control over nondairy products. We can only hope that the use of the terms "no lactose" or "lactose-free" will soon get equal attention. I've seen a sugar-free candy that displays "NO LACTOSE" in big letters across the package front. On the back, however, it is revealed that the second ingredient is unsalted butter. Although it is possible to find sources to back up a claim that butter is lactose-free, even a specially-made butter is almost certain to contain some percentage of lactose, however tiny.

The NLEA recognizes food processing realities when it redefines the word "free" to mean minimal. "Fat-free" or "sodium-free" foods may have a tiny amount of residual fat or sodium, in other words. As yet, "lactose-free" has no such official reinterpreted meaning. Free here still means free. Technically, according to state and FDA regulators I've talked to, the presence of any lactose whatsoever should preclude the use of a lactose-free label, although none knew of any formal complaints. What may appear to be pedantic quibbling becomes a true issue when applied to products that use caseins. In one of the few acknowledgments of LI in mainstream packaged foods, a number of companies have taken to stating specifically in ingredients lists that the sodium caseinate they use is "not a source of lactose." This assuredly means that it is not a significant source of lactose (*see box on previous page*). Can we take this as a guarantee that no lactose at all truly remains?

The state and federal officials I spoke with weren't sure, noting that the availability of new ultrasensitive analysis techniques capable of detecting one lactose molecule among a billion others would make it likely that they could find some lactose in any dairy-derived product. We are venturing into realms that verge on the metaphysical here. It is probably beyond the bounds of physical possibility to know that every last lactose molecule has been removed from any test sample. Even if the sample passed the one-in-a-billion test, how could anyone know if it would also pass a one-in-a-trillion test?

Once again, the issue is not a very meaningful one for the LI and I hope I've apprised those others who are looking to avoid milk of the snares and dangers. Write to the FDA if you want your opinion to be considered in future regulation changes. In the meantime, write to manufacturers if you have complaints about their labeling or want reassurances about the absolute purity of their products. And you can take notice of the good examples out there.

Gisé Crème Glacé, a frozen dessert competitor to ice cream (that Crème alone is an indication that it is a dairy alternative as only real dairy products can use the actual word Cream) is made from "delactosed sweet milk whey." Nonetheless, its brochure is overlaid with a fine tracing of lawyer tracks. The claims made are modest, careful and undoubtedly true: Gisé, it says, contains *low* lactose and can be enjoyed by *most* lactose intolerants.

It's nice to know that companies are becoming well enough aware of LI to want our business and market their products to us. It's even nicer when they understand exactly what our needs are.

THE NEW NUTRITION LABEL

There it is (Figure 1) in all its glory, 41 numbers or percentages crammed into a space about the size of your TV's remote control. Thousands of hours of testing, controversy and compromise went into its creation. The result is a label that hits just about every hot issue in the national debate over nutrition and health. I like the new labels: I think they're a vast improvement over the old ones. People who read the labels regularly can make intelligent and informed decisions about where the foods they eat fit into their overall diet, and that was the whole point of the exercise. But there are also subtleties and stories behind virtually every item on the label that are worth looking into.

SERVING SIZE

How many of you drink half of a can of soda pop and put the rest away for later? Or eat half a brownie? Or a third of a can of soup? The old labels allowed manufacturers who couldn't make their foods look healthy any other way to play games with the serving size. Most 12 ounce cans of cola used a 6 ounce serving size, thereby cutting the Calorie count down to something that looked respectable. Soup companies used servings too tiny for a child, probably because their sodium content would seem gigantic otherwise. They assumed, rightly, that few people would bother to do the math needed to multiply all the information by 2 or 3 to get the true, and unappetizing, numbers.

THE NEW FOOD LABEL

Nutrition Facts

Serving Size 1 cup (228g)
Servings Per Container 2

Amount Per Serving

Calories 260   Calories from Fat 120

% Daily Value*

Total Fat 13g	**20**%
Saturated Fat 5g	**25**%
Cholesterol 30mg	**10**%
Sodium 660mg	**28**%
Total Carbohydrate 31g	**10**%
Dietary Fiber 0g	**0**%
Sugars 5g	
Protein 5g	

Vitamin A 4%   •   Vitamin C 2%

Calcium 15%   •   Iron 4%

* Percent Daily Values are based on a 2,000 calorie diet. Your daily values may be higher or lower depending on your calorie needs.

	Calories:	2,000	2,500
Total Fat	Less than	65g	80g
Sat Fat	Less than	20g	25g
Cholesterol	Less than	300mg	300mg
Sodium	Less than	2,400mg	2,400mg
Total Carbohydrate		300g	375g
Dietary Fiber		25g	30g

Calories per gram:
Fat 9 • Carbohydrate 4 • Protein 4

This scam is over, mostly. The FDA actually went out and did national food consumption surveys to find out how many ounces of soup or how much of a can of soda people are likely to eat at one sitting, or, in the romantic jargon of the bureaucrat, one "eating occasion." As a result, the NLEA creates "Reference Amounts" (short for "Reference Amounts Customarily Consumed Per Eating Occasion") for 139 FDA-regulated food product categories. Serving sizes now have to relate to these reference amounts, grounding them in reality rather than manufacturers' whims. Moreover, with fairly uniform serving sizes, comparisons between different brand names of similar foods become meaningful, as do the health claims (such as reduced fat) that have also been regulated.

The serving sizes are still not quite perfect. The sample nutrition label in Figure 1 (from a frozen macaroni and cheese product, if you're curious) lists a serving size of ½ cup. Perhaps it's just my limited experience with macaroni and cheese but neither 1 cup nor the weight equivalent of 228 g is a meaningful amount to me. Like it or not, all weights and volumes on the new labels will be in metric measures. If you have your calculator handy and know that there are 28.375 grams to the ounce, it all becomes clear: This serving is almost exactly a quarter pound of macaroni and cheese. Table 1 lists the reference amounts and their equivalent household

TABLE 1
REFERENCE AMOUNTS AND EQUIVALENTS FOR DAIRY PRODUCTS

PRODUCT CATEGORY	REFERENCE AMOUNT	HOUSEHOLD MEASURE
Milk	240 milliliters (ml)	1 cup
Eggnog	120 milliliters (ml)	½ cup
Half & Half	30 milliliters (ml)	2 tablespoons (Tbsp)
Cream (fluid)	15 milliliters (ml)	1 tablespoon (Tbsp)
Cottage Cheese	10 grams (g)	½ cup
Grated Hard Cheese	5 grams (g)	1 tablespoon (Tbsp)
All Other Cheese	30 grams (g)	1 slice; 1 ounce (oz)
Butter	1 tablespoon (Tbsp)	1 tablespoon (Tbsp)
Dairy Dips	2 tablespoons (Tbsp)	2 tablespoons (Tbsp)
Ice Cream; Frozen Yogurt	½ cup	½ cup
Sour Cream	25 grams (g)	2 tablespoons (Tbsp)
Yogurt	225 grams (g)	1 cup

OTHER EQUIVALENTS
1,000 milliliters (ml) equal 1 liter (l), or just over 1 quart.
1,000 milligrams (mg) equal 1 gram (g).
1 pound (lb) equals 454 grams (g).
1 ounce (oz) equals 28 grams (g).
1 cup (liquid measure) equals 8 fluid ounces, 16 tablespoons or ½ pint.
1 fluid ounce (fl oz) equals 30 milliliters (ml).
1 teaspoon (tsp) equals 5 milliliters (ml).

measures for some common dairy products, along with a few other useful equivalents.

Nutrition Facts and Daily Values

Important as serving sizes are, they're just a base on which to build the information we really want: Nutrition Facts, as the FDA calls them. Here's where the new labels shine, providing more and better information than before.

The sample label shown as Figure 1 gives the amounts of 14 nutrients (or dietary components, in FDA-speak) the absolute minimum required by law. These mandatory components cover the hottest nutrition issues: fat, cholesterol, sodium, fiber. Manufacturers can, if they wish, cater to other constituencies by voluntarily listing certain other components. The complete roster of mandatory and voluntary components is given in Table 2. No other components than those shown in Table 2 can appear on any label, at least for the present. I'll have more to say about that in a moment.

TABLE 2 DIETARY COMPONENTS LEGALLY ALLOWABLE ON THE NEW NUTRITION LABELS	
MANDATORY COMPONENTS	**VOLUNTARY COMPONENTS**
Total Calories	
Calories from fat	Calories from saturated fat
Total fat	
Saturated fat	Polyunsaturated fat
	Monounsaturated fat
	Stearic acid (meat & poultry products only)
Cholesterol	
Sodium	Potassium
Total carbohydrate	
Dietary fiber	Soluble fiber
	Insoluble fiber
Sugars	Sugar alcohol (from sugar substitutes like xylitol, mannitol and sorbitol)
	Other carbohydrate (the difference between total carbohydrate and the sum of dietary fiber, sugars and sugar alcohols, if declared)
Protein	
Vitamin A	% of Vitamin A present as beta-carotene
Vitamin C	
Calcium	
Iron	Other essential vitamins and minerals
NOTE: If food is fortified or enriched with an otherwise optional component, listing that information becomes mandatory.	

The value of the makeover rests in the new label elements. They're worth the fuss and expense because they put into perspective the difficult-to-interpret raw numbers of the mandatory components. Look at the sample in Figure 1. Yes, even the old nutrition labels would have told you that our frozen macaroni and cheese has 13 g of fat. But how meaningful was that? Could you have said whether that made it a high-fat food? And, since 13 g is the equivalent of only a half-ounce of fat, would you have known whether that was enough to make a difference in your diet?

Questions like these prompted the FDA to add the "Calories from Fat" line and the "% Daily Value" column to the new labels, giving you a fair chance to come up with the answers. In this example, we can see at a glance that a 260 Calorie serving has 120 Calories from fat. I think it's fair to say that a macaroni and cheese dinner that has 46% of its Calories from fat is a high-fat food. But so is a potato chip. The question remains, what will eating a serving do to your diet? Check the % Daily Value column. That seemingly tiny half-ounce of fat is 20% of the *maximum* amount of fat you should eat in a day. If the rest of your diet is fairly low in fat, that's okay. If not, you may be heading for some potentially serious health problems.

In general, then, the % Daily Values give you the information you need to try to keep down those dietary components that are bad for you (fat, saturated fat, cholesterol and sodium) and boost the nutrients that are good for you (fiber, vitamins and minerals).

Between standardized serving sizes and % Daily Values, it's now much easier to determine how healthful a food really is. Moreover, it's a snap making direct comparisons between similar foods from different companies to see which best fits your personal dietary needs. And they've even gone to the trouble of printing right on the labels some suggested goals for a 2,000 Calorie diet (and a 2,500 Calorie one on larger labels).

Voluntary Dietary Components

Labels that include some or all of the voluntary components should make it even easier to fine-tune a diet to your individual needs. The amounts of total fat and saturated fat in a food are mandatory components because their intake is known to be a risk factor for coronary heart disease. There are many other types of fats, of course, and all of them seem to be in the headlines at one time or another. Their seeming ability to lower cholesterol counts make polyunsaturated and monounsaturated fats the ones of most interest, and so the FDA allows manufacturers to voluntarily break these out on their labels. You say you don't find them listed specifically on some of your favorite foods? Write to the manufacturers involved and encourage them to do so.

But what about the triglycerides which caused a recent scare over margarine, or the omega-3 fatty acids which may allow you to safely eat even a high-fat diet? As of this writing, manufacturers can't mention them at all on a label. The FDA's position is that there is simply not enough evidence to say whether these fats are good or bad. Unless and until there is, including the information implies hopes or warnings that may not be warranted.

There is one other dietary component that I would love to see specifically listed on every food product in the universe. You guessed it: lactose. Because lactose is not on the voluntary list, manufacturers cannot put it onto a nutrition label if they want to. (They can, of course, slap a big "lactose-free" across the package front if they choose—and if it's true.) There is only one way to make this happen. All of us who are LI must write to the FDA, requesting that lactose be included as a voluntary— maybe even someday a mandatory—component. The address to write to is:

Director
Office of Food Labeling
Food and Drug Administration
200 C Street SW
Washington, DC 20204

Customizing the Nutrition Facts
Now the bad news. There's still some work left for you to do.

Men and women have very different dietary needs. So do the young and old, overweight and underweight, athlete and couch potato. One set of Daily Values can't possibly be right for all of them. Indeed, in the search for a one-size-fits-all compromise, the FDA emerged with a set of recommendations based on the needs of a population segment that might not be your first guess of the national average: postmenopausal women.

Here's their reasoning. We know, says the FDA, that the % Daily Values have to be based on something, and that something has to be the number of Calories eaten in a day. The national average daily Calorie count is 2,350. So we proposed that and got shot down. You need a round number as a base, we were told, or else ordinary consumers will find it too hard to scale the numbers up or down to match their own diets. Well, 2,000 Calories is a nice round number. And it just happens to approximate the maintenance Calorie requirements of postmenopausal women. Hmmm, they're the group most often targeted for weight reduction, and we're trying to change everybody's habits so that they eat less fat and cholesterol anyway. Sounds perfect. Now, does anyone want to volunteer to explain all this to the public?

Everybody else took one step backwards, leaving me to do the dirty work. So how do the % Daily Values apply to you? First, you have to know approximately how many Calories you eat in a day. Unless you're on a strict and probably supervised diet, you probably have no idea. I certainly don't. National studies, though, show that virtually everybody over the age of puberty, except the few keeping those strict and supervised diets, eats well over 2,000 Calories a day. Men, especially growing teenage boys, may eat a full 3,000 Calories a day.

In short, if you normally eat well over 2,000 Calories a day, attempting to keep your % Daily Values of such nasties as fat, saturated fat, cholesterol and sodium down to the levels suggested on nutrition labels will force a healthier diet by drastically cutting these negatives. The flip side is that you may wind up skimping yourself on fiber, vitamins, minerals and other such good stuff by keeping to artificially low suggested values. A close reading and understanding of the label is a requirement for those who don't conform to the national average. You might also want to doublecheck your needs for vitamins and minerals by paying attention to the Recommended Dietary Allowances (RDA) that were talked about in Chapter 4. But even with some extra work involved, the added information is not a bad bargain.

A Few Other Facts About the Nutrition Facts

Other Label Types

- Packages too small for the full nutrition label (tuna cans, e.g.) can use a simplified label that only contains the basic required dietary components.
- Foods that basically have no nutritional value except for Calories (soda pop, e.g.) can use an even simpler label, to spare consumers the ugly sight of all those zeros where the % Daily Values would be.
- Labels of foods for children under 2 will carry no information about fat. Too many parents seem to think that the restrictions on fat in their diet should also apply to their children's. Very young children need fat for adequate growth and development, so the FDA doesn't want to do anything to discourage their getting it.
- Foods in weird packages (egg cartons, e.g.) can have the nutrition label as an insert or on a hanging tag.

Foods Which Will Not be Labeled

- Foods produced by small businesses.
- Foods served for immediate consumption (restaurants, sidewalk vendors, cafeterias, airplanes, etc.).
- Ready-to-eat (not pre-packaged) foods from bakeries, delis and candy stores.
- Bulk foods.
- Foods which contain no significant amounts of any nutrients (plain coffee and tea, flavor extracts, food colors, spices, etc.).

▌ LET'S PLAY DICTIONARY

Nutrition Claims

Have you ever picked up a bag of potato chips that had the words "LOW FAT" plastered across its front in letters as large and brightly colored as those on the side of the Goodyear blimp and wondered, "Low fat? Compared to what? Deep-fried mozzarella sticks?"

Wonder no more. Under the new FDA rules, a product can only claim "low fat" if it has three or fewer grams of fat in a serving. A "reduced fat" bag of potato chips has to have at least 25% less fat than its original counterpart. Nothing can be called "fat free" unless it has less than 0.5 g. of fat per serving.

By pairing nine core terms from column A (fewer, free, good source, high, less, light [or lite], low, more [or added] and reduced) with six nutrition categories from column B (Calories, cholesterol, fat, fiber, sodium and sugar) the FDA created a series of definitions as long as a Chinese menu and with much of the same kind of overlap. Just as moo shu chicken and moo shu pork are the same dish except for the meat used, "reduced Calories" and "reduced sugar" both have the same definition (at least 25% less than the original) applied to different types of foods.

Few of these terms have any direct connection to LI as far as I can see, so there's no need to spend pages listing them all here. (*See the box earlier in this chapter for sources of more detailed information.*) But I do want to issue warnings about a couple.

* "Free," as in "Calorie free" or "fat free," does not necessarily mean zero. It can mean merely extremely low, or a dietarily negligible amount. A "Calorie free" beverage, for example, is one with five or fewer Calories per serving. People who want to avoid any amount, no matter how small, had still better read the ingredients and nutrition labels very carefully.
* "No added" is not the same as no. The term is used when that item is already naturally present in the food. A food (applesauce, e.g.) claiming "no added sugar" cannot have had any sugar, nor any ingredient containing sugar, added to its recipe, but that doesn't necessarily mean it's sugar-free.
* Terms that apply to foods with standards of identity have special restrictions. A "low-fat" or "light" version of such a food must be nutritionally equal to the original. For example, the standard for sour cream requires that it be 18% fat. A manufacturer can't just remove half the fat and then market the resulting product as "light" sour cream because in the process of removing the fat some of the vitamin A is also lost. To avoid calling the product "imitation light" sour cream, vitamin A must be put back in.

Health Claims

Companies trumpeting claims that things bad for you have been taken out of their products (or never added in the first place) are likely to try to convince you that their products can actually make you healthier. The slightest hint that a food will cure a disease has historically been one of the FDA's biggest no-nos, a sure way to summon the government's wrath. But with the feds themselves busily saying that a healthy diet can help lower the risk of such major killers as cancer and heart disease, preventing manufacturers from repeating those claims came to look more and more hypocritical. The NLEA completely reversed the FDA's former position, making the U.S. the first country in the world to allow health claims on food labels. Only seven very specific, and very limited, claims about the relationship between diet and disease are being allowed, but more may be added as the evidence warrants. Note that claims can only say "may" or "might," not "will."

The seven claims are:

- Limiting your sodium intake may help reduce your risk of hypertension (high blood pressure).
- Limiting your saturated fat and cholesterol intake may help reduce your risk of heart attacks.
- Limiting your total fat intake may help reduce your risk of cancer.
- Eating fruits, vegetables and fiber-containing grain products, particularly soluble fibers, may help reduce your risk of coronary heart disease.
- Eating fruits, vegetables and fiber-containing grain products may help reduce your risk of cancer.
- An adequate supply of calcium may help reduce your risk of osteoporosis.

Obviously, it's that last claim that has the most relevance for those trying to cut back on or avoid milk. Exactly when and how it may be used is subject to a maze of "if"'s, "but"'s, "only if"'s, "never"'s and "wait a minute, I thought you said"'s that keep food companys' lawyers working overtime.

The tripwires lie in the FDA's efforts to encourage the use of positive nutrients (calcium, e.g.) and discourage the use of negative ones (fat, e.g.). To qualify for a health claim, a food has to have both sufficiently large quantities of the positive nutrients *and* sufficiently low quantities of the negatives. Whole milk is naturally high in calcium but it doesn't qualify for the calcium health claim. Why? It's too high in fat. Nor can the calcium claim be used if the product contains more phosphorus than calcium.

So where will you see the calcium claim? On skim, 1% and 2% milks and variations thereof, and on yogurt, tofu, calcium-fortified citrus drinks and even some calcium supplements.

What the claim can say is wrapped up in almost as many qualifiers as where it can be used. The FDA says the wording of calcium claims must say that:

- The chances of developing osteoporosis vary with race, sex and age;
- Regular exercise and a healthy diet are essentials for reducing risk;
- Raising bone mass early in life reduces the risk of fractures later on;
- Those at greatest risk for developing osteoporosis later on are white and Asian teenage and young adult women; and
- There's no sense in overdoing the calcium since a daily intake of over 2,000 mg doesn't add any extra protection.

How easy will that be to accomplish? Here's a sample claim provided by the FDA:

> "Regular exercise and a healthy diet with enough calcium helps teens and young adult white and Asian women maintain good bone health, and may reduce their high risk of osteoporosis later in life."

I think that's a fine job of cramming the most information into the smallest possible space, but you'll notice that they still left out the bit about not overdoing it.

In general, foods carrying health claims must contain at least 10% of the Daily Value of any of the positive nutrients (calcium, fiber, iron, protein, vitamin A and vitamin C). They also can contain no more than 20% of the Daily Value of the negatives (cholesterol, fat, saturated fat and sodium). Products that combine several different foods into a whole meal (TV dinners, e.g.) are allowed somewhat higher negatives.

Health claims do not apply to infant formulas, foods intended for children under 2 years, medical foods or foods regulated as drugs.

11

MILK ON AISLE 1,
AND 2, 3, 4, 5, 6, . . .

My neighborhood supermarket contains 15 long aisles of products, not including the separate bakery, deli, gourmet shoppe, meat and produce sections. Conservatively, some 50,000 different products line the shelves. And it's one of the smaller stores in the chain. The larger stores have more selection, more products from smaller companies, more international foods, more bulk items, more variety of every kind.

That's the good news. Maximizing one's variety and breadth of selection is critical whenever you're on a special or restricted diet. Dairy products are the norm in this country, remember. Standard national brands are likely to include them in their recipes as a matter of course. It will be the smaller brands, the niche products needing to differentiate themselves from the giants as tastier, healthier, cheaper or vegetarian that offer you the best chance of finding milk-free alternatives. (The best place to find large numbers of these niche products, conspicuously displayed and compactly grouped, is at a health food store. They may be the only place to locate certain problematic milk-free alternatives, such as frozen onion rings or waffles.)

The bad news is that you have to find them yourselves. Nobody publishes listings of lactose-free products: Any such list, even if someone were foolish, er, courageous enough to attempt such a gargantuan task, given the thousands of food suppliers in this country, many only local or regional, would be out of date before it hit paper. (Perhaps in some distant high-tech future an instantly updateable on-line service will solve this aspect of the problem.) Adding to the confusion, some brands adapt their recipes to variations in regional tastes. A product that's milk-free in the Northeast may not be so in the Southwest, or vice versa.

The reason for this turmoil is that supermarkets run on tiny profit margins, with packaged goods contributing the least to the bottom line. Stores are far more likely to expand their meat or produce departments than add another long middle aisle (called a prison in the trade) that keeps the customer away from the high profit zones around the store's perimeter. With an annual horde of 10,000 new items jockeying for position on a fixed quantity of shelf space, only the strongest survive. The few major food conglomerates always have the edge in this competition. Smaller and niche brands, doomed without advertising clout, money to pay stocking fees or the ability to lower wholesale costs, are usually the first to go in the neverending shelf wars. Every year brings a cry of anguish as I find that another product I had depended upon has vanished from the shelves. Even the majors constantly evolve to meet shifting tastes, and if that means changing a familiar recipe so that it now contains milk, so be it. Supermarkets are like glaciers: They may appear unchanged with each visit, but they're really always on the move.

Dividing 50,000 products by one of you may seem like an overwhelming task, especially if you're just discovering that you or someone in your family is LI and you want to cut back on—or at least get a better idea of—the amount of milk products you've been getting from packaged food. To make it manageable, first cut back on the clutter. You know best whether you cook everything from scratch, depend on frozen foods or ignore supermarkets entirely in favor of natural or health food stores. Concentrate at first on what you use most. No one person or family, however large, uses every single product category. Nor does it matter how many brands of toilet tissue or hair spray a store carries. Only food items count.

If you've been taking those foods for granted before, however, you can no longer do so. Most of us spend a good deal of our time in supermarkets anyway. Use that time wisely. Search out new foods, new brands, new varieties. Go beyond eye level, where the most popular products are shelved, and scour the bottom and top shelves for less familiar items that can replace old favorites. Handle everything, especially in the beginning. You should train yourself to read the ingredients lists on every product you plan to buy, every single time, both to guard against recipe changes and to develop a better feel for which product types are most likely to contain milk products. Check the adjacent nutritional information as well. You may find yourself eating better without even meaning to.

After 16 years and countless hours of walking the aisles, I sometimes forget these rules myself. Occasionally I'll even bring home a product that turns out to have milk in it after all. I get mad at myself when I do that, though not because of the milk. My goal is not to fanatically avoid all milk products in all forms, but to make when, where and how much milk I consume a conscious and deliberate set of decisions. My decisions, not those of an anonymous food technician. Buying lactose-free foods is a convenience. By doing so I only have to check ingredients labels once, in the store, rather than again at home. And I never have to kick myself for forgetting to take a lactase pill with dinner.

You will undoubtedly evolve your own conveniences, rules and exceptions. In the meantime, I'll be happy to pass along a few things I've learned over the years to guide you through the supermarket maze, starting with the magic word that guarantees lactose-free safety every single time.

PAREVE: SAFETY WITH A CAPITAL P

Many groups of people other than those who are LI have an urgent need to know exactly what is—and isn't—in the food they eat. Long before the food industry started putting "lactose free" labels on their products, it responded to the urgings of another group. It did so only because the group, though small in sheer numbers, was sufficiently large, cohesive and motivated to make its wishes known—and because its members were willing to follow through by swinging their purchasing might toward companies who catered to their needs. It's a lesson those of us with LI should take to heart.

This influential group consists of people who follow the Jewish dietary laws, which from the time of the Old Testament have called for a strict prohibition against mixing milk and meat in the same meal. Fortunately for variety, the dietary laws also always recognized a broad third category of neutral foods. Neutral foods, those which are completely free of either milk or meat, are known as "pareve" or "parve" and may be so listed on packages.

English borrowed the term from Yiddish, and that is perhaps why no one can agree on its pronunciation or spelling. Dictionaries give it three syllables, *PAH-ruh-vuh*, but in everyday parlance it might be reduced to *PAR-vuh* or even just *parv*. It probably doesn't matter. Like the new name for the singer once known as Prince, "pareve" is more a symbol for the purposes of print than a word to be voiced. In my experience, most supermarket employees will give you a blank look however you pronounce it.

Because of its origins as a religious prohibition, pareve-ness is an absolute concept. Something can't be slightly pareve; it either is or isn't. The slightest taint of a dairy product will keep a food from being pareve. It is not used lightly even though no one national organization oversees the use of the term. (Nor is there any accepted symbol or abbreviation that indicates that a food is pareve. The word must be written out in full.) Each individual manufacturer must decide whether to put the word on its packaging: Many foods on the market are therefore safely pareve but just not marked that way. Whenever you do see the word on a food label, though, you have a guarantee that no milk whatsoever is to be found inside.

You may have noticed that I haven't yet used the word kosher at all. That's to try to keep the confusion to a minimum. Kosher foods—foods prepared according to the Jewish dietary laws—are not at all the same thing as pareve foods. Pareve foods do not have to be kosher. Many, perhaps most, are not. And kosher foods do not have to be pareve. It is quite possible to have kosher dairy products. Many references misunderstand this difference and erroneously claim that all kosher foods are safe for the LI.

The misunderstanding probably stems from the fact that any kosher food that has meat in it is guaranteed not to have any taint of milk, and any meal that contains meat that is served in a kosher household or restaurant must be similarly completely milk-free. True kosher delis and bakeries are therefore excellent sources of breads, rolls, cookies, cakes, salads and other normally milk-laden foods that have been formulated to be pareve so that they can be used when meats are being served. (On the other hand, they will serve sour cream on a baked potato or cream cheese on a bagel or milk in coffee if no meat is present.) I say true kosher because the time and expense of keeping kosher is so great that some delis are only "kosher-style." These vary as much in their closeness to the real thing as "New York" delis around the country do.

The intricacies of kosher food labeling may also be to blame for some confusion. A "U" in a circle indicates that a food has been certified kosher by the Union of Orthodox Jewish Congregations of America. A "U" in a circle followed by a capital "D," however, has two meanings. It may mean that the food is kosher and contains milk products. It may also mean that the food is kosher and contains no milk products but cannot be considered pareve because it has been manufactured using the same machinery which is used at other times for dairy foods. You should always check the ingredients list on a food package labeled "U, D" to see whether any dairy products are in fact present. This fine religious distinction serendipitously serves a secular medical need as well. There are several cases on record of children with extreme sensitivities to milk proteins having allergic reactions to pareve or nondairy foods which had been processed on such equipment. The "U,D" designation protects them in a way that no ingredient listing ever could. (The "U,P" symbol indicates that a food is kosher for Passover, by the way, not that it is pareve.)

■ LACTOSE IN THE SUPERMARKET

When it comes to searching out lactose in packaged foods, the only rule is that there are no rules. Dairy ingredients are used everywhere, in every kind of product, but without any consistency. One product may be milk-free, while a seemingly identical product from the same company sitting next to it on a shelf may be loaded with lactose. For example, when I last checked, Pepperidge Farm stuffing mixes—including the Herb Seasoned variety—intended for cooking inside poultry were milk-free. Someone not paying very close attention may mistake the inside variety for a second Herb Seasoned Stuffing in a look-alike package that is designed for "top of stove preparation." It lists nonfat milk, butter and cultured buttermilk among its ingredients. Or glance at two varieties of the Mueslix cereal Kellogg's makes. One, Golden Crunch, contains whey; the other, Crispy Blend, does not. Supermarkets are filled with similar pitfalls.

Ingredients lists have a second advantage beyond merely itemizing dairy products. Ingredients in packaged foods must be listed in order by weight. It is physically impossible for more than the first few items to be present in large quantities. A cream soup with milk as the first ingredient is probably mostly milk. A cake listing milk near the bottom probably uses just a smidgen. Even lactose itself, which is found surprisingly often in packaged foods, may not bother you if it's down among the emulsifiers and preservatives.

There is a large gray area between entirely eliminating lactose from your diet and indulging in foods that might lead to a long and unpleasant evening. For those seeking that middle ground, try these rules of thumb:

- Avoid foods in which any dairy product is one of the first three ingredients.
- Avoid products in which dried milk or dried whey in any form is one of the top half dozen ingredients.
- Avoid products which have dried milk or whey plus a second dairy product or which have three or more dairy products of any kind.
- Avoid foods which might tempt you to eat several servings, thereby multiplying the total lactose consumed.

Since I can't possibly take you through a store product by product, let me do the next best thing and give general guidelines by product category.

Beverages

Plain tea, coffee and cocoa are to my knowledge milk-free without exception. Cocoa mixes and flavored "international" coffees will usually have powdered milk mixed in, along with heaps of sugar.

Pasteurizing milk for a short time at very high temperatures allows it to remain at room temperature for long periods without spoiling, as long as it is in a hermetically sealed, aseptic package. The chocolate drinks on the shelf next to the familiar brick packs long used for juices really are milk-based. Milk itself can now be found in that form.

Creme de menthe, creme de cacao or creme de anything are not milk products, either as syrups for topping desserts or as liqueurs. A few liqueurs with cream properly spelled in their titles really do have cream added. Check the spelling to be sure.

Egg "creams" and "cream" sodas do not contain milk. Coconut "milk" is the liquid center of a coconut. Coconut "cream" is made from coconut meat. Piña colada mixes should contain coconut cream and pineapple juice. Some may contain some real milk or cream instead.

Breads

As a general rule, crusty breads and rolls (French, Italian, Vienna, pumpernickel, rye), pita breads and other flatbreads are made without milk. Soft breads are not so easily classifiable. Soft versions of crusty breads are usually milk-free. White breads, along with hot dog and hamburg rolls, vary by baker. You can find milk-free varieties but you'll have to look. Milk-free commercial bread crumbs are very hard to find. If you don't want to make your own by crumbling dry bread, hunt down a Jewish bakery.

Cakes, Pies, Muffins and Doughnuts

A quick course in cooking would be more help than I can provide here, but I'll toss out a few generalizations nonetheless. Cream and pumpkin pies require milk as part of the filling; fruit and meringue pies do not. Lard was once part of the secret of obtaining the lightest, flakiest crust but butter is far more likely to take its place today. Those in-store bakeries may indeed bake some of their own goodies but if the home-made looking pies carry a printed nutrition label you can bet that they've been shipped in frozen. That proved to be the distinction between the milk-free blueberry pies and the adjacent milk-in-the-crust grape pies I ran across yesterday. A few pies in the freezer case can also be found milk-free.

Most store-baked muffins and doughnuts will contain some variety of dairy product. Doughnuts' cream and custard fillings are also milk-based. Brownies and cookies are also likely to contain some lactose, although recipes vary widely.

Angel cakes and the cake part of strawberry shortcakes are normally milk-free. Not so pound cakes, which originally were so named for the pound of butter used in their recipes.

Sheet or layer cakes themselves may or may not be milk-free depending on the personal predilections of the chef. Can't imagine a cake without frosting? Standard frostings on store-bought cakes are whipped cream or buttercream-based. (An alternative is to locate a Jewish bakery, where pareve cakes and pies are common, although they may need to be special-ordered. One I know of celebrates the arrival of fall with a milk-free pumpkin pie, of all amazing things.)

You're better off heading for the packaged cake mix aisle. Basic cake mixes are overwhelmingly likely to be milk-free. Most don't even ask you to add milk to the mix. Still can't imagine a cake without frosting? Except for milk chocolate and white chocolate varieties, most canned frostings are surprisingly milk-free. Pound cakes, coffee cakes, angel cakes and other variations can also be found that don't contain lactose.

Most brownie and cookie mixes are also milk-free, again once you cull out those which use milk chocolate, but be careful to read the very fine print. There's a wild new category that sprouts new flavors and varieties almost daily. I suppose you could call them dessert cakes, since they're full of fruits or candies or fudge. These you'll have to go through one by one, but the majority do have some milk.

Most bread mixes are milk-free, though I found a pumpkin bread that was not. Milk-free muffin mixes, on the other hand, were the exception.

Canned Foods

Although most spaghetti and other pasta products contain cheese in their sauces, a few can be found that are milk-free. Canned chilis, hashes and stews contain no milk, except for chicken stews, which can come in a milk-based gravy. A similar pattern is common among the individual-serving luncheon meals. Beef meals are generally dairy-free, chicken meals often contain milk, spaghettis and pastas almost always do. Canned tuna is lactose-free, but may contain hydrolyzed casein protein, although all the ones I checked recently had hydrolyzed vegetable protein instead.

The use of cheese in spaghetti sauces is common, although it is heavily brand-dependent: some brands almost always use them, some almost never. Most clam sauces are milk-free, unless the name indicates otherwise.

Gravies are likely to contain milk. All the barbecue sauces I've checked have been lactose-free. I don't know of any commercial marinades with milk products but these are more likely to have local or regional brands and variations, so should be checked carefully.

Older lactose-free diets sometimes warn against canned peas. I've never found any reason why. Most canned peas do list sugar among their ingredients, but sugar always means sucrose, not lactose.

"Cream"-style corn is actually packed in a food starch-based paste. I know of no brands which use actual cream. Neither butter beans, butter-flavor potatoes, butternut squash nor buttercup squash contain lactose.

Cereal

A surprising number of cereals contain nonfat milk, nonfat dry milk or whey. If there is a pattern to which do and which do not, I have been unable to detect it. If you put real milk on your cereal, this tiny additional quantity of lactose is insignificant. Ironically, "cream" of wheat or rice cereals tend to be milk-free (although some flavored instants may contain milk products).

Chocolate

Everything about chocolate is designed to produce confusion. It comes from the cacao tree, whose seeds are called beans and misspelled as cocoa. The seeds contain cocoa butter, a fat similar to coconut oil. Just as peanut butter is a paste made from ground-up peanuts and not a milk product, cocoa butter is entirely milk-free. If you grind up cocoa seeds, you also get a pasty substance. This semi-liquid is referred to as chocolate liquor, although it is not alcoholic. Squeeze some of the cocoa butter out of chocolate liquor and you wind up with cocoa powder. Solidifying the chocolate liquor makes baking chocolate. None of those variations contain any milk.

Both chocolate liquor and cocoa powder are used in a huge number of commercial products. Both are also too bitter to be eaten straight so sweeteners must be added to turn them into candy. Dark, semi-sweet and bittersweet chocolate have the least amount of sweetener and are usually milk-free whether they are used as coatings on candy or candy bars, as solid chocolate bars or as chocolate chips. Unfortunately, there are exceptions. For those who conscientiously avoid all dairy products, please note that it is very common to find milk fat or butterfat added to dark chocolates.

While most chocolate chips are semi-sweet unless otherwise marked, you should assume that most chocolate candy bars and candy coatings are milk chocolate until you learn differently.

The beautifully oxymoronic white "chocolate" cannot technically be considered a chocolate, as only cocoa butter and not chocolate liquor is used in its manufacture. In fact, if you look closely, you'll notice that it is usually referred to as a white "confection." It contains a variety of milk solids nonetheless. A wide variety. One brand's ingredients include milk, whey, nonfat milk, lactose, cream and milk fat.

Chocolate or fudge toppings are usually made with milk; chocolate syrups are not. Caramel always implies the use of milk, unless the product is just caramel flavored.

Condiments

"Creamy" mustards refer to their consistency; they do not contain milk. Ketchups, salsas, relishes, horseradish sauces, mayonnaise and similar accoutrements for burgers and sandwiches are equally milk-free.

Cookies and Crackers

Most commercial cookies, especially any with chocolate or chocolate chips, contain whey. (For inexplicable reasons, those same companies' chocolate chocolate chip cookies usually do not.) Old-fashioned vanilla, oatmeal, molasses or ginger cookies are more likely to be milk-free. One warning: The higher-priced the cookie, the more likely it will contain true milk and butter to give it that gourmet cachet. House brands or generics are better bets in this respect.

Standard saltine-style crackers are almost always milk-free, with just enough exceptions to be frustrating. Graham crackers used to be milk-free until they started coming in flavors. A growing trend is for reduced fat or fat-free crackers—and many other products as well—to add whey or non-fat dry milk for flavor, even when the corresponding full fat product is milk-free. Milk crackers and butter crackers are a European style that are often found in gourmet sections. In general, you'll need to examine crackers as thoroughly and individually as you do cookies.

Frozen Foods

The TV dinner has come a long way since the 1950s, and has mostly transcended its earlier state as a near-food experience. Both because frozen dinners (and their entree and individual serving relatives) are a hot segment of the marketplace and because it is so hard to make low-fat frozen food taste better than cardboard, supermarket freezer cases are about as stable as the pictures on a slot machine. New brands, new dishes, new recipes pop up with the monotonous regularity of the target in a shooting arcade—and they are shot down just as quickly. Commenting on anything so volatile requires either taking the risk of being immediately outdated or overgeneralizing the subject down to mush. Mush it is: The vast majority of brands and varieties contain some milk. Reading sufficient ingredients lists to find milk-free dinners means being willing to brave frostbitten fingers but it can be done. Not caring about a bit of butter improves your chances considerably. Less expensive brands are more likely to be milk-free.

Sightings of frozen fish and seafood not covered in a layer of deep-fried flour are slightly more common in the modern low-fat world than in olden days, but still extremely rare. Whether battered or breaded, coatings are likely to contain some milk products, although diligent searching may turn up a few milk-free mavericks. Uncoated fish dishes have a distressing tendency to substitute a butter sauce instead.

French fried potatoes are naturally white. Their deep golden glow comes from a sprayed-on layer of sugar caramelized by the heat of cooking. French fry makers could theoretically use lactose for the purpose, and many lactose-free diets insist that they do, but I've never seen lactose listed on any of the many bags of fries I've examined over the years. Dextrose, the commercial name for good old glucose, is universally used instead. A better use of your time is checking the ingredients lists on those newer varieties of fries made from diced and reformed potatoes. These may well contain milk. Onion ring breadings almost always contains milk.

Plain frozen vegetables virtually never contain lactose, but those that come with sauces almost always involve cheese or butter. No sauce vegetable packages are a recent trend, starting the circle anew, albeit at a higher price. Other vegetable dishes (spinach souffle or scalloped potatoes, e.g.) may have more milk than vegetable.

Virtually all frozen pancakes, waffles and breakfasts contain whey and other milk products. Look for alternative brands in the gourmet section or in health food stores instead.

Surprisingly, not all frozen desserts contain milk, but most do, so choose carefully. Skip the ice cream and sherbets in all their multitude of forms: quarts, bars, sticks and sandwiches. Look for pure frozen fruit bars, sorbets or Italian ices (but not spumonis) instead. I've already tried to sort through the thorny questions about frozen yogurts in Chapter 7, and a discussion of nondairy frozen desserts is found in Chapter 10.

Hot Dogs and Cold Cuts

An old joke tells us that if we want to avoid losing our appetites, we should never look too closely into what went into the making of sausage or legislation. Both have been forced to clean up their acts in recent years.

From our LI point of view, the problem lay not in the various odd portions of hogs and cattle that found a home in the deli case, but in the non-meat fillers that got thrown in both to cheaply bulk out hot dogs and salamis and to add a modicum of taste and protein and other such desirable qualities. Non-fat dry milk was a common filler.

The only sure way to avoid dairy products is to go after kosher meats. Most supermarkets in large cities will carry at least a small selection of kosher hot dogs and cold cuts, although these are usually limited to salami, bologna or pastrami. All are guaranteed not to have any lactose, and most have a minimum at most of other filler. The meat is also sure to be from recognizable parts of an animal because the Jewish dietary laws greatly restrict those portions of a cow that can be considered as kosher.

For those who want a vastly larger array of choices, the non-kosher selection of packaged cold cuts, hot dogs and luncheon meats is less of a minefield than it once may have been. The recent emphasis on health has brought forth a host of low-fat turkey and chicken analogues of ham, salami, pastrami and frankfurters. I just completed a package-by-package survey in a large nearby supermarket and not one of them listed any dairy products among their ingredients.

In fact, even the old-fashioned beef and pork luncheon meats were remarkably lactose-free. Only one or two salami products contained any non-fat dry milk, and those were clearly marked on the front of the package label.

Much the same can be said for the hot dogs. A few companies listed non-fat dry milk among the ingredients; most did not. For some reason, the beef and pork blends were more apt to have added milk. Cheese dogs and variations are obviously not for anyone whose goal is the complete avoidance of dairy products.

Head cheese is not cheese. My dictionary defines it as "A jellied loaf or sausage made from chopped and boiled parts of the feet, head, and sometimes the tongue and heart of an animal, usually a hog." Which is why kosher cold cut firms stay in business.

Salad Dressings

Broadly speaking, there are three types of salad dressings: oil & vinegar-based, mayonnaise-based and milk-based. Even when gussied up, vinaigrettes are unlikely to contain any milk. Commercial mayonnaise-based dressings are the norm: They're usually identifiable by the use of soybean oil high on the ingredients list. Even when self-styled as "creamy" Italian, French, Russian or Thousand Island, these dressings seldom contain milk. On the other hand, virtually every dressing with buttermilk, ranch or caesar in its name will contain milk or cheese, even if it is otherwise mostly soybean oil. True cream-based dressings are rare on supermarket shelves, but less so in restaurants. If in doubt, ask.

Snacks

Good old-fashioned plain pretzels and potato chips will be lactose-free. Unfortunately, this is another hot area in the marketplace in which manufacturers compete by showing off their technical prowess. The latest fad is incorporating the dip into the chip. Any snacks with sour cream, ranch, cheese or nacho as part of the brand name probably contain some milk products. On the other hand, butter-flavored snacks may contain butter flavor without being tainted by any actual butter.

Instant pudding mixes are instant because the milk is already added. Cooked pudding mixes have no milk, but most milk substitutes will not set and so cannot be used. Try a reduced-lactose milk or a soy milk instead. Most ready-to-eat puddings already have milk added.

Soups

Yes, all "cream of . . . ." soups will contain milk, if not cream itself. Unfortunately, so will most other varieties of canned soup, even if cream is not mentioned as part of the name. Nor is there any consistency from brand to brand about which soups are generally milk-free, and even within brands one variety of chicken soup may include milk while another seemingly similar variation does not.

Clear soups—broths and bouillons—are milk-free across the line, as are the various ramen soups. New England clam (or other seafood) chowders are milk-based; Manhattan clam chowders are tomato-based.

Packaged soup mixes may commonly have been lactose-free at one time, but no more. Today as many of them use dairy products—though often in tiny quantities—as do the canned soups.

Spices

Lactose is prized as an anti-caking agent. Spices need to be free-flowing. Is there likely to be a connection? Maybe. Salt substitutes often blend a number of spices to titillate the taste buds in lieu of the flavor-enhancing salt. I've seen brands containing lactose in the past, though none in a recent check. I once even found lactose used in containers of orange and lemon peel.

Other spices are more straightforward. Many brands of butter granules designed for shaking onto baked potatoes (and the like) really do use butter.

List after list of lactose-containing foods include warnings against monosodium glutamate (MSG). I've never been able to actually verify this, and no store brand I've ever looked at lists any lactose. MSG is a flavor-enhancer that is itself tasteless so it is often used in packaged foods in lieu of salt but I know of no reason to believe that any of these foods therefore contain lactose. Given the outcry in recent years over other potential ill-effects of MSG, fewer restaurants automatically add it to their dishes than in the past and virtually all will leave it out upon request.

Packaged spice mixes, like gravy mixes or premixed chili or taco seasoning, often contain milk products. Lactose-free alternatives are almost always available.

"Cream" of tartar is not a dairy product.

Miscellaneous
Many commercial tortillas contain milk.

Butterscotch candies contain butter, although butter rum do not. For that matter, most candies (except clear sour balls, gumdrops, licorice, lollypops and the like) contain some type of milk product.

Peanut butter, like almond butter and the many other types of nut butters, gets its name from its consistency rather than from the presence of any dairy product. The same is true for apple butter and other fruit butters.

In the past, some ready to cook hams and prebasted turkeys were injected with butter or milk to baste from the inside out. Those I checked on a recent supermarket trip used vegetable oil instead.

"Milk" of magnesia is not real milk.

The list of dairy-free foods with milk or cream or butter in their names could probably be long extended (and might make a fun supermarket game for LI kids). The length of the list is tribute to the high regard in which dairy products are held in our culture: A "creamy" product will be considered, at least unconsciously, superior to an ordinary one. There should be little confusion for the LI over the vast majority of these products, but their existence indicates the distance we have yet to travel to win equality with the milk drinkers.

12

EATING IN AND DINING OUT

In a world with 100% lactose-free milk available in every supermarket, where restaurants will customize dishes to accommodate every special dietary need and when commercials for lactase products appear on national television, it is hard even for me to remember the days when LI was akin to a culinary prison sentence in solitary confinement.

Back then I was a special case, both to friends and family and to the chefs and waiters I quizzed about what might be hidden behind innocuous names on menus. Every food seemed forbidden or perilous. I had to relearn what little I knew about cooking. The few special diets aimed at the LI I could find were badly mimeographed handouts put together by a doctor or hospital nutritionist and combined the appetite-whetting appeal of silage with warnings about every food that somebody, somewhere, thought might contain lactose—whether it did or not.

I won't go on. Still, there are a few things I've learned over the years which might be of benefit to some of you, especially those who must for whatever reasons avoid all dairy products. I'll start by passing along a few ideas that can be used to keep your diet as varied as it was before you learned you were LI, even if you don't or can't use reduced-lactose milks, and I'll follow that with a quick glance at the perils of restaurant dining.

▌ HOME COOKING

Basic Sauces
Hundreds of dishes you can't eat at a restaurant are available to you at home—including souffles, casseroles, soups, mousses and croquettes— once you learn two variations on a crucial basic recipe.

This starter recipe comes in two guises: a white sauce and a broth-based variation, known as velouté sauce. These sauces are exceptionally versatile:

1. Just as is, they can be the foundation for casseroles or a seafood mousse;

BASIC VELOUTE SAUCE

2 Tbsp milk-free margarine   2 Tbsp all-purpose flour
Dash each: salt and pepper   1 cup chicken broth or stock

In small saucepan, melt margarine over low heat. Stir flour, salt, and pepper into margarine until smooth and bubbly. Slowly stir in chicken broth. (If you use bouillon from a cube or powder instead of canned or homemade chicken broth, do not add additional salt.) Increase heat and bring to a boil. Stir while boiling one minute or until thick. Makes 1 cup.

---

2. Add other ingredients to flavor them and they can be poured over food to complete a dish;
3. Thicken them, and they become binders for making souffles and croquettes;
4. With liquids and cooked vegetables added, they become soups.

A term you'll see in many cream sauce recipes is *roux*. Normally, a roux is a mixture of melted butter and flour, cooked and used as a thickener to form the base of the sauce. Just substitute a milk-free margarine for the butter.

For a thicker sauce or a souffle base, double the amount of margarine and flour without changing the liquid used in either recipe.

It's difficult, though not impossible, to ruin either sauce. The most common errors are using too high a heat or leaving the sauce unattended on the stove, both of which can cause the sauce to burn. I find I can turn the heat up to medium, and stir only occasionally (especially if I'm preparing another part of the meal), without destroying the sauce. You've got to catch it as it starts boiling, however.

A few more hints. Cook the roux for a minute or so before adding the

---

BASIC WHITE SAUCE

2 Tbsp milk-free margarine   2 Tbsp all-purpose flour
Dash each: salt and pepper   ½ cup (4 oz.) milk substitute
½ cup water

In small saucepan, melt margarine over low heat. Remove from heat and stir in flour, salt, and pepper until smooth. Slowly stir in milk substitute and water. Cook over low heat, stirring constantly, until mixture just comes to a boil. (This will take much longer than you think, and you may want to increase the heat just a *little* to speed things up.) Makes 1 cup.

liquid; otherwise you may taste raw flour in the final product. You can increase the ratio of flour to margarine, increase or decrease the ratio of roux to liquid, or add flavoring at any step in the process to create interesting variations or meet the needs of a particular recipe. Too much margarine unbalanced by flour, however, may make the sauce taste greasy.

The two sauces do have some subtle differences between them. Any plain white sauce is quite bland (some cookbooks compare it to library paste) but this very blandness prevents its taste from competing with the flavors of the added ingredients. Overboiling may leave a scorched taste from the milk substitute. Veloute sauce has a stronger intrinsic flavor from its chicken stock and is lower in Calories and saturated fats than the white sauce (unless a low-fat milk substitute is used). The natural flavor will enhance the flavor of meat or vegetables because of the stock or broth used as a base. Chicken croquettes, for example, are best based on a veloute sauce as the chicken stock improves the flavor of the entire croquette.

Once you learn to adjust to a milk substitute, there is no reason why you cannot go back to your favorite cookbooks and adapt those recipes directly, provided that you realize that heavily milk-dependent meals may not come out quite the same.

A few dishes are hard to duplicate simply by substituting an equal amount of milk substitute since they do not always behave exactly as their dairy counterparts. Ingenuity and dedicated cooks have developed recipes for virtually every situation.

Substitutions

Nondairy creamers and soy and nut milks, along with the various alternative butters, cheeses, yogurts and toppings discussed in Chapter 9 should provide adequate substitutes for dairy products in almost any recipe, including those in your favorite cookbooks. While you might certainly want to check out specialty nondairy cookbooks (especially those discussed in Chapter 15), I no longer rely on them the way I did when I first learned I was LI. (The one important exception: Puddings and custards do not always set well with nondairy creamers, so it is worthwhile to follow the lead of nondairy experts.) Adapting regular recipes is usually easy enough even for kitchen klutzes like me. For creative nondairy cooking, focus on the cuisines of those countries or ethnic groups who traditionally have never incorporated milk into their cooking, from Japanese to Native American.

If you're just beginning to adapt to a dairy-free kitchen, you may find yourself without the proper commercial nondairy substitute on hand. Don't panic: Every well-stocked kitchen cabinet is filled with ingenious solutions. Some changes in flavor will no doubt result, especially if large quantities of the substitute are used, but that can be part of the fun. Professional chefs do this all the time and get raises and acclaim whenever it works. And if it doesn't? Well, there are 1,094 meals left in the year. You'll get many more chances.

General Tips:

- Milk's major role in many recipes is simply that of a liquid. Try water or fruit juice, beer or wine, coconut milk or syrup drained from canned fruits.
- Beef bouillon or chicken broth work well in sauces. They're salty, so scant on any additional salt the recipe may call for.
- What's the difference between New England and Manhattan clam chowders? The first uses milk as a base, while the latter uses tomato. Tomato bases add flavor to many soups and stews.
- Milk-free margarine can often substitute for butter, but the whipped varieties may scorch at high temperatures. Oil heats well, but should not be used in baking unless specifically stated.
- If you plan to cook with a milk substitute, read the label carefully; it should say how well it will stand up to heat. Yogurt may need to be mixed with cornstarch, for example.
- Whipping nondairy substitutes rarely work; some nondairy whips can be found on the market, however.
- If you can have dairy products, try plain yogurt in recipes or salad dressings in place of sour cream or buttermilk.
- If you have questions about cooking with particular products, for heaven's sake, don't call me; call the manufacturer either at the number given on the label or listed in Chapter 9. If you have complaints or compliments, by all means call with those, too.

■ RESTAURANT DINING

For the LI, changes in restaurants over the past decade are best described in a lyric from gloomy New Jersey bard Bruce Springsteen: "one step forward, two steps back." Most fast food establishments now provide ingredients lists but seem to be adding cheese to every new dish introduced. Menus are much better about describing the contents of entrees than in the past, but that may lull you into failing to quiz the waiter about what might be missing from what made it into print. (A menu I recently ordered from temptingly depicted a grilled swordfish in a wine sauce but neglected to mention that the sauce was one part wine to nine parts cream.) Healthy dishes with less butter and cream sit elbow to elbow with comfort food favorites made dripping with tasty milkfats. The expanded menus in many restaurants are made possible by the import of frozen dishes premade at a central kitchen, about whose ingredients the staffs know little or nothing. French, Mexican and Italian restaurants, with their heavily sauced and cheesed delights, are competing with ever increasing numbers of restaurants featuring cuisines from Asian countries that have traditionally used little milk in their cooking—but which are adding more to accommodate American tastes. Creative and tasty dinners can now be found even at neighborhood diners but leave you at the mercy of their chefs' penchants for putting personal stamps onto standard recipes: cream in the salad dressing, perhaps; sour cream in the cole slaw; real mashed potatoes whipped with real milk and real butter.

Perhaps the best example is to be found in the once humble realm of coffee. The standard accompaniment to a cup of coffee plopped on a diner counter used to be a packet of nondairy creamer. Most diners now have upscaled to the point of using containers of half-and-half instead. And the plague of cappuccino and espresso bars introduces a new hazard for the unwary. Giant-sized double lattes and similar extravaganzas of caffeine may require steaming up to 10 ounces of milk, more than enough to give many people with LI an unpleasant surprise later that night. Well, at least you would be up anyway.

If you don't want to settle for the compromise of having lactase pills always at the ready, you can get lactose-free meals in most restaurants by following four basic steps: 1) have a good working knowledge of where dairy products are most likely to be used; 2) have your waiter check on the ingredients of one or two dishes you're not sure about (don't abuse this by forcing an accounting of every item on the menu); 3) be willing to eat what is available rather than exactly what you're in the mood for; and 4) ask if the chef is willing to create a special meal or variation that leaves out the milk.

It also helps to become a regular at a handful of restaurants. Not only does this allow you to know what accommodations they can make, but through familiarity the chef will become better acquainted to your special needs. (Avoid high-volume times so that you don't become an imposition or take the risk that they will forget your instructions in the rush.) Restaurants always take better care of customers they know, for it keeps them coming back. Tipping well doesn't hurt either. Needless to say, "have it your way" or not, fast food restaurants are less likely to be able to arrange special meals than restaurants in which the manager is attentive, the staff knows what goes into the food and the chef has a reputation of quality to maintain.

You can increase your range of choices by cultivating a taste for those cuisines least likely to use dairy products in the first place. In approximate order of safety, these include:

Kosher Restaurants

True kosher restaurants, and even many kosher-style delis, make a point of religiously separating all dairy products from all meat dishes and from pareve (neutral) foods. Dairy foods can be kosher, contrary to some misinformation on the subject, but should be clearly marked on the menu. A word to your server will preclude any mixups.

Vegetarian Restaurants

Advocates of vegetarian cuisine come in as many levels as a step pyramid, from those whose only proscription is against red meats to true vegans who refuse to eat any food of animal origin. Much vegetarian food is really lacto- or lacto-ovo-vegetarian, the lacto indicating that dairy products are acceptable. But most vegetarian restaurants do feature vegan dishes or can easily prepare them in that fashion. Waiters and chefs are usually knowledgeable and sensitive to individual needs.

Asian Restaurants

East Asian cuisines (Chinese and Japanese) are least likely to use milk in any of their dishes (except possibly desserts). Dairy ingredients begin to sneak into foods that originate farther south and west in Asia (Thai, Vietnamese and Indonesian cuisines, e.g.) but are still a distinct minority on menus. Indian cooking in America is usually that of northern India, a region that has had cattle for thousands of years. Yogurt (and occasionally cream) is commonly used in sauces, breads are layered with butter and Indian tea comes premixed with milk. Desserts are almost all milk-based. It is still very easy to find non-milk dishes, but some quizzing of the waiter may be necessary. Southern Indian cooking, if you can find any, is far less likely to use milk.

Fast Food Restaurants

One of the nicest trends over the past few years is the increasing ease with which it is possible to get a full accounting of the ingredients in fast foods. This is especially important now that they have taken over from more traditional cafeterias in airports and stores (even in schools) as well as highway rest stops. You may find that not every part of every meal is noted on the ingredients lists. Most fast food franchises are so huge and so widely dispersed that they must rely on local suppliers. The availability of milk-free McDonalds' hamburger buns, for example, once varied from spot to spot, although the company announced several years ago that they would all be milk-free in the future.

▌ TRAVEL TO OTHER LANDS

There can be no excuse for not laying in a large supply of lactase pills before embarking on any trip. Taking them regularly should markedly alleviate LI symptoms no matter where you travel. Investing in a good phrase book or menu guide is also a must. While it will not hurt to take lactase with every meal, there's no reason to do so if it's not needed. I've also found waiters generally very willing to help me out, or to find English speakers where necessary if I can't get my point across any other way.

Lactase enzyme products and reduced-lactose milks originated in Europe and are now sold widely there under a number of brand names, most of which will be unfamiliar to Americans. Ask where you are staying for the names of those to be found locally. Neighborhood shops may not carry them, but hypermarkets, comparable in size and number of products sold to our largest supermarkets, will, and they are springing up in and around most large European cities. Pharmacies are another good place to search. Lactase products can also easily be found in Australia and other English-speaking countries.

Soy milks and other soy products will be found all over Asia, although they may not have the same taste or consistency as commercial American products. A number of American health food companies are beginning to market their products in other countries, however, including Pacific Rim countries.

The Central and South American countries are currently tempting targets for expansion, and they are regularly mentioned as locations that companies who make products of interest to the LI have moved into or are planning to do so.

13

DOCTORS, DIAGNOSES, DRUGS AND DISEASES

Is there anything in the world that *doesn't* upset your stomach? When it comes to digestive distress milk must stand in line along with sugar, caffeine, beans, fiber, spicy foods, carbonated beverages and general overindulgence. Worried because you spot some of your favorite foods on that list? Better take a deep breath to stay calm. Too much stress can manifest itself in diarrhea even when stress isn't implicated in Irritable Bowel Syndrome (IBS), whose familiar symptoms of painful spasms and bloating along with diarrhea and/or constipation have been called the leading cause of missed work days. Take some medication to alleviate your problems? Check the fine print that comes with the container. Clinical testing will have shown that a few percent of people will suffer from at least some of the following adverse reactions to almost any drug: abdominal pain, acid regurgitation, bloating, constipation, diarrhea, flatulence, nausea and vomiting. Don't even think about using any of the illicit drugs to blot out that reality. Alcohol goes right to work on the stomach, while the side effects of amphetamines include diarrhea. And all of this is in addition to the possibility of truly serious gastrointestinal diseases, from colitis to diverticulosis to Crohn's disease to colon cancer and many more.

With so many possible causes and so many similar symptoms, pinpointing exact cause and effect is not an easy matter, either for doctors or for amateur diagnosticians. Not everyone quickly makes the association of gas, bloating and diarrhea with milk. Some doctors never even suggest it as a possibility, while others on the lookout for LI may hit on the problem the first visit. (LI testing appears to increase in the summer, perhaps because overindulging in ice cream triggers noticeable symptoms in people who otherwise have few dairy products.) Stopping milk drinking on the assumption that LI is to blame, on the other hand, may not eliminate symptoms; gastrointestinal problems are so common in our society that overlap of LI with other problems is guaranteed. LI does not cause any disease, but is known to be associated with many, simply because of the sensitivity of the lactase-producing areas of the intestines.

I've been stressing throughout this book the importance of seeing a doctor whenever you have chronic intestinal problems, even though I realistically know that many, perhaps most people won't do so because they've found that changing their diet to reduce or eliminate lactose alleviated their symptoms. I hope that if so, LI was the only cause of your distress. For everyone else, it's time to make that appointment.

▌ TALKING WITH YOUR DOCTOR

As I've just indicated, studies show that the people who go see their doctors about digestive symptoms that may be caused by LI are not typical of the whole LI population. Those who have already eliminated milk and been cured and those who never see a doctor short of total bodily collapse (a surprisingly high number) have already been selected out. The ones who are left are usually those whose symptoms are in as much of a muddle as their innards. According to Dr. Robert Kornfield, a specialist in gastroenterology, a good family physician familiar with a patient's history can easily diagnose LI. He notes, therefore, that most of the people that family physicians refer to him have a complex of symptoms not so easily interpreted. This complexity undoubtedly accounts for the vast gap between the anecdotal evidence of people who have been going to doctor after doctor for years without ever getting properly diagnosed as LI and some doctors' assurances that LI is easy to spot and that most people already know they need to go off milk.

In truth, according to a fascinating study of people referred to specialists for chronic undiagnosed abdominal complaints ("Prediction of Lactose Malabsorption in Referral Patients," Jack A. DiPalma and Roberto M. Narvaez, *Digestive Diseases and Sciences*, 1988;33:303–7), it is extremely difficult to make any distinctions whatsoever between the LI and the LP without formal testing.

Once tests had confirmed who was LI and who was LP, the doctors compared the two populations. The two groups were, on average, the same age and had similar ratios of males to females (about one to three, interestingly). They were of various racial and ethnic backgrounds, but trying to sort them into groups known to be high or low LI didn't work. (In fact, the same percentages of northwestern European whites tested LI as did Asians and Native Americans.) All had had chronic symptoms for an average of five years, and both groups reported essentially the same symptoms in the same percentages. Nor did a food history present any clues. No real differences could be found in the percentages of those reporting symptoms from milk, ice cream, cheese or yogurt, or from foods with little or no lactose. It's true that just over half of the LP said they never had associated any specific food with their symptoms. But so did over 40% of those who proved to be LI, preventing the difference from being statistically significant. Only actual laboratory testing could distinguish those with low lactase activity. A full two-thirds of the test group were found to be LI.

And as for the claim that everyone who is LI already knows it, the study concludes that "less than 30% of our malabsorbers were aware of the relationship between lactose-containing foods and their presenting complaints." Even more amazing, "The percent of absorbers claiming lactose intolerance was similar and not statistically different from the malabsorbers."

A little knowledge may be a dangerous thing. Once you know about the connection between milk and intestinal distress the temptation always exists to blame every flare-up on LI, whether justified or not. Only testing can provide a definitive answer.

Prepare for your visit ahead of time by thinking about the various problems you've had. Symptoms alone may not enable your doctor to

---

LACTOSE AND MEDICATIONS

With inert, tasteless lactose a nearly ideal filler and coating, its use in prescription and over-the-counter (OTC) drugs has long been widespread but not commonly known. Fortunately, the amount of lactose in any one pill is truly minuscule. It is unlikely to be sufficient to affect anyone with LI, even when that amount is added to the other lactose in one's diet. Unlikely is not impossible: Reports of LI directly associated with medication containing tiny amounts of lactose can be found in the medical literature. The elderly and others who may routinely take up to several dozen pills a day may receive a cumulative dose that creates noticeable symptoms. Lactose used as a filler is also a concern for people who have galactosemia or other diseases which require a complete prohibition of dairy products. Those who have concerns about the use of any animal-derived product and those who must refrain from lactose for religious reasons also need to know when lactose is being used. (Note that people with milk allergies should not be affected in any way, as only lactose and not milk protein is used.)

Most major manufacturers of OTC drugs adhere to voluntary industry guidelines and print a list of inactive ingredients somewhere on their packages. I have a feeling these lists get read about as often as the fine print on the back of a sweepstakes entry blank, but at least they're there for you now self-aware consumers to find. According to my investigations, the use of lactose in OTC drugs is common but erratic. Big brand-name drugs come in so many variations of size, type and combinations of ingredients that even when one contains lactose, you're almost certain to find several others that do not. In addition, many drugs appear on the OTC market only after their patents have expired, allowing several firms to compete with their own versions of the drug. This allows you to choose from among several different brand names and different manufacturing techniques, improving your chances of finding one that does not use lactose.

Those ranks of vitamins, minerals and other nutritional supplements found in supermarkets, pharmacies and natural foods stores are just as likely to be specially formulated house brands or from small or regional companies as national brand names, making it impossible for me to proffer much in the way of useful advice. Compounding the problem is that vitamins and such are somewhat less likely to come with inactive ingredients listed. I can't even guarantee that a label reading "no sugar" means no lactose; it could simply be referring to sucrose. Check with the pharmacist or a knowledgeable clerk or write to the manufacturer for more information.

Prescription medications present a more difficult and potentially serious problem. Pharmacy bottles now come with ever-longer lists of instructions and warnings, but you don't get to see the original package and its list of inactive ingredients. Your pharmacist should have direct access to these, however, and your doctor will certainly subscribe to one or more of the various publications that compile this information. With the help of the people who put out one of these, the familiar *Physician's Desk Reference*, I've compiled a list of over 300 lactose-containing medications. You'll find it, along with other useful information, in Appendix III.

If you want or need to avoid prescription medications that contain lactose, you still have a number of options. As with OTC drugs, many brand names offer alternate forms or dosages that do not use lactose. There is also far more direct competition among drug companies than most people think. According to *The New York Times*, half to three-quarters of the revenues of large drug companies now come from so-called "me too" drugs, competing and all-but-identical patented versions of popular medicines. "Me too" drugs may well contain different inactive ingredients, however. In addition, drug companies just as often compete by coming up with totally different techniques for combating ailments as by dancing around each other's patents.

The real problem is not so much the lack of competing drugs as doctors' very understandable biases toward medications that they have had good experiences with, feel comfortable about, or that may cost less or be easier to cover under a prescription plan. Giving your doctor the freedom to prescribe the best medication for your individual needs should take precedence over the possible presence of lactose in all but extraordinary cases. For many ailments, doctors often need to try several drugs before hitting on the right one for you. Unduly refusing any medication with lactose may overly circumscribe your choices. Perhaps the most restricted category is that of oral contraceptives, where there appears to be but a single lactose-free option, G. D. Searle's Demulen.

If you feel strongly about barring lactose-containing medications, be sure to thoroughly discuss your preferences and alternatives with your doctor and be aware of the potential consequences of limiting your choices.

diagnose LI, but they can provide important clues. Give as much detail as possible. Here are some questions to ask yourself. Which symptoms bother you the most? How long have you noticed these symptoms? Do they appear to be associated with particular foods? Do you notice them especially after visiting a restaurant or eating at a friend's or relative's or while on vacation? Do they occur at particular times of the day? Do they ever wake you up in the middle of the night? Are the symptoms consistent? Do you alternate diarrhea with constipation, for example? Do you ever notice blood in your stool? Do you suffer from hemorrhoids? Are you losing weight? Do you feel pain? If so, exactly where?

Your doctor's response will vary depending on your answers to these and other questions. You may be asked to try a lactose-free diet for a while. A report of debilitating symptoms or the presence of blood may prompt a referral to a gastroenterologist or other specialist. And it is very likely that somewhere along the way you will be tested for LI.

LACTOSE INTOLERANCE TESTS

The Breath Hydrogen Test

Thumbing through the medical literature, I've come across descriptions of at least 18 separate and distinct tests for LI. Each has had a place and purpose, if only as part of medical research. For those of you who, like me, can't stand loose ends, I'll get around to mentioning all of them sooner or later but one so towers over all the others that it is the only one you are ever likely to encounter. It's called the breath hydrogen test (BHT).

The test makes use of the fact that hydrogen gas is extremely rare in the human body. Only one reaction will create a comparatively large supply of it: the fermentation of carbohydrates by bacteria in the colon, exactly what happens when a load of undigested lactose hits. Testing for hydrogen in the colon itself would no doubt be unpleasant, so give thanks for the development of a much easier and more convenient test that measures the hydrogen in our breath instead. Hydrogen exists in our exhaled breath because some 14%–21% of the gas produced diffuses through the walls of the colon into the bloodstream, where it eventually filters out through the lungs. So rare are even tiny amounts of hydrogen that a measurement of more than 20 parts per million (ppm) of hydrogen in the breath is an extremely reliable and sensitive indicator of a failure to digest lactose.

The incredibly simple test puts no more demands on you than the ability to exhale. Testing is typically done first thing in the morning after a 12-hour fast. You'll likely be asked to blow into a small mouthpiece connected to a laminated foil bag that resembles a pillow-shaped mylar balloon, although numerous variations like a nasal prong that shunts air into glass syringes or rubber-stoppered tubes may be found. After blowing up one bag with air to be used as a reference baseline, you'll be asked to drink a solution of lactose in water, although some doctors have been experimenting with using milk to better approximate everyday conditions. The amount of lactose may range from 10 to 50 grams: The larger amounts will identify a greater number of people as LI but will also cause more symptoms in those who are sensitive.

A certain amount of time is needed for the lactose to reach the colon and for the fermentation to create a buildup of hydrogen in the breath. Various labs will take further breath samples at intervals of 15–60 minutes and for up to two to six hours. Longer is usually better, as some people will not show an effect before three hours, although a quick rise is often meaningful. The use of milk instead of a lactose solution also demands a longer test, because the milk solids tend to delay gastric emptying. Any symptoms that occur while the test is being run should be noted, but as we've seen neither the presence of symptoms or their absence is necessarily related to being LI.

While the test itself is so simple that it can be done almost anywhere, the collected samples are usually shipped off to a specialized laboratory that can afford the several thousand dollars need to purchase the analyzer. Testing is accurate to within 2 ppm but don't bother to ask for an exact number. All that matters is whether you exceed the 20 ppm threshold. Higher numbers do not correlate with greater symptoms nor can you learn how much lactase you have left from the test results.

Machines have recently come onto the market that can simultaneously analyze both the hydrogen and methane in your breath samples. Methane gas is produced by a different set of colonic bacteria from those that produce the hydrogen because they work on the hydrogen and carbon dioxide gases that result from the other bacteria's fermentation of lactose and similar undigested carbohydrates. Only one-third to two-thirds of the population exhibit this so-called methanogenesis, but those who do will show a rise in breath methane that seems to parallel the rise in breath hydrogen.

The ability to simultaneously test for methane is a bonus for your doctor. Methanogenesis has been shown to be correlated with various gastrointestinal diseases, including Crohn's disease, ulcerative colitis, IBS, diverticulosis and polyposis. The presence of methane therefore may signal that your symptoms come from serious problems instead of or in addition to LI.

The BHT is a superior test both from the patient's and doctor's point of view. A good medical test should meet five criteria: It should be non-invasive, direct, simple, inexpensive and physiologic. The BHT is non-invasive, because it does not involve needles, probes or any other devices inserted into the body. It is a direct measure, as it directly measures a result of the maldigestion of lactose. It is simple, being a single measurement of a single substance. The cost of the test equipment precludes it from being inexpensive, although there are far more expensive tests around. The last criterion is more of a problem. A physiologic test is one that approximates actual bodily conditions. Drinking a huge lactose load on an empty stomach is hardly similar to the way most of us have dairy products on a regular basis. A 50 g solution of lactose is the equivalent of drinking a quart of milk in a single gulp, but without the buffering of the milk solids or of a full meal that would make the lactose better tolerated by almost everyone. It is for this reason that some doctors are looking at switching over to glasses of milk for the test. However, none of the other tests for lactose is any different in this regard. The use of milk or lactose depends on the tester and not on the test.

The BHT is such a good test for LI that it has almost completely taken over the field in the last few years. Good as it is, the BHT does have a few flaws. People on antibiotics should not take it because the antibiotics may knock out the very bacteria that would otherwise produce the hydrogen. Using aspirin before the test may create a misleading rise in hydrogen. Smoking will do the same, and it can be very difficult to insure that the dedicated smoker completely refrains for the many hours both before and during this long test. The true unknown is whether your intestines even contain the right bacteria in the first place. A certain percentage of the population, some 2%–20% in various studies, seem to be colonized with bacteria incapable of producing hydrogen. Obviously, these people will get a negative reading on the test whether they are LI or not. Techniques exist that will reveal who lacks such bacteria. If you are among them, you may need to fall back on one of the 17 other tests for LI.

The Blood Glucose Test

Doctors are understandably conservative in choosing which tests to apply and to believe in. New tests, new techniques need time to prove themselves, especially considering the number of variables that can muddle the accuracy of the results. Given the choice, most doctors would prefer to stick to old standbys. Indeed, for many years, doctors so relied on one of the most basic tests in the entire medical repertoire that it became known as *the* Lactose Tolerance Test (LTT), capital letters and all. Even today, the LTT, more accurately referred to as a blood glucose test, is the only LI test other than the BHT you are likely to be given. With only a few older doctors sticking with it, though, a busy lab may see hundreds of hydrogen tests for every blood glucose test it does for LI.

Glucose, as explained in Chapter 5, is the basic energy source of the body, distributed to every cell by the bloodstream. The body insures a constant supply of glucose through the digestion of all sugars and carbohydrates, as well as the breakdown of stored fat if the dietary glucose supply is insufficient. Changes in the level of glucose in the blood, or the lack of them, are indicative of a wide range of possible bodily processes, one reason for its ubiquity. Since digestion breaks lactose down into glucose and galactose, a rise in the level of blood glucose should be evident immediately after a lactose load. Without sufficient lactase, however, there is no digestion and no rise in glucose.

For you the patient, the blood glucose test is identical to a BHT, except that blood samples substitute for the breath samples. The LTT is also given on an empty stomach after an overnight fast and the same restrictions against eating during the test apply. You're in and out in less time, though, since the blood samples are taken usually every 30 minutes for two hours.

Another advantage of the test that made it a doctors' favorite is that blood analysis does not require the complex and expensive machinery that hydrogen detection does. Virtually every lab in the world can do a blood glucose test.

The reason for the LTT's fall from prominence in LI testing is as simple and straightforward as the test itself. It is just not a very reliable indicator of LI. Measuring glucose in blood is an exact science; applying that measure to LI failed in any number of ways. Individual differences in the time taken to move the lactose load out of the stomach and into the intestines as well as in the rate of blood-glucose metabolism will affect whether and how much of a rise in the blood glucose will be seen. Drawing the blood from veins created systematic errors but so did taking it from capillaries. The test did not work on diabetics.

And so on. The LTT was right in the majority of cases but its error rate was far higher than the tiny percentage shown by the BHT. Even if it had been as accurate and reliable, the LTT might still have been superseded because it failed a greater number of the five criteria for a good test. While simple and inexpensive, it was invasive, requiring half a dozen blood samples; indirect, since a positive reading was evidence of lactose digestion rather than of LI itself; and as unphysiologic as the BHT.

In short, blood glucose testing may still be a standard tool for many things but it has outlived its usefulness for LI testing. You are only likely to see it if you are one of those people for whom the BHT will not work or perhaps if you live in an area with limited access to the kind of major medical facility that can do hydrogen analysis.

The low accuracy rate of the LTT along with its near universal use in the past inevitably lead to the conclusion that many people were misdiagnosed, either as being LI when they were not or as not being LI when they in truth were. If you have come to doubt the accuracy of an old diagnosis that was based on a blood glucose test, you may want to think about taking a BHT as a confirmation.

Other LI Tests

If one of the problems with the LTT is that too many other reactions in the body also involve glucose, then an obvious alternative would be to concentrate on the second product of lactose digestion: galactose. In theory galactose provides a unique and direct marker of lactose digestion because lactose is the only source of galactose in the diet. (Note that it is still an *indirect* sign of lactose *mal*digestion, however.)

The drawback to the search for galactose is that it moves almost directly from the intestines to the liver, where it is rapidly converted into, what else, glucose. Researchers have found that it is fairly easy to short circuit the conversion and keep the galactose moving through the blood or have it pass into the urine. In either case a single test 40 minutes after the ingestion of a lactose load gives an extremely reliable indicator of LI. Several studies in fact suggest that a number of the variations on galactose tests are even better determiners of LI than the BHT.

One problem clouds this rosy picture. Getting the liver to turn off its galactose metabolism requires the use of ethanol, the alcohol found in most liquor. An amount of ethanol approximately equal to that in one beer is used for adults; a proportionally lesser amount for children. All the studies I've seen touting the virtues of galactose tests come from Europe, where any concern over the use of a small amount of ethanol is simply dismissed. "We have used this method for children for nearly 15 years . . . and have had no difficulties," concludes one study. Another says "the physical and metabolic impairment caused by the amount of alcohol ingested after an overnight fast seemed to be negligible even in elderly diabetic patients."

In the U.S., however, the use of alcohol appears to make galactose testing an absolute taboo. It is not discussed even in clinical research articles. American investigators also appear to have a much higher regard for the accuracy of the BHT than do the Europeans. Whether future research and direct comparisons of the various tests will change anyone's mind is unclear. For all practical purposes, use of any of the galactose tests (including the LTT with ethanol and several urine tests) in the U.S. is currently somewhere between negligible and nonexistent.

You're even less likely to see any of the other LI tests, as most are remnants of the early days of LI research. They represent a variety of ingenious approaches to the basic problem of measuring the results of a digestive process but have virtually no applications outside of the laboratory. Many of them use radioactive carbon (C^{14}) as a tracer so that they are unacceptable even for experimental work these days. Table 1 summarizes the advantages and disadvantages of the whole vast array of possible tests. (Some variants have been combined for clarity.)

Most of the tests listed need no further comment. Stool tests are sometimes used for infants too young for any of the other tests. The next chapter discusses children and LI.

I've saved one test for last. I hope some of you have wondered how, if all the tests have flaws, doctors could possibly know just how reliable and accurate they were. They would be like a teacher grading a roomful of math quizzes without access to the answer sheet. There is one test that

TABLE 1
ADVANTAGES AND DISADVANTAGES OF THE VARIOUS LACTOSE
TOLERANCE TESTS

TEST	ADVANTAGE(S)	DISADVANTAGE(S)
Blood tests		
Lactose tolerance test (LTT)	Possible anywhere	Unreliable
LTT with ethanol (LTTE)	More reliable	Requires alcohol
LTT + LTTE	Reliable	Requires alcohol
Breath tests		
Breath hydrogen test (BHT)	Noninvasive; reliable	Needs large lab for analysis; takes longest to do
$^{14}CO_2$ breath test	None	Unreliable; radiation
$^{13}CO_2$ breath test	No radiation	Unreliable; expensive
Intestinal examination		
Lactase assay (intestinal biopsy)	"Gold Standard"	Invasive; radiation
Perfusion studies	Quantitative	Invasive
Barium X-ray	None	Radiation
Patient examination		
Doctor's assessment of symptoms	Easy	Difficult to interpret symptoms
Stool tests		
Stool pH	Easy	Unreliable
Fecal reducing sugars	Easy	Unreliable
Fecal ^{14}C	None	Unreliable; radiation
Urine tests		
Urinary galactose test	Easy; convenient	Requires alcohol
Urinary galactose strip test	Easy; reliable; convenient; quick	Requires alcohol

(Adapted from H. Arola *et al.*, "Comparison of Indirect Diagnostic Methods for Hypolactasia," *Scandinavian Journal of Gastroenterology*, 1988; 23:351–7.)

appears to meet this standard of absolute accuracy so that it can serve as the reference for all other tests. It's the Gold Standard of lactose tolerance tests. And it is—fortunately—rarely used.

The "Gold Standard" for LI

LI is caused by the natural tendency of the intestines to stop producing the lactase enzyme as people age. Wouldn't it seem much more sensible to directly measure lactase output rather than fuss with the messy uncertainties of lactose byproducts? No more worries about whether you have the right colonic bacteria or if your stomach empties at the standard speed. For that matter, no more drinking a mammoth lactose solution that can churn up your insides for hours after the test.

Think what this would mean, though. Lactase is a true homebody among enzymes. It doesn't circulate in the blood or in the lymphatic system or even in the intestines. The enzyme forms on the inside surface of the jejunum, the middle section of the small intestine, and remains bound there. Getting at the lactase requires direct access to the inside of the jejunum, about as inconvenient a site as exists in the human body. Since slicing through the abdomen is frowned upon in the best medical circles, the jejunum can be reached only by sending a probe down the throat and through the stomach or backwards from the rectum and through many feet of intestine. Manoeuvering the probe and landing in the best spot for taking a measurement is a challenge in and of itself. Once there, the problem of measuring the lactase output remains. In an intestinal perfusion study, a tube is inserted into the jejunum and lactose pumped through, allowing a precise rate of absorption to be determined. This takes up rather more time than most people would prefer so the usual technique is to snip off a few samples of the intestinal wall to take back to the lab for testing there.

Taking a slice for testing is a roundabout way of describing a biopsy. Doctors like biopsies because it gives them a chance to look directly at live tissue or take it apart in ways not possible in the body. Lactase itself is not visible, of course, but damage to the mucosa, the inside layer of the intestine, will show up under a dissecting microscope. Those of us who have lost lactase activity with time will have normal mucosa, so the other samples taken can be brought to a lab for analysis. Either the lactase activity can be directly measured or a ratio of lactase to sucrase, the enzyme that digests sucrose, is determined. This is a actually a better measure because lactase activity varies along the length of the intestine, but the ratio between enzymes stays constant. Both methods reveal that a person with LI has only about 10% as much lactase as a person who is LP.

Despite the almost unquestioned accuracy[1] of an intestinal biopsy (formally known as assay of mucosal disaccharidases), it is highly unlikely that any doctor would ever ask you to undergo one just to test for LI, although a lactase test might be added if a biopsy was already scheduled to be done to check for more serious problems. The increase in accuracy over easy and non-invasive tests like the BHT is tiny. Even doctors call the procedure "moderately unpleasant," their way of saying "better you than

---

[1]Note for the technical-minded: A few researchers have recently begun to doubt the perfection even of biopsies, citing three potential problems: 1) lactase production varies from spot to spot in the jejunum; 2) damages to the mucosa from injury or disease may be too patchy to sample; 3) rapid transit of lactose through the intestine may result in LI even if lactase activity is high.

me." Positioning the probe often requires X-ray control, which means a slight dose of radiation. As with any invasive procedure, the possibility of complications exists, though probably no oftener than once in every 500 biopsies. And in a small percentage of cases the tube "cannot be persuaded to leave the stomach." The mental picture of a group of doctors, fake smiles on their faces, offering the tube candy or a spot on Oprah if only it would come out of hiding is a pretty one, but if my stomach were involved I would be more like to go directly from persuasion to threats, mostly of lawsuits. Biopsies are an extremely important medical tool, but LI testing has gone off the Gold Standard just as much as the U.S. government has.

WHAT IF YOU DO TURN OUT TO BE LI?

Go back to Chapter 1. Start reading.

WHAT IF YOU DON'T TURN OUT TO BE LI?

If not lactose, then what is causing all that gastrointestinal distress? A whole other book is needed at this point, so all I can do is suggest a few explanations and encourage you to continue seeing your doctor.

Secondary LI
One possibility is that you have been suffering from a temporary lactase deficiency. Acute gastroenteritis is perhaps the most common cause, but any number of drugs, diseases, surgical procedures and long-term abuse of the intestines can knock out the body's ability to make lactase [see box]. Recover from the disease or surgery, stop taking the drugs and lactase production will slowly return to previous levels. Your BHT may reflect this renewed lactase activity even though your memories are of past symptoms.

Irritable Bowel Syndrome (IBS)
Much more probable is that your symptoms are a sign of IBS, aka irritable colon, spastic colon, mucous colitis and many others. IBS symptoms exactly parallel those of LI: "Painful spasms and bloating, usually in the lower abdomen, and diarrhea or constipation—very commonly, diarrhea alternating with constipation," according to Dr. Steven Peikin. Pain may decrease after a bowel movement or increase when more frequent loose bowel movements occur. Some people suffer from a feeling that their bowel movements are incomplete and return to the bathroom for relief that never quite comes. When probing for IBS, doctors will likely ask if you ever are awakened by middle-of-the-night symptoms. A yes answer is a sign of more serious organic diseases; an IBS oddity is that even people with otherwise severe symptoms will rarely find themselves awakened from a sound sleep by the need to reach a bathroom.

SECONDARY LACTOSE INTOLERANCE

How fragile our intestines are, how precarious their grip on whatever lactase they might have, is nowhere better shown than in the extraordinary length and breadth of the list of items that can temporarily knock out the body's ability to manufacture lactase. Since the normal reduction of lactase production is often called primary lactose intolerance, this type of lactose maldigestion is usually referred to as secondary lactose intolerance (SLI). The name fits in many ways: SLI is less prevalent, usually short-lived, often less severe.

The most common cause of SLI is acute infectious diarrhea. Any number of bacteria, viruses and protozoa can damage the intestinal lining, inflaming it to the point where lactase production decreases. Up to age three, children are so susceptible to these attacks that SLI is far more prevalent than primary LI. (More on this in the next chapter.) A lactose-free diet is recommended for the several weeks necessary for the intestines to slowly heal.

In celiac disease, under any of its many names (gluten-sensitive [or gluten-induced] enteropathy; gluten intolerance; nontropical sprue; celiac sprue), an intolerance to gluten, or protein, in wheat or rye causes damage to the villi, making absorption impossible. Although treatment consists of a permanent gluten-free diet, lactase activity will normally return within a few months for anyone who is not naturally LI. (Those who are intolerant to both milk and wheat will have significantly worse symptoms before treatment than those who only have gluten intolerance.)

Crohn's disease, giardiasis, tropical sprue, cystic fibrosis, Whipple's disease and a host of other, fortunately equally rare, diseases can also cause SLI.

Physical damage to the intestines can come from many other sources as well. Chronic alcohol consumption, pelvic irradiation and malnutrition have been linked to SLI. Drugs such as colchicine, neomycin, kanamycin and even plain old aspirin can do similar damage. Any surgical procedure which shocks the villi may temporarily knock out lactase activity.

In a category of its own is surgical-caused permanent intolerance, which is the likely result of the removal of any major portion of the intestinal track or a smaller piece that centers around the jejunum where lactase activity is highest.

Any true secondary intolerance will clear up shortly after its cause has been taken care of. Any unusual sensitivity to dairy products after an intestinal disease or surgery should be reported to your doctor immediately to see if a lactose-free diet is required so as not to further strain your system.

No one appears to be quite sure what causes IBS, although the fact that a high-fiber diet and stress reduction are the best cures surely offers a clue. What is known is that IBS is one of the commonest ailments in the country. Dr. Thomas Almy of the Dartmouth Medical School ranks IBS just behind the common cold as the leading reason people miss work. With tens of millions suffering from LI and an equal number from IBS, the odds are enormously high that many people will have both. (I do myself.) There does not seem to be any actual connection between the two, however, as studies of IBS patients have found LI in anywhere from 5% to 86% of their test subjects. If you've been diagnosed as having IBS but have never been tested for LI, you may want to ask for a test. A substantial minority of IBS patients can get relief by reducing lactose consumption.

Two points need to be emphasized. First, doctors cannot distinguish LI from IBS just by listening to your symptoms. Testing is a necessity. Second, a simple change in diet may not prove anything. Going off milk may not do much to reduce overall symptoms in people who have both LI and IBS, while a sudden increase in fiber intake may result in worsened diarrhea or bloating. And any intestinal symptoms from either LI or IBS may be masking those of truly serious diseases.

Diseases of the Intestines

Crohn's disease, diverticulitis, diverticulosis, ulcerative colitis, colon cancer, the list of potential intestinal diseases is long and scary. All involve actual damage to the intestines and may require changes in diet, medications or surgery. The best news I can give is that they are generally rare, afflicting a tiny fraction of the numbers that LI and IBS do. The best reason to go to a doctor for any long-term gastrointestinal complaints is to rule out these true diseases—or get an early start on their treatment.

The possibility of intestinal disease is what motivates your doctor to ask a series of question like those I suggested you think about earlier in this chapter. Some are designed to zero in on certain diseases; others to eliminate various possibilities. A seemingly off-the-wall question about whether you have pencil-thin stools is actually a probe toward a possible blockage of the colon by a tumor. Rectal bleeding is most probably a sign of hemorrhoids, but bloody diarrhea may mean ulcerative colitis while blood in the stool requires a check for polyps or tumors. The exact location of pain helps distinguish between IBS, diverticulitis and Crohn's disease.

Don't second-guess answers, anticipate questions or make a self-diagnosis. Do pay attention to your particular pattern of symptoms so that you can give answers that are exact and complete. Hope for the best. By comparison, LI is a light and easy burden to bear.

14

BABIES WITHOUT MILK:
THE LACTOSE
INTOLERANT CHILD

A fter hearing me say over and over for an entire book that virtually all babies make sufficient lactase to digest milk, you may wonder what this chapter is doing here.

I stand on my record. Babies do indeed make all the lactase they need and do so from birth. Congenital LI, the total absence of lactase from birth, is an exceptionally rare disorder and is almost unknown in the U.S. In all the world, only about 40 cases have been reported in the past 35 years.[1]

Even so, milk can become an issue for both infants and for older children, and in some ways that most adults never have to deal with. In this chapter I'll take a look at four different problems that might require your taking your child off lactose, and even off milk itself, whether cow's milk or breast milk:

1. Temporary or Secondary LI created by gastrointestinal infections or other damage to fragile intestines;
2. Rare diseases and disorders involving glucose and galactose;
3. Cow's milk protein (CMP) intolerance and true CMP allergy; and
4. LI itself, which can develop in children as young as three to five years old.

Problems one through three will likely first appear in infants under two years of age, necessitating a lactose-free infant formula for feedings. Rather than go over the same ground three separate times, I'll discuss lactose-free infant formulas following the section on CMP.

---

[1] About half of all known cases have been reported in Finland, a country with one of the world's lowest rates of LI. Finland's impenetrable forests, which have historically isolated towns and generated highly inbred populations, are the reason for this apparent anomaly. Congenital illnesses are rare because they stem from recessive genes. The condition manifests itself only if a child inherits that gene from both parents. Inbred populations greatly increase this risk over time. Finland is known for having local centers of inborn disease almost unheard of elsewhere.

▌ TEMPORARY LI

Your poor baby has just gotten over a case of severe diarrhea. A diet of clear liquids and electrolytes has helped but you now hope to get back to the regular routine of breast or bottle feeding. To your dismay, the diarrhea recurs in large volumes, with general gas and bloating and perhaps with greasy, foul-smelling stools that are difficult to flush. You've been warned that a slight increase in diarrhea is to be expected in any case, because milk is less easily digested than clear liquids, so you may be more resigned than concerned at first. But what are you to think if it doesn't stop, if, in fact your baby seems to be suffering from diarrhea almost as severe as during the original malady? Is it a repeat of that ailment or is this something new?

The second bout could have many causes, but the odds are that it is an indirect outgrowth of the earlier diarrhea, especially if that proved to be a case of acute gastroenteritis, more familiarly known as a stomach virus. We all seem to get them from time to time, but they are much more serious in infants and young children than in either older children or adults. The reason for this did not emerge until the particular viruses involved were identified in the 1970s as a family known as the rotavirus.

PREMATURE BABIES AND LI

Babies are born genetically programmed to exist solely on mother's milk, the highest lactose milk of all. You might expect lactase production to be high well before birth to ensure that that first crucial meal can be digested even if the baby doesn't wait the full nine months to be born. For reasons not completely clear, however, lactase is one of the *last* digestive enzymes the fetus begins to manufacture in sufficient quantities to be of much use.

Lactase activity in a six month fetus is only 30% of what it will be when the baby is born. As late as the eighth month of pregnancy activity is still only 70% of the newborn level. It is only in the last weeks before birth that lactase production shoots skyward. This means that a premature baby weighing three pounds will only absorb 30%–40% of the lactose he or she takes in. A two pound premature infant will absorb effectively none.

Logically, then, all premature babies should suffer the ravaging symptoms of acute LI. To everyone's relief, they don't. Several factors appear to be at work. The first feedings evidently stimulate premies' bodies to produce more lactase. Mothers' very first drops of milk are lower in lactose than they will be in the coming weeks. And many of the symptoms of LI come from the bacteria in the colon fermenting the undigested lactose. Babies are born with essentially sterile guts; they have no bacteria to run amok on them.

Premature infants may fall prey to many problems, but even though it can be shown that the lactose they're drinking is mostly not being absorbed, LI is not among them.

The rotavirus preferentially attacks the lactase-rich cells at the ends of villi, the finger-like protrusions that cover the inside of the small intestine (*see Chapter 5*). With lactase activity higher and intestines more delicate in infants than in most adults, children under two get hit the hardest. The rotaviral infection produces the severe original diarrhea. Fortunately, the duration of the illness is self-limiting because the viruses kill off their host cells. The mature cells that were invaded are replaced by new, immature ones that do not offer as hospitable a home to the virus. When all the mature cells are gone, so is the virus. The infection ends along with the diarrhea.

A problem remains. The definition of an immature cell in that location is one that is not enzymatically active; that is, one that does not produce any enzyme. Lactase is the most vulnerable enzyme, so it is always the first to go and the last to return. Your infant may now be perfectly healthy but left without a means of digesting lactose. LI caused by an illness or injury to the intestines is usually called Secondary LI, but I am referring to it in this chapter by its alternate name of Temporary LI to emphasize its transient nature. Immature cells mature very quickly, and lactase production may restart a week or so after the end of the infection, almost certainly within a month. Once the cells mature and resume producing lactase, the LI will go away.

(Usually, at least. There is one possible exception to this general rule. Children whose heritage predisposes them toward losing their lactase ability at an early age may never fully regain production of the enzyme after they suffer a rotavirus infection at six months or older. Asian children seem particularly subject to this permanent loss.)

Very young infants, those under six months, are much less affected by rotaviral infections, possibly because breastfeeding mothers pass along antibodies in their milk. The scarceness of breastfeeding after that point is another possible explanation of why infants in the 6–18 month age group are most likely to suffer from the virus. Toddlers' distressing habit of touching most everything and then bringing their hands to their months without washing likely also plays a role, because it provides a convenient route for the virus to reenter the system. Children susceptible to rotaviral infections have been known to get them and the ensuing LI several times over. Removing the offending milk from the diet and replacing it with a lactose-free formula is critical. Malnutrition and weight loss may result if the diarrhea is allowed to linger for long periods.

It's very difficult to say how common this type of Temporary LI is. Since most diarrheas run themselves out after two weeks in any case, parents may not think this episode serious enough to warrant a return visit to the pediatrician. Dr. Richard Lawrence, a pediatric gastroenterologist, estimates that 10%–15% of the children in his practice suffer from some kind of infectious condition, and 10%–15% of that group will become LI. Only about 1% of the infant population has Temporary LI from the

LI TESTS FOR INFANTS AND CHILDREN

The breath hydrogen test (BHT) discussed in Chapter 13 as the best test for adults is the best for children as well. A noninvasive test—no needles—the BHT requires no more of the child than drinking some lactose (a much smaller amount than given to an adult, scaled down proportionately to the child's weight). Older children can exhale into a collecting bag through a mouthpiece as adults do; your doctor may use a nasal prong or infant face mask to shunt air from younger children into an especially tiny bag. The BHT is suitable for children six months and older, thereby covering the entire age range of children most prone to rotavirus infections. It has even been used with success on hospitalized infants under three months of age. The one drawback is that prolonged diarrhea can disrupt the colonic bacteria which manufacture the hydrogen that the test measures. The test is not accurate for the first few days of recovery after such an illness. Normally, however, Temporary LI would not manifest itself until after this period had passed in any case, since the bacteria must be present for symptoms to occur.

Children too young even for the BHT need to be evaluated by other means. If a sufficiently serious problem is suspected, an intestinal biopsy may be taken for laboratory examination. Such an invasive procedure would be rare.

Much more likely would be a time-honored screening test for LI, one which uses a substance diarrhetic infants readily produce in great abundance. Stool testing makes use of two handy facts: 1) only carbohydrates produce acidic stools in small children, and 2) the only carbohydrate in breast milk or milk-based formula is lactose. The test is so simple that it can be performed right at the bedside. Stool tests are not accurate enough to be good diagnostic measures, but they can be useful in indicating whether a lactose-free formula should be tried.

aftermath of an infection at any given time. The odds are somewhat greater that your infant will develop Temporary LI at least once during the two years of greatest susceptibility, however.

Although acute gastroenteritis is the most common cause of Temporary LI, children are also vulnerable to the vast number of drugs, diseases, surgeries or intestinal shocks that I mentioned in the last chapter as affecting the lactase output of adults, with new ones being discovered all the time. Babies born infected with the HIV virus, for example, often suffer from severe gastrointestinal dysfunction, leading to chronic diarrhea and malnutrition and damage to lactase and other enzymes. Your pediatrician should be able to alert you if LI is likely to be a consequence of anything else your child is going through.

One side note: LI is probably not causing what even doctors call "the distressing syndrome of infantile colic." Lactase drops and low-lactose milks have been tried with no significant effect on crying or fussing.

▍ GLUCOSE AND GALACTOSE DISORDERS

Glucose-galactose Malabsorption

Lactose must be split into its component parts, glucose and galactose, to be absorbed by the body. The failure to do so results in LI. Turn that problem around. What if the lactose split perfectly well, but the resulting glucose and galactose could not be absorbed? That is precisely the condition known as glucose-galactose malabsorption.

Symptoms are similar to those of LI but cannot be alleviated as easily by switching formulas. The substitute sweeteners in lactose-free formulas, including sucrose, corn syrups and starches, will also break down to form glucose. Fortunately, fructose sugar is tolerated by most sufferers of glucose-galactose malabsorption and formulas can be adapted to use it instead. By the age of three to five years, the body usually learns to live with the problem and the chronic diarrhea disappears.

Because the inability to drink any milk is potentially life-threatening, this condition is usually diagnosed almost immediately in infants. A few older children and even some adults may develop it, however. Diet must be strictly regulated to exclude not only lactose, but most other carbohydrates as well.

Galactosemia

This disorder is similar in many ways to glucose-galactose malabsorption. Again, lactose is easily broken down to glucose and galactose. In galactosemia, however, it is the liver enzyme that converts galactose to glucose that is missing. After a few days on either mother's milk or a lactose-containing formula, the affected infant will suffer from persistent vomiting, jaundice, weight loss and enlargement of the liver. If left untreated, the consequences can be dire. The galactose rapidly accumulates in the blood and body tissues, leading to liver damage or mental retardation. It is, thankfully, an extremely rare disease, occurring approximately once in every 60,000 births in North America.

Because this is a genetic disease, doctors actively look for it even before the baby is born. Tests have also been developed to screen for it at birth by examining blood in the umbilical cord. The availability of lactose-free formulas should prevent recurrence of the effects of the galactose.

People with galactosemia must expect to follow a completely lactose-free diet for life. This requires special precautions beyond those needed for LI. Reduced-lactose milks, whether store-bought or made at home through the use of lactase drops, are actively dangerous for persons with this condition, because the lactase will create galactose when it splits the lactose. And unless the manufacturing process has been exceedingly strict, small amounts of lactose may remain in products that use casein in any of its forms. Care will be needed to impress upon children the importance of never accepting snacks or desserts from others. Parents will also need to work with schools to get them to understand the dietary limitations so that school lunches can be handled appropriately.

▌ COW'S MILK PROTEIN ALLERGY AND INTOLERANCE

Babies' bodies are designed to expect nothing but mother's milk for their first vulnerable months of life. Mothers who do not exclusively breastfeed their babies will expose their children to nutrients, first in formulas and later on in solid foods, not found in mother's milk. Normally innocuous sugars and other carbohydrates create problems in certain children, and corn, soy, egg and peanut proteins are also known to produce reactions.

The first non-human protein the vast majority of babies in the U.S. eat is cow's milk protein (CMP), and because cow's milk contains more than 40 different proteins to which infants can react, CMP reactions are the most common and the best known. These reactions can be classified into two large groups depending upon which internal mechanisms are involved. (This holds true for all food reactions, not just those caused by CMP.)

Allergic reactions are the first major group. CMP allergies involve the body's immune system. Digestion normally breaks food proteins back down into individual amino acids, which the body readily accepts. If whole proteins happen to leak into the bloodstream, however, the immune system manufactures antibodies that attack those foreign proteins. These antibodies thereafter stay in the bloodstream to protect against another invasion, sensitizing it. If even a tiny amount of that protein finds its way back into the bloodstream, the body gears up and produces massive amounts of antibodies whether they're really needed or not. The result can be a stupendous variety of symptoms, most of them unpleasant, a few of them life-threatening.

True allergies are associated with one specific antibody, IgE (or immunoglobulin E). IgE-associated immune reactions are the dangerous ones, appearing immediately or within minutes of contact with the offending food, and creating the hives, rashes or blocked nasal passages that characterize what most people think of as allergic reactions as well as the anaphylactic shock that can kill victims who do not get immediate treatment.

The potential seriousness of allergic reactions has created a false impression that they are omnipresent, permanent and the source of all food reactions. In fact, true food allergies are extremely rare, caused by relatively few foods and will very likely be outgrown before the end of childhood.

The confusion stems from lack of familiarity with the many other mechanisms through which the body can react to foods. This large second group of mechanisms are called food intolerances. LI is an example of a carbohydrate intolerance. Specific CMP intolerance can be also identified.

CMP intolerance reactions are distinguishable from CMP allergies in several ways. Parents are most likely to note that intolerance symptoms take much longer to manifest and typically affect only the gastrointestinal system. As intestines strengthen with age, intolerance reactions will diminish. They rarely last past the pre-school years. Table 1 summarizes the major differences between CMP intolerances and CMP allergies.

If you're confused, you're not alone. Dr. Robert H. Schwartz, a specialist in pediatric allergies, has written that

> Many people, some physicians and nurses, and even some registered dieticians do not always appreciate the differences between cow's milk protein hypersensitivity[2] [allergy], cow's milk protein intolerance, and cow's milk sugar (lactose) intolerance.

You are likely to see the first symptoms of these three reactions to cow's milk at different times and in different ways. Babies who are immediately placed on cow's milk formulas will typically develop symptoms from CMP intolerance in the first three months of life if they do so at all. Most breast-fed babies who display CMP allergy symptoms will react almost immediately after being given their first taste of cow's milk, but not until then. The age allergic symptoms first manifest may vary, however. About 70% of children with CMP allergy develop symptoms while still under 2 years of age but in 10% the symptoms do not begin until the children are 7–14 years old. (It is possible, although rare, for CMP from the mother's diet to enter her breast milk and so cause an allergic reaction before the child has actually tasted milk.)

A parent can perform a quick CMP allergy test by noticing if a drop of milk falling on the infant's skin raises a hive. The skin-prick test an allergist performs is just a formal variation. In this test the skin is literally pricked with a pin where a drop of formula has been placed. A positive reaction produces a wheal of at least 3 mm after 15 minutes.

LI, as we saw earlier, is associated with the aftermath of gastroenteritis or other disease rather than with the introduction of cow's milk into the diet.

One similarity among the three types of reactions is important to emphasize. Both CMP intolerances and allergies are as comparatively rare

---

[2]Adding to the confusion, some doctors apply the term hypersensitivity to allergic responses; others use it to mean an intolerance rather than a true IgE reaction. I will avoid it entirely and speak only of allergies and intolerances. Be sure to ask your doctor how he or she defines hypersensitivity if the word gets used in relation to your child.

TABLE 1 DIFFERENT REACTIONS TO COW'S MILK PROTEINS (CMP)		
	CMP ALLERGY	**CMP INTOLERANCE**
Reaction Time:	Immediate (within 45 minutes)	Intermediate (45 minutes to 20 hours)
Trigger:	Trace amounts of CMP	Large amounts of CMP
Symptoms:	Cutaneous (skin); Respiratory—Hives, swelling, rashes, coughing, wheezing	Gastrointestinal— Vomiting, diarrhea, colic
Skin-prick test:	Positive	Negative
IgE levels:	Elevated	Normal
Develops in:	Breast-fed babies	Formula-fed babies
Prognosis:	Persists for several years, possibly into adulthood	Subsides after infancy

(Adapted from "Allergy, Intolerance and Other Adverse Reactions to Foods," Robert H. Schwartz, *Pediatric Annals*, 1992; 21:654–74)

as Temporary LI. CMP allergy may be "the most common food sensitivity issue confronting pediatricians today," but the consensus of current opinion is that it affects only about 1%–3% of infants, with CMP intolerance at that level or below. Perhaps 20% of that small group will continue to be allergic through adulthood.

 LACTOSE-FREE INFANT FORMULAS

As if life with a baby weren't complicated enough, CMP allergy, CMP intolerance and Temporary LI will force about 20% of all infants temporary or permanently onto a specialized formula in the first year of life. Which formula is best will depend upon the exact nature of the problem.

All formulas are created equal in the sense that all must satisfy the complete known set of infants' nutritional needs. Their nutrient composition must conform to published recommendations of the American Academy of Pediatrics's Committee on Nutrition (AAP-CN). Formulas are perhaps the FDA's most closely regulated food. This does not mean that all formulas are alike. On the contrary, each takes a unique route toward its nutritional goal. I haven't found anyone willing to say in print that one brand is better than the rest, but your baby may well prefer the taste of one formula over another because each uses a slightly different mix of fats and carbohydrates. Special problems or allergies may also steer you toward or away from certain formulas.

BREASTFEEDING VS. FORMULA FEEDING

With CMP allergy a possibility from breastfeeding and CMP intolerance a possibility from formula feeding, mothers face a dilemma and potential guilt whichever they choose. The medical literature offers little of value to base a decision upon. The issue has been thoroughly studied, "almost to the point of tedium," according to one journal, but results remain jumbled.

Dr. Schwartz reviewed a series of studies and concluded that: "There is compelling evidence that breast-feeding, as it is commonly practiced today, is a major risk factor in the development of IgE-mediated cow's milk allergy," although he also says that the virtues of breastfeeding "are numerous, and in most instances, the advantages outweigh the disadvantages."

But a Swedish team ("Does Breast-Feeding Prevent Food Allergy?" Bengt Björkstén & N-I Max Kjellman, *Allergy Proceedings*, 1991; 12:233–7) pulled a different set of studies out of the same journals to support this conclusion:

> Most prospective studies indicate that breast-feeding delays the onset of allergy for several years in infants with a clear family history of atopic [allergic] disease. . . . Although allergy does not seem to be prevented by breast-feeding, merely delaying the onset of disease in children is important. This delay in onset seems to be associated with a lessening in disease severity. Parents with a severely affected infant or child would agree that postponed onset of disease is of great value in itself. . . . Breast-feeding should be combined with an avoidance of solid foods for at least [the first] 4 months.

An editorial on "Cow's Milk Allergy" in the journal *Clinical and Experimental Allergy* (1993; 23:79–80) agreed that the evidence was at best equivocal:

> It is remarkable that infants totally nourished by cows' milk cannot usually be distinguished, either in growth or in biochemical profile, from those who have been exclusively breast fed in the first months of life. . . . Whole population studies have not been able to demonstrate less allergy in breast fed infants even when all confounding factors are included in the analysis.

My interpretation of this conflicting morass of statements is that while virtually everyone agrees that breastfeeding is superior to any of the alternatives ("breast is best," the editorial concludes), breastfeeding is a critical issue only for high-risk infants. Even then breastfeeding alone is insufficient. Mothers may have to avoid drinking milk themselves while ensuring that the baby is kept off solid foods for as much as six months after birth to significantly lessen the danger.

Breastfeeding does have one other advantage that needs to be mentioned here. Breast-fed infants have significantly fewer gastrointestinal infections, which would cut down on the possibility of their developing Temporary LI as a result.

Three major categories of lactose-free formula exist (*see box*). Soy-based formulas are the most numerous and probably the best known. They are based on soy-protein isolates, unlike the troublesome soy-flour formulas of the 1960s and '70s. All are completely lactose-free and CMP-free. By also being completely free of any animal-derived products, they can be used by vegans and are pareve. Babies without other problems will thrive on soy formulas for as long as they are needed.

One warning: Ordinary soy "milks" are NOT the equivalent of specially-fortified soy formulas. They lack many vital nutrients and have others in quantities smaller than infants need. Babies fed exclusively on soy milk from birth will develop severe malnutrition and a host of other problems, which could prove fatal.

Soy formulas would be the first choice for infants with galactosemia. They are also suitable for babies with Temporary LI and for most infants with CMP intolerance or mild allergy.

Table 2 lists a soy-based formula named RCF. Those initials stand for Ross Carbohydrate-free Formula. Babies with glucose-galactose intolerance who must avoid other formulas because their carbohydrates break down into the forbidden glucose can use this formula, usually with fructose added by the parent.

A second alternative is the newest. Techniques now exist by which the lactose in a cow's milk-based formula can be completely removed and replaced by corn syrup solids (glucose polymers). (This is a completely different process from the hydrolysis of lactose by lactase used in making

---

VARIETIES OF LACTOSE-FREE INFANT FORMULAS

Soy-based formulas:
  Gerber Soy Formula
  Isomil (also available in Canada)
  Isomil DF
  Nursoy (also available in Canada)
  ProSobee (also available in Canada)
  RCF (also available in Canada)
  Soyalac
Hypoallergenic hydrolysate formulas:
  Alimentum (also available in Canada)
  Nutramigen (also available in Canada)
  Pregestimil (also available in Canada)
Cow's milk-based formula:
  Lactofree (available in Canada as Alactimil)

(Sources: *USP DI-Volume II, Advice for the Parent: Drug Information in Lay Language*, edition 14, 1994; Mead Johnson. Brand name products continually leave and enter the market. This listing is indicative rather than comprehensive.)

reduced-lactose milks.) Soy formulas have the disadvantage, for the pediatrician at least, of alleviating symptoms without exposing their cause. A lactose-free milk formula is a halfway step that can help diagnose whether LI or a protein sensitivity is the culprit. If protein is the problem, the baby can then be switched to a soy formula. LI was probably at fault if the symptoms do stop. Some pediatricians also prefer cow's milk formulas over soy formulas because they believe the proteins or minerals may be better digested. No cow's milk formula, not even one without lactose, should ever be used if a severe CMP allergy is suspected.

Infants who are highly or multiply allergic, as well as those unable to digest intact protein for other reasons, can be put on hydrolysate-based formulas. In these, casein protein is hydrolyzed (predigested) by being broken down into its component parts. A mild disadvantage of hydrolysates is a taste and smell that even parents who have gotten used to cow's milk formulas find disagreeable. Very young babies don't seem to care and readily accept hydrolysates, but they may start to reject them when older. As casein-derivatives, however, they can neither be considered pareve nor acceptable to vegans.

Soy formulas are less expensive and more palatable than casein-hydrolysate formulas so they have been the first choice when the infant is taken off milk, especially if CMP is the suspect. True allergies to soy protein are as rare as true allergies to milk protein but soy protein intolerance may occur in up to 25% of infants with CMP intolerance. Hydrolysates are the preferred option in these cases. Most doctors would also start a severely allergic baby or one from a family with a known history of CMP allergy directly on a hydrolysate formula because of the dangers of cross-sensitivity.

Parents of milk-sensitive infants may hear mention of partially hydrolyzed whey protein formulas. (These formulas are not suitable for LI babies because they contain lactose. No lactose-free whey-based hydrolysates are currently available in the U.S.) The advantage of these formulas is that they are far more palatable than the casein hydrolysates. The disadvantages are more notable. Partially hydrolyzed formulas are considered less hypoallergenic and even dangerous in children with true CMP allergy, probably because they retain some casein despite the predominantly whey base. Perhaps if fully hydrolyzed whey protein formulas are introduced into the U.S. they will provide a better fourth alternative.

Parents should remember that hydrolysate formulas are hypoallergenic, not non-allergenic. The AAP-CN allows a formula to be labeled hypoallergenic if it is tolerated by 90% of milk-allergic infants. All three hydrolysate formulas listed in Table 2 meet this criterion. Severe allergic reactions have been reported with every type and brand of infant formula, however.

If all else fails, the infant may be put onto an elemental diet whose protein consists of synthesized amino acids. So non-allergenic and predigested are these formulas (marketed under the brand names Vivonex or Tolerex) that they were developed for postoperative nutrition of infants following major intestinal surgery. Doctors may try them as a temporary elimination diet when multiple food allergies make other formulas unusable. They are usually a last resort because they are unpalatable and not well accepted by older children.

LI IN OLDER CHILDREN

Children are the forgotten group in the LI world, as most attention gets focused on the special needs of infants or the gradual loss of lactase by adults. Once past the crises of infancy, children are assumed to be able to have milk. So associated is milk-drinking with childhood (to the annoyance of the dairy industry) that many adults stop to avoid possible ridicule.

The idyllic picture of a child snacking on milk and cookies has been undermined by our growing understanding of how many children are actually LI. Who these children are is determined by their ethnic heritage. Children from groups that become almost universally LI as adults will likely start losing their ability to produce lactase by the time they are five years old.

Although there are many causes of childhood gastrointestinal distress, the possibility of LI should be on the minds of both parents and doctors whenever a child over the age of five shows persistent symptoms of diarrhea and abdominal pain. Researchers now believe that a full 15% of American school-age children are LI. Knowing how to treat LI not only alleviates their uncomfortable and discomforting symptoms (what child would possibly wish to have to face schoolmates while suffering from stool leakage?) but also can keep high-calcium dairy products in the diet at a crucial period of bone growth and development.

I addressed the earlier chapters in this book to adults but just about everything I've said about LI applies equally to children. The symptoms of diarrhea, gas, borborygmi and bloating are the same, although vomiting is more often seen in children than adults. The tests used to detect LI, especially the breath hydrogen test, can be performed on all children more than a few months old. Lactase pills, lactase drops to remove lactose from milk and store-bought reduced-lactose milks can be given to children as soon as they go off formula, usually after age one. The tolerance to lactose from a change in colonic bacteria that can result from regular consumption of milk products may be even more evident in children than adults because they are the group most likely to have milk on a daily basis.

Education is the key, both of your children and those they must deal with. Make sure they understand all about LI. Help them learn which dairy products are likely to be better tolerated than others and why overindulging in milk or ice cream can cause them pain. Let schools know if you want your child to go onto a milk-free diet. School cafeteria personnel should be extremely sensitive to LI, but they'll want a parent's note rather than the child's say-so to substitute other beverages for milk. Teach your child how to say no. A polite, "I'm sorry, but I can't eat that," will deflect a lot of potentially troublesome food. Neither you nor they will be able to guard against all food all the time, but making them aware of the problem and of the consequences will give them the strength and the ammunition to fend off a lot of well-intentioned but ignorant adults.

Given the enormous range of alternatives and options available to the LI today, there is no reason for a child's life to be more than minimally disrupted by LI. Milk allergies or other problems which do call for a complete ban on dairy products will be more difficult to cope with, but all the casein-free nondairy alternatives I've talked about are suitable for children and can provide just as healthy and nutritionally fulfilling a diet for them as they do for many adults.

Children are not entirely miniature adults, of course, and a few issues remain that are of special relevance to children.

Calcium and Growing Bones
In the past, the most critical issue facing children who did not drink milk was a lack of calcium just at the time their growing bodies most needed it for building the solid bone structure that would carry them through later life. The current Recommended Dietary Allowance (RDA) for calcium is 800 mg per day for children aged one through ten and 1,200 mg for adolescents aged 11 through 24. These are proportionally huge amounts, with a one-year old infant needing as much calcium as a full-grown adult weighing five or six times as much. It is believed that much osteoporosis in older women will be prevented if girls get their full RDA of calcium. At present, the average teenage girl does not, even if she isn't LI.

While it is possible to get calcium from other dietary sources, few among them are high on the favorite food lists of young children. Kids who increase soda drinking because they (or their parents) associate milk with stomach distress are at a double disadvantage because the high levels of phosphorus in many carbonated beverages prevent the body from using calcium efficiently. As few as three to four cans of soda a day can threaten bones.

Calcium-enriched bread and orange juice can provide a fair amount of the missing calcium. But the best alternative is keeping milk in your child's diet. Lactose has the wonderful property of increasing the body's calcium absorption. Reduced-lactose milks, along with easily tolerated foods like yogurt or cheese, are much better for your child than adding calcium supplements to a diet than contains no lactose. The extra sweetness of reduced-lactose milks that sometimes make them unpalatable for adults is a bonus for kids. Lactase pills can be used with other dairy products to reduce potential LI symptoms from these high-calcium foods.

Recurrent Abdominal Pain

Recurrent abdominal pain (RAP), pain serious enough to interfere with a child's activities and which recurs a number of times over a period of months, is one of the most common problems encountered by pediatricians. An estimated 10%–15% of school-age children suffer from it. In some ways RAP appears to be the child's equivalent of irritable bowel syndrome (IBS) in adults, since both are more a collection of miscellaneous symptoms with large numbers of possible causes both physical and psychological than an identifiable disease. Both, of course, are serious enough to their sufferers, with many RAP victims missing more than one day of school out of every ten.

The potential connection of abdominal pain with LI has not been lost on doctors, but results of past studies have been mixed and inconclusive. The blinkered mentality of non-LI researchers might have been to blame. Most of those early studies were conducted on subjects of Anglo-Saxon or Scandinavian heritage, groups with the lowest levels of LI in the world. Other doctors decided that it might make more sense to try looking at populations with high levels of LI instead. Lo and behold, researchers in both India and Italy concluded that LI appears to be a major cause of RAP in those countries. Today's consensus among doctors is that LI is probably a significant factor in RAP wherever high-LI populations are found.

Trying an RAP child on a low-lactose or lactose-free diet should always be considered, whatever the child's ethnic heritage. As with adult IBS, however, the removal of lactose may not always ease symptoms. One recent U.S. study determined that about one-quarter of children with RAP may also be LI. Those children were placed on a lactose-free diet, but only 50%–60% later reported improvement. That's intriguingly similar to another study's report that 43% of IBS adults had their symptoms relieved by a lactose-restricted diet. Both reports are encouraging, but more research obviously needs to be done.

THE FUTURE

LI children will grow up to be LI adults, swelling our ranks. Changing immigration patterns and the general aging of the U.S. population insure that a greater and greater percentage of adults will be LI for the foreseeable future. They will share our benefits of having a wide range of lactase, low-lactose and lactose-free products at our disposal. Our increasing numbers should mean that ever more attention will be paid to us and our special needs. Children taught about LI—where it comes from, what it means, what can be done about it—become the kind of educated consumers who can ensure that this will indeed happen. The long years of ignorance about LI are over. The years of understanding have already begun.

APPENDIX I

PERCENTAGES OF LACTOSE INTOLERANCE AMONG THE WORLD'S POPULATION GROUPS

Hundreds of studies have been conducted to determine the frequency of lactose intolerance (LI) in groups whose members share common ancestry. High percentages of LI among adults, adolescents and children past the age of weaning prove to be the norm almost everywhere in the world. There are only two major exceptions to this general pattern: members of nomadic tribes in desert areas in northern Africa and the Middle East, and people whose ancestors lived in northern or western Europe. Since many separate studies, done at different times by different researchers using different methods, give remarkably similar answers, researchers have great confidence in the accuracy of this mass of data. It is this accumulated body of evidence that has led scientists to conclude that the vast majority of people in the world are naturally LI.

Several compilations of the results of dozens or hundreds of these studies exist; all show similar patterns. This table has been adapted from "The Acceptability of Milk and Milk Products in Populations with a High Prevalence of Lactose Intolerance," Nevin S. Scrimshaw & Edwina B. Murray, *American Journal of Clinical Nutrition*, 1988; 48:1080–1159. I have arranged the data so that it more clearly shows some of the patterns of most interest.

For example, very young children in all populations are almost never found to be LI, lending support to the conclusion that humans are genetically designed to be able to safely drink mother's milk for the first several years of their lives. Because I have listed studies within each group by the age of the test population, a gradual rise in the percentage of LI as the population ages should be evident. For this reason, LI is assumed to be a condition associated with aging, due to a loss of the lactase enzyme that allows infants to digest milk. The age at which a majority of the population becomes LI is also an important indicator. In general, populations with the highest percentages of adult LI also show the earliest loss of lactase.

Negative patterns can also be meaningful. There appears to be only a slight correlation between the percent testing as maldigesters and percent showing symptoms for any given study. In some studies many people who test as maldigesters show none of the symptoms associated with LI; in others a large number of people who do not test as maldigesters exhibit symptoms anyway. The variances demonstrated by these studies illustrate the importance of a proper diagnosis to insure that the true underlying cause of one's problems has been determined.

While the general population patterns are clear and striking, individual variations abound. Two studies of seemingly the same population may have very different LI percentages. Studies can even be found in which older populations have lower levels of LI than younger ones. There are many reasons for this:

- Some studies use test populations so small that they may not be representative of their group.
- Studies of people with medical problems often produce very different results from studies of healthy populations with similar ancestry.
- Studies using larger lactose loads will usually identify a greater percentage of their subjects as LI.
- Early studies were often done using tests less accurate than those available today, and so tended to underestimate the number of people who were LI.

Real world problems such as these are the reason that compilations of hundreds of studies must be done to provide statistically significant results. It is unlikely that every study of a particular group will show the same biases or be flawed in exactly the same manner. The totality of studies paints a picture that no individual study can hope to match.

Long as this table is (and it does not include every LI population study that has ever been performed), many corners of the world and many individual populations remain to be surveyed. Additional studies may yet provide answers to some of the questions concerning LI scientists still wonder about. How long ago did the ability to safely drink milk as an adult appear? Where did milk drinking first start, and when, and why? Are worldwide levels of LI decreasing due to intermarriage between those who are LI and those who are not? Can anything be done to slow or stop the loss of lactase with age? Much of interest surely is waiting to be discovered.

WORLD LACTOSE INTOLERANCE

CONTINENT COUNTRY	POPULATION	AGES	PERCENT TESTING AS MALDIGESTERS	PERCENT SHOWING SYMPTOMS	SIZE OF TOTAL SAMPLE
North America					
United States	General	Adults	35%	92%	34
United States	General	Elderly	16	—	75
United States	Asian, African, Hispanic	2–3	0	—	33
United States	Asian, African, Hispanic	3–4	0	—	1
United States	Asian, African, Hispanic	4–5	0	—	3
United States	Asian, African, Hispanic	5–6	33	—	6
United States	Asian, African, Hispanic	6–7	67	—	3
United States	Asian	23–38	100	95	20
United States	Chinese	22–49	75	87	20
United States	Vietnamese	22–63	100	65	31
United States	Black (grades 1–6)	Children	40	—	312
United States	Black	11mo–11yr	30	35	20
United States	Black	13mo–59mo	29	18	116
United States	Black	4–5	11	—	9
United States	Black	5–9	58	11	48
United States	Black	6–7	50	—	24
United States	Black	6–13	54	73	89
United States	Black	8–9	72	—	29
United States	Black	11–18	58	68	33
United States	Black	13–19	69	91	32
United States	Black	14–78	73	—	41

CONTINENT COUNTRY	POPULATION	AGES	PERCENT TESTING AS MALDIGESTERS	PERCENT SHOWING SYMPTOMS	SIZE OF TOTAL SAMPLE
North America					
United States	Black	17–53	100%	83%	6
United States	Black	18–54	75	90	20
United States	Black	24–75	64	64	11
United States	Caucasian (grades 1–6)	Children	9	–	221
United States	Caucasian	14mo–11yr	5	10	20
United States	Caucasian	2–5	0	–	3
United States	Caucasian	4–5	0	–	2
United States	Caucasian	6–7	0	–	14
United States	Caucasian	6–9	6	–	31
United States	Caucasian	8–9	20	–	10
United States	Caucasian	10–14	12	–	17
United States	Caucasian	14–78	16	43	19
United States	Caucasian	18–48	75	50	8
United States	Caucasian	18–54	10	10	20
United States	Caucasian	18–59	10	10	20
United States	Caucasian	18–82	15	76	142
United States	Caucasian	24–75	45	–	11
United States	Caucasian	Adults	25	6	16
United States	Mexican-American	2–5	18	31	88
United States	Mexican-American	6–9	39	68	119
United States	Mexican-American	>9	50	100	16
United States	Mexican-American	10–11	56	83	75
United States	Mexican-American	18–94	53	88	277

CONTINENT COUNTRY	POPULATION	AGES	PERCENT TESTING AS MALDIGESTERS	PERCENT SHOWING SYMPTOMS	SIZE OF TOTAL SAMPLE
North America					
United States	Mexican-American	19–57	26%	20%	19
United States	Mexican-American	Adults <60	47	47	17
United States	Puerto Rican	Adults	54	33	50
United States	Native American	3–5	20	–	10
United States	Native American	6–12	10	–	10
United States	Native American	13–19	70	–	10
United States	Native American	18–57	81	83	36
United States	Chippewa Indian	5–6	63	–	16
United States	Chippewa Indian	5–62	100	88	59
United States	Chippewa Indian	7–8	72	–	18
United States	Chippewa Indian	9–10	67	–	18
United States	Chippewa Indian	11–12	67	–	15
United States	Chippewa Indian	13–14	64	–	14
United States	Chippewa Indian	15–17	74	–	23
United States	Chippewa Indian	>18	62	–	52
United States	Indian and Eskimo	Adults	81	–	36
United States	Pima Indian	3–7	31	–	122
Canada	Canadian Eskimo	0–3	22	–	9
Canada	Canadian Eskimo	4–7	91	–	11
Canada	Canadian Eskimo	8–11	89	–	9
Canada	Canadian Eskimo	12–15	100	–	7
Canada	Canadian Eskimo	16–19	64	–	11
Canada	Canadian Eskimo	>20	83	–	12

CONTINENT COUNTRY	POPULATION	AGES	PERCENT TESTING AS MALDIGESTERS	PERCENT SHOWING SYMPTOMS	SIZE OF TOTAL SAMPLE
North America					
Canada	Canadian Indian	0–3	38%	–%	8
Canada	Canadian Indian	4–7	25	–	8
Canada	Canadian Indian	8–11	38	–	8
Canada	Canadian Indian	12–15	50	–	10
Canada	Canadian Indian	14–24	63	68	30
Canada	Canadian Indian	16–19	100	–	10
Canada	Canadian Indian	>20	85	–	13
Canada	General Non-Indian	15–26	6	0	16
Canada	General	18–39	52	–	21
Canada	Jewish	Adults	69	95	32
Guatemala	General	>18	65	65	20
Jamaica	Rural	Preschool	56	34	94
Jamaica	Urban	Preschool	70	50	20
Mexico	Rural	13–17	69	40	108
Mexico	Rural	13–21	77	66	193
Mexico	Rural	18–72	74	68	100
Trinidad	East Indian	Adult	67	90	30
South America					
Argentina	General	6–12	50	29	96
Brazil	General	19–39	46	–	24
Brazil	Black	Adults	95	85	20
Brazil	Caucasian	Adults	45	45	40

CONTINENT COUNTRY	POPULATION	AGES	PERCENT TESTING AS MALDIGESTERS	PERCENT SHOWING SYMPTOMS	SIZE OF TOTAL SAMPLE
South America					
Brazil	Hospitalized Caucasian	Adults	69%	–%	32
Brazil	Hospitalized Non-Caucasian	Adults	94	–	18
Brazil	Japanese	Adults	100	100	20
Chile	Chilean Indian	6–80	56	–	64
Chile	Men	18–20	70	–	195
Colombia	Chami Indian	15–55	58	58	24
Peru	Mestizo	23mo–82mo	67	67	6
Peru	Mestizo	<3	27	0	11
Peru	Mestizo	3–5	88	64	25
Peru	Mestizo	6–8	92	77	24
Peru	Mestizo	9–12	95	90	21
Peru	Previously malnourished	<3	0	0	2
Peru	Previously malnourished	3–5	100	33	3
Peru	Previously malnourished	6–8	88	86	8
Peru	Previously malnourished	9–12	100	100	5
Peru	General	16–54	80	80	50
Surinam	Creole	1–3	90	–	20
Surinam	Hindustani	7–12	96	–	27
Surinam	Bushnegro	Adults	100	–	29
Surinam	Creole soldiers	Adults	92	–	12
Surinam	Dutch soldiers	Adults	36	–	14
Surinam	Urban Creole	Adults	84	–	19

CONTINENT COUNTRY	POPULATION	AGES	PERCENT TESTING AS MALDIGESTERS	PERCENT SHOWING SYMPTOMS	SIZE OF TOTAL SAMPLE
Europe					
Austria	General	Adults	20%	–%	528
Denmark	Hospital patients	Adults	100	100	18
Denmark	Greenland Eskimo	13–75	72	74	32
Denmark	Greenland Eskimo	Adults	74	–	19
England	Gastric patients	<70	34	26	35
England	Greek Cypriot	Adults	88	–	17
Finland	Servicemen	14–25	18	–	134
Finland	Hospital patients	15–69	28	–	121
Finland	Students, Finnish	21–30	17	–	156
Finland	Students, Swedish	21–30	8	–	91
Finland	General	21–65	17	81	159
France	Caucasian	7–15	47	57	30
France	General	18–21	37	–	131
France	General	Adults	7	–	14
Germany	General	8–10	15	–	124
Germany	General	Adults	15	–	1805
Greece	General	Infants	26	0	50
Greece	General	7–13	54	46	24
Greece	Continental Greek	15–78	45	44	600
Greece	Cretan	15–78	56	56	50
Greece	General	15–80	75	–	200
Greece	Greek Cypriot	Adults	66	66	50

CONTINENT COUNTRY	POPULATION	AGES	PERCENT TESTING AS MALDIGESTERS	PERCENT SHOWING SYMPTOMS	SIZE OF TOTAL SAMPLE
Europe					
Greece	Students, Americans	Adults	0%	-%	13
Greece	Students, Greek	Adults	38	–	16
Greenland	General	Adults	55	78	219
Hungary	Women	16–54	63	–	172
Hungary	General	17–39	37	–	535
Hungary	Romai (Gypsy)	Adults	56	–	113
Italy	General	16–73	62	–	42
Italy	General (Healthy)	Adults	38	–	40
Italy	General	Adults	39	83	218
Italy	IBS patients	22–70	88	–	40
Italy	Neapolitan	15–45	100	100	9
Italy	Central Italians	Adults	18	–	65
Italy	Northern Italians	Adults	51	–	208
Italy	Northern Italians	Adults	52	–	89
Italy	Sicilian	Adults	75	65	20
Italy	Southern Italians	Adults	41	–	51
Netherlands	General	4–15	19	90	52
Turkey	Students	18–37	37	91	30
North Africa and Middle East					
Egypt	Men	14–34	73	16	570
Iraq	General	18–36	86	85	69

CONTINENT COUNTRY	POPULATION	AGES	PERCENT TESTING AS MALDIGESTERS	PERCENT SHOWING SYMPTOMS	SIZE OF TOTAL SAMPLE
North Africa and Middle East					
Iran	General	<3	31%	19%	16
Iran	General	3–5	67	25	12
Iran	General	6–11	70	32	37
Iran	General	12–15	79	47	19
Israel	General	3–16	4	–	100
Israel	Iraqi	17–65	84	–	38
Israel	North African (Sephardi)	17–69	63	–	32
Israel	Other (Sephardi)	17–69	72	–	36
Israel	Ashkenazi	20–70	78	–	55
Israel	Yemenite	20–70	44	–	36
Israel	Asian	24–64	85	–	20
Israel	General	38–49	80	–	93
Israel	Arab	Adult	81	–	67
Jordan	General	1–12mo	30	–	46
Jordan	General	1–12	66	–	140
Jordan	Jordanian Arab	17–48	77	64	56
Jordan	General	Adults	75	–	148
Jordan	Jordanian Bedouin	Adults	24	–	162
Lebanon	General	17–43	78	71	74
Lebanon	Caucasian	Adults	33	–	15
Lebanon	"Mediterranean lymphoma" patients	Adults	100	–	12

CONTINENT COUNTRY	POPULATION	AGES	PERCENT TESTING AS MALDIGESTERS	PERCENT SHOWING SYMPTOMS	SIZE OF TOTAL SAMPLE
North Africa and Middle East					
Saudi Arabia	Bedouin	14–65	86%	–%	14
Saudi Arabia	Khadir (mixed African)	14–65	22	–	9
Saudi Arabia	Urban Saudi	14–65	88	–	8
Saudi Arabia	Yemenite	14–65	75	–	8
Tunisia	General	0–6mo	0	–	6
Tunisia	General	6–18mo	12	–	9
Tunisia	General	18–36mo	33	–	12
Tunisia	General	3–5	40	–	10
Tunisia	General	5–7	67	–	9
Tunisia	General	7–13	63	–	24
Africa					
(General Africa)	Healthy Zulu	Adults	93	–	14
	Hospitalized Zulu	Adults	89	–	47
Botswana	Hawi	Children	100	–	3
Botswana	Hawi	Adults	91	–	22
Ghana	General	2–6	73	–	100
Kenya	General	5–15	73	–	71
Nigeria	General (unweaned)	1–14mo	32	0	28
Nigeria	General	8–30mo	79	29	38
Nigeria	Protein-energy malnourished	2–6	30	30	23

CONTINENT COUNTRY	POPULATION	AGES	PERCENT TESTING AS MALDIGESTERS	PERCENT SHOWING SYMPTOMS	SIZE OF TOTAL SAMPLE
Africa					
Nigeria	Caucasian (in Lagos)	>4	36%	–%	11
Nigeria	Fulani (in Lagos)	>4	58	–	33
Nigeria	Hausa (in Lagos)	>4	76	–	17
Nigeria	Yoruba	>4	98	–	41
Nigeria	Ibo	13–38	82	73	11
Nigeria	Yoruba	13–70	83	65	48
Nigeria	Hausa and Fulani	17–60	60	60	15
Nigeria	General non-tribal	18–49	100	78	9
South Africa	Hospital patients	Adults	91	0	22
South Africa	Shangaan	Adults	86	14	7
South Africa	Sotho	Adults	65	26	23
South Africa	Swazi	Adults	75	17	12
South Africa	Tswana	Adults	83	33	24
South Africa	Xhosa	Adults	82	29	17
South Africa	Zulu	Adults	81	31	32
South-West Africa	Nama	Children	19	–	21
Sudan	Beja	14–18	19	–	124
Sudan	Nilote	14–18	73	–	98
Sudan	Beja	19–30	15	–	141
Sudan	Nilote	19–30	75	–	154
Sudan	Beja	>30	18	–	38
Sudan	Nilote	>30	73	–	30

CONTINENT COUNTRY	POPULATION	AGES	PERCENT TESTING AS MALDIGESTERS	PERCENT SHOWING SYMPTOMS	SIZE OF TOTAL SAMPLE
Africa					
Tanzania	Arab	5–14	100%	–%	2
Tanzania	Bantu	5–14	92	–	127
Tanzania	European	5–14	0	–	4
Tanzania	Masai	5–14	62	–	21
Uganda	General	<1wk	0	–	22
Uganda	General	36–47mo	60	–	5
Uganda	General	48–60mo	100	–	5
Uganda	General	7–9	100	–	4
Uganda	Hamite	13–18	33	0	6
Uganda	Bantu	13–43	100	75	12
Zaire	Twa	15–58	77	–	22
Zaire	Shi	19–26	96	–	28
Zaire	Hutu	20–41	58	–	36
Zaire	Mixed Tutsi and Hutu	20–41	55	–	11
Zaire	Tutsi	20–41	10	–	27
Zambia	General	17–59	96	80	26
Asia					
Bangladesh	General	0–6mo	0	–	18
Bangladesh	General	7–18mo	10	–	29
Bangladesh	General	19–36mo	59	–	34
Bangladesh	General	>36mo	80	–	108
Bangladesh	General	5–7	100	83	12

CONTINENT COUNTRY	POPULATION	AGES	PERCENT TESTING AS MALDIGESTERS	PERCENT SHOWING SYMPTOMS	SIZE OF TOTAL SAMPLE
Asia					
Sri Lanka	General	16–78	73%	–%	200
India	General	7mo–7yr	41	37	54
India	General	46–157mo	18	16	50
India	General	15–58	28	100	25
India	General	Adults	61	50	18
India	General	Adults	64	62	100
India	Patients	Adults	97	97	32
India	Trivandrum	10–63	67	90	30
India	Pundicheng	13–70	67	90	30
India	North Indian	15–30	19	–	54
India	North Indian	31–50	33	–	51
India	North Indian	51–70	46	–	13
India	North Indian	>70	50	–	2
Japan	General	15–64	100	17	35
Korea	General	17–83	75	–	300
Singapore	General	<5	0	–	6
Singapore	General	1–3	36	–	11
Singapore	General	3–5	21	–	14
Singapore	General	5–7	50	–	14
Singapore	General	5–10	87	–	15
Singapore	General	7–9	71	–	17

CONTINENT COUNTRY	POPULATION	AGES	PERCENT TESTING AS MALDIGESTERS	PERCENT SHOWING SYMPTOMS	SIZE OF TOTAL SAMPLE
Asia					
Singapore	General	9–15	93%	–%	14
Singapore	General	15–42	100	–	22
Thailand	Healthy	<2	29	–	41
Thailand	Malnourished	<2	66	–	41
Thailand	Institutionalized	1mo–1yr	41	–	49
Thailand	Institutionalized	1–2	75	–	36
Thailand	Institutionalized	>2	87	–	30
Thailand	Village	1mo–1yr	14	–	21
Thailand	Village	1–2	30	–	20
Thailand	Village	>2	88	–	16
Thailand	Northern Thai	2–4	54	–	13
Thailand	Northern Thai	4–12	100		24
Thailand	Northern Thai	Adults	100	97	75
Thailand	Americans	Adults	24	–	58
Thailand	General	Adults	100	85	140
Oceania					
Australia	Aboriginal	6–7	75	–	16
Australia	Aboriginal	8–9	84	–	19
Australia	Aboriginal	10–11	64	–	14
Australia	Aboriginal	12–14	50	–	14
Australia	Aboriginal (at Manigrida)	<15	84	–	62

CONTINENT COUNTRY	POPULATION	AGES	PERCENT TESTING AS MALDIGESTERS	PERCENT SHOWING SYMPTOMS	SIZE OF TOTAL SAMPLE
Oceania					
Australia	Aboriginal (at Papunga preschool)	<15	95%	-%	324
Australia	Aboriginal	15–75	84	64	45
Australia	Controls	6–12	9	–	46
Australia	General	18–40	17	35	100
Australia	General	Adults	4	0	23
Australia	Nonaboriginal	15–75	19	19	37
Australia	Caucasian	19–31	20	–	10
Australia	Caucasian students	Adults	17	17	12
Australia	Chinese residents	13–34	56	–	34
Australia	Australian-born Chinese	17–30	80		10
Australia	Chinese residents	18–27	90	80	10
Australia	Asian students	Adults	95	95	20
Australia	Southeast Asian	Adults	95	–	43
Papua New Guinea	General	Adults	77	–	35
Papua New Guinea	Goodenough Islanders	Adults	83	–	29

APPENDIX II

NUTRITIVE VALUE
OF SELECTED FOODS

Good health depends on the proverbial balanced diet. Whether based on the old Four Food Groups or the newer Food Pyramid, a balanced diet has traditionally been assumed to include dairy products in general, and milk in particular. Milk is an excellent source of a wide range of nutrients, some of which are not easy to find in alternative foods that are as popular and as palatable as milk.

If your reactions to lactose intolerance have made you decide to reduce the amount of milk in your diet or eliminate it altogether, whether you realize it or not, you have cut out one of the major sources of phosphorus, riboflavin, and vitamin A in the American diet, as well as the source of three-fourths of all the calcium eaten in this country. You should be looking at alternative foods rather than supplement pills as your first choice for replacing these missing nutrients.

To guide you to those foods which best serve your individual needs, likes and dislikes, I've put together the following chart, adapted from the authoritative *Nutritive Values of Food*, put out by the U.S. Department of Agriculture. It's designed specifically for the needs of the low-dairy product-consuming lactose intolerant diet. Nutrients that milk is not a major source of have been eliminated to avoid confusion, while calcium is a special focus.

Notes on use:

- Uniform measures — 1 ounce or 1 cup — have been used wherever possible so that comparisons within a group can be made. The equivalent weight in grams for each portion size is also given. There are 28 grams in an ounce, 454 grams to the pound.
- Vitamin A is actually a group of compounds, usually retinols from animal sources and beta-carotene from plant sources, that are absorbed somewhat differently in the intestines. Expressing vitamin A activity in International Units (IU), while still frequently seen listed on the labels of many packaged foods and vitamin supplements, obscures these differences. The Recommended Dietary

Allowances (RDAs) now give vitamin A activity as micrograms of retinol equivalents (RE). Typically, for plants 10 IU = 1 RE, while for animals 3 IU = 1 RE. I give both measures here for your convenience.

- The last two columns, calcium [in milligrams] per 100 grams and calcium [in milligrams] per 100 Calories, allow you to make better comparisons of the calcium density of different foods. For example, one cup of parsnips has almost exactly as much calcium as one cup of cooked onions, but the lower Calorie onions have twice as much calcium per Calorie. Similarly, the yolk of a chicken egg has about the same amount of calcium as a cup of mixed light and dark chicken meat, but the yolk is a much more concentrated source of the calcium, with almost ten times the calcium per gram of weight.

NUTRITIVE VALUES OF SELECTED FOODS

CATEGORY	STYLE	TYPE	SIZE OR NUMBER	GRAMS	CALORIES	PHOSPHORUS (MILLIGRAMS)	VITAMIN A (INTERNATIONAL UNITS)	VITAMIN A (RETINOL EQUIVALENTS)	RIBOFLAVIN (MILLIGRAMS)	CALCIUM (MILLIGRAMS)	CALCIUM PER 100 GRAMS	CALCIUM PER 100 CALORIES
BREADS												
Boston Brown	Canned		1 slice	45	95	72	0	0	0.04	41	91	43
French		enriched	1 slice	35	100	30	Trace	Trace	0.12	39	111	39
Italian		enriched	1 slice	30	85	23	0	0	0.07	5	17	6
Mixed grain		enriched	1 slice	25	65	55	Trace	Trace	0.10	27	108	42
Oatmeal		enriched	1 slice	25	65	31	0	0	0.07	15	60	23
Pita	White	enriched	1 pita	60	165	60	0	0	0.12	49	82	30
Pumpernickel		enriched	1 slice	32	80	71	0	0	0.17	23	72	29
Raisin		enriched	1 slice	25	65	22	Trace	Trace	0.15	25	100	38
Rye	Light	enriched	1 slice	25	65	36	0	0	0.08	20	80	31
Vienna		enriched	1 slice	25	70	21	Trace	Trace	0.09	28	112	40
Wheat		enriched	1 slice	25	65	47	Trace	Trace	0.08	32	128	49
White		enriched	1 slice	25	65	27	Trace	Trace	0.08	32	128	49
Whole-wheat			1 slice	28	70	74	Trace	Trace	0.06	20	71	29
DAIRY PRODUCTS												
Butter	Regular		1 stick	113	810	26	3460	852	0.04	27	24	3
Margarine	Regular	hard, 80% fat	1 stick	113	810	26	3740	1122	0.04	34	30	4
			1 tbsp	14	100	3	460	139	Trace	4	29	4
		soft, 80% fat	8 oz	227	1625	46	7510	2254	0.07	60	26	4
			1 tbsp	14	100	3	460	139	Trace	4	29	4
	Spread	hard, 60% fat	1 stick	113	610	18	3740	1122	0.03	24	21	4
			1 tbsp	14	75	2	460	139	Trace	3	21	4

DAIRY PRODUCTS

CATEGORY	STYLE	TYPE	SIZE OR NUMBER	GRAMS	CALORIES	PHOSPHORUS (MILLIGRAMS)	VITAMIN A		RIBOFLAVIN (MILLIGRAMS)	CALCIUM (MILLIGRAMS)	CALCIUM PER 100 GRAMS	CALCIUM PER 100 CALORIES
							(INTERNATIONAL UNITS)	(RETINOL EQUIVALENTS)				
Margarine	Spread	soft, 60% fat	8 oz	227	1225	37	7510	2254	0.06	47	21	4
			1 tbsp	14	75	2	460	139	Trace	3	21	4
		Imitation soft, 40% fat	8 oz	227	785	31	7510	2254	0.05	40	18	5
			1 tbsp	14	50	2	460	139	Trace	2	14	4
Cheese	Blue		1 oz	28	100	110	200	65	0.11	150	536	150
	Camembert		1 wedge	38	115	132	350	96	0.19	147	387	128
	Cheddar	piece	1 oz	28	115	145	300	86	0.11	204	729	177
		shredded	1 cup	113	455	579	1200	342	0.42	815	721	179
	Cottage Cheese	4% fat large curd	1 cup	225	235	297	370	108	0.37	135	60	57
		4% fat small curd	1 cup	210	215	277	340	101	0.34	126	60	59
		2% fat	1 cup	226	205	340	160	45	0.42	155	20	37
		uncreamed, nonfat	1 cup	145	125	151	40	12	0.21	46	16	23
	Cream Cheese		1 oz	28	100	30	400	124	0.06	23	82	23
	Feta		1 oz	28	75	96	130	36	0.24	140	500	187

DAIRY PRODUCTS

CATEGORY	STYLE	TYPE	SIZE OR NUMBER	GRAMS	CAL-ORIES	PHOS-PHORUS (MILLI-GRAMS)	VITAMIN A (INTER-NATIONAL UNITS)	VITAMIN A (RETINOL EQUIVA-LENTS)	RIBO-FLAVIN (MILLI-GRAMS)	CALCIUM (MILLI-GRAMS)	CALCIUM PER 100 GRAMS	CALCIUM PER 100 CALORIES
Cheese	Mozzarella	whole milk	1 oz	28	80	105	220	68	0.07	147	525	184
		part skim milk	1 oz	28	80	149	180	54	0.10	207	739	259
	Muenster		1 oz	28	105	133	320	90	0.09	203	725	193
	Parmesan grated		1 cup	100	455	807	700	173	0.39	1376	1376	302
	Provolone		1 oz	28	100	141	230	75	0.09	214	764	214
	Ricotta	whole milk	1 cup	246	430	389	1210	330	0.48	509	207	118
		part skim milk	1 cup	246	340	449	1060	278	0.46	669	272	197
	Swiss		1 oz	28	105	171	240	72	0.10	272	971	259
	Pasteurized process cheese	American	1 oz	28	105	211	340	82	0.10	174	621	166
		Swiss	1 oz	28	95	216	230	65	0.08	219	782	231
	Pasteurized process cheese food		1 oz	28	95	130	260	62	0.13	163	582	172
	Pasteurized process cheese spread		1 oz	28	80	202	220	54	0.12	159	568	199
Milk, Canned	Evaporated, unsweetened	whole milk	1 cup	252	340	510	610	136	0.80	657	261	193
		skim milk	1 cup	255	200	497	1000	298	0.79	738	195	67
	Sweetened, condensed		1 cup	306	980	775	1000	248	1.27	868	284	89

DAIRY PRODUCTS

CATEGORY	STYLE	TYPE	SIZE OR NUMBER	GRAMS	CALORIES	PHOSPHORUS (MILLIGRAMS)	VITAMIN A (INTERNATIONAL UNITS)	VITAMIN A (RETINOL EQUIVALENTS)	RIBOFLAVIN (MILLIGRAMS)	CALCIUM (MILLIGRAMS)	CALCIUM PER 100 GRAMS	CALCIUM PER 100 CALORIES
Milk, Dried	Buttermilk		1 cup	120	465	1119	260	65	1.89	1421	241	79
	Nonfat	instant	1 cup	68	245	670	1610	483	1.19	837	1231	342
Milk, Fluid	Whole	3.3% fat milk	1 cup	244	150	228	310	76	0.40	291	119	194
	Lowfat milk	2% fat	1 cup	244	120	232	500	139	0.40	297	122	248
		1% fat	1 cup	244	100	235	500	140	0.41	300	123	300
	Nonfat (skim)		1 cup	245	85	247	500	144	0.34	302	123	355
	Buttermilk		1 cup	245	100	219	80	20	0.38	285	116	285
	Chocolate milk	regular	1 cup	250	210	251	300	73	0.41	280	112	133
		2% fat	1 cup	250	180	254	500	143	0.41	284	114	158
		1% fat	1 cup	250	160	226	500	148	0.42	287	115	179
	Eggnog		1 cup	254	340	278	890	203	0.48	330	130	97
Sweet Cream	Half-and-Half		1 cup	242	315	230	1050	259	0.36	254	105	81
			1 tbsp	15	20	14	70	16	0.02	16	107	80
	Light cream		1 cup	240	470	192	1730	437	0.36	231	96	49
			1 tbsp	15	30	12	110	27	0.02	14	93	47
	Whipping cream light, unwhipped		1 cup	239	700	146	2690	705	0.30	166	69	24
			1 tbsp	15	45	9	170	44	0.02	10	67	22

DAIRY PRODUCTS

CATEGORY	STYLE	TYPE	SIZE OR NUMBER	GRAMS	CALORIES	PHOSPHORUS (MILLIGRAMS)	VITAMIN A (INTERNATIONAL UNITS)	VITAMIN A (RETINOL EQUIVALENTS)	RIBOFLAVIN (MILLIGRAMS)	CALCIUM (MILLIGRAMS)	CALCIUM PER 100 GRAMS	CALCIUM PER 100 CALORIES
Sweet Cream	Whipping cream	heavy, unwhipped	1 cup	238	820	149	3500	1002	0.26	154	65	19
			1 tbsp	15	50	9	220	63	0.02	10	67	20
	Whipped topping	pressurized can	1 cup	60	155	54	550	124	0.04	61	102	39
			1 tbsp	3	10	1	30	6	Trace	3	100	30
Ice Cream, vanilla	Regular	hard, 11% fat	1/2 gal	1064	2155	1075	4340	1064	2.63	1406	132	65
			1 cup	133	270	134	540	133	0.33	176	132	65
	Rich	hard, 16% fat	1/2 gal	1188	2805	927	7200	1758	2.27	1213	102	43
			1 cup	148	350	115	900	219	0.28	151	102	43
	Soft serve	frozen custard	1 cup	173	375	199	790	199	0.45	236	136	63
Ice Milk, vanilla	Regular	hard, 4% fat	1/2 gal	1048	1470	1035	1710	419	2.78	1409	134	96
			1 cup	131	185	129	210	52	0.35	176	134	95
		soft serve, 3% fat	1 cup	175	225	202	175	44	0.54	274	157	122
Sherbet		2% fat	1/2 gal	1542	2160	594	1480	308	0.71	827	54	38
			1 cup	193	270	74	190	39	0.09	103	53	38

CATEGORY	STYLE	TYPE	SIZE OR NUMBER	GRAMS	CALORIES	PHOSPHORUS (MILLIGRAMS)	VITAMIN A (INTERNATIONAL UNITS)	VITAMIN A (RETINOL EQUIVALENTS)	RIBOFLAVIN (MILLIGRAMS)	CALCIUM (MILLIGRAMS)	CALCIUM PER 100 GRAMS	CALCIUM PER 100 CALORIES
DAIRY PRODUCTS												
Sour Cream			1 cup	230	495	195	1820	448	0.34	268	117	54
			1 tbsp	12	25	10	90	23	0.02	14	117	56
Yogurt	lowfat milk	fruit-flavored	8 oz	227	230	271	100	25	0.40	345	152	150
		plain	8 oz	227	145	326	150	36	0.49	415	183	286
	nonfat milk		8 oz	227	125	355	20	5	0.53	452	199	362
FISH AND SHELLFISH												
Clams	Raw		3 oz	85	65	138	90	26	0.15	59	69	91
	Canned		3 oz	85	85	116	90	26	0.15	47	55	55
Crabmeat	Canned		1 cup	135	135	246	50	14	0.11	61	45	45
Fish sticks		breaded, cooked	1 stick	28	70	58	20	5	0.05	11	39	16
Flounder or Sole		baked, no added fat	3 oz	85	80	197	30	10	0.08	13	15	16
Haddock		breaded, fried	3 oz	85	175	183	70	20	0.10	34	40	19
Halibut		broiled, butter/lemon juice	3 oz	85	140	206	610	174	0.07	14	16	10
Herring		pickled	3 oz	85	190	128	110	33	0.18	29	34	15
Ocean perch		breaded, fried	3 oz	85	185	191	70	20	0.11	31	36	17

CATEGORY	STYLE	TYPE	SIZE OR NUMBER	GRAMS	CALORIES	PHOSPHORUS (MILLIGRAMS)	VITAMIN A (INTERNATIONAL UNITS)	VITAMIN A (RETINOL EQUIVALENTS)	RIBOFLAVIN (MILLIGRAMS)	CALCIUM (MILLIGRAMS)	CALCIUM PER 100 GRAMS	CALCIUM PER 100 CALORIES
FISH AND SHELLFISH												
Oysters	Raw		1 cup	240	160	343	740	223	0.43	226	94	141
Salmon	Canned	pink	3 oz	85	120	243	60	18	0.15	167	196	139
	Baked	red	3 oz	85	140	269	290	87	0.14	26	31	19
	Smoked		3 oz	85	150	208	260	77	0.17	12	14	8
Sardines	Canned	in oil, drained	3 oz	85	175	424	190	56	0.17	371	436	212
Scallops		breaded	6	90	195	203	70	21	0.11	39	43	20
Shrimp	Canned		3 oz	85	100	224	50	15	0.03	98	115	98
	Fresh	breaded, fried	3 oz	85	200	154	90	26	0.09	61	77	252
Tuna	Canned	in oil, drained, chunk light	3 oz	85	165	199	70	20	0.09	7	8	4
		in water, solid white	3 oz	85	135	202	110	32	0.10	17	20	13
FRUITS												
Apple		peeled, sliced	1 cup	110	65	8	50	5	0.01	4	4	6
Apple-sauce		sweetened	1 cup	255	195	18	30	3	0.07	10	4	5
		unsweetened	1 cup	244	105	17	70	7	0.06	7	3	7
Apricot			3	106	50	20	2770	277	0.04	15	14	30

FRUITS

CATEGORY	STYLE	TYPE	SIZE OR NUMBER	GRAMS	CALORIES	PHOSPHORUS (MILLIGRAMS)	VITAMIN A (INTERNATIONAL UNITS)	(RETINOL EQUIVALENTS)	RIBOFLAVIN (MILLIGRAMS)	CALCIUM (MILLIGRAMS)	CALCIUM PER 100 GRAMS	CALCIUM PER 100 CALORIES
Apricot	Canned	in heavy syrup	1 cup	258	215	31	3170	317	0.06	23	9	11
		in heavy syrup	3 halves	85	70	10	1050	105	0.02	8	9	11
	Canned	in juice	1 cup	248	120	50	4190	419	0.05	30	12	25
		in juice	3 halves	84	40	17	1420	142	0.02	10	12	25
	Dried	uncooked	1 cup	130	310	152	9410	941	0.20	59	45	19
		cooked, unsweetened	1 cup	250	210	103	5910	591	0.08	40	16	19
Avocados	California	no skin or seed	1	173	305	73	1060	106	0.21	19	11	6
	Florida	no skin or seed	1	304	340	119	1860	186	0.37	33	11	10
Bananas		no peel	1	114	105	23	90	9	0.11	7	6	7
		sliced, no peel	1 cup	150	140	30	120	12	0.15	9	6	6
Blackberries			1 cup	144	75	30	240	24	0.06	46	32	61
Blueberries			1 cup	145	80	15	150	15	0.07	9	6	11
Cantaloupes			1/2	267	95	45	8610	861	0.06	29	11	31
Cherries		whole (no pits)	10	68	50	13	150	15	0.04	10	15	20

FRUITS

CATEGORY	STYLE	TYPE	SIZE OR NUMBER	GRAMS	CALORIES	PHOSPHORUS (MILLIGRAMS)	VITAMIN A (INTERNATIONAL UNITS)	VITAMIN A (RETINOL EQUIVALENTS)	RIBOFLAVIN (MILLIGRAMS)	CALCIUM (MILLIGRAMS)	CALCIUM PER 100 GRAMS	CALCIUM PER 100 CALORIES
Dates		whole (no pits)	10	83	230	33	40	4	0.08	27	33	12
		chopped	1 cup	178	490	71	90	9	0.18	57	32	12
Figs		dried	10	187	475	127	250	25	0.16	269	144	57
Grapefruit			1/2	120	40	10	10	1	0.02	14	12	35
Grapes	Thompson seedless		10	50	35	7	40	4	0.03	6	12	17
	Tokay or Emperor seeded		10	57	40	7	40	4	0.03	6	11	15
Honeydew			1/10	129	45	13	50	5	0.02	8	6	18
Kiwifruit			1	76	45	30	130	13	0.04	20	26	44
Lemons			1	58	15	9	20	2	0.01	15	26	100
Mangoes			1	207	135	23	8060	806	0.12	21	10	16
Nectarines			1	136	65	22	1000	100	0.06	7	5	11
Oranges			1	131	60	18	270	27	0.05	52	40	87
Papayas			1 cup	140	65	12	400	40	0.04	35	25	54
Peaches	Fresh		1	87	35	10	470	47	0.04	4	5	11
	Canned	in heavy syrup	1 cup	256	190	28	850	85	0.06	8	3	4
			1 half	81	60	9	270	27	0.02	2	2	3
		in juice	1 cup	248	110	42	940	94	0.04	15	6	14
			1 half	77	35	13	290	29	0.01	5	6	14
	Dried	uncooked	1 cup	160	380	190	3460	346	0.34	45	28	12

FRUITS

CATEGORY	STYLE	TYPE	SIZE OR NUMBER	GRAMS	CALORIES	PHOSPHORUS (MILLIGRAMS)	VITAMIN A (INTERNATIONAL UNITS)	VITAMIN A (RETINOL EQUIVALENTS)	RIBOFLAVIN (MILLIGRAMS)	CALCIUM (MILLIGRAMS)	CALCIUM PER 100 GRAMS	CALCIUM PER 100 CALORIES
Peaches	Dried	cooked, unsweetened	1 cup	258	200	98	510	51	0.05	23	9	12
Pears	Bartlett		1	166	100	18	30	3	0.07	18	11	18
	Bosc		1	141	85	16	30	3	0.06	16	11	19
	D'Anjou		1	200	120	22	40	4	0.08	22	11	18
	Canned	in heavy syrup	1 cup	255	190	18	10	1	0.06	13	5	7
			1 half	79	60	6	Trace	Trace	0.02	4	5	7
		in juice	1 cup	248	125	30	10	1	0.03	22	9	18
			1 half	77	40	9	Trace	Trace	0.01	7	9	18
		diced	1 cup	155	75	11	40	4	0.06	11	7	15
Pineapples	Canned	in heavy syrup, chunks	1 cup	255	200	18	40	4	0.06	36	14	18
		in heavy syrup, slices	1 slice	58	45	4	10	1	0.01	8	14	18
		in juice, chunks	1 cup	250	150	15	100	10	0.05	35	14	23
		in juice, slices	1 slice	58	35	3	20	2	0.01	8	14	23
Plantains			1	179	220	61	2020	202	0.10	5	3	2
			1 cup	154	180	43	1400	140	0.08	3	2	2
Plums	boiled		1	66	35	7	210	21	0.06	3	5	9

CATEGORY	STYLE	TYPE	SIZE OR NUMBER	GRAMS	CALORIES	PHOSPHORUS (MILLIGRAMS)	VITAMIN A (INTERNATIONAL UNITS)	VITAMIN A (RETINOL EQUIVALENTS)	RIBOFLAVIN (MILLIGRAMS)	CALCIUM (MILLIGRAMS)	CALCIUM PER 100 GRAMS	CALCIUM PER 100 CALORIES
FRUITS												
Plums	Canned	in heavy syrup	1 cup	258	230	34	670	67	0.10	23	9	10
			3 plums	133	120	17	340	34	0.05	12	9	10
		in juice	1 cup	252	145	38	2540	254	0.15	25	10	17
			3 plums	95	55	14	960	96	0.06	10	11	18
Prunes			5	49	115	39	970	97	0.08	25	51	22
		cooked, unsweetened	1 cup	212	225	74	650	65	0.21	49	23	22
Raisins		seedless	1 cup	145	435	141	10	1	0.13	71	49	16
Raspberries			1 cup	123	60	15	160	16	0.11	27	22	45
Rhubarb		cooked, with sugar	1 cup	240	280	19	170	17	0.06	348	145	124
Strawberries			1 cup	149	45	28	40	4	0.10	21	14	47
Tangerines			1	84	35	8	770	77	0.02	12	14	34
	Canned	in light syrup	1 cup	252	155	25	2120	212	0.11	18	7	12
Watermelons			1 piece	482	155	43	1760	176	0.10	39	8	25
FRUIT JUICES												
Apple juice	Canned		1 cup	248	115	17	Trace	Trace	0.04	17	7	15
Apricot nectar	Canned		1 cup	251	140	23	3300	330	0.04	18	7	13
Cranberry juice cocktail		sweetened	1 cup	253	145	3	10	1	0.04	8	3	6

FRUIT JUICES

CATEGORY	STYLE	TYPE	SIZE OR NUMBER	GRAMS	CALORIES	PHOSPHORUS (MILLIGRAMS)	VITAMIN A (INTERNATIONAL UNITS)	VITAMIN A (RETINOL EQUIVALENTS)	RIBOFLAVIN (MILLIGRAMS)	CALCIUM (MILLIGRAMS)	CALCIUM PER 100 GRAMS	CALCIUM PER 100 CALORIES
Grapefruit juice		fresh	1 cup	247	95	37	20	2	0.05	22	9	23
	Canned	unsweetened	1 cup	247	95	27	20	2	0.05	17	7	18
		sweetened	1 cup	250	115	28	20	2	0.06	20	8	17
	Frozen	unsweetened, w/ water	1 cup	247	100	35	20	2	0.05	20	8	20
Grape juice	Canned		1 cup	253	155	28	20	2	0.09	23	18	122
	Frozen	sweetened, w/ water	1 cup	250	125	10	20	2	0.07	10	4	8
Lemon juice		fresh	1 cup	244	60	15	50	5	0.02	17	7	28
	Canned	unsweetened	1 cup	244	50	22	40	4	0.02	27	11	54
Lime juice		fresh	1 cup	246	65	17	20	2	0.02	22	9	34
	Canned	unsweetened	1 cup	246	50	25	40	4	0.01	30	12	60
Orange juice		fresh	1 cup	248	110	42	500	50	0.07	27	11	25
	Canned	unsweetened	1 cup	249	105	35	440	44	0.07	20	8	19
	Frozen	unsweetened, w/ water	1 cup	249	110	40	190	19	0.04	22	9	20
Pineapple juice	Canned	unsweetened	1 cup	250	140	20	10	1	0.06	43	17	31
Prune juice	Canned		1 cup	256	180	64	10	1	0.18	31	12	17
Tangerine juice	Canned	sweetened	1 cup	249	125	35	1050	105	0.05	45	18	36

GRAINS AND PASTAS

CATEGORY	STYLE	TYPE	SIZE OR NUMBER	GRAMS	CALORIES	PHOSPHORUS (MILLIGRAMS)	VITAMIN A (INTERNATIONAL UNITS)	VITAMIN A (RETINOL EQUIVALENTS)	RIBOFLAVIN (MILLIGRAMS)	CALCIUM (MILLIGRAMS)	CALCIUM PER 100 GRAMS	CALCIUM PER 100 CALORIES
Barley	Pearled	light, uncooked	1 cup	200	700	378	0	0	0.10	32	16	5
Buckwheat	flour	light, sifted	1 cup	98	340	86	0	0	0.04	11	11	3
Bulgur		uncooked	1 cup	170	600	575	0	0	0.24	49	29	8
Cornmeal	Whole-ground	unbolted, dry form	1 cup	122	435	312	620	62	0.13	24	20	6
	Bolted	dry form	1 cup	122	440	272	590	59	0.10	21	17	5
	Degermed enriched	dry form	1 cup	138	500	137	610	61	0.36	8	6	2
		cooked	1 cup	240	120	34	140	14	0.10	2	1	2
Egg Noodles	Enriched	cooked	1 cup	160	200	94	110	34	0.13	16	10	8
Macaroni	Enriched	cooked, firm stage, hot	1 cup	130	190	85	0	0	0.13	14	11	7
	Enriched	cooked, tender stage, hot	1 cup	140	155	70	0	0	0.11	11	8	7
Rice	Brown	cooked	1 cup	185	670	174	0	0	0.06	44	24	7
	White	cooked	1 cup	205	225	57	0	0	0.02	21	10	9
		Instant, cooked	1 cup	165	180	31	0	0	0.02	5	3	3

CATEGORY	STYLE	TYPE	SIZE OR NUMBER	GRAMS	CALORIES	PHOSPHORUS (MILLIGRAMS)	VITAMIN A (INTERNATIONAL UNITS)	VITAMIN A (RETINOL EQUIVALENTS)	RIBOFLAVIN (MILLIGRAMS)	CALCIUM (MILLIGRAMS)	CALCIUM PER 100 GRAMS	CALCIUM PER 100 CALORIES
GRAINS AND PASTAS												
Rice		Parboiled, cooked	1 cup	175	185	100	0	0	0.02	33	19	18
Spaghetti	Enriched	cooked, firm stage, hot	1 cup	130	190	85	0	0	0.13	14	11	7
		cooked, tender stage, hot	1 cup	140	155	70	0	0	0.11	11	8	7
Wheat flours	All-purpose	enriched, sifted	1 cup	115	420	100	0	0	0.46	18	16	4
		enriched, unsifted	1 cup	125	455	109	0	0	0.50	20	16	4
	Cake or Pastry	enriched, sifted	1 cup	96	350	70	0	0	0.38	16	17	5
	Self-rising	enriched, unsifted	1 cup	125	440	583	0	0	0.50	331	265	75
	Whole-wheat	from hard wheats	1 cup	120	400	446	0	0	0.14	49	41	12
LEGUMES, NUTS AND SEEDS												
Almonds	Shelled	slivered, packed	1 cup	135	795	702	0	0	1.05	359	266	45
		whole	1 oz	28	165	147	0	0	0.22	75	268	45
Beans	Black	cooked	1 cup	171	225	239	Trace	Trace	0.05	47	27	21

LEGUMES, NUTS AND SEEDS

CATEGORY	STYLE	TYPE	SIZE OR NUMBER	GRAMS	CALORIES	PHOSPHORUS (MILLIGRAMS)	VITAMIN A (INTERNATIONAL UNITS)	(RETINOL EQUIVALENTS)	RIBOFLAVIN (MILLIGRAMS)	CALCIUM (MILLIGRAMS)	CALCIUM PER 100 GRAMS	CALCIUM PER 100 CALORIES
Beans	Great Northern	cooked	1 cup	180	210	266	0	0	0.13	90	50	43
	Lima	cooked	1 cup	190	260	293	0	0	0.11	55	29	21
	Pea (navy)	cooked	1 cup	190	225	281	0	0	0.13	95	50	42
	Pinto	cooked	1 cup	180	265	296	Trace	Trace	0.16	86	48	32
	Red Kidney	canned	1 cup	255	230	278	10	1	0.10	74	29	32
Black-eyed Peas		cooked	1 cup	250	190	238	30	3	0.10	43	17	23
Brazil Nuts	Shelled		1 oz	28	185	170	Trace	Trace	0.03	50	179	27
Cashew Nuts		dry roasted	1 oz	28	165	139	0	0	0.06	12	43	7
		roasted in oil	1 oz	28	165	121	0	0	0.05	12	589	7
Chestnuts	European roasted,	shelled	1 cup	143	350	153	30	3	0.25	41	245	12
Chickpeas		cooked	1 cup	163	270	273	Trace	Trace	0.09	80	49	30
Coconut	raw,	shredded	1 cup	80	285	90	0	0	0.02	11	14	4
	dried, sweetened,	shredded	1 cup	93	470	99	0	0	0.02	14	15	3

LEGUMES, NUTS AND SEEDS

CATEGORY	STYLE	TYPE	SIZE OR NUMBER	GRAMS	CALORIES	PHOSPHORUS (MILLIGRAMS)	VITAMIN A (INTERNATIONAL UNITS)	VITAMIN A (RETINOL EQUIVALENTS)	RIBOFLAVIN (MILLIGRAMS)	CALCIUM (MILLIGRAMS)	CALCIUM PER 100 GRAMS	CALCIUM PER 100 CALORIES
Filberts (Hazelnuts)		chopped	1 oz	28	180	88	20	2	0.03	53	189	29
Lentils		cooked	1 cup	200	215	238	40	4	0.12	50	25	23
Macadamia Nuts		roasted in oil	1 oz	28	205	57	Trace	Trace	0.03	13	46	6
Peanuts		roasted in oil	1 oz	28	165	143	0	0	0.03	24	86	15
Peanut Butter			1 tbsp	16	95	60	0	0	0.02	5	31	5
Peas, Split		cooked	1 cup	200	230	178	80	8	0.18	22	11	10
Pecans			1 oz	28	190	83	40	4	0.04	10	36	5
Pine Nuts	Shelled		1 oz	28	160	10	10	1	0.06	2	7	1
Pistachio Nuts	Shelled	dried	1 oz	28	165	143	70	7	0.05	38	136	23
Soybeans		cooked	1 cup	180	235	322	50	5	0.16	131	73	56
Walnuts	Black	chopped	1 oz	28	170	132	80	8	0.03	16	57	9
	English	pieces	1 oz	28	180	90	40	4	0.04	27	96	15

MEAT AND MEAT PRODUCTS

CATEGORY	STYLE	TYPE	SIZE OR NUMBER	GRAMS	CALORIES	PHOSPHORUS (MILLIGRAMS)	VITAMIN A (INTERNATIONAL UNITS)	VITAMIN A (RETINOL EQUIVALENTS)	RIBOFLAVIN (MILLIGRAMS)	CALCIUM (MILLIGRAMS)	CALCIUM PER 100 GRAMS	CALCIUM PER 100 CALORIES
Beef	Chuck Blade	pot roasted, lean only	2.2 oz	62	170	146	Trace	Trace	0.17	8	13	5
	Bottom Round	pot roasted, lean only	2.8 oz	78	175	212	Trace	Trace	0.20	4	5	2
	Ground	broiled, lean	3 oz	85	230	134	Trace	Trace	0.18	9	11	4
		broiled, regular	3 oz	85	245	144	Trace	Trace	0.16	9	11	4

MEAT AND MEAT PRODUCTS

CATEGORY	STYLE	TYPE	SIZE OR NUMBER	GRAMS	CALORIES	PHOSPHORUS (MILLIGRAMS)	VITAMIN A (INTERNATIONAL UNITS)	VITAMIN A (RETINOL EQUIVALENTS)	RIBOFLAVIN (MILLIGRAMS)	CALCIUM (MILLIGRAMS)	CALCIUM PER 100 GRAMS	CALCIUM PER 100 CALORIES
	Rib Roast	oven roasted, lean only	2.2 oz	61	150	177	Trace	Trace	0.13	5	8	3
	Eye of Round Roast	oven roasted, lean only	2.6 oz	75	135	170	Trace	Trace	0.13	3	4	2
	Sirloin steak	broiled, lean only	2.5 oz	72	150	176	Trace	Trace	0.22	8	11	5
	Heart	braised	3 oz	85	150	213	Trace	Trace	1.31	5	6	3
	Liver	fried	3 oz	85	185	392	30690	9120	3.52	9	11	5
Lamb	Arm chop	braised, lean only	1.7 oz	48	135	111	Trace	Trace	0.13	12	25	9
	Loin chop	broiled, lean only	2.3 oz	64	140	145	Trace	Trace	0.18	12	19	9
	Leg	roasted, lean only	2.6 oz	73	140	150	Trace	Trace	0.20	6	8	4
	Rib	roasted, lean only	2 oz	57	130	111	Trace	Trace	0.13	12	21	9
Pork, cured, cooked	Bacon	Regular	3 slices	19	110	64	0	0	0.05	2	11	2
		Canadian-style	2 slices	46	85	136	0	0	0.09	5	11	6

MEAT AND MEAT PRODUCTS

CATEGORY	STYLE	TYPE	SIZE OR NUMBER	GRAMS	CALORIES	PHOSPHORUS (MILLIGRAMS)	VITAMIN A (INTERNATIONAL UNITS)	VITAMIN A (RETINOL EQUIVALENTS)	RIBOFLAVIN (MILLIGRAMS)	CALCIUM (MILLIGRAMS)	CALCIUM PER 100 GRAMS	CALCIUM PER 100 CALORIES
Pork, cured, cooked												
	Ham	roasted, lean only	2.4 oz	68	105	154	0	0	0.17	5	7	5
		canned, roasted	3 oz	85	140	188	0	0	0.21	6	7	4
	Luncheon meat	canned	2 slices	42	140	34	0	0	0.08	3	7	2
		chopped ham	2 slices	42	95	65	0	0	0.09	3	7	3
		cooked ham, regular	2 slices	57	105	141	0	0	0.14	4	7	4
		cooked ham, extra lean	2 slices	57	75	124	0	0	0.13	4	7	5
Pork, fresh, cooked												
	Loin chop	broiled, lean only	2.5 oz	72	165	176	10	1	0.22	4	6	2
		panfried, lean only	2.4 oz	67	180	178	10	1	0.22	3	4	2
	Ham leg	roasted, lean only	2.5 oz	72	160	202	10	1	0.25	5	7	3
	Rib	roasted, lean only	2.5 oz	71	175	182	10	1	0.22	8	11	5
	Shoulder	braised, lean only	2.4 oz	67	165	151	10	1	0.24	5	7	3

CATEGORY	STYLE	TYPE	SIZE OR NUMBER	GRAMS	CALORIES	PHOSPHORUS (MILLIGRAMS)	VITAMIN A (INTERNATIONAL UNITS)	VITAMIN A (RETINOL EQUIVALENTS)	RIBOFLAVIN (MILLIGRAMS)	CALCIUM (MILLIGRAMS)	CALCIUM PER 100 GRAMS	CALCIUM PER 100 CALORIES
MEAT AND MEAT PRODUCTS												
Pork sausages												
	Bologna		2 slices	57	180	52	0	0	0.08	7	12	4
	Braunschweiger		2 slices	57	205	96	8010	2405	0.87	5	9	2
	Brown and serve	browned	1 link	13	50	14	0	0	0.02	1	8	2
	Frankfurter	cooked	1 frank	45	145	39	0	0	0.05	5	11	3
	Pork link	cooked	1 link	13	50	24	0	0	0.03	4	31	8
	Salami	cooked-type	2 slices	57	145	66	0	0	0.21	7	12	5
		dry-type	2 slices	20	85	28	0	0	0.06	2	10	2
	Sandwich spread	pork, beef	1 tbsp	15	35	9	10	1	0.02	2	13	6
	Vienna sausage		1 sausage	16	45	8	0	0	0.02	2	13	4
Veal	Cutlet	braised or broiled	3 oz	85	185	196	Trace	Trace	0.21	9	11	5
	Rib	roasted	3 oz	85	230	211	Trace	Trace	0.26	10	12	4
POULTRY AND POULTRY PRODUCTS												
Chicken	Breast	fried, batter dipped	4.9 oz	140	365	259	90	28	0.20	28	20	8
		fried, flour coated	3.5 oz	98	220	228	50	15	0.13	16	16	7

POULTRY AND POULTRY PRODUCTS

CATEGORY	STYLE	TYPE	SIZE OR NUMBER	GRAMS	CALORIES	PHOSPHORUS (MILLIGRAMS)	VITAMIN A (INTERNATIONAL UNITS)	VITAMIN A (RETINOL EQUIVALENTS)	RIBOFLAVIN (MILLIGRAMS)	CALCIUM (MILLIGRAMS)	CALCIUM PER 100 GRAMS	CALCIUM PER 100 CALORIES
Chicken	Breast	roasted, flesh only	3.0 oz	86	140	196	20	5	0.10	13	15	9
	Drumstick	fried, batter dipped	2.5 oz	72	195	106	60	19	0.15	12	17	6
		fried, flour coated	1.7 oz	49	120	86	40	12	0.11	6	12	5
		roasted, flesh only	1.6 oz	44	75	81	30	8	0.10	5	11	7
	Light and dark meat	stewed, flesh only	1 cup	140	250	210	70	21	0.23	20	14	8
	Liver	cooked	1 liver	20	30	62	3270	983	0.35	3	15	10
	Canned	boneless	5 oz	142	235	158	170	51	0.18	20	14	9
	Frankfurter		1 frank	45	115	48	60	17	0.05	43	96	37
	Roll	light	2 slices	57	90	89	50	14	0.07	24	42	27
	Egg	whole	1	50	75	89	320	95	0.25	25	50	33
		white only	1	33	15	4	0	0	0.15	2	6	13
		yolk only	1	17	60	81	320	97	0.11	23	135	38
Turkey	Dark meat	roasted, flesh only	3 oz	85	160	173	0	0	0.21	27	32	17
	Light meat	roasted, flesh only	3 oz	85	135	186	0	0	0.11	16	19	12

POULTRY AND POULTRY PRODUCTS

CATEGORY	STYLE	TYPE	SIZE OR NUMBER	GRAMS	CAL-ORIES	PHOS-PHORUS (MILLI-GRAMS)	VITAMIN A (INTER-NATIONAL UNITS)	VITAMIN A (RETINOL EQUIVA-LENTS)	RIBO-FLAVIN (MILLI-GRAMS)	CALCIUM (MILLI-GRAMS)	CALCIUM PER 100 GRAMS	CALCIUM PER 100 CALORIES
Turkey	Frozen	gravy and turkey boneless	5 oz	142	95	115	60	18	0.18	20	14	21
		roast, cooked	3 oz	85	130	207	0	0	0.14	4	5	3
	Loaf	breast meat	2 slices	42	45	97	0	0	0.05	3	7	7
	Patties	breaded, fried	1 patty	64	180	173	20	7	0.12	9	14	5
VEGETABLES												
Artichokes		cooked, from raw	1	120	55	72	170	17	0.06	47	39	85
Asparagus	Green	cooked, from raw	1 cup	180	45	110	1490	149	0.22	43	24	96
		cooked, from frozen	1 cup	180	50	99	1470	147	0.19	41	23	82
Bamboo Shoots		canned	1 cup	131	25	33	10	1	0.03	10	8	40
Bean Sprouts	Mung	cooked, from raw	1 cup	124	25	35	20	2	0.13	15	12	60
Beets		cooked, diced	1 cup	170	55	53	20	2	0.02	19	11	35
		canned, diced	1 cup	170	55	29	20	2	0.07	26	15	47

CATEGORY	STYLE	TYPE	SIZE OR NUMBER	GRAMS	CALORIES	PHOSPHORUS (MILLIGRAMS)	VITAMIN A (INTERNATIONAL UNITS)	VITAMIN A (RETINOL EQUIVALENTS)	RIBOFLAVIN (MILLIGRAMS)	CALCIUM (MILLIGRAMS)	CALCIUM PER 100 GRAMS	CALCIUM PER 100 CALORIES
VEGETABLES												
Beet Greens		cooked, from raw	1 cup	144	40	59	7340	734	0.42	164	114	410
Black-eyed Peas		cooked, from raw	1 cup	165	180	196	1050	105	0.18	46	28	26
Broccoli		cooked, from frozen	1 cup	170	225	207	130	13	0.11	39	23	17
		raw	1 spear	151	40	100	2330	233	0.18	72	48	180
		cooked, from raw	1 cup	155	45	74	2180	218	0.32	71	46	158
		cooked, from frozen	1 cup	185	50	102	3500	350	0.15	94	51	188
Brussels Sprouts		cooked, from raw	1 cup	155	60	87	1110	111	0.12	56	36	93
		cooked, from frozen	1 cup	155	65	84	910	91	0.18	37	24	57
Cabbage		raw, shredded	1 cup	70	15	16	90	9	0.02	33	47	220
		cooked, from raw	1 cup	150	30	38	130	13	0.08	50	33	167
	Red	raw, shredded	1 cup	70	20	29	30	3	0.02	36	51	180
	Savoy	raw, shredded	1 cup	70	20	29	700	70	0.02	25	36	125

CATEGORY	STYLE	TYPE	SIZE OR NUMBER	GRAMS	CALORIES	PHOSPHORUS (MILLIGRAMS)	VITAMIN A (INTERNATIONAL UNITS)	(RETINOL EQUIVALENTS)	RIBOFLAVIN (MILLIGRAMS)	CALCIUM (MILLIGRAMS)	CALCIUM PER 100 GRAMS	CALCIUM PER 100 CALORIES
VEGETABLES												
Carrots		raw, grated	1 cup	110	45	48	30940	3094	0.06	30	27	67
		cooked, from raw	1 cup	156	70	47	38300	3830	0.09	48	31	69
Cauliflower		cooked, from frozen	1 cup	146	55	38	25850	2585	0.05	41	28	75
		raw, flowerets	1 cup	100	25	46	20	2	0.06	29	29	116
		cooked, from raw	1 cup	125	30	44	20	2	0.07	34	27	113
		cooked, from frozen	1 cup	180	35	43	40	4	0.10	31	17	89
Celery	Pascal	raw, diced	1 cup	120	20	31	150	15	0.04	43	36	215
Chinese Cabbage	Pak-choi,	cooked	1 cup	170	20	49	4370	437	0.11	158	93	790
		Pe-tsai, raw	1 cup	76	10	22	910	91	0.04	59	78	590
Collard Greens		cooked, from raw	1 cup	190	25	19	4220	422	0.08	148	78	592
		cooked, from frozen	1 cup	170	60	46	10170	1017	0.20	357	210	595
Corn	Sweet	raw	1 ear	77	85	79	170	17	0.06	2	3	2
		cooked, from frozen	1 ear	63	60	47	130	13	0.04	2	3	3

CATEGORY	STYLE	TYPE	SIZE OR NUMBER	GRAMS	CALORIES	PHOSPHORUS (MILLIGRAMS)	VITAMIN A (INTERNATIONAL UNITS)	VITAMIN A (RETINOL EQUIVALENTS)	RIBOFLAVIN (MILLIGRAMS)	CALCIUM (MILLIGRAMS)	CALCIUM PER 100 GRAMS	CALCIUM PER 100 CALORIES
VEGETABLES												
Corn		cooked, frozen kernels	1 cup	165	135	78	410	41	0.12	3	2	2
	Canned	cream style	1 cup	256	185	131	250	25	0.14	8	3	4
		whole kernel	1 cup	210	165	134	510	51	0.15	11	5	7
Cucumber		raw, with peel	1 oz	28	5	5	10	1	0.01	4	14	80
Dandelion Greens		cooked, from raw	1 cup	105	35	44	12290	1229	0.18	147	140	420
Eggplant		cooked, steamed	1 cup	96	25	21	60	6	0.02	6	6	24
Endive or Escarole		raw	1 cup	50	10	14	1030	103	0.04	26	52	260
Jerusalem Artichoke		raw, sliced	1 cup	150	115	117	30	3	0.09	21	14	18
Kale		cooked, from raw	1 cup	130	40	36	9620	962	0.09	94	72	235
		cooked, from frozen	1 cup	130	40	36	8260	826	0.15	179	138	448
Kohlrabi		cooked, diced	1 cup	165	50	74	60	6	0.03	41	25	82
Lettuce	Boston	raw	1 head	163	20	38	1580	158	0.10	52	32	260

VEGETABLES

CATEGORY	STYLE	TYPE	SIZE OR NUMBER	GRAMS	CAL-ORIES	PHOS-PHORUS (MILLI-GRAMS)	VITAMIN A (INTER-NATIONAL UNITS)	(RETINOL EQUIVA-LENTS)	RIBO-FLAVIN (MILLI-GRAMS)	CALCIUM (MILLI-GRAMS)	CALCIUM PER 100 GRAMS	CALCIUM PER 100 CALORIES
Lettuce	Iceberg	raw	1 head	539	70	108	1780	178	0.16	102	19	146
	Romaine	raw	1 cup	56	10	14	1060	106	0.04	38	68	380
Lima Beans	Ford-hook	cooked, from frozen	1 cup	170	170	37	320	32	0.10	32	19	19
Mushrooms		raw, chopped	1 cup	70	20	73	0	0	0.31	4	6	20
		cooked, from raw	1 cup	156	40	136	0	0	0.47	9	6	23
		canned	1 cup	156	35	103	0	0	0.03	17	11	49
Mustard Greens		cooked, no stems	1 cup	140	20	57	4240	424	0.09	104	74	520
Okra		cooked, from raw	8 pods	85	25	48	490	49	0.05	54	64	216
Onions		raw, chopped	1 cup	160	55	46	0	0	0.02	40	25	73
		cooked	1 cup	210	60	48	0	0	0.02	57	27	95
Parsley		raw	10 sprigs	10	5	4	520	52	0.01	13	130	260
Parsnips		cooked, diced	1 cup	156	125	108	0	0	0.08	58	37	46
Peas	Green	canned	1 cup	170	115	114	1310	131	0.13	34	20	30
		cooked, from frozen	1 cup	160	125	144	1070	107	0.16	38	24	30

VEGETABLES

CATEGORY	STYLE	TYPE	SIZE OR NUMBER	GRAMS	CALORIES	PHOSPHORUS (MILLIGRAMS)	VITAMIN A (INTERNATIONAL UNITS)	VITAMIN A (RETINOL EQUIVALENTS)	RIBOFLAVIN (MILLIGRAMS)	CALCIUM (MILLIGRAMS)	CALCIUM PER 100 GRAMS	CALCIUM PER 100 CALORIES
Peppers	Red Chili	raw	1	45	20	21	4840	484	0.04	8	18	40
	Sweet Red	raw	1	74	20	16	390	39	0.04	4	5	20
		cooked, from raw	1	73	15	11	280	28	0.03	3	4	20
Potatoes	Fresh	baked, with skin	1	202	220	115	0	0	0.07	20	10	9
		baked, no skin	1	156	145	78	0	0	0.03	8	5	6
		boiled, no skin	1	135	115	54	0	0	0.03	11	8	10
	French Fries	oven heated	10	50	110	43	0	0	0.02	5	10	5
		fried in oil	10	50	160	47	0	0	0.01	10	20	6
Pumpkin		cooked, from raw	1 cup	245	50	74	2650	265	0.19	37	15	74
		canned	1 cup	245	85	86	54040	5404	0.13	64	26	75
Radishes		raw	4	18	5	3	Trace	0	0.01	4	22	80
Spinach		raw, chopped	1 cup	55	10	27	3690	369	0.10	54	98	540
		cooked, from raw	1 cup	180	40	101	14740	1474	0.42	245	136	613
		cooked, from frozen	1 cup	190	55	91	14790	1479	0.32	277	146	504

CATEGORY	STYLE	TYPE	SIZE OR NUMBER	GRAMS	CALORIES	PHOSPHORUS (MILLIGRAMS)	VITAMIN A (INTERNATIONAL UNITS)	(RETINOL EQUIVALENTS)	RIBOFLAVIN (MILLIGRAMS)	CALCIUM (MILLIGRAMS)	CALCIUM PER 100 GRAMS	CALCIUM PER 100 CALORIES
VEGETABLES												
Squash	Summer	cooked, from raw	1 cup	180	35	70	520	52	0.07	49	27	140
	Winter	cooked, from raw	1 cup	205	80	41	7290	729	0.05	29	14	36
Sweet Potatoes		baked, no skin	1	114	115	63	24880	2488	0.14	32	28	28
		boiled, no skin	1	151	160	41	25750	2575	0.21	32	21	20
		canned	1 cup	255	260	133	38570	3857	0.23	77	30	30
Tomatoes		raw	1	123	25	28	1390	139	0.06	9	7	36
		canned, whole	1 cup	240	50	46	1450	145	0.07	62	26	124
		canned, paste	1 cup	262	220	207	6470	647	0.50	92	35	42
		canned, puree	1 cup	250	105	100	3400	340	0.14	38	15	36
		canned, sauce	1 cup	245	75	78	2400	240	0.14	34	14	45
Turnip Greens		cooked, from raw	1 cup	144	30	42	7920	792	0.10	197	137	657
		cooked, from frozen	1 cup	164	50	56	13080	1308	0.12	249	152	498
Turnips		cooked, diced	1 cup	156	30	30	0	0	0.04	34	22	113
Water Chestnuts		canned	1 cup	140	70	27	10	1	0.03	6	4	9

APPENDIX III

LACTOSE-CONTAINING PRESCRIPTION MEDICATIONS

The use of lactose as an inactive ingredient in medications of all kinds is a common practice in the pharmaceutical industry. An estimated 20% of prescription drugs and 6% of over-the-counter medicines use lactose. It is even possible that the medicine you unwittingly take to control symptoms of lactose intolerance such as diarrhea will itself contain lactose.

The amount of lactose in any individual pill is small, far below the level required to cause symptoms in all but the most exceptionally sensitive lactose intolerant people. Documented cases of such intolerance do appear in the medical literature, however. It is also possible that the cumulative amount of lactose ingested by those who must take large numbers of medications each day may produce symptoms in some, especially when added to the lactose they consume in foods.

I am in no way advocating against the use of any medications just because they contain lactose. On the contrary, needed medication should never be avoided just because it contains lactose, nor should anyone unduly restrict a doctor's choices for the best medication for one's needs. However, I do believe that those who are lactose intolerant should be aware of hidden sources of lactose so that they may make informed decisions about their use of any lactose-containing product. If you discover a medication you are taking on this listing and want to eliminate even the small risk of any additional lactose intake or have religious or philosophical

PLEASE NOTE: Information is provided to the PDR by the manufacturers. Neither the publisher nor the author is responsible for the misuse of a product due to typographic error. Not every drug is listed in the PDR, nor have all manufacturers of listed drugs identified inactive ingredients. Formulations are subject to change without notice. New medications come onto and are taken off the market continually: No printed listing can be completely up-to-date. Although the alternate forms of medications listed here as not containing lactose should be chemically identical to those that do, they may NOT in fact be equivalent in their effectiveness in the body. Always consult your physician before making any substitution.

reasons for refraining from the use of animal-derived products, ask your physician whether it would be possible to prescribe the drug in a different, non-lactose containing format or replace it with a different product.

This listing is designed to serve only as a convenient compilation of lactose-containing medications. Only prescription medications designed for oral administration are included. The medications listed were compiled from entries in the CD-ROM version of the 1994 *Physicians' Desk Reference* (PDR). (Copyright *Physicians' Desk Reference* 1994, 48th Edition, published by Medical Economics Data, Montvale, New Jersey 07645. Used by permission. All rights reserved.)

How to read these listings:

Name of Drug	PDR Product Category & Subcategories	Varieties Containing Lactose	Varieties Which Do NOT Contain Lactose	Manufacturer
Benadryl	Antihistamine Nausea Medication Parkinsonism Drug Sedative Non-Barbiturate	25 mg capsules	50 mg capsules Injection	Parke-Davis
Ser-Ap-Es	Cardiovascular Agent Rauwolfia Derivative/ Combination	0.1/25/15 mg tablets		Ciba Consumer Pharmaceuticals

Benadryl: Benadryl is listed in the PDR Product Category Index as an Antihistamine, as a Nausea Medication and as a Parkinsonism Drug. It is also listed as a Sedative, under the subcategory Non-Barbiturate. Benadryl comes in several physical forms, with only the capsule with the dosage level of 25 milligrams (mg) containing lactose among its inactive ingredients. Lactose is not listed as being among the inactive ingredients of either the 50 mg capsule or the Benadryl injection. All forms share the same active ingredient. The manufacturer of Benadryl is Parke-Davis.

Ser-Ap-Es: Ser-Ap-Es is listed in the PDR Product Category Index as a Cardiovascular Agent, under the subcategory Rauwolfia Derivatives and Combinations. It comes in only a single format, a tablet with three active ingredients, whose strengths are respectively 0.1 mg, 25 mg and 15 mg. There are no non-lactose containing forms. The manufacturer of Ser-Ap-Es is Ciba Consumer Pharmaceuticals.

Abbreviations: mg = milligrams; mcg = micrograms.

A LISTING OF CERTAIN PRESCRIPTION MEDICATIONS WHICH CONTAIN LACTOSE AS AN INACTIVE INGREDIENT

NAME OF DRUG	PDR PRODUCT CATEGORY & SUBCATEGORIES	VARIETIES CONTAINING LACTOSE (AS AN INACTIVE INGREDIENT)	VARIETIES WHICH DO NOT CONTAIN LACTOSE	MANUFACTURER
Accupril	Cardiovascular Agent Angiotensin Converting Enzyme Inhibitor	5, 10, 20, 40 mg tablets		Parke-Davis
Achromycin V	Antibiotic, Systemic Tetracycline	250, 500 mg capsules		Lederle Laboratories
Adalat CC	Cardiovascular Agent Calcium Channel Blocker	30, 60, 90 mg extended release capsules	10, 20 mg Adalat capsules	Miles
Adipex-P	Appetite Suppressant Non-Amphetamine	37.5 mg capsules; 37.5 mg tablets		Gate Pharmaceuticals
Akineton	Parasympatholytic Parkinsonism Drug	2 mg tablets		Knoll Pharmaceutical
Alkeran	Antineoplastic Nitrogen Mustard Derivative	2 mg tablets		Burroughs Wellcome
Alupent	Respiratory Drug Sympathomimetic/Combination	10, 20 mg tablets	Inhalation Aerosol; Inhalation Solution; Syrup	Boehringer Ingelheim Pharmaceuticals
Ambien	Hypnotic	5, 10 mg tablets		G. D. Searle
Anadrol-50	Hormone Androgen	50 mg tablets		Syntex Laboratories

NAME OF DRUG	PDR PRODUCT CATEGORY & SUBCATEGORIES	VARIETIES CONTAINING LACTOSE (AS AN INACTIVE INGREDIENT)	VARIETIES WHICH DO NOT CONTAIN LACTOSE	MANUFACTURER
Anaprox	Analgesic NSAID Anti-Inflammatory Agent Non-Steroidal Arthritis Medication NSAID	275 mg tablets	550 mg DS tablets	Syntex Puerto Rico
Ancobon	Fungal Medication, Systemic	250, 500 mg capsules		Roche Laboratories
Android	Hormone Androgen	10, 25 mg tablets		ICN Pharmaceuticals
Ansaid	Anti-Inflammatory Agent Non-Steroidal Arthritis Medication NSAID	50, 100 mg tablets		The Upjohn Company
Antivert	Nausea Medication Vertigo Agent	50 mg chewable tablets	12.5, 25 mg tablets	Roerig Division/Pfizer
Anturane	Gout Treatment Uricosuric Agent	100 mg tablets; 200 mg capsules		Ciba Pharmaceutical Company
Apresoline	Cardiovascular Agent Vasodilator, Peripheral/Combination	10, 25, 50, 100 mg tablets	Ampuls	Ciba Pharmaceutical Company
Asacol	Anti-Inflammatory Agent Salicylate	400 mg tablets		Procter & Gamble Pharmaceuticals

NAME OF DRUG	PDR PRODUCT CATEGORY & SUBCATEGORIES	VARIETIES CONTAINING LACTOSE (AS AN INACTIVE INGREDIENT)	VARIETIES WHICH DO NOT CONTAIN LACTOSE	MANUFACTURER
Atarax	Antihistamine Nausea Medication Pruritus Medication Psychotropic Antianxiety Agent	10, 25, 50, 100 mg tablets	Syrup	Roerig Division/Pfizer
Ativan	Psychotropic Antianxiety Agent	0.5, 1, 2 mg tablets	Injection	Wyeth-Ayerst Laboratories
Atretol	Seizure Disorder Miscellaneous	200 mg tablets		Athena Neurosciences
Atrohist Plus	Antihistamine Cold & Cough Preparation Antihistamine/Combination Oral/Combination Sympathomimetic/Combination	Tablets		Adams Laboratories
Aygestin	Hormone Progestogen	5 mg tablets		Wyeth-Ayerst Laboratories
Bellergal-S	Parasympatholytic Sympatholytic	40/0.6/0.2 mg tablets		Sandoz Pharmaceuticals
Benadryl	Antihistamine Nausea Medication Parkinsonism Drug Sedative Non-Barbiturate	25 mg capsules	50 mg capsules	Parke-Davis

NAME OF DRUG	PDR PRODUCT CATEGORY & SUBCATEGORIES	VARIETIES CONTAINING LACTOSE (AS AN INACTIVE INGREDIENT)	VARIETIES WHICH DO NOT CONTAIN LACTOSE	MANUFACTURER
Bentyl	Antispasmodic/Anticholinergic Gastrointestinal Parasympatholytic	10 mg capsules; 20 mg tablets	Injection; Syrup	Marion Merrell Dow
Betapace	Cardiovascular Agent Antiarrhythmic: Group III Beta Blocker	80, 160, 240 mg tablets		Berlex Laboratories
Biphetamine	Appetite Suppressant Amphetamine	12.5, 20 mg capsules		Fisons Corporation
Brethine	Respiratory Drug Sympathomimetic/Combination Sympathomimetic/Combination	2.5, 5 mg tablets	Inhalation Aerosol; Injection	Geigy Pharmaceuticals
Brevicon	Contraceptive, Oral Hormone Progestogen & Estrogen Combination	21 & 28 day-tablets		Syntex (F. P)
Bricanyl	Respiratory Drug Sympathomimetic/Combination Sympathomimetic/Combination	2.5, 5 mg tablets	Injection	Marion Merrell Dow
Bromfed	Antihistamine Cold & Cough Preparation Oral/Combination	4/60 mg tablets	Capsules; PD-capsules	Muro Pharmaceutical
Bumex	Cardiovascular Agent Diuretic: Loop Diuretic	0.5, 1, 2 mg tablets	Injection	Roche Laboratories

NAME OF DRUG	PDR PRODUCT CATEGORY & SUBCATEGORIES	VARIETIES CONTAINING LACTOSE (AS AN INACTIVE INGREDIENT)	VARIETIES WHICH DO NOT CONTAIN LACTOSE	MANUFACTURER
BuSpar	Psychotropic Antianxiety Agent	5, 10 mg tablets		Mead Johnson Pharmaceuticals
Cafergot	Ergot Preparation Migraine Preparation Migraine Preparation Ergot Derivative/Combination	1/100 mg tablets	Suppositories	Sandoz Pharmaceuticals
Calan	Cardiovascular Agent Antiarrhythmic: Group IV Calcium Channel Blocker	40, 80, 120 mg tablets	SR oral caplets	G. D. Searle
Cantil	Antispasmodic/Anticholinergic Gastrointestinal Parasympatholytic	25 mg tablets		Marion Merrell Dow
Capoten	Cardiovascular Agent Angiotensin Converting Enzyme Inhibitor	12.5, 25, 50, 100 mg tablets		E. R. Squibb & Sons
Capozide	Cardiovascular Agent Angiotensin Converting Enzyme Inhibitor with Diuretic	25/15, 25/25, 50/15, 50/25 mg tablets		E. R. Squibb & Sons
Cardene SR	Cardiovascular Agent Calcium Channel Blocker	30, 45, 60 mg capsules	Cardene capsules	Syntex Laboratories
Cardilate	Cardiovascular Agent Vasodilator, Coronary	10 mg tablets		Burroughs Wellcome

NAME OF DRUG	PDR PRODUCT CATEGORY & SUBCATEGORIES	VARIETIES CONTAINING LACTOSE (AS AN INACTIVE INGREDIENT)	VARIETIES WHICH DO NOT CONTAIN LACTOSE	MANUFACTURER
Cardioquin	Cardiovascular Agent Antiarrhythmic: Group I	275 mg tablets		Purdue Frederick
Cardizem	Cardiovascular Agent Calcium Channel Blocker	30, 60, 90, 120 mg tablets	CD capsules; Injectable; SR capsules	Marion Merrill Dow
Cardura	Cardiovascular Agent Adrenergic Blocker, Peripheral/Combination	1, 2, 4, 8 mg tablets		Roerig Division/Pfizer
Cartrol	Cardiovascular Agent Beta Blocker	2.5, 5 mg tablets		Abbott Laboratories
Catapres	Cardiovascular Agent Adrenergic Stimulant, Central/Combination	0.1, 0.2, 0.3 mg tablets		Boehringer Ingelheim Pharmaceuticals
Centrax	Psychotropic Antianxiety Agent	5, 10, 20 mg capsules		Parke-Davis
Cephulac	Hyperammonia Reduction	Syrup		Marion Merrill Dow
Chloromycetin	Antibiotic, Systemic Miscellaneous Antibiotic	250 mg capsules		Parke-Davis
Chronulac	Laxative Osmotic	Syrup		Marion Merrill Dow
Claritin	Antihistamine	10 mg tablets		Schering
Cleocin HCl	Antibiotic, Systemic Miscellaneous Antibiotic	75, 150, 300 mg capsules		The Upjohn Company
Clozaril	Psychotropic Antipsychotic Medication	25, 100 mg tablets		Sandoz Pharmaceuticals

NAME OF DRUG	PDR PRODUCT CATEGORY & SUBCATEGORIES	VARIETIES CONTAINING LACTOSE (AS AN INACTIVE INGREDIENT)	VARIETIES WHICH DO NOT CONTAIN LACTOSE	MANUFACTURER
Cogentin	Parkinsonism Drug	0.5, 1, 2 mg tablets	Injection	Merck & Co.
Combipres	Cardiovascular Agent Adrenergic Stimulant, Central/Combination	0.1, 0.2, 0.3 mg tablets		Boehringer Ingelheim Pharmaceuticals
Compazine	Nausea Medication Psychotropic Antipsychotic Medication	5, 10 mg tablets	25 mg tablets; Disposable syringes; Spansule capsules; Suppositories; Syrup; Vials	SmithKline Beecham Pharmaceuticals
Cordarone	Cardiovascular Agent Antiarrhythmic: Group III	200 mg tablets		Wyeth-Ayerst Laboratories
Cortone Acetate	Anti-Inflammatory Agent Steroid/Combination Arthritis Medication Steroid Hormone Glucocorticoid	25 mg tablets	Sterile suspension	Merck & Co.
Corzide	Cardiovascular Agent Beta Blocker with Diuretic	40/5, 80/5 mg tablets		Bristol Laboratories
Coumadin	Anticoagulant	1, 2, 2.5, 5, 7.5, 10 mg tablets		Du Pont Pharma
Crystodigin	Cardiovascular Agent Inotropic Agent	0.05, 0.1 mg tablets		Eli Lilly and Company

NAME OF DRUG	PDR PRODUCT CATEGORY & SUBCATEGORIES	VARIETIES CONTAINING LACTOSE (AS AN INACTIVE INGREDIENT)	VARIETIES WHICH DO NOT CONTAIN LACTOSE	MANUFACTURER
Cuprimine	Antidote Metal Poisoning Arthritis Medication Other	125, 250 mg capsules		Merck & Co.
Cycrin	Hormone Progesterone	2.5, 5, 10 mg tablets		ESI-Pharma
Cylert	Central Nervous System Stimulant Psychotropic Psychostimulant	18.75, 37.5, 75 mg tablets	37.5 mg chewable tablets	Abbott Laboratories
Cystospaz	Antispasmodic/Anticholinergic Gastrointestinal Urinary Tract Agent Antispasmodic	0.15 mg tablets		Webcon Uriceutical
Cytoxan	Antineoplastic Cytotoxic Agent	25, 50 mg tablets	Injection	Bristol-Myers Oncology
Dalmane	Hypnotic	15, 30 mg capsules		Roche Products
Danocrine	Endometriosis Management Gonadotropin Inhibitor Hormones, Suppression of	50, 100, 200 mg capsules		Sanofi Winthrop Pharmaceuticals
Dantrium	Muscle Relaxant Skeletal Muscle Relaxant	25, 50, 100 mg capsules	Intravenous	Procter & Gamble Pharmaceuticals

NAME OF DRUG	PDR PRODUCT CATEGORY & SUBCATEGORIES	VARIETIES CONTAINING LACTOSE (AS AN INACTIVE INGREDIENT)	VARIETIES WHICH DO NOT CONTAIN LACTOSE	MANUFACTURER
Daranide	Cardiovascular Agent Diuretic: Carbonic Anhydrase Inhibitor Ophthalmic Preparation Carbonic Anhydrase Inhibitor	50 mg tablets		Merck & Co.
Daraprim	Antiparasitic Protozoa Malaria Toxoplasma	25 mg tablets		Burroughs Wellcome
Darvon-N	Analgesic Narcotic, Synthetic/Combination	100 mg tablets	Suspension	Eli Lilly and Company
Decadron	Anti-Inflammatory Agent Steroid/Combination Arthritis Medication Steroid Hormone Glucocorticoid	0.25, 0.5, 0.75, 1.5, 4, 6 mg tablets	Elixir	Merck & Co.
Deltasone	Anti-Inflammatory Agent Steroid/Combination	2.5, 5, 10, 20, 50 mg tablets		The Upjohn Company
Depen	Antidote Metal Poisoning Arthritis Medication Other	250 mg tablets		Wallace Laboratories

NAME OF DRUG	PDR PRODUCT CATEGORY & SUBCATEGORIES	VARIETIES CONTAINING LACTOSE (AS AN INACTIVE INGREDIENT)	VARIETIES WHICH DO NOT CONTAIN LACTOSE	MANUFACTURER
Desogen	Contraceptive, Oral Hormone Progestogen & Estrogen Combination	21 & 28-day tablets		Organon
Desyrel	Psychotropic Antidepressant: Miscellaneous	50, 100 mg tablets	150, 300 mg tablets	Apothecon
Dexedrine	Appetite Suppressant Amphetamine Sympathomimetic/Combination	5 mg tablets	Capsules	SmithKline Beecham Pharmaceuticals
Dibenzyline	Cardiovascular Agent Adrenergic Blocker, Peripheral/Combination	10 mg capsules		SmithKline Beecham Pharmaceuticals
Didrex	Appetite Suppressant Amphetamine Sympathomimetic/Combination	25, 50 mg tablets		The Upjohn Company
Diethylstilbestrol	Hormone Estrogen	1, 5 mg enseals; 1, 5 mg tablets		Eli Lilly and Company
Dilantin	Seizure Disorder Hydantoin Derivative	30, 100 mg capsules	Injection	Parke-Davis
Dilaudid	Analgesic Narcotic, Synthetic/Combination	2, 4, 8 mg tablets	Ampules; HP Injection; Multiple dose vials; Non-sterile powder; Oral liquid; Suppositories	Knoll Pharmaceutical

NAME OF DRUG	PDR PRODUCT CATEGORY & SUBCATEGORIES	VARIETIES CONTAINING LACTOSE (AS AN INACTIVE INGREDIENT)	VARIETIES WHICH DO NOT CONTAIN LACTOSE	MANUFACTURER
Ditropan	Urinary Tract Agent Antispasmodic	5 mg tablets	Syrup	Marion Merrell Dow
Diucardin	Cardiovascular Agent Diuretic: Thiazide/Related Diuretic	50 mg tablets		Wyeth-Ayerst Laboratories
Diupres	Cardiovascular Agent Rauwolfia Derivative/Combination	250, 500 mg tablets		Merck & Co.
Diuril	Cardiovascular Agent Diuretic: Thiazide/Related Diuretic	250 mg tablets	500 mg tablets; Oral suspension	Merck & Co.
Dolophine Hydrochloride	Analgesic Narcotic, Synthetic/ Combination	5, 10 mg tablets	Injection	Eli Lilly and Company
Donnatal	Antispasmodic/Anticholinergic Gastrointestinal	16.2 mg capsules	16.2 mg tablets; Elixir	A. H. Robins
Dopar	Parkinsonism Drug	100, 250, 500 mg capsules		Roberts Pharmaceutical
Doral	Hypnotic	7.5, 15 mg tablets		Wallace Laboratories
Doryx	Antibiotic, Systemic Tetracycline	100 mg capsules		Parke-Davis
Dulcolax	Laxative Stimulant	5 mg tablets	Suppository	CIBA Consumer Pharmaceuticals

NAME OF DRUG	PDR PRODUCT CATEGORY & SUBCATEGORIES	VARIETIES CONTAINING LACTOSE (AS AN INACTIVE INGREDIENT)	VARIETIES WHICH DO NOT CONTAIN LACTOSE	MANUFACTURER
Dyazide	Cardiovascular Agent Diuretic: Combination Diuretic	25/50 mg capsules		SmithKline Beecham Pharmaceuticals
DynaCirc	Cardiovascular Agent Calcium Channel Blocker	2.5, 5 mg capsules		Sandoz Pharmaceuticals
Dyrenium	Cardiovascular Agent Diuretic: Potassium-Sparing Diuretic	50, 100 mg capsules		SmithKline Beecham Pharmaceuticals
E-Mycin	Antibiotic, Systemic Macrolide: Erythromycin	250, 333 mg tablets		Boots Laboratories
Edecrin	Cardiovascular Agent Diuretic: Loop Diuretic	25, 50 mg tablets	Intravenous	Merck & Co.
Elavil	Psychotropic Antidepressant: Tricyclic/Combination	10, 25, 50, 75, 100, 150 mg tablets	Injection	Stuart Pharmaceuticals
Eldepryl	Parkinsonism Drug	5 mg tablets		Somerset Pharmaceuticals
Endep	Psychotropic Antidepressant: Tricyclic/Combination	10, 25, 50, 75, 100, 150 mg tablets		Roche Products
Enduron	Cardiovascular Agent Diuretic: Thiazide/Related Diuretic	2.5, 5 mg tablets		Abbott Laboratories

NAME OF DRUG	PDR PRODUCT CATEGORY & SUBCATEGORIES	VARIETIES CONTAINING LACTOSE (AS AN INACTIVE INGREDIENT)	VARIETIES WHICH DO NOT CONTAIN LACTOSE	MANUFACTURER
Ergamisol	Antineoplastic Adjunct Immunomodulator	50 mg tablets		Janssen Pharmaceutica
Ergomar	Ergot Preparation Migraine Preparation Migraine Preparation	2 mg tablets		Lotus Biochemical
Ergostat	Ergot Preparation Migraine Preparation Migraine Preparation Ergot Derivative/Combination	2 mg tablets		Parke-Davis
Esidrix	Cardiovascular Agent Diuretic: Thiazide/Related Diuretic	25, 50, 100 mg tablets		Ciba Pharmaceutical Company
Esimil	Cardiovascular Agent Adrenergic Blocker, Peripheral/Combination	10/25 mg tablets		Ciba Pharmaceutical Company
Eskalith	Psychotropic Antimanic Agent	300 mg capsules; 300 mg tablets	CR tablets	SmithKline Beecham Pharmaceuticals
Estrace	Antineoplastic Hormone Hormone Estrogen	1, 2 mg tablets	Vaginal cream	Mead Johnson Laboratories

NAME OF DRUG	PDR PRODUCT CATEGORY & SUBCATEGORIES	VARIETIES CONTAINING LACTOSE (AS AN INACTIVE INGREDIENT)	VARIETIES WHICH DO NOT CONTAIN LACTOSE	MANUFACTURER
Estratab	Hormone Estrogen	0.3, 0.625, 1.25, 2.5 mg tablets		Solvay Pharmaceuticals
Estratest	Hormone Androgen & Estrogen Combination	0.625/1.25, 1.25/2.5 mg tablets		Solvay Pharmaceuticals
Estrovis	Hormone Estrogen	100 mcg tablets		Parke-Davis
Ethmozine	Cardiovascular Agent Antiarrhythmic: Group I	200, 250, 300 mg tablets		Roberts Pharmaceutical
Etrafon	Psychotropic Antidepressant: Tricyclic/Combination	2/10, 2/25, 4/25 mg tablets		Schering Corporation
Eulexin	Antineoplastic Androgen Inhibitor	125 mg capsules		Schering Corporation
Exna	Cardiovascular Agent Diuretic: Thiazide/Related Diuretic	50 mg tablets		A. H. Robins
Fansidar	Antiparasitic Protozoa: Malaria	500/25 mg tablets		Roche Laboratories
Felbatol	Seizure Disorder	400, 600 mg tablets	Oral suspension	Wallace Laboratories
Feldene	Anti-Inflammatory Agent Non-Steroidal Arthritis Medication NSAID	10, 20 mg capsules		Pratt Pharmaceuticals

NAME OF DRUG	PDR PRODUCT CATEGORY & SUBCATEGORIES	VARIETIES CONTAINING LACTOSE (AS AN INACTIVE INGREDIENT)	VARIETIES WHICH DO NOT CONTAIN LACTOSE	MANUFACTURER
Ferro-Sequels	Hematinic Iron/Combination	150/100 mg tablets		Lederle Laboratories
Fiorinal	Analgesic Non-Narcotic/Anxiolytic	50 mg tablets	50 mg capsules	Sandoz Pharmaceuticals
Flexeril	Muscle Relaxant Skeletal Muscle Relaxant	10 mg tablets		Merck & Co.
Florinef Acetate	Hormone Mineralocorticoid	0.1 mg tablets		Apothecon
Floxin	Quinolone, Systemic	200, 300, 400 mg tablets	Injection	McNeil Pharmaceutical
Fulvicin P/G	Fungal Medication, Systemic	125, 165, 250, 330 mg tablets		Schering Corporation
Gantrisin	Sulfonamide/Combination, Systemic; Urinary Tract Agent Antibacterial	0.5 g tablets		Roche Laboratories
Glucotrol	Diabetes Agent Oral	5, 10 mg tablets		Pratt Pharmaceuticals
Glynase	Diabetes Agent Oral	1.5, 3 mg tablets		The Upjohn Company
Gris-PEG	Fungal Medication, Systemic	125 mg tablets	250 mg tablets	Allergan Herbert
Grisactin	Fungal Medication, Systemic	250 mg capsules	500 mg tablets	Wyeth-Ayerst Laboratories

NAME OF DRUG	PDR PRODUCT CATEGORY & SUBCATEGORIES	VARIETIES CONTAINING LACTOSE (AS AN INACTIVE INGREDIENT)	VARIETIES WHICH DO NOT CONTAIN LACTOSE	MANUFACTURER
Grisactin Ultra	Fungal Medication, Systemic	250, 330 mg tablets		Wyeth-Ayerst Laboratories
Halcion	Hypnotic	0.125, 0.25 mg tablets		The Upjohn Company
Halotestin	Hormone Androgen & Estrogen Combination	2, 5, 10 mg tablets		The Upjohn Company
Hexalen	Antineoplastic Cytotoxic Agent	50 mg capsules		U. S. Bioscience
Hismanal	Antihistamine	10 mg tablets		Janssen Pharmaceutica
Hivid	AIDS Chemotherapeutic Agent	0.375, 0.750 mg tablets		Roche Laboratories
Hycodan	Cold & Cough Preparation Antitussive/Combination with Narcotic	5/1.5 mg tablets	Syrup	Du Pont Multi-Source Products
Hydergine	Cerebral Metabolic Enhancer	1 mg oral tablets	Liquid; Liquid capsules; Sublingual tablets	Sandoz Pharmaceuticals
Hydrea	Antineoplastic Cytotoxic Agent	500 mg capsules		Immunex Corporation
Hydrocortone	Anti-Inflammatory Agent Steroid/Combination Arthritis Medication Steroid Hormone Glucocorticoid	10, 20 mg tablets		Merck & Co.

NAME OF DRUG	PDR PRODUCT CATEGORY & SUBCATEGORIES	VARIETIES CONTAINING LACTOSE (AS AN INACTIVE INGREDIENT)	VARIETIES WHICH DO NOT CONTAIN LACTOSE	MANUFACTURER
HydroDIURIL	Cardiovascular Agent Diuretic: Thiazide/Related Diuretic	25, 50, 100 mg tablets		Merck & Co.
Hydropres	Cardiovascular Agent Rauwolfia Derivative/ Combination	25/0.125, 50/0.125 mg tablets		Merck & Co.
HydroStat IR	Analgesic Narcotic, Synthetic/ Combination	1, 2, 3, 4 mg tablets		Richwood Pharmaceutical
Hylorel	Cardiovascular Agent Adrenergic Blocker, Peripheral/Combination	10, 25 mg tablets		Fisons Corporation
Hytrin	Cardiovascular Agent Adrenergic Blocker, Peripheral/Combination	1, 2, 5, 10 mg tablets		Abbott Laboratories
IBU	Analgesic NSAID Anti-Inflammatory Agent Non-Steroidal	800 mg tablets	400, 600 mg tablets	Boots Laboratories
Imodium	Diarrhea Medication	2 mg capsules		Janssen Pharmaceutica
Imodium A-D	Diarrhea Medication	2 mg caplet	Liquid	McNeil Consumer Products

NAME OF DRUG	PDR PRODUCT CATEGORY & SUBCATEGORIES	VARIETIES CONTAINING LACTOSE (AS AN INACTIVE INGREDIENT)	VARIETIES WHICH DO NOT CONTAIN LACTOSE	MANUFACTURER
Imuran	Arthritis Medication Other Immunosuppressive	50 mg tablets	Injection	Burroughs Wellcome
Inderal	Cardiovascular Agent Antiarrhythmic: Group II Beta Blocker Migraine Preparation Beta Blocker Tremor Preparation	10, 20, 40, 60, 80 mg tablets	LA capsules	Wyeth-Ayerst Laboratories
Inderide	Cardiovascular Agent Beta Blocker with Diuretic	40/25, 80/25 mg tablets; 80/50, 120/50, 160/50 mg LA capsules		Wyeth-Ayerst Laboratories
Indocin	Anti-Inflammatory Agent Non-Steroidal Arthritis Medication	25, 50 mg capsules	Oral suspension; SR capsules; suppositories	Merck & Co.
Intal	Mast Cell Stabilizer Respiratory Drug Anti Inflammatory Agent, Non-Steroidal	20 mg capsules	Inhaler, Nebulizer solution	Fisons Corporation
Inversine	Cardiovascular Agent Miscellaneous Cardiovascular Agents	2.5 mg tablets		Merck & Co.

NAME OF DRUG	PDR PRODUCT CATEGORY & SUBCATEGORIES	VARIETIES CONTAINING LACTOSE (AS AN INACTIVE INGREDIENT)	VARIETIES WHICH DO NOT CONTAIN LACTOSE	MANUFACTURER
Ionamin	Appetite Suppressant Non-Amphetamine	15, 30 mg capsules		Fisons Corporation
Ismelin	Cardiovascular Agent Adrenergic Blocker, Peripheral/Combination	10, 25 mg tablets		Ciba Pharmaceutical Company
Ismo	Cardiovascular Agent Vasodilator, Coronary	20 mg tablets		Wyeth-Ayerst Laboratories
Isoptin	Cardiovascular Agent Antiarrhythmic: Group IV Calcium Channel Blocker	40, 80, 120 mg tablets	Injection; SR tablets	Knoll Pharmaceutical
Isordil	Cardiovascular Agent Vasodilator, Coronary	2.5, 5, 10 mg sublingual tablets; 40 mg Tembids tablets; 5, 10, 20, 30, 40 mg Titradose tablets	40 mg Tembids capsules	Wyeth-Ayerst Laboratories
Kemadrin	Parkinsonism Drug	50 mg tablets		Burroughs Wellcome
Kerlone	Cardiovascular Agent Beta Blocker	10, 20 mg tablets		G. D. Searle
Kinesed	Antispasmodic/Anticholinergic Gastrointestinal Parasympatholytic	16/0.12/0.007 mg tablets		Stuart Pharmaceuticals
Klonopin	Seizure Disorder Benzodiazepine	0.5, 1, 2 mg tablets		Roche Laboratories

NAME OF DRUG	PDR PRODUCT CATEGORY & SUBCATEGORIES	VARIETIES CONTAINING LACTOSE (AS AN INACTIVE INGREDIENT)	VARIETIES WHICH DO NOT CONTAIN LACTOSE	MANUFACTURER
Ku-Zyme	Enzyme/Digestant Digestant	Capsules		Schwarz Pharma
Ku-Zyme HP	Enzyme/Digestant Digestant	Capsules		Schwarz Pharma
Kutrase	Antispasmodic/Anticholinergic Gastrointestinal Enzyme/Digestant Digestant	Capsules		Schwarz Pharma
Lanoxin	Cardiovascular Agent Antiarrhythmic: Misc. Antiarrhythmic Inotropic Agent	125, 250, 500 mcg tablets	Lanoxicaps capsules; Elixir pediatric; Injection; Injection pediatric	Burroughs Wellcome
Lariam	Antiparasitic Protozoa: Malaria	250 mg tablets		Roche Laboratories
Lasix	Cardiovascular Agent Diuretic: Loop Diuretic	20, 40, 80 mg tablets	Injection	Hoechst-Roussel Pharmaceuticals
Leucovorin Calcium (Wellcovorin brand)	Vitamin Anti-Folic Acid Antagonist Other	5, 25 mg tablets	Injection	Burroughs Wellcome
Leucovorin Calcium	Antineoplastic Other Vitamin Anti-Folic Acid Antagonist Other	10, 15 mg tablets	5 mg tablets; Injection	Immunex Corporation

NAME OF DRUG	PDR PRODUCT CATEGORY & SUBCATEGORIES	VARIETIES CONTAINING LACTOSE (AS AN INACTIVE INGREDIENT)	VARIETIES WHICH DO NOT CONTAIN LACTOSE	MANUFACTURER
Leukeran	Antineoplastic Nitrogen Mustard Derivative	2 mg tablets		Burroughs Wellcome
Levatol	Cardiovascular Agent Beta Blocker	20 mg tablets		Reed & Carnrick
Levlen	Contraceptive, Oral	21 & 28-day tablets		Berlex Laboratories
Levo-Dromoran	Analgesic Narcotic, Synthetic/Combination	2 mg tablets	Ampuls; Vials	Roche Laboratories
Levothroid	Hormone Thyroid Preparation: Synthetic T4	25, 50, 75, 88, 100, 112, 125, 137, 150, 175, 200, 300 mcg tablets		Forest Pharmaceuticals
Levoxine	Hormone Thyroid Preparation: Synthetic T4	25, 50, 75, 88, 100, 112, 125, 150, 175, 200, 300 mcg tablets	Injection	Daniels Pharmaceuticals
Levsin	Antispasmodic/Anticholinergic Gastrointestinal Parasympatholytic Parkinsonism Drug Urinary Tract Agent Antispasmodic	0.125 mg tablets	Drops; Elixir; Injection; Levsinex Timecaps; SL tablets	Schwarz Pharma
Librax	Antispasmodic/Anticholinergic Gastrointestinal Psychotropic Antianxiety Agent	5/2.5 mg capsules		Roche Products

NAME OF DRUG	PDR PRODUCT CATEGORY & SUBCATEGORIES	VARIETIES CONTAINING LACTOSE (AS AN INACTIVE INGREDIENT)	VARIETIES WHICH DO NOT CONTAIN LACTOSE	MANUFACTURER
Libritabs	Psychotropic Antianxiety Agent	5, 10, 25 mg tablets		Roche Products
Librium	Psychotropic Antianxiety Agent	5, 10, 25 mg capsules	Injectable	Roche Products
Limbitrol	Psychotropic Antianxiety Agent Antidepressant: Tricyclic/Combination	5/12.5 mg, 10/25 mg tablets		Roche Products
Lincocin	Antibiotic, Systemic Miscellaneous Antibiotic	250, 500 mg capsules	Sterile solution	The Upjohn Company
Lo/Ovral	Contraceptive, Oral Hormone Progestogen & Estrogen Combination	21 & 28-day tablets		Wyeth-Ayerst Laboratories
Lodine	Analgesic NSAID Anti-Inflammatory Non-Steroidal Arthritis Medication	200, 300 mg capsules; 400 mg tablets		Wyeth-Ayerst Laboratories
Loestrin 21	Contraceptive, Oral Hormone Progestogen & Estrogen Combination	1/20, 1.5/30 tablets		Parke-Davis

NAME OF DRUG	PDR PRODUCT CATEGORY & SUBCATEGORIES	VARIETIES CONTAINING LACTOSE (AS AN INACTIVE INGREDIENT)	VARIETIES WHICH DO NOT CONTAIN LACTOSE	MANUFACTURER
Loestrin Fe	Contraceptive, Oral Hormone Progestogen & Estrogen Combination	1/20, 1.5/30 tablets		Parke-Davis
Loniten	Cardiovascular Agent Vasodilator, Peripheral/ Combination	2.5, 10 mg tablets		The Upjohn Company
Lopressor	Cardiovascular Agent Beta Blocker	50, 100 mg tablets	Ampuls	Geigy Pharmaceuticals
Lopressor HCT	Cardiovascular Agent Beta Blocker with Diuretic	50/25, 100/25, 100/50 mg tablets		Geigy Pharmaceuticals
Lorelco	Hypolipidemic Other	250, 500 mg tablets		Marion Merrell Dow
Lotensin	Cardiovascular Agent Angiotensin Converting Enzyme Inhibitor	5, 10, 20, 40 mg tablets		Ciba Pharmaceutical Company
Loxitane	Psychotropic Antipsychotic Medication	5, 10, 25, 50 mg capsules		Lederle Laboratories
Lozol	Cardiovascular Agent Diuretic: Thiazide/Related Diuretic	1.25, 2.5 mg tablets		Rhône-Poulenc Rorer Pharmaceuticals
Ludiomil	Psychotropic Antidepressant: Tetracyclic	25, 50, 75 mg tablets		Ciba Pharmaceutical Company

NAME OF DRUG	PDR PRODUCT CATEGORY & SUBCATEGORIES	VARIETIES CONTAINING LACTOSE (AS AN INACTIVE INGREDIENT)	VARIETIES WHICH DO NOT CONTAIN LACTOSE	MANUFACTURER
Macrobid	Urinary Tract Agent Antibacterial	100 mg capsules		Procter & Gamble Pharmaceuticals
Macrodantin	Urinary Anti-Infective & Analgesic Combination	25, 50, 100 mg capsules		Procter & Gamble Pharmaceuticals
Marplan	Psychotropic Antidepressant: MAO Inhibitor	10 mg tablets		Roche Laboratories
Materna	Vitamin Prenatal	tablets		Lederle Laboratories
Maxaquin	Anti-Infective, Miscellaneous Systemic Quinolone, Systemic Urinary Tract Agent Antibacterial	400 mg tablets		G. D. Searle
Mebaral	Psychotropic Antianxiety Agent Sedative Barbiturate Seizure Disorder Barbiturate	32, 50, 100 mg tablets		Sanofi Winthrop Pharmaceuticals
Meclomen	Analgesic NSAID Anti-Inflammatory Agent Non-Steroidal Arthritis Medication NSAID	50, 100 mg capsules		Parke-Davis

NAME OF DRUG	PDR PRODUCT CATEGORY & SUBCATEGORIES	VARIETIES CONTAINING LACTOSE (AS AN INACTIVE INGREDIENT)	VARIETIES WHICH DO NOT CONTAIN LACTOSE	MANUFACTURER
Medrol	Anti-Inflammatory Agent Steroid/Combination Arthritis Medication Steroid Hormone Glucocorticoid	2, 4, 8, 16, 24, 32 mg tablets		The Upjohn Company
Megace	Antineoplastic Hormone	20, 40 mg tablets		Bristol-Myers Oncology
Mellaril	Psychotropic Antipsychotic Medication	10, 15, 25, 50, 100, 150, 200 mg tablets	Concentrate; Oral suspension	Sandoz Pharmaceuticals
Menest	Hormone Estrogen	0.3, 0.625, 1.25, 2.5 mg tablets		SmithKline Beecham Pharmaceuticals
Mephyton	Anticoagulant Antagonist Vitamin Other	5 mg tablets		Merck & Co.
Mesantoin	Seizure Disorder Hydantoin Derivative	100 mg tablets		Sandoz Pharmaceuticals
Mestinon	Cholinesterase Inhibitor Muscle Relaxant Antagonist	60 mg tablets	Injectable, Syrup, Timespan tablets	ICN Pharmaceuticals
Metaprel	Respiratory Drug Sympathomimetic/Combination	10, 20 mg tablets	Inhalation aerosol; Inhalation solution; Syrup	Sandoz Pharmaceuticals

NAME OF DRUG	PDR PRODUCT CATEGORY & SUBCATEGORIES	VARIETIES CONTAINING LACTOSE (AS AN INACTIVE INGREDIENT)	VARIETIES WHICH DO NOT CONTAIN LACTOSE	MANUFACTURER
Methergine	Ergot Preparation Uterine Contractant Oxytocic	0.2 mg tablets	Injection	Sandoz Pharmaceuticals
Methotrexate	Antineoplastic Antimetabolite	2.5 mg tablets	LPF; for Injection; Injection	Immunex Corporation
Mevacor	Hypolipidemic HMG-COA Reductase Inhibitor	10, 20, 40 mg tablets		Merck & Co.
Micronor	Contraceptive, Oral Hormone Progestogen	28-day tablets		Ortho Pharmaceutical
Midamor	Cardiovascular Agent Diuretic: Potassium-Sparing Diuretic	5 mg tablets		Merck & Co.
Mintezol	Antiparasitic Ascaris (Roundworm) Enterobius (Pinworm) Hookworm Strongyloids (Threadworm) Trichuris (Whipworm)	500 mg tablets	Suspension	Merck & Co.
Moban	Psychotropic Antipsychotic Medication	5, 10, 25, 50, 100 mg tablets		Gate Pharmaceuticals

NAME OF DRUG	PDR PRODUCT CATEGORY & SUBCATEGORIES	VARIETIES CONTAINING LACTOSE (AS AN INACTIVE INGREDIENT)	VARIETIES WHICH DO NOT CONTAIN LACTOSE	MANUFACTURER
Modicon	Contraceptive, Oral Hormone / Progestogen & Estrogen Combination	21 & 28-day tablets		Ortho Pharmaceutical
Moduretic	Cardiovascular Agent Diuretic: Combination Diuretic	5/50 mg tablets		Merck & Co.
Monoket	Cardiovascular Agent Vasodilator, Coronary	10, 20 mg tablets		Schwarz Pharma
Monopril	Cardiovascular Agent Angiotensin Converting Enzyme Inhibitor	10, 20 mg tablets		Mead Johnson Pharmaceuticals
Motofen	Diarrhea Medication	1/0.025 mg tablets		Carnrick Laboratories
MS Contin	Analgesic Narcotic, Synthetic/ Combination	15, 30, 60 mg tablets	100 mg tablets	Purdue Frederick
MSIR	Analgesic Narcotic, Synthetic/ Combination	15, 30 mg capsules; 15, 30 mg tablets	Oral solution; Oral solution concentrate	Purdue Frederick
Mysoline	Seizure Disorder Miscellaneous	50, 250 mg tablets	Suspension	Wyeth-Ayerst Laboratories
Navane	Psychotropic Antipsychotic Medication	1, 2, 5, 10, 20 mg capsules		Roerig Division/Pfizer

NAME OF DRUG	PDR PRODUCT CATEGORY & SUBCATEGORIES	VARIETIES CONTAINING LACTOSE (AS AN INACTIVE INGREDIENT)	VARIETIES WHICH DO NOT CONTAIN LACTOSE	MANUFACTURER
Nembutal Sodium	Hypnotic Sedative Barbiturate	50 mg capsules	100 mg capsules; Solution; Suppositories	Abbott Laboratories
Niacor	Hypolipidemic Nicotinic Acid Vitamin Therapeutic	500 mg tablets		Upsher-Smith Laboratories
Nitrostat	Cardiovascular Agent Vasodilator, Coronary	0.15, 0.3, 0.4, 0.6 mg tablets		Parke-Davis
Nizoral	Fungal Medication, Systemic	200 mg tablets	Cream; Shampoo	Janssen Pharmaceutica
Nor-QD	Contraceptive, Oral Hormone Progestogen	21 & 28 day-tablets		Syntex (F. P.)
Nordette	Contraceptive, Oral Hormone Progestogen & Estrogen Combination	21 & 28-day tablets		Wyeth-Ayerst Laboratories
Norflex	Analgesic Other	100 mg tablets	Injection	3M Pharmaceuticals
Norgesic	Analgesic Aspirin Combination	25/385/30, 50/770/60 mg tablets		3M Pharmaceuticals

NAME OF DRUG	PDR PRODUCT CATEGORY & SUBCATEGORIES	VARIETIES CONTAINING LACTOSE (AS AN INACTIVE INGREDIENT)	VARIETIES WHICH DO NOT CONTAIN LACTOSE	MANUFACTURER
Norinyl 1 + 35	Contraceptive, Oral Hormone Progestogen & Estrogen Combination	21 & 28 day-tablets		Syntex (F. P.)
Norinyl 1 + 50	Contraceptive, Oral Hormone Progestogen & Estrogen Combination	21 & 28 day-tablets		Syntex (F. P.)
Norlutate	Hormone Progestogen	5 mg tablets		Parke-Davis
Normodyne	Cardiovascular Agent Alpha/Beta Adrenergic Blocker	100, 200, 300 mg tablets	Injection	Schering Corporation
Norpace	Cardiovascular Agent Antiarrhythmic: Group I	100, 150 mg capsules	CR capsules	G. D. Searle
Nucofed	Cold & Cough Preparation Antitussive/Combination with Narcotic	20 mg capsules	Expectorant syrup; Pediatric expectorant syrup; Syrup	Roberts Pharmaceutical
Obetrol	Appetite Suppressant Amphetamine Psychotropic Psychostimulant	10, 20 mg tablets		Rexar Pharmacal
Ogen	Hormone Estrogen	0.75, 1.5, 3 mg tablets	Vaginal cream	Abbott Laboratories

NAME OF DRUG	PDR PRODUCT CATEGORY & SUBCATEGORIES	VARIETIES CONTAINING LACTOSE (AS AN INACTIVE INGREDIENT)	VARIETIES WHICH DO NOT CONTAIN LACTOSE	MANUFACTURER
Omnipen	Antibiotic, Systemic Penicillin	250, 500 mg capsules	Oral suspension	Wyeth-Ayerst Laboratories
Oramorph SR	Analgesic Narcotic, Synthetic/Combination	30, 60, 100 mg tablets		Roxane Laboratories
Orap	Tourettes Syndrome Agent	2 mg tablets		Gate Pharmaceuticals
Oretic	Cardiovascular Agent Diuretic: Thiazide/Related Diuretic	25, 50 mg tablets		Abbott Laboratories
Ortho-Cept	Contraceptive, Oral Hormone Progestogen & Estrogen Combination	21 & 28-day tablets		Ortho Pharmaceutical
Ortho-Cyclen	Contraceptive, Oral Hormone Progestogen & Estrogen Combination	21 & 28-day tablets		Ortho Pharmaceutical
Ortho-Est 0.625	Hormone Estrogen	0.75 mg tablets		Ortho Pharmaceutical
Ortho-Est 1.25	Hormone Estrogen	1.5 mg tablets		Ortho Pharmaceutical

NAME OF DRUG	PDR PRODUCT CATEGORY & SUBCATEGORIES	VARIETIES CONTAINING LACTOSE (AS AN INACTIVE INGREDIENT)	VARIETIES WHICH DO NOT CONTAIN LACTOSE	MANUFACTURER
Ortho-Novum	Contraceptive, Oral Hormone Progestogen & Estrogen Combination	7/7/7 21 & 28-day tablets; 10/11 21 & 28-day tablets; 1/35 21 & 28-day tablets; 1/50 21 & 28-day tablets		Ortho Pharmaceutical
Ortho Tri-Cyclen	Contraceptive, Oral Hormone Progestogen & Estrogen Combination	21 & 28-day tablets		Ortho Pharmaceutical
Orudis	Anti-Inflammatory Agent Non-Steroidal Arthritis Medication NSAID	25, 50, 75 mg capsules		Wyeth-Ayerst Laboratories
Ovcon 35	Contraceptive, Oral Hormone Progestogen & Estrogen Combination	21 & 28-day tablets		Mead Johnson Laboratories
Ovcon 50	Contraceptive, Oral Hormone Progestogen & Estrogen Combination	21 & 28-day tablets		Mead Johnson Laboratories

NAME OF DRUG	PDR PRODUCT CATEGORY & SUBCATEGORIES	VARIETIES CONTAINING LACTOSE (AS AN INACTIVE INGREDIENT)	VARIETIES WHICH DO NOT CONTAIN LACTOSE	MANUFACTURER
Ovral	Contraceptive, Oral Hormone Progestogen & Estrogen Combination	21-day tablets		Wyeth-Ayerst Laboratories
Ovrette	Contraceptive, Oral Hormone Progestogen	28-day tablets		Wyeth-Ayerst Laboratories
Paraflex	Muscle Relaxant Skeletal Muscle Relaxant	250 mg caplets		McNeil Pharmaceutical
Parafon Forte DSC	Analgesic Other Muscle Relaxant Skeletal Muscle Relaxant	500 mg caplets		McNeil Pharmaceutical
Parlodel	Dopamine Receptor Agonist Galactorrhea Inhibitor Parkinsonism Drug	5 mg capsules; 2.5 mg tablets		Sandoz Pharmaceuticals
Parnate	Psychotropic Antidepressant: MAO Inhibitor	10 mg tablets		SmithKline Beecham Pharmaceuticals
Pathocil	Antibiotic, Systemic Penicillin	250, 500 mg capsules	Oral suspension	Wyeth-Ayerst Laboratories
PBZ	Antihistamine	25, 50 mg tablets	100 mg SR tablets	Geigy Pharmaceuticals

NAME OF DRUG	PDR PRODUCT CATEGORY & SUBCATEGORIES	VARIETIES CONTAINING LACTOSE (AS AN INACTIVE INGREDIENT)	VARIETIES WHICH DO NOT CONTAIN LACTOSE	MANUFACTURER
PCE	Antibiotic, Systemic Macrolide: Erythromycin	333 mg tablets	500 mg tablets	Abbott Laboratories
Peganone	Seizure Disorder Hydantoin Derivative	250, 500 mg tablets		Abbott Laboratories
Pen Vee K	Antibiotic, Systemic Penicillin	250 mg tablets	500 mg tablets; Oral suspension	Wyeth-Ayerst Laboratories
Periactin	Antihistamine	4 mg tablets		Merck & Co.
Permax	Dopamine Receptor Agonist Parkinsonism Drug	0.05, 0.25, 1 mg tablets		Athena Neurosciences
Persantine	Platelet Inhibitor	25, 50, 75 mg tablets		Boehringer Ingelheim Pharmaceuticals
Phenaphen with Codeine	Analgesic Narcotic, Synthetic/ Combination	325/60 mg capsules	325/15 mg capsules; 325/30 mg capsules; 650/30 mg tablets	A. H. Robins
Phenergan	Antihistamine Motion Sickness Remedy Nausea Medication Sedative Non-Barbiturate	12.5, 25, 50 mg tablets	Injection; Suppositories; Syrup Fortis; Syrup Plain	Wyeth-Ayerst Laboratories
Phenobarbital	Sedative Barbiturate Seizure Disorder Barbiturate	15, 30, 60, 100 mg tablets	Elixir	Eli Lilly and Company

NAME OF DRUG	PDR PRODUCT CATEGORY & SUBCATEGORIES	VARIETIES CONTAINING LACTOSE (AS AN INACTIVE INGREDIENT)	VARIETIES WHICH DO NOT CONTAIN LACTOSE	MANUFACTURER
Phenurone	Seizure Disorder / Miscellaneous	500 mg tablets		Abbott Laboratories
Plegine	Appetite Suppressant / Non-Amphetamine	35 mg tablets		Wyeth-Ayerst Laboratories
Plendil	Cardiovascular Agent / Calcium Channel Blocker	5, 10 mg tablets		Merck & Co.
PMB	Hormone / Estrogen / Psychotropic / Antianxiety Agent	0.45/200, 0.45/400 mg tablets		Wyeth-Ayerst Laboratories
Ponstel	Analgesic / NSAID / Anti-Inflammatory Agent / Non-Steroidal	250 mg capsules		Parke-Davis
Pravachol	Hypolipidemic / HMG-COA Reductase Inhibitor	10, 20, 40 mg tablets		E. R. Squibb & Sons
Premarin	Hormone / Estrogen	0.3, 0.625, 0.9, 1.25, 2.5 mg tablets	Vaginal cream	Wyeth-Ayerst Laboratories
Premarin with Methyltestosterone	Hormone / Androgen & Estrogen Combination	0.625/5, 1.25/10 mg tablets		Wyeth-Ayerst Laboratories
Prilosec	Proton Pump Inhibitor	20 mg capsules		Merck & Co.

NAME OF DRUG	PDR PRODUCT CATEGORY & SUBCATEGORIES	VARIETIES CONTAINING LACTOSE (AS AN INACTIVE INGREDIENT)	VARIETIES WHICH DO NOT CONTAIN LACTOSE	MANUFACTURER
Pro-Banthine	Antispasmodic/Anticholinergic Gastrointestinal	7.5, 15 mg tablets		Roberts Pharmaceutical
Procan SR	Cardiovascular Agent Antiarrhythmic: Group I	250 mg tablets	500, 750, 1000 mg tablets	Parke-Davis
Prolixin	Psychotropic Antipsychotic Medication	1, 2.5, 5, 10 mg tablets	Elixir; Injection; Oral concentrate	Apothecon
Proloprim	Antibiotics, Systemic Miscellaneous Antibiotic Urinary Tract Agent Antibacterial	100 mg tablets	200 mg tablets	Burroughs Wellcome
Proscar	Urinary Tract Agent Prostatic Hypertrophy Modifier	5 mg tablets		Merck & Co.
ProSom	Hypnotic Sedative Non-Barbiturate	1, 2 mg tablets		Abbott Laboratories
Prostigmin	Cholinesterase Inhibitor Muscle Relaxant Antagonist	15 mg tablets		ICN Pharmaceuticals
Protostat	Antiparasitic Protozoa Ameba, Extraintestinal Ameba, Intestinal Trichomonas	250, 500 mg tablets		Ortho Pharmaceutical

NAME OF DRUG	PDR PRODUCT CATEGORY & SUBCATEGORIES	VARIETIES CONTAINING LACTOSE (AS AN INACTIVE INGREDIENT)	VARIETIES WHICH DO NOT CONTAIN LACTOSE	MANUFACTURER
Proventil	Respiratory Drug Sympathomimetic/Combination	2, 4 mg tablets; 4 mg extended-release tablets	Inhalation solution; Solution for inhalation; Syrup	Schering Corporation
Provera	Hormone Progestogen	2.5, 5, 10 mg tablets		The Upjohn Company
Purinethol	Antineoplastic Antimetabolite	50 mg tablets		Burroughs Wellcome
Pyridium	Urinary Anti-Infective & Analgesic Combination	100, 200 mg tablets		Parke-Davis
Quarzan	Antispasmodic/Anticholinergic Gastrointestinal	2.5, 5 mg capsules		Roche Products
Quibron-T	Respiratory Drug Xanthine Derivative/Combination	300 mg tablets	SR tablets	Roberts Pharmaceutical
Reglan	Gastrointestinal Motility Factor	5 mg tablets	10 mg tablets; Injectable; Syrup	A. H. Robins
Respbid	Respiratory Drug Xanthine Derivative/Combination	250, 500 mg tablets		Boehringer Ingelheim Pharmaceuticals
Restoril	Hypnotic Sedative Non-Barbiturate	7.5, 15, 30 mg capsules		Sandoz Pharmaceuticals
Rheumatrex	Arthritis Medication Other	5, 7.5, 10, 12.5, 15 mg tablets	LPF; Injection; for Injection	Immunex Corporation

NAME OF DRUG	PDR PRODUCT CATEGORY & SUBCATEGORIES	VARIETIES CONTAINING LACTOSE (AS AN INACTIVE INGREDIENT)	VARIETIES WHICH DO NOT CONTAIN LACTOSE	MANUFACTURER
Proventil	Respiratory Drug Sympathomimetic/Combination	2, 4 mg tablets; 4 mg extended-release tablets	Inhalation solution; Solution for inhalation; Syrup	Schering Corporation
Provera	Hormone Progestogen	2.5, 5, 10 mg tablets		The Upjohn Company
Purinethol	Antineoplastic Antimetabolite	50 mg tablets		Burroughs Wellcome
Pyridium	Urinary Anti-Infective & Analgesic Combination	100, 200 mg tablets		Parke-Davis
Quarzan	Antispasmodic/Anticholinergic Gastrointestinal	2.5, 5 mg capsules		Roche Products
Quibron-T	Respiratory Drug Xanthine Derivative/Combination	300 mg tablets	SR tablets	Roberts Pharmaceutical
Reglan	Gastrointestinal Motility Factor	5 mg tablets	10 mg tablets; Injectable; Syrup	A. H. Robins
Respbid	Respiratory Drug Xanthine Derivative/Combination	250, 500 mg tablets		Boehringer Ingelheim Pharmaceuticals
Restoril	Hypnotic Sedative Non-Barbiturate	7.5, 15, 30 mg capsules		Sandoz Pharmaceuticals
Rheumatrex	Arthritis Medication Other	5, 7.5, 10, 12.5, 15 mg tablets	LPF; Injection; for Injection	Immunex Corporation

NAME OF DRUG	PDR PRODUCT CATEGORY & SUBCATEGORIES	VARIETIES CONTAINING LACTOSE (AS AN INACTIVE INGREDIENT)	VARIETIES WHICH DO NOT CONTAIN LACTOSE	MANUFACTURER
Seldane-D	Antihistamine Cold & Cough Preparation Oral/Combination	60/10 mg tablets		Marion Merrell Dow
Ser-Ap-Es	Cardiovascular Agent Rauwolfia Derivative/Combination	0.1/25/15 mg tablets		Ciba Pharmaceutical Company
Serax	Psychotropic Antianxiety Agent	10, 15, 30 mg capsules; 15 mg tablets		Wyeth-Ayerst Laboratories
Serentil	Psychotropic Antipsychotic Medication	10, 25, 50, 100 mg tablets	Ampuls; Concentrate	Boehringer Ingelheim Pharmaceuticals
Slow Fe	Hematinic Folic Acid	160 mg tablets		CIBA Consumer Pharmaceuticals
SMA Infant Formula	Infant Formula, Regular Liquid Concentrate Liquid Ready-to-Feed Powder Infant Formula, Special Purpose Iron Supplement Liquid Concentrate Liquid Ready-to-Feed Powder Low Iron Liquid Concentrate Liquid Ready-to-Feed Powder	Concentrated liquid; Powder; Ready-to-feed		Wyeth-Ayerst Laboratories

NAME OF DRUG	PDR PRODUCT CATEGORY & SUBCATEGORIES	VARIETIES CONTAINING LACTOSE (AS AN INACTIVE INGREDIENT)	VARIETIES WHICH DO NOT CONTAIN LACTOSE	MANUFACTURER
Sorbitrate	Cardiovascular Agent Vasodilator, Coronary	5, 10, 20, 30, 40 mg oral tablets; 2.5, 5, 10 sublingual tablets; 40 mg SA tablets	5, 10 mg chewable tablets	Zeneca Pharmaceuticals
Spectrobid	Antibiotic, Systemic Penicillin	400 mg tablets		Roerig Division/Pfizer
Stelazine	Psychotropic Antipsychotic Medication	1, 2, 5, 10 mg tablets	Concentrate; Multi-dose vials	SmithKline Beecham Pharmaceuticals
Stilphostrol	Antineoplastic Hormone	50 mg tablets		Miles
Surmontil	Psychotropic Antidepressant: Tricyclic/Combination	25, 50, 100 mg capsules		Wyeth-Ayerst Laboratories
Synthroid	Hormone Thyroid Preparation: Synthetic T4	25, 50, 75, 88, 100, 112, 125, 150, 175, 200, 300 mcg tablets		Boots Pharmaceuticals
Tabloid	Antineoplastic Antimetabolite	40 mg tablets		Burroughs Wellcome
Tao	Antibiotic, Systemic Macrolide: Other	250 mg capsules		Roerig Division/Pfizer
Tapazole	Hormone Thyroid Preparation: Thyroid Suppressant	5, 10 mg tablets		Eli Lilly and Company

NAME OF DRUG	PDR PRODUCT CATEGORY & SUBCATEGORIES	VARIETIES CONTAINING LACTOSE (AS AN INACTIVE INGREDIENT)	VARIETIES WHICH DO NOT CONTAIN LACTOSE	MANUFACTURER
Tavist	Antihistamine Pruritus Medication	1.34, 2.68 mg tablets	Syrup	Sandoz Pharmaceuticals
Tegison	Dermatological Psoriasis Agent	10, 25 mg capsules		Roche Dermatologics
Tenex	Cardiovascular Agent Adrenergic Stimulant, Central/Combination	1, 2 mg tablets		A. H. Robins
Tenuate	Appetite Suppressant Non-Amphetamine	25 mg tablets	Dospan tablets	Marion Merrell Dow
Teslac	Antineoplastic Hormone Hormone Anabolic	50 mg tablets		Bristol-Myers Oncology
Thalitone	Cardiovascular Agent Diuretic: Thiazide/Related Diuretic	15, 25 mg tablets		Horus Therapeutics
Theo-Dur	Respiratory Drug Xanthine Derivative/Combination	100, 200, 300, 450 mg tablets	Capsules	Key Pharmaceuticals
Theo-X	Respiratory Drug Xanthine Derivative/Combination	100, 200, 300 mg tablets		Carnrick Laboratories

NAME OF DRUG	PDR PRODUCT CATEGORY & SUBCATEGORIES	VARIETIES CONTAINING LACTOSE (AS AN INACTIVE INGREDIENT)	VARIETIES WHICH DO NOT CONTAIN LACTOSE	MANUFACTURER
Theolair	Respiratory Drug Xanthine Derivative/Combination	125, 250 mg tablets	Liquid	3M Pharmaceuticals
Theolair-SR	Respiratory Drug Xanthine Derivative/Combination	200, 250, 300, 500 mg tablets		3M Pharmaceuticals
Thorazine	Nausea Medication Psychotropic Antipsychotic Medication	10, 25, 50, 100, 200 mg tablets	Ampuls; Capsules; Concentrate; Multi-dose vials; Suppositories; Syrup	SmithKline Beecham Pharmaceuticals
Tigan	Nausea Medication	100, 250 mg capsules	Ampuls; Disposable syringes; Multiple dose vials; Pediatric suppositories; Suppositories	SmithKline Beecham Pharmaceuticals
Toprol XL	Cardiovascular Agent Beta Blocker	50, 100, 200 mg tablets		Astra USA
Toradol	Analgesic NSAID Anti-Inflammatory Agent Non-Steroidal	10 mg tablets	Intramuscular	Syntex Laboratories
Torecan	Nausea Medication	10 mg tablets	Injection; Suppository	Roxane Laboratories
Trandate	Cardiovascular Agent Alpha/Beta Adrenergic Blocker	100, 200, 300 mg tablets	Injection	Allen & Hanburys
Tranxene-SD	Psychotropic Antianxiety Agent	11.25, 22.5 mg tablets	T-Tabs	Abbott Laboratories

NAME OF DRUG	PDR PRODUCT CATEGORY & SUBCATEGORIES	VARIETIES CONTAINING LACTOSE (AS AN INACTIVE INGREDIENT)	VARIETIES WHICH DO NOT CONTAIN LACTOSE	MANUFACTURER
Trecator-SC	Tuberculosis Preparation	250 mg tablets		Wyeth-Ayerst Laboratories
Tri-Levlen	Contraceptive, Oral	21 & 28 day-tablets		Berlex Laboratories
Tri-Norinyl	Contraceptive, Oral Hormone Progestogen & Estrogen Combination	21 & 28 day-tablets		Syntex (F. P.)
Triavil	Psychotropic Antidepressant: Tricyclic/Combination	2/10, 2/25, 4/10, 4/25, 4/50 mg tablets		Merck & Co.
Tridione	Seizure Disorder Oxazolidinedione	150 mg tablets	300 mg capsules; Solution	Abbott Laboratories
Trilafon	Nausea Medication Psychotropic Antipsychotic Medication	2, 4, 8, 16 mg tablets	Concentrate; Injection	Schering Corporation
Trimpex	Urinary Tract Agent Antibacterial	100 mg tablets		Roche Laboratories
Trinalin	Antihistamine Cold & Cough Preparation Oral/Combination Decongestant Expectorant/Combination	1/120 mg tablets		Key Pharmaceuticals
Triphasil	Contraceptive, Oral Hormone Progestogen & Estrogen Combination	21 & 28-day tablets		Wyeth-Ayerst Laboratories

NAME OF DRUG	PDR PRODUCT CATEGORY & SUBCATEGORIES	VARIETIES CONTAINING LACTOSE (AS AN INACTIVE INGREDIENT)	VARIETIES WHICH DO NOT CONTAIN LACTOSE	MANUFACTURER
Unipen	Antibiotic, Systemic Penicillin	500 mg tablets	Capsules; Injection	Wyeth-Ayerst Laboratories
Urecholine	Parasympathomimetic	5, 10, 25, 50 mg tablets	Injection	Merck & Co.
Vantin	Antibiotic, Systemic Cephalosporin: 3rd Generation	50, 100 mg oral suspension; 100, 200 mg tablets		The Upjohn Company
Vascor	Cardiovascular Agent Calcium Channel Blocker	200, 300, 400 mg caplets		McNeil Pharmaceutical
Vaseretic	Cardiovascular Agent Angiotensin Converting Enzyme Inhibitor with Diuretic	10/25 mg tablets		Merck & Co.
Vasotec	Cardiovascular Agent Angiotensin Converting Enzyme Inhibitor	2.5, 5, 10, 20 mg tablets		Merck & Co.
Ventolin	Respiratory Drug Sympathomimetic/Combination Sympathomimetic/Combination	2, 4 mg tablets	Inhalation solution; Nebules inhalation solution; Rotacaps for inhalation; Syrup	Allen & Hanburys

NAME OF DRUG	PDR PRODUCT CATEGORY & SUBCATEGORIES	VARIETIES CONTAINING LACTOSE (AS AN INACTIVE INGREDIENT)	VARIETIES WHICH DO NOT CONTAIN LACTOSE	MANUFACTURER
Vicon Forte	Hematinic Cyanocobalamin Folic Acid Vitamin B_{12} Mineral Nutritional Supplement Vitamin Geriatric Multivitamin Multivitamin with Mineral	Capsules		Whitby Pharmaceuticals
Viokase	Enzyme/Digestant Digestant	Powder; Tablets		A. H. Robins
Vivactil	Psychotropic Antidepressant: Tricyclic/Combination	5, 10 mg tablets		Merck & Co.
Voltaren	Anti-Inflammatory Agent Non-Steroidal Arthritis medication NSAID	25, 50, 75 mg tablets		Geigy Pharmaceuticals
Wigraine	Ergot Preparation Migraine Preparation Migraine Preparation Ergot Derivative/Combination	1/100 mg tablets	Suppositories	Organon

NAME OF DRUG	PDR PRODUCT CATEGORY & SUBCATEGORIES	VARIETIES CONTAINING LACTOSE (AS AN INACTIVE INGREDIENT)	VARIETIES WHICH DO NOT CONTAIN LACTOSE	MANUFACTURER
Winstrol	Hormone Anabolic	2 mg tablets		Sanofi Winthrop Pharmaceuticals
Wytensin	Cardiovascular Agent Adrenergic Stimulant, Central/Combination	4, 8 mg tablets		Wyeth-Ayerst Laboratories
Xanax	Psychotropic Antianxiety Agent Antipanic Medication	0.25, 0.5, 1, 2 mg tablets		The Upjohn Company
Yutopar	Uterine Relaxant	10 mg tablets	Injection	Astra USA
Zithromax	Antibiotic, Systemic Macrolide: Other	250 mg capsules		Pfizer Labs
Zocor	Hypolipidemic HMG-COA Reductase Inhibitor	5, 10, 20, 40 mg tablets		Merck & Co.
Zofran	Antineoplastic Adjunct Nausea Medication	4, 8 mg tablets	Injection	Cerenex Pharmaceuticals
Zovirax	Antiviral, Systemic Herpes Treatment Nucleoside Analogue	200 mg capsules	Ointment; Sterile Powder; Suspension; Tablets	Burroughs Wellcome
Zyloprim	Gout Treatment Urinary Tract Agent Calcium Oxalate Stone Preventive	100, 300 mg tablets		Burroughs Wellcome

GLOSSARY

Chronic Diarrhea (Also called: Protracted Diarrhea)   The passage of more than 200 g of stool per day for more than three weeks.

Congenital Lactose Intolerance   Recessive genetic condition in which virtually no lactase is produced from birth. Extremely rare.

Cow's Milk Protein (CMP) Allergy   Reaction of the body's immune system to either the whey or casein proteins in cow's milk. Similar reactions may occur to the proteins in other animal milks. Not known to occur from mother's milk. Can last through adulthood. Reactions can be extremely severe and may force a complete ban on milk protein-containing products.

Cow's Milk Protein (CMP) Intolerance   Non-immune system response to the proteins in cow's milk. Usually outgrown after early childhood as intestines strengthen.

Cow's Milk-Sensitive Enteropathy [CMSE]   The intestinal damage and corresponding diarrhea and other symptoms induced by CMP.

Hypersensitivity   Usually used synonymously with allergic reaction. May, however, be applied to protein intolerance reactions.

Hypoallergenic   Applied to products with a greatly reduced likelihood of creating an allergic reaction. Does not mean nonallergenic. An infant formula may be deemed hypoallergenic if it is tolerated by 90% of milk-allergic infants.

Hypolactasia (Also called: Lactase Restriction)   A state of very low lactase activity in the small intestine. Commonly used in medical journals published outside the U.S. as the general term for lactose intolerance.

Lactase (Also called: Lactase-Phlorizin Hydrolase [LPH]; Lactase-Glycosylceramidase)   Natural intestinal digestive enzyme that splits lactose into glucose and galactose.

Lactase Deficiency (Also called: Alactasia)   A state of total lack of lactase activity in the small intestine. Unlikely unless physical damage to or removal of the intestines occurs.

Lactase Persistence [LP] (Also called: Lactase Sufficiency; Normolactasia; High Lactose Digestion Capacity)   Adult state in which lactase activity has not declined from the high levels of early childhood.

Lactose (Also called: Milk Sugar)   The sugar found in the milk of most mammals, including humans, and nowhere else. Lactose is a disaccharide, a double sugar, because it is composed of two simple sugars, glucose and galactose.

Lactose Hydrolysis   The splitting, or digestion, of the lactose molecule into glucose and galactose by the lactase enzyme.

Lactose Intolerance [LI]   Technically, the appearance of symptoms (usually gas, bloating or diarrhea) from whatever cause after the ingestion of lactose-containing dairy products. Commonly used to refer both to those symptoms and to the condition of reduced lactase production due to Primary Lactose Intolerance (*see below*), but may occur even with a technically sufficient lactase supply.

The following table lists related terms:

PAIRS OF TERMS USED TO DISTINGUISH THOSE WHO CAN DRINK MILK WITHOUT SUFFERING SYMPTOMS FROM THOSE WHO CAN'T	
CAN'T	CAN
Lactose intolerance	Lactose tolerance
Lactase restriction	Lactase persistence
Lactase deficiency	Lactase sufficiency
Hypolactasia	Normolactasia
Lactose maldigester	Lactose digester
Low lactose digestion capacity (low LDC)	High lactose digestion capacity (high LDC)
Lactose malabsorption	Lactose absorption

Lactose Maldigestion (Also called: Lactose Malabsorption; Low Lactose Digestion Capacity)   The inability to digest molecules of lactose. May be caused by the natural decline of lactase production, by reduced lactase activity caused by damage to the intestines or by other intestinal ailments which prevent even a sufficient lactase supply from working properly. Symptoms of LI may or may not be present. The term implies a medical diagnosis following clinical testing.

Pareve (Also called: Parve)   Neutral foods permitted under the Jewish dietary laws to be eaten either with meals containing meat or meals containing milk. To qualify as pareve, a food must not contain any animal-derived product or be made in equipment that is also used to produce food that contains any animal-derived product. Pareve foods therefore contain no dairy products of any kind in any amount.

Premature Lactose Intolerance   Low lactase production found in premature babies due to the lack of development of full lactase activity until the ninth month of pregnancy. Normally does not create noticeable symptoms.

Primary Lactose Intolerance (Also called: Adult-Onset Lactose Intolerance; Late-Onset Lactose Intolerance; Delayed-Onset Lactose Intolerance)   Slow decline in the production of the lactase enzyme with age. Found in approximately 70% of the world's population. May start in early childhood.

Secondary Lactose Intolerance (Also called: Temporary Lactose Intolerance; Acquired Lactose Intolerance)   A loss of lactase production following damage to the intestines from drugs, disease, surgery or other systemic shocks. Usually temporary. Lactase production will normally resume once the cause for the loss has ended.

Vegans   People who refrain from the use of any animal-derived food products.

BIBLIOGRAPHY

ACADEMIC AND TECHNICAL RESOURCES

Books

No academic book has ever been written specifically on LI or any aspect of it, although one has been done on milk allergies. The LI shelf in my library consists only of collections of articles or compilations of papers from conferences, and even those often bring in side issues like milk fat intolerance or starch intolerance. The books listed below tend to focus on very narrow and extremely technical aspects of LI and are all but unreadable by anyone not a specialist in the field. The same is true for the books on such related issues as milk allergies and galactosemia. I don't actually recommend any of these, but if you're a health professional or are determined to work your way through every major item on LI that has ever been put inside hard covers, you should be able to track these down at larger medical libraries or through interlibrary loan. A few are even listed in *Books in Print*.

Bahna, Sami L., and Douglas C. Heiner. *Allergies to Milk*. New York: Grune & Stratton, 1980.

Delmont, J., ed. *Milk Intolerances and Rejection*. Basel: S. Karger, 1983.

Hsia, David Yi-yung, ed. *Galactosemia*. Springfield, IL: Charles C Thomas, Pub., 1969.

Lebenthal, Emanuel, ed. *Digestive Diseases in Children*. New York: Grune & Stratton, 1978.

Lifschitz, Fima, ed. *Carbohydrate Intolerance in Infancy*. New York: Marcel Dekker, 1982.

Mestecky, Jiri, Claudia Blair, and Pearay L. Ogra, eds. *Immunology of Milk and the Neonate,* volume 310 in the series Advances in Experimental Medicine and Biology. New York: Plenum Press, 1991.

Paige, David M., and Theodore M. Bayless, eds. *Lactose Digestion: Clinical and Nutritional Implications*. Baltimore: Johns Hopkins University Press, 1981.

Journal Articles and Overviews

Doctors, understandably, concentrate their time and attention on the most urgent and dire problems. LI is neither, so it has never been a hot issue in the medical community. The monthly updates of the *Index Medicus*, which provides a subject index reference to an unbelievable number of medical journals, often fail to contain a single reference to LI. Even so, over the years the literature on LI has grown to number in the hundreds if not thousands of articles, and that's not even including papers on calcium absorption, osteoporosis or the many other areas that an interest in LI leads one to. Out of this wealth of material, I've selected only a handful of overviews, those covering—or at least touching on—most issues of importance. I would recommend these over any of the books above if only because they are not as narrowly focused. Except for the *Scientific American* piece, however, expect them to be nearly as technical. A good medical dictionary is advised.

Esteban, Manuel Martín, ed. "Adverse Reactions to Foods in Infancy and Childhood." *The Journal of Pediatrics*. 1992; 121(5,Pt.2):S1–S121. Proceedings of a symposium on food allergies.

Flatz, Gebhard. "Genetics of Lactose Digestion in Humans." Chapter 1 in *Advances in Human Genetics*, Harris, Harry, and Kurt Hirschhorn, eds. New York: Plenum Press, 1987. [Medical libraries are likely to treat this annual volume as a journal rather than as a book.]

Kretchmer, Norman. "Lactose and Lactase." *Scientific American*. October 1972.

Sahi, T., and A. Tamm, eds. "Hypolactasia: Epidemiology, Diagnosis, Clinical Picture and Management." *Scandinavian Journal of Gastroenterology*. 1994; 29 (suppl 202):1–62. A series of six articles on LI by various authors.

Scrimshaw, Nevin S., and Edwina B. Murray. "The Acceptability of Milk and Milk Products in Populations with a High Prevalence of Lactose Intolerance." *American Journal of Clinical Nutrition*. 1988; 48:1080–1159.

All of the above have some information on the origins of LI. I'm not aware of any recent major articles that focus solely on that aspect of LI that are less than 90% solid math. Probably the most readable older articles are by Frederick J. Simoons, especially the following:

Simoons, Frederick J. "The Geographic Hypothesis and Lactose Malabsorption: A Weighing of the Evidence." *Digestive Diseases*. 1978; 23(11):963–980.

Johnson, John D., Norman Kretchmer and Frederick J. Simoons. "Lactose Malabsorption: Its Biology and History." *Advances in Pediatrics*. 1974; 21:197–237.

Other
The slogan, "Every Body Needs Milk," is so thoroughly etched into the consciousness of every media-cognizant American that most people would be amazed to learn that it hasn't been used since the 1970s. Oddly, this slogan does not come from a national ad campaign from the American

Dairy Council or any such group you might logically suspect, but from the California Milk Producers Advisory Board of Modesto, CA. They hired the ad agency of Cunningham & Walsh, who succeeded beyond the Advisory Board's wildest dreams in bringing milk to the public's consciousness. The series of ads, starring well-known 1970s personalities including Vida Blue, Mark Spitz and Abigail Van Buren, was a smash, although, as often happens, the campaign was a success but the patient died. Milk consumption has continued to fall despite the slogans and jingles. In other ways, however, the ads succeeded too well.

The campaign brought so many complaints that the Federal Trade Commission jumped in to accuse the Board of, essentially, false advertising. Namely, as the title of this book puts it, *Milk Is Not for Every Body,* especially those bodies with LI or milk allergies. The case went before Judge Daniel H. Hanscom, an administrative-law judge for the FTC. As *Fortune* magazine put it in 1979, "His opinion reflects the sensibilities of a man who has been thinking milk, breathing milk, and possibly even drinking milk, for thirteen months [and] a determination to share with the world everything that he has been learning about milk." In the end, Judge Hanscom dismissed the FTC complaint on the ground that, while true, the government itself had for years been telling the public that it *should* drink milk, so it was in no position to throw stones.

Filled with ads, expert testimony and more obscure facts than even I've been able to squeeze in here, the decision (*In the Matter of California Milk Producers Advisory Board, et al.*, Federal Trade Commission Decisions, 94 F.T.C. 429, Final Order, Sept. 21, 1979) is a weirdly wonderful delight to read, although somewhat dated today.

■ POPULAR BOOKS, PAMPHLETS AND PUBLICATIONS

Lactose Intolerance – General

If the book-length medical literature on LI is relatively small, the number of popular books is positively minuscule. A decade ago, I wrote what I modestly believe to be the most comprehensive book on the subject, *No Milk Today: How to Live with Lactose Intolerance*, but it has been out of print for years.

The only other general book on LI ever written, to my knowledge, is *The Milk Sugar Dilemma: Living with Lactose Intolerance*, by Richard A. Martens & Sherlyn Martens, E. Lansing, MI: Medi-Ed Press, revised and expanded 2nd edition, 1987, $13.95. To order, write to 716 E. Empire, Suite A, Bloomington, IL 61701 or call 800–500–8205.

Many organizations (including some of the ones listed later), producers of milk substitutes, even individual supermarkets put out pamphlets, brochures, flyers or other minor pieces on LI. They range from good to awful. The only one individually listed in *Books In Print* is from the usually top-notch American Dietetic Association. Unfortunately, their brochure (*Lactose Intolerance*, by Merri Lou Dobler, revised edition, 1991) is wildly overpriced at $5.50 ($9.00 including shipping and handling) for 21 pages, half of which are irrelevant recipes.

The most readable popular explanation of the origins of lactase persistence and the spread of milk-drinking populations can be found in Marvin Harris's *The Sacred Cow and the Abominable Pig: Riddles of Food and Culture* (originally published as *Good to Eat*), NY: Touchstone/Simon & Schuster, 1985.

For ongoing information on LI, I can think of no better source than Jane Zukin's *The Newsletter for People With Lactose Intolerance and Milk Allergy*. Each bimonthly issue has eight pages of useful information ranging from new dairy-free products to reports on the latest findings from medical journals to articles on overall health and wellness. She answers readers' questions on all aspects of LI and allergies and has a recipe insert as well. Subscriptions are currently $15.00 for one year, with discounts offered for longer-term subscriptions. Write to: Jane Zukin/Commercial Writing Service, P.O. Box 3129, Ann Arbor, MI 48106.

Lactaid now puts out a newsletter of its own: *The Lactaid Digest*. It's mostly a long commercial for Lactaid, but it does contain some useful advice for those who plan to keep dairy in their diets. To get a free copy, call 800-LACTAID, or write to: The Lactaid Digest, McNeil Consumer Products Company, 7050 Camp Hill Road, Fort Washington, PA 19034.

Cookbooks for Dairy-free Recipes
Whether you need a cookbook depends too much on your cooking habits and level of intolerance for me to give a definitive answer. If you are trying to rigorously avoid milk products, some favorite recipes will certainly need altering, either by eliminating the need for milk or substituting for the dairy content. Milk-free desserts are especially difficult to concoct if you're not used to doing so. On the other hand, does anyone really need milk-free recipes for chili, lamb stew, fruit salad, Jello molds or lemon-ade[!], all of which have appeared in milk-free cookbooks in the past?

Most ordinary cookbooks contain numerous recipes which require no milk products or ones easily substituted for, but if you're just starting to cope with LI you may want cookbooks whose recipes have been designed from scratch not to need milk. Three types exist: 1) LI cookbooks; 2) vegetarian cookbooks; and 3) allergy cookbooks. (All the books listed here were in print at the time of writing. I've included the publishers' addresses and phone numbers for the books from smaller presses, since they are often harder to find in bookstores.)

Lactose Intolerance Cookbooks

Small LI cookbooks from even smaller publishers abound, but are usually too limited in scope or too difficult to find for me to want to recommend any. Fortunately, two writers experienced in the field have recently brought out revisions of their earlier smaller books, so greatly expanded as to count as new and important books in and of themselves. Both include some general information about LI and a wide range of recipes covering just about every kind of dairy product substitution situation you might encounter. If you're looking for a cookbook, start here.

Kidder, Beth. *The Milk-Free Kitchen: Living Well Without Dairy Products.* New York: Henry Holt, 1991, 480 p., trade paper, $15.95.

Zukin, Jane. *Dairy-Free Cookbook.* P. O. Box 1260JZ, Rocklin, CA 95677: Prima Publishing & Communications (916–624-5718), 1991, 300 p., trade paper, $14.95.

Vegetarian Cookbooks

Although all vegetarian cookbooks would seem to be equally good sources of milk-free recipes, a glance through a representative sample will show that they cover an enormous range, from those whose only concession is to omit red meat to those which shun any form of animal-derived product. The latter are known as vegan cookbooks. Variations exist even among these: Some will allow honey, others will not. The two listed here are ones that specifically formulate substitutions for dairy products.

Cole, Candia L. *Not Milk . . . Nut Milks! Forty of the Most Original Dairy-Free Recipes Ever!* P. O. Box 6189, Santa Barbara, CA 93160: Woodbridge Press Pub. Co. (800–287-6053), 128 p., paperback, $7.95.

Stepaniak, Joanne. *The Uncheese Cookbook.* P. O. Box 99, Summertown, TN 38483: Book Pub. Co. (800–695-2241), 1994, 160 p., paperback, $10.95.

Allergy Cookbooks

Many people, especially children, who are allergic to milk protein are also allergic to a variety of other foods, making mealtimes a constant trial. Allergy cookbooks often have a string of "-free"s in their titles—not just milk-free, but egg-free, corn-free, wheat-free and more—to highlight the potential scope of the problem. Unfortunately, allergy cookbooks are usually less convenient to those concerned solely about LI, as the milk-free recipes are not always segregated from those eliminating other problem foods. If allergies are your problem, however, they can be invaluable. Far more allergy cookbooks than LI cookbooks exist; upon consideration, I decided not to list any individual titles since your particular needs should take precedence. The McNicol book is a more general treatment of the subject, although some sample recipes are included.

McNicol, Jane. *Your Child's Food Allergies*. New York: John Wiley & Sons, 1992, 160 p., trade paper, $9.95.

Milk

The best source of information on milk comes from, where else, The National Dairy Council. Every few years they put out an edition of *Newer Knowledge of Milk and Other Fluid Dairy Products* that's a fascinating mine of milk facts and figures. (National Dairy Council, 6300 N. River Rd., Rosemont, IL 60018, $6.00.) Their bi-monthly publication, *Dairy Council Digest*, does a good job of covering at a technical level nutritional issues relating to milk. Periodic reports on LI summarize the medical literature. (National Dairy Council, Order Department, O'Hare International Center, 10255 West Higgins Rd., Suite 900, Rosemont, IL 60018–5616, one-year subscription for $12.00.)

ORGANIZATIONS

The *Encyclopedia of Associations* runs to three fat volumes annually. Unless you're a serial killer, I guarantee that you will find something in here that matches your personal or professional needs. For those who have specialized health problems or questions about matters beyond the scope of this book, these organizations can provide reams of information, referrals or reassurance that you are not alone.

Health Organizations – United States

American Allergy Association
P.O. Box 7273
Menlo Park, CA 94026
415–322-1663

American College of Nutrition
P.O. Box 831
White Plains, NY 10602
914–948-4848

American Dietetic Association
216 West Jackson Blvd.
Chicago, IL 60606–6995
312–899-0040

American Digestive Disease Society
7720 Wisconsin Ave.
Bethesda, MD 20014
301–652-9293

Digestive Disease National Coalition
711 Second St. NE, Suite 200
Washington, DC 20002
202–544-7497

National Foundation for Ileitis and Colitis
Crohn's Colitis Foundation of America
444 Park Ave. South, 11th floor
New York, NY 10016–7374
212–685-3440

National Osteoporosis Foundation
2100 M Street NW, Suite 602
Washington, DC 20037
202–223-2226

United States Government Agencies

Food and Drug Administration
Office of Consumer Affairs
5600 Fishers Lane, HFE-88
Rockville, MD 20857

National Digestive Diseases Education and Information Clearinghouse
Box NDDIC
7000 Rockville Pike
Bethesda, MD 20892
301–468-6344

Health Organizations – Canada

Canadian Foundation for Ileitis and Colitis
21 St. Clair Ave. East, Suite 301
Toronto, Ontario M4T 1L9
416–920-5035

National Institute of Nutrition
1565 Carling Ave., Suite 400
Ottawa, Ontario K1Z 8R1
613–725-1889

Osteoporosis Society of Canada
76 St. Clair Ave. West, Suite 502
Toronto, Ontario M4V 1N2
416–922-1358

Dairy Product Organizations

American Butter Institute—202–659-1454
American Cultured Dairy Products Institute—202–223-1931
International Ice Cream Association—202–296-4250
National Cheese Institute—202–659-1454
888 16th St. NW
Washington, DC 2006

American Dairy Association—708–696-1880
National Dairy Council—708–696-1020
United Dairy Industry Association—708–696-1860
6300 N. River Rd.
Rosemont, IL 60018

American Dairy Products Institute
130 N. Franklin St.
Chicago, IL 60606
312–782-4888

National Ice Cream and Yogurt Retailers Association
1429 King Ave., Suite 210
Columbus, OH 43212
614-486-1444

National Yogurt Association
1764 Old Meadow Lane, Suite 350
McLean, VA 22102
703-821-0770